RENAISSANCE SOCIETY OF AMERICA REPRINT TEXTS 7

Vespasiano da Bisticci

THE VESPASIANO MEMOIRS: LIVES OF ILLUSTRIOUS MEN OF THE XVTH CENTURY

Translated by William George and Emily Waters
Introduction by Myron P. Gilmore

Published by University of Toronto Press
Toronto Buffalo London
in association with the Renaissance Society of America

© Renaissance Society of America 1997
Printed in Canada
ISBN 0-8020-7968-7

First complete edition of the 15th century manuscript published (in Italian) by Cardinal Angelo Mai in 1837, from a manuscript in the Vatican Library.

English translation published by George Routledge & Sons, Ltd., London, in 1926, under the title *The Vespasiano Memoirs*.

First Harper Torchbook edition published in 1963 by Harper & Row, Publishers, Incorporated. Introduction to the Torchbook edition copyright © 1963 by Myron P. Gilmore.

Canadian Cataloguing in Publication Data

Vespasiano da Bisticci, Fiorentino,
1421–1498
The Vespasiano memoirs

(Renaissance Society of America reprint texts ; 7)
Originally published under title: Vite de uomini illustri del scolo XV.
Reprint of: Renaissance princes, popes, and prelates.   New York : Harper & Row, 1963.   (Harper torchbooks.   The Academy library).
Includes bibliographical references and index.
ISBN 0-8020-7968-7

l. Italy – History – 15th century – Biography.
I. Waters, W. G. (William George), 1844–1928.
II. Waters, Emily.   III. Renaissance Society of America.   IV. Title.   V. Series.

DG537.8.A1V4713 1997   945'.05'0922   C97-930552-7

CONTENTS

CONTENTS

vi

CONTENTS

CONTENTS

LIST OF ILLUSTRATIONS

PLATE I

THE EMPEROR JOHN PALAEOLOGUS, JOURNEYING TO THE COUNCIL OF FLORENCE

INTRODUCTION TO THE TORCHBOOK EDITION
by
MYRON P. GILMORE

I N MARCH, 1895, Ludwig von Pastor, the historian of the papacy, came to Basel to visit Jacob Burckhardt, the historian of the Italian Renaissance. The latter was then an old man and Pastor was interested to inquire into the genesis of his famous essay, *The Civilization of the Renaissance in Italy,* published in 1860. In the conversation that followed, Burckhardt, brushing aside a suggestion that his inspiration had been due to his travels in Italy and also to his earlier description of Italian works of art, recalled that the first idea for his great book had come to him in Rome in 1847 on reading a copy loaned to him of Vespasiano da Bisticci's *Lives of Illustrious Men.* Thus is established by the most direct testimony the place of the Florentine bookseller's biographies in the genesis of the most famous of modern works on the Renaissance.

Of Vespasiano's life we know comparatively little. He was born in Florence in 1421 of a family which had originated in Bisticci, a little village near Florence, from which he took his name. We do not know whether family circumstances prevented his completing a higher education and so entering into one of the recognized higher professions or whether his own

xi

inclination led him to the stationers' guild. At all events it is clear that in the trade of *cartolaio* he discovered his vocation and in his subsequent career so took advantage of the various opportunities then open to the bookseller or stationer that he was eventually known not only in Florence and in Italy but even beyond the Italian borders as the most celebrated dealer in books and manuscripts of his generation. It was a case of a happy coincidence between the tastes and abilities of the man and the Italian cultural situation. In the preceding century Petrarch and his associates and followers had given a powerful stimulus to the study of ancient civilization. Rejecting the scholastic dependence on commentaries, the humanists emphasized the importance of studying the original texts of Greek and Roman authors and of the Church Fathers. The renewed interest in the teaching of Greek which had made itself felt in Florence and other centers of northern Italy before the end of the fifteenth century, was accelerated as the Turkish pressure on Byzantium increased. In these circumstances it became fashionable to collect libraries of manuscripts beautifully copied in the hand which had been developed by the humanist educators. Rulers and wealthy private individuals sought codices which embodied the best texts of ancient and early Christian authors, many of which had been recently discovered and circulated. Vespasiano's shop supplied these needs. One of his foremost patrons was Cosimo de' Medici and Vespasiano tells us himself how at Cosimo's request and regardless of expense, he hired forty-five scribes to complete in twenty-two months the library that Cosimo had commanded. Many of these manuscripts remain today in the Laurentian Library in Florence. Among Vespasiano's other friends and patrons were Florentine bibliophiles like Niccolo Niccoli, two popes, Eugenius IV and Nicholas V, and Alfonso the Magnanimous, King of Naples. In his later years he had particularly close relations with the great Duke of Urbino, Federigo de Montefeltro of whose career he has left so detailed and admiring an account. For the Duke Vespasiano's copyists assembled many of the manuscripts which made of the library at Urbino a model foundation for

Christian and classical learning and which constitute today one of the most important collections of humanist manuscripts in the Vatican. As Vespasiano proudly tells us, the Duke had an ambition to do what no one had done in a thousand years, that is, create the finest library since antiquity. Vespasiano lovingly dwells on the catalog and the beautiful bindings which were designed to be of an elegance worthy of the manuscripts they enclosed.

Among the clients of Vespasiano north of the Alps were John Tiptoft, Earl of Worcester, and Mathias Corvinus, King of Hungary. The former, influenced by the intellectual enthusiasm he found in Italy, assembled a splendid collection of manuscripts which he bequeathed to the University of Oxford. The King of Hungary was one of the first of those northern monarchs who sought to introduce Italian learning and Italian arts in their courts and he imitated Italian rulers in his effort to assemble a library of manuscripts which reflected the interests of humanist educators.

In 1480 the bookshop which had for so many years been a center for the meeting of learned men in Florence passed from the hands of Vespasiano to those of Andrea de Lorenzo. The effects of printing had begun to be felt and it was already obvious by this time that beautifully copied manuscripts were no longer able to compete with printed books nor to command the price they had bought in the heyday of Vespasiano's career. Vespasiano deplored this development and his attitude is reflected on many pages of the *Lives*. In his encomium on the library of Urbino, for example, we read that, "had there been one printed volume, it would have been ashamed in such company." Not wishing to continue his trade under such changed conditions, the bookseller gave up his shop and retired to the village of Antella where he devoted his last years to writing.

During this period he composed several moral treatises, a collection of sketches of illustrious ladies and a lament on behalf of Italy on the fall of Otranto, which had been captured by the Turks in 1480. His principal work was, however, the *Lives of Illustrious Men,* for most of which he drew on his personal recollections. The form of his work may have been dictated by the traditional compositions, *de virie illustribus,* which had come down from antiquity and been revived and imitated by the humanists. In writing his *Lives* in the vernacular, however, and without much attention either to elegance of style or to wide historical generalizations or parallels, he was able to preserve the vivid and intimate details which enhance the value of his work as a historical source.

His last years brought disillusionment. Not only did he deplore the changed conditions of intellectual life brought about by the printing press, but also he felt that the political life of Florence had degenerated. In spite of his admiration for Cosimo de' Medici he had reservations about his exercise of political power and he had condemned the changes in the traditional Florentine government brought about by the Medici rule after 1434. His originally conservative political views were reinforced by the experience of the events after the French invasion sixty years later. In the end he lived to see the collapse of the Medicean government and the installation of Savonarola's dictatorship. In a letter written a year before his death he uttered a melancholy warning on the evils of mob rule.

Although Vespasiano's *Lives* were known to scholars and some few of them were published or extracted in the seventeenth and eighteenth centuries, the collection as a whole remained in manuscript till 1839 when it was published by Cardinal Angelo Mai from a manuscript in the Vatican. It was a copy of this edition, loaned to Jacob Burckhardt in 1847, which inspired his ideas on a cultural history of the Italian Renaissance.

Even without Burckhardt's avowal of the importance of Vespasiano, it would be possible to suggest a relationship between the biographies of the Florentine bookseller and the synthesis of the Swiss historian. In the first place, the lives of the rulers, statesmen, ecclesiastics, and men of letters presented by Vespasiano exhibit certain common characteristics which may easily be taken to suggest an ideal type, a set of qualities which in the abstract represent the mentality of the age. Generalization based on a series of illuminating anecdotes about individuals is a large part of Burckhardt's method. Vespasiano's lives of Renaissance men thus contributed to the conception of Renaissance *man*.

It is furthermore remarkable how much Vespasiano suggests many of those "general" features of Italian Renaissance society which were used by Burckhardt as the titles for the various parts of his essay and which form the organizing principle of the work. Many of the characteristics of what Burckhardt describes under the rubric "The State as a Work of Art" are to be found in the careers of such rulers as Pope Nicholas V, Alfonso of Naples, Federigo of Urbino and Cosimo de' Medici. The creative aspects of the revival of antiquity are abundantly illustrated in the lives of the humanist scholars, such as Lionardo Bruni, Poggio Bracciolini, and Giannozzo Manetti. Again and again Vespasiano reiterates the belief—so characteristic of earlier quattrocento humanism—in the compatibility of the best of classical with Christian ideals. Such a figure as Federigo of Urbino unites classical learning with Christian piety and applies the lessons of both to his career as a soldier and statesman. In this way Vespasiano's biographies offer the materials for that combination of political and intellectual history which Burckhardt achieved in his masterpiece.

Vespasiano says in his own brief preface that he has been moved to record the lives of illustrious men he has known for two reasons: "First, that their fame may not perish; Second, that if anyone should take the trouble to write their lives in Latin, he should find before him a material from which such work could be modelled." Of his first reason, it may be said that if some of his heroes have been forgotten, yet fame has dealt kindly with the ones for whom he cared most. Of his second reason, although he could not imagine an age in which Latin would have ceased to be the language of communication among educated men, nevertheless, his "material" has found its way into a history which has been translated into all modern languages. The judgment pronounced upon him in that history is perhaps the most just appreciation of his importance. "For

TORCHBOOK INTRODUCTION

further information as to the learned citizens of Florence at this period the reader must all the more be referred to Vespasiano, who knew them all personally, because the tone and atmosphere in which he writes, and the terms and conditions on which he mixed in their society, are of even more importance than the facts which he records. . . . Without being a great writer, he was thoroughly familiar with the subject he wrote on, and had a deep sense of its intellectual significance."*

Harvard University
June 1963

BIBLIOGRAPHY

*Jacob Burckhardt, *The Civilization of the Renaissance in Italy* (New York, Harper Torchbooks, 1958) I, 226-7.

Caprin, Giulio, *"Il libraio fiorentino degli umanisti, Vespasiano da Bisticci,"* in *Il Quattrocento* (Florence, 1954).

Frizzi, E., *"Di Vespasiano da Bisticci e delle sue biografie,"* *Annale della R. Scuola Normale Superiore di Pisa,* III, 1-137.

Kaegi, Werner, *Jacob Burckhardt, Eine Biographie* (Basel, 1956) III, 647.

Neidhart, C., *"Vespasiano da Bisticci und seine Papstleben,"* *Schweizerische Rundschau,* XXVI², 897 ff and 982 ff.

Rossi, *Il Quattrocento* (5th ed., Milan, 1956) 37, 191 ff.

TRANSLATORS'
INTRODUCTION

IF the *Vite* of Vespasiano da Bisticci are not entirely forgotten, they are only known to few, even of those who are students of history. In certain instances they have been effectively used to impart piquant details to standard works which, but for the tincture of his artless gossip, might have lost some of their interest. His rich storehouse of remarkable events and shrewd observations is a quarry fully as serviceable to the historian and the biographer as is Vasari to the writer on art. In suggesting an English equivalent to the *Vite*, the *Short Lives* of John Aubrey seem to be the most appropriate.

The *Vite di uomini illustri del Secolo XV* are contemporary memoirs written by Vespasiano da Bisticci, a Florentine bookseller whose life lasted from 1421 to 1498. They were first printed from a collection of manuscript biographies called the *Spicilegium Romanum*, discovered by Cardinal Angelo Mai in the Vatican Library. One hundred and three lives were first published under his editorship in Rome, 1839. But Mai was not the first to recognise him, for Gibbon had quoted him (Chap. LXVI) in writing of Pope Nicolas V. Gibbon's reference, however, is made to the Pope's life by Vespasiano, printed by Muratori—*Rerum Italic. Script.*, XXV, pp. 267, 290. Mai affixed to his book a Latin preface in which he professed to give a complete account of Vespasiano. This was largely taken from an introduction to the Epistles of Ambrogio Camaldolese, written by the Abbate Lionardo Mehus in 1759. In a later edition, brought out by Adolfo Bartoli in 1859, two extra lives are given, bringing the number up to one hundred and five. In an introduction of his own, Bartoli corrects certain errors made by Mai and amends some of the lives by collation with a MS. which Mai apparently had not seen, but he generally follows him, though he hints that his text may have been somewhat over-modernized.

I

TRANSLATORS' INTRODUCTION

Little is known of Vespasiano apart from the *Vite* and his bookshop. He was probably of a family belonging to Bisticci, a village near Florence. In the Archivio Centrale there is an entry of his burial in S. Croce in 1498 as *Vespasiano Cartolaio*. It is clear that he had a passion for books, and that inclination may have swayed him in the choice of a calling. There have been many booksellers who have risen to a level far above that of a trader, and Vespasiano was one of them. He was a man of wide, if superficial, reading, and a skilled expert in rare MSS. of Greek authors which were then arriving in large quantities from Constantinople. His reputation increased, as did the demand for copies of Greek writings in the original or in Latin translations, and as he frequently speaks of making copies there is little doubt that he extended his business by engaging a large number of scribes who reproduced these for his patrons. In several of the lives, notably in those of the Sclavonic bishops of Strigonia and the Five Churches ; of the English protonotary, the Earl of Worcester, and of the Bishop of Ely, he writes of the large purchases made by these bibliophiles regardless of cost and of their eagerness to get possession of their treasures ; and how the protonotary Andrew Hollis bought so largely that he was forced to charter a ship at Leghorn to convey his library to England. Vespasiano was evidently the leading bibliophile of the age, and the lettered travellers who went to Florence would naturally make his *bottega* their meeting-place during their stay ; it was to Florence what the bookshop of the Sosii was to classic Rome. This qualification will explain the close and friendly relations he established with all the great men of the time who happened also to be book-collectors. We learn in the *Lives* of the Greek, Latin and Hebrew MSS. he supplied at the instance of Nicolas V to the Vatican Library : of the many fine books he collected for Cosimo de Medici which formed the nucleus of the Laurentian Library, and of the great purchases he made for Alessandro Sforza and Federigo of Urbino ; others were the Cardinal of Portugal, who died all too soon, and John Tiptoft, Earl of Worcester, who, according to Calvo, despoiled the libraries of Italy to enrich England. As a Balliol man he rightly gave his books to Oxford, and one of them—alas, one only !—a commentary on Juvenal, is still in the Bodleian. Of all the Englishmen named by Vespasiano, Tiptoft (Duca di Worcestri) is by far the most interesting figure. He had recently gone to Italy on a mission of state and incidentally had heard Guarino lecture at Ferrara. He is a most elusive and fascinating figure, an English Pico della Mirandola, moving amongst the dismal wreck and ruin of his country like one born out of due time. His name crops up in the matter-of-fact pages of the Paston Letters, but there and in the Chronicles we are told little about him save of his cruelty and unjust dealing with captive Lancastrians, and how he had learned these nefarious ways through association with the corrupt and treacherous Italians. He is said to have cited some provision of " the Law Padowe " to justify the mutilation and slaughter of his foes, when he could find no such authority in the law of the land. This, in any case, was the accusation lodged against him by his Lancastrian enemies at his trial. But Tiptoft had evidently found time amongst the cares of state to cultivate the friendship of Caxton, who passes by his sins as a politician, and pours out enthusiasm over his learning and munificence, and grief over the untimely death which overtook him. In the Epilogue to the Orations of Cornelius Scipio, Caxton writes, " I mene the right vertuo and noble Erle, Therle of Worcestre, whiche late pytously lost his lyf whos sowle I recommende unto your special prayers, and also in his tyme made many other vertuous workys which I have hered of. O good blessyd lord God, what grete loss was it of that noble vertuous and wel disposed lord. Whan I remember and advertyse his lyf, his science and vertue, methynketh God not displesyd overgrete a losse of such a man, consyderying his estate and cunnyng. And also the exercise of the same with the grete laboures in gooying one pylgremage to Jherusalem, visyting there the holy places that oure blessyd Lord haloued thith his blessyd presence. . . . And what worship had he at Rome in the presence of oure holy fadyr the pope." Fuller ignores the charges of cruelty and records only his literary merits : " Then did the axe at one blow cut off more learning in England than was left in the heads of all the surviving nobility." He affirms that Tiptoft quitted England in order to avoid participation in the strife between the king *de facto* and the

3

Yorkist leader to whom he was unflinchingly loyal, a statement which Vespasiano repeats, but he does not record the
episode, given by Leland, of Tiptoft's oration before Pius II,
so eloquent that it brought the Pope to tears, but he adds
certain details about him which are lacking in the English
chronicles. He tells how Tiptoft was attended on the scaffold
by an Italian Dominican friar, who possibly may have carried
back these details to Florence, where later on they came to
Vespasiano's hearing.

Vespasiano judges Tiptoft more severely than either Caxton
or Fuller, whether more justly it is difficult to say. Edward IV,
his master, was merciless, and Tiptoft, in spite of his human-
istic learning may have become deadened to the horrors of
cruelty by Italian teaching and English practice. But no
man could call him traitor. He remained a loyal Yorkist, no
treason like that of Clarence or Scrope or Stanley sullied his
name. These men, though they had never sojourned in
" Circe's Court," might justly have been set beside him on the
scaffold.

William Gray (Guglielmo Graim) was also one of Guarino's
pupils. He was of noble birth, a son of Lord Gray of Codnor
in Derbyshire and a scholar of Balliol. He probably went to
Italy about 1440, and met with varied adventures on the
journey which are described in his life. He won the favour
of Nicolas V, who tried unsuccessfully to gain for him the
Bishopric of Lincoln in 1450, and in 1454 appointed him
Bishop of Ely. He made large purchases of books by the
advice of Vespasiano, which he subsequently gave to Balliol
College, and about 152 of these still remain. The most interesting episode of his Italian journey was his friendship with
Niccolo Perotto, one of Guarino's most accomplished scholars,
which is told in the life of the Bishop of Siponto. Gray went as
king's proctor to Rome in 1449. After his return to England
to assume his duties at Ely neither the cares of his new office
nor the troubles of the realm made him forget the claims of
learning, for he sent to Ferrara John Free and John Gunthorpe, two Balliol scholars, who subsequently rose to fame.
Free became a distinguished physician at Padua and dedicated
two of his books to Tiptoft, praising the learning and virtues
of his patron. Subsequently he became Bishop of Bath and

TRANSLATORS' INTRODUCTION

Wells, while Gunthorpe, after discharging diplomatic missions in various countries, was preferred to the same see after Free's death.

The only other Englishman noted by Vespasiano is Andrew Hollis, under the style of Andrea Ols. He probably won the high praise given to him by Vespasiano because he was a scholar, a patron of learning and a collector of books. Hollis was king's proctor to Eugenius IV and followed the papal court to Florence, where no doubt he met and did business with Vespasiano. We are told that after his return he withdrew from all temporal affairs to a benefice which he possessed in order to find leisure to occupy himself with his library. It would be interesting to lay hands on one of his volumes, but the multitude of his benefices make any search after them difficult. He was chancellor of Salisbury, Archdeacon of Anglesey, Canon of S. Asaph, Lichfield, Southwell and York, and Rector of Davenham, and of S. Dunstan's, London.

To return to the *Lives*. Independently of the vast store of facts scattered about in Vespasiano's pages, the wonderful group of men he commemorates and his shrewd judgment on their actions, there is to be reckoned the value of the light they throw on the complicated politics of the time. Here is a rich store for the historian of statecraft, of warfare or of Churchmanship and, considering the inextricable tangle of treaties, alliances, intrigues and the vagaries of the Captains of Free Companies he had to chronicle, his errors are trifling and unimportant. So much for the matter : with regard to his method of revelation any commendation would be out of place. With all his acuteness of observation and industry he had no literary gift, and this defect may partially explain why his writings had little vogue in his lifetime. He wrote in the vulgar tongue and not in Latin, which was then the fashion, and he constantly apologises for this practice and remarks that he is merely giving notes of the life of some distinguished man for the edification of the unlearned and for the use of scholars, who, in future times, may wish to produce a complete biography in a learned language. Mai attributes the badness of his style to his want of a liberal education, and describes his Italian as diffuse, lacking in polish, difficult to understand, and not always grammatical : his spelling and punctuation as

5

defective, his proper names often mutilated and his composition full of solecisms. These strictures are severe, but they are deserved, for worse prose than Vespasiano's has rarely been written, and by ill luck the conservation of it fell into the hands of very careless copyists. Besides this he often disregards the sequence of the events and scarcely ever gives a date or the birth or the death of any of his subjects. He is unduly prodigal of adjectives and prone to repetition, frequently making the same statement more than once on the same page. Another defect of his is the trick of putting into the mouths of his subjects turgid rhapsodies, and long dissertation on things in general, which must have been his own invention.*

He was free from egoism, and has very little to say about himself. He shows that he is reasonably pleased when he is in the company of the great men of his time, Cosimo de' Medici, Pope Nicolas, Manetti, Palla Strozzi and the rest, but there is no sense of snobbery. His life appears to have been a very happy one : everyone must have liked the garrulous good-tempered bookseller, delighting in his wares, profoundly learned as to their origin and production, and knowing very little of their contents. Of all his memories the happiest must have been that he was chosen by Cosimo, by Nicolas V, by Federigo of Urbino and by Alessandro Sforza to arrange the noble libraries they had collected.

Vespasiano is mentioned by many Italian writers, the most distinguished of whom are Sozomen, the author of the *Chronicle*, and Muratori, who wrote long after his death. Sozomen declares that, had Cicero been his contemporary, he would have commemorated him in his golden periods, and Muratori praises him highly and laments the disappearance of the Life of King Alfonso, which was subsequently rediscovered by Cardinal Mai. After the strictures which have been made on Vespasiano's methods, it is only just to add that, faulty as his instrument is, he knows how to use it with effect. Recent writers of eminence who have consulted him have acknowledged their debt in generous terms, and testified to the truth and clarity of the descriptions of events given in his

* In certain instances a slight concentration has been deemed legitimate.

homely and disjointed sentences. He had mastered the secret of selecting for treatment the most appropriate details of any episode he might have under treatment, and in a few simple words in the Life of Alfonso of Naples he explains his method. He says that Fazi, the recognised biographer of the king, wrote only of Alfonso's deeds of arms and left untold the story of his everyday life. He himself was minded to tell of these humbler details which Fazi had ignored. He was as good as his word, for Alfonso's life is the most anecdotic of all, and he lets us into the secret of his method by relating how, soon after the king's death, he waited on Messer Ferrando, the priest who was with him at the last, and gathered from him the minute details of Alfonso's last illness. His portrait of Nicolas V is the most complete, and displays the Pope not so much as the skilful diplomatist and pacificator of Italy as the bookman, the humble priest, simple-minded and shrewd, at the same time joking with his friend about the astonishment of the Florentines at his elevation to the Papal throne. Then he tells how Thomas of Sarzana had come back from Germany without a coin in his pocket, having spent all the money authorized by the letter of credit, generously given him by Cosimo by Vespasiano's management, and how another hundred florins was forthcoming to carry him on to Rome— also by the intervention of Vespasiano. His portrait of Nicolas and of the others with whom he was well acquainted suggest that he had within him something of the spirit of Boswell ; the sympathetic insight which could divine what points of a great man's character would best attract the attention of the public at large, and decide as to the most effective method of presentation. Nicolas would never have gained the reverence and affection of every successive generation had his biographer laid stress only on his knowledge of the Fathers and of the Civil and Canon Law. He and the sage of Fleet Street both owe much to the pen of the *Vates sacer*.

In his preface Vespasiano writes that he intends to set the life of Nicolas at the head of his volume *uno degno capitano* and a worthy leader of those who are to follow, but the copyist, following chronology, placed that of Eugenius IV first, and this order has always been maintained. The change was not a happy one. Vespasiano knew nothing personally of Eugenius, who indeed was scantily endowed with the qualities which would have attracted him. What kindly consideration he gave to Eugenius was given to him as the patron of Thomas of Sarzana, rather than to the reformer of the mendicant order and the would-be unifier of the Churches. The opening life is not particularly interesting, as it is largely taken up by descriptions of the ceremonies at Florence during the Council of the Greeks, and the establishment of the Observantist rule.

The lives contained in the *Specilegium Romanum* were first published in Cardinal Mai's volume in 1839, in which also appears the important life of Alfonso of Naples, reprinted by Mai from a MS. in the Biblioteca Marucelliana. He gives but few details of his investigations and no hints that he knew of the existence of certain of the lives in other codices. Of the lives in his volume six had already appeared; those of Eugenius IV and Nicolas V in Muratori, that of Cardinal Cesarini in *Italia Sacra*, edited by Ughelli (Venice, 1717), that of Niccolo Albergati, published by Ruggieri from the Vatican Codex, that of Agnolo Pandolfini, printed as an introduction to his *Trattato del Governo* (Florence, 1734) and that of Franceso Filelfo by Riccomano (Rome, 1775).

Besides being included in the Vatican Codex the lives of Piero dei Pazzi, Agnolo Acciaiuoli, Lorenzo Ridolfi, Bernardo Giugni, Bartolemeo dei Fortini and Giannozzo Manetti exist in the Laurentian Library at Florence. In the Magliabecchian are those of Eugenius IV, Lionardo d' Arezzo, Pandolfo and Agnolo Pandolfini, Alessandra dei Bardi and Palla Strozzi. In the Marucelliana are the first five lives given in the Laurentian list as well as those of King Alfonso, the Cardinal of Piacenza, Nicolas V, Donato Acciaiuoli, Cardinal Cesarini and Eugenius IV. Bartoli has added to his edition two extra lives, those of Alessandra dei Bardi and of Bartolemeo dei Fortini. Fortini was a meritorious public servant, but nothing more: the story of Alessandra is of greater interest, but it is marred by inordinate rhapsodizing and repetition and the dragging in of meaningless episodes. The picture given of festivities in Florence at the time of the Emperor Sigismund's coronation progress is interesting, but beyond this there is little else than a rambling narrative of the misfortunes which

8

befel the unhappy lady, written by a hand evidently stricken by senility, and long prayers and lamentations which she is supposed to have uttered.

According to Mai, Vespasiano was for a long time comparatively unknown. The publication of his life of Agnolo Pandolfini as the introduction to the *Trattato del Governo* and the commendation of the Abbate Mehus in his introduction to the life of Ambrogio Camaldolesi in 1759, brought him into notice, and he was hailed as the Italian Plutarch, but for some unaccountable reason oblivion soon fell upon him and his work.

On the whole he shows himself at his best in the last section of his book where he treats of those he knew intimately, men who produced the wares in which he dealt. Here his personal references are most effective, and here he best reveals his own personality; that of a shrewd, good-tempered, straightforward trader with a touch of legitimate pride that Fate had brought him into contact with the finest intellects of the age. Nothing here of the guile and finesse of the traditional Italian, or of the newly fledged humanist revelling in the prospect of a revival of the Greek literature and of its religion also. Paganism had no attraction for him, for every page shows him to have been, before all, an ardent and unquestioning Catholic ; probably sufficiently well furnished with common sense to talk to the advanced spirits who haunted his *bottega* about codices and palimpsests rather than theology. Only two or three of his clients were suspect as to their orthodoxy. One of these, Matteo Palmieri, he lectures sharply in the style of a preaching friar for having gone astray with Origen over the nature of the soul. In life and conduct he is always on the side of what he styles *laudabili costumi*. Mai rises to eloquence over his good qualities, his love of justice, of decent life, of munificence in spiritual and temporal dignitaries, of industry, gentleness and love of our country. Especially he commends prayer, fasting, almsgiving, forgiveness of injuries and the contempt of worldly splendour. Sometimes in pointing a moral over the death-beds of the righteous he overstresses his language till it becomes mawkish—notably in the cases of Eugenius IV, King Alfonso and Niccolao Niccoli, and it must be remembered that the descriptions he has provided can only have been penned from hearsay report.

9

TRANSLATORS' INTRODUCTION

He is an incorrigible eulogist and has a good word for all who are not pronounced malefactors or sceptics—he never censures a brutal ruffian like Ferdinand of Naples. But now and then he is reticent as to the doings of powerful personages, and omits proper names when a clear presentment might have brought unpleasant consequences. In Florence then, the dictatorship of the proletariat used the same measures as it uses in Moscow to-day. The banishment of his neighbours taught him the value of silence on occasions when speech might have affected the prosperity of the bookshop by the relegation of its proprietor to some remote hill-town for an indefinite visit. Early in life Vespasiano must have had experience of the stormy times of the '33 and '34 : of Cosimo's banishment and recall, for the details given in the lives of Cosimo and Palla Strozzi are amongst the most interesting in the book. They are written with caution, but are fairly outspoken. Cosimo probably knew him as a bookseller only and rated him as politically insignificant ; but had these lives, with their frank sympathy with the victims of '34, come under his observation, Vespasiano might not have come off so easily as he did. He is much better as a portraitist than as a chronicler, for while his human figures stand out clearly with all the impress of truth, his descriptions of the scenes in which they may have taken part are often meagre and even unintelligible.

It is sometimes argued that a biography is better written fifty years after the death of the subject, in order that the personality of a man of action may be viewed in juster relation to the results of his career. There is something to be said in favour of this view, but it too often happens that a biography written on these lines, through the introduction of too many ancillary causes and effects, and the operation of forces which have come into being since the death of the person commemorated, becomes less a biography than a section of history.

He omits many lives which might well have been given Rinaldo degli Albizzi, Niccolo d' Uzzano, Pius II, Leo Battista Alberti, Corio, the Milanese historian, Landino, Platina, Laurentius Valla and Pontano. These would have better filled the space which Vespasiano has given to a dozen or so insignificant cardinals and bishops. A place too might have been found for Masuccio Salernitano, the rival of Boccaccio, and the castigator rather than the apologist of profligacy. But the picture Masuccio gives of the morality of the Neapolitan clergy probably convinced the good Vespasiano that he had no title to a place amongst the illustrious.* Most remarkable of all it is that Vespasiano never realised that fame and honour could come to a man who was an architect, a sculptor or a painter. Donatello, Brunelleschi and a few others are mentioned as the recipients of Cosimo's bounty and no more. He was insensible that all around him a band of immortal artists were working to fill the treasure-house of Florence with masterpieces which have held succeeding generations spellbound by their beauty. In comparison with this glorious harvest how meagre is the contribution of the band of writers he commemorates, often in fulsome terms. Who ever turns to them now, except to verify a reference? Lionardo Aretino was a careful compiler of annals, and one of the first to cultivate Greek letters and—together with his fellow-Aretines, Carlo and Benedetto—to translate them into Latin. Poggio's letters are good reading, but probably he is best known by his *Facetiæ*, which often appears in booksellers' catalogues. Immortality, however, does not come this way. Giannozzo Manetti we must admire on account of his noble life and dauntless constancy under malignant persecution—and Palla Strozzi may well stand beside him—but we do not read any of their works.

Even if Vespasiano had included the names suggested above it is not likely that the gain to letters would have been more imposing. The fourteenth century in Italy had witnessed the great outburst of literature—Guido Guinicelli, Dante, Petrarch and Boccaccio—but the momentum was spent with the advent of the fifteenth, just as this same century in England can only show writers of the calibre of Occleve, Lydgate and Malory, the most barren period in our annals.

In Italy things were little better before the closing decade. The treasure-houses of learning had just been reopened, and the finer and more eager spirits were dazzled and fascinated by the newly found jewels : men like Valla, Poggio or Pontano

* Every clerical person Vespasiano notices he praises, except Sixtus IV.

did not deign to waste time over Dante and Petrarch or to follow in their track ; study and scholarship held the field against original work, but in the closing years of the *cinquecento* evidence of the new outburst began to appear.

In 1481 Cristofero Landino, then an old man, advanced the art of criticism by the publication of his Commentary on Dante. As professor of rhetoric and poetry in Florence he had upheld the claim of Dante and Petrarch in his lectures while the rest of the *literati* were poring over Greek codices. Lorenzo now gathered him, together with Pico della Mirandola, Marsilio Ficino, Poliziano and Pulci into the famous circle out of which modern Italian letters may be held to spring. Beyond this point it will not be permissible to go as the term of Vespasiano's activity has already been passed.

Of the other writings of Vespasiano the Magliabecchian Library in Florence possesses : *Trattato della vita e conversazione dei Cristiani a Jacopo Gianfigliazzi* and a *Trattato contro all' ingratitudine, mandato a Luca degli Albizzi.* The Ricciardiana Library has *Libro delle lodi e commendazioni delle Donne illustri, rammentate nel Vecchio e nel Nuovo Testamento e di quelle ancora che furono celebri nelle greche, latine e italiane istorie.* Signor Luigi Polidoro has published " Frammenti di un Trattato storico morale, e notizie di alcune illustri Donne del secolo XV scritti da Vespasiano Bisticci, i.e. Proemio di Vespasiano nel Libro delle lode e commendazione delle Donne mandato a Monna Maria donna di Pierfilippo Pandolfini," also some short notices of " Donne state in Italia degne Andrea degli Acciaiuoli contessa d'Altavilla ; Battista Malatesti ; Pagola Malatesti nei Gonzaga ; Cecilia Gonzaga ; Caterina Alberti nei Corsini : Francesca Acciaiuoli. Alessandra Bardi negli Strozzi ; Giovanna Valori nei Pandolfini ; Caterina Strozzi negli Ardinghelli ; Saracina Acciaiuoli." Vespasiano's last work was the " Lamento d' Italia per la presa d' Otranto fatta nel 1480."

I: *A DISCOURSE BY THE AUTHOR*

I HAVE often considered how great is the value of the light which learned writers, in times both ancient and modern, have thrown upon the actions of illustrious men; how that the fame of many worthies has come to naught because there was no one to preserve in writing the memory of their deeds, and that, if Livy and Sallust and other writers of excellence had not lived in the time of Scipio Africanus, the renown of that great man would have perished with his life. Neither would there have been any record of Metellus, or of Lycurgus, or of Cato, or of Epaminondas the Theban, or of the infinite number of men of mark who lived in Greece and Rome. But because many illustrious writers flourished amongst these people, the lives and actions of their great men have been displayed and published abroad, so that they are as real to us as if they had lived to-day, whereas they happened a thousand years and more ago. For this reason great men may well lament that, in their lifetime, there should be living no writers to record their deeds.

As to the origin of Florence, it is the opinion of Messer Lionardo* and of many other learned men that the Florentines are sprung from the horse-soldiers of Sylla, but this view is difficult to justify. Pliny holds that the city must be of great antiquity, and that the Florentines were called Fluentini because their city was placed between the streams of Arno and Mugone. This is a valid testimony of its antiquity. Moreover, he cites, by way of further proof, the shape of the theatre which still exists, the Temple of Mars, now S. Giovanni a very ancient building, and certain aqueducts which are still partially standing; but all these instances depend only on conjecture, seeing that no learned scribes have ever put the matter on record. For this reason Messer Lionardo, in writing his history of Florence, was put to much trouble through lack

* Lionardo d' Arezzo, the author of a History of Florence, Villani Chron., I, pp. 5, 7, 30–38.

A DISCOURSE BY THE AUTHOR

of documents, except for a period of some hundred and fifty years, and elsewhere he had to base his facts upon such authorities as I have named above.

We find in Florence no writers from the foundation to the time of Dante, that is for more than a thousand years. Following Dante came Petrarch and then Boccaccio, but these tell nothing of the origin of the city because they found no records. After Dante came two other poets, Messer Coluccio and Maestro Luigi Marsigli, who was also a theologian and very learned also in astrology, geometry and arithmetic. Of the lives of these we have no detailed record, but they are mentioned occasionally by all writers. The present age has produced many distinguished men in all the faculties, as will appear to posterity if a record be kept of them, as was the practice in old times when learned writers were plentiful. In this age all the seven liberal arts have been fruitful in men of distinction, not only in Latin, but also in Hebrew and Greek ; men most learned and eloquent and equal to the best of any age. In painting, sculpture and architecture we find art on its highest level, as we may see from the works which have been wrought amongst us. An immense number of these great men we cannot call by name ; their fame has perished simply because no one has written of them. And this loss did not arise through lack of writers ; eloquent and learned men abounded, but they were loth to undertake the burden of literature, knowing that in the end they would enjoy neither the repute nor the appreciation they deserved.

We may see how numerous men of learning were in the times of Pope Nicolas of happy memory, and of King Alfonso, because they were well rewarded and held in the highest esteem, and how many excellent works they composed or copied through the munificence of princes so liberal as the two I have named, whose fame will last for ever. Moreover, beyond the money they gave, they paid honour to men of letters and advanced them to high station. In addition to these two princes must be named a worthy successor, the Duke of Urbino, who, having followed their example in honouring and rewarding and promoting men of letters, became their protector in every respect, so that all were wont to fly to him in case of need. Thus, to help them in their labours, he paid them well for their work, so that he gained immortal fame by their writings. But when there was no longer a Duke of Urbino, and when neither the court of Rome nor any of the other courts showed any favour for letters, they perished, and men withdrew to some other calling, seeing that, as I have said, letters no longer led to profit or reward.

As it has chanced that I myself am of this same age, and that from time to time I have met many illustrious men, whom I have come to know well, I have set down a record of these in the form of a short commentary to preserve their memory, though such work is foreign to my calling. I have been moved thereto by two reasons. *First*, that their fame may not perish : *Second*, that if anyone should take the trouble to write their lives in Latin he should find before him a material from which such work could be modelled. And in order that these men of light and leading may be under a worthy chief, whom they may well follow, and because in all cases the spiritual ought to hold the first place, I will assign to Pope Nicolas* the leadership of all the rest, and I will tell what I have to say concerning His Holiness with all the brevity possible, considering the praise which is his due. Had this task of mine been undertaken in ancient times, the Pope must have been portrayed as an illustrious man by anyone who might have done it. It will appear from the life of this excellent Pope how great is the power of virtue, because everyone must see that he could only have attained to his high position by virtuous dealing.

* References to Nicolo Secondino occur in the lives of Eugenius IV and of Nicolas V. A comparison of these will show that the life of Nicolas V must have been written first. The life of Eugenius IV was an afterthought, and it was the action of the copyist of the Codex which fixed the lives in the chronological order which, with more or less accuracy, they still follow.

15

Pope Eugenius IV (1383–1447)

ESSER GABRIELLO CONDULMERI, a citizen
of Venice who afterwards became Pope Eugenius
IV, was a man of the saintliest life and carriage.
His father died while he was still a youth, leaving
him rich in temporal possessions, and it came to pass that,
having been brought early to realise the worthlessness of this
life, he determined to free himself from the tenacious bonds
of earthly riches which bind men in this unhappy world, by
giving away twenty thousand ducats for the love of God.
After he had got rid of his temporal goods, he determined to
become heir of those which are eternal, and he ordered his
doings in this wise. He was well acquainted with Messer
Antonio Coreri, a young Venetian gentleman who afterwards
became Cardinal of Bologna, also on the threshold of manhood
and greatly esteemed by all, and the two friends resolved to
renounce the world and its pomps, and put themselves under
the yoke of obedience by becoming brethren of S. Giorgio
d' Alga, those friars who wear the blue habit. After they had
entered this house they made themselves perfect in the
spiritual life, setting about their duties like the other brethren
with the utmost humility. Pope Eugenius had an excellent
knowledge of the Latin tongue, and Messer Antonio likewise.
Both by day and by night every hour was fully employed, not a
moment being lost, either in saying the office, or in reading,
or in prayer or in writing. He was a very fine penman, and
whenever he could find time he would occupy himself in
inscribing with his own hand a breviary, out of which he read
the office after he became Pope.

Thus the two friends lived in the monastery of S. Giorgio,
and every day there came some fresh report of their beneficence.
In each monastery of the Observantists* it was the custom

* By the middle of the fourteenth century the Franciscan order
had become corrupt and degenerate, whereupon a company of holy

that, besides the porter, one of the brethren should stand at the gate—in some houses for a day at a time, and in some for a week—to receive any strangers who might arrive, and to answer their enquiries. One day when Messer Gabriello was on duty there came and knocked at the door one in the garb of a hermit. When he had entered the cloister Messer Gabriello, as was the custom, took him by the hand and gave him a friendly welcome, and then, according to their wont, withdrew to the church for prayer. When they came out of the church, as they were traversing the cloister, the hermit turned towards Messer Gabriello and predicted his elevation to the pontificate. Afterwards, when they had conversed, the hermit said, " You will be made Cardinal and afterwards Pope, and during your pontificate you will know much trouble. You will attain to your eighteenth year of power and then you will die." When the hermit had thus spoken he took leave of Messer Gabriello and went his way, and no man ever saw him after, or knew who he was.

This saying Pope Eugenius often repeated in after life and we may observe that the prophecy of the hermit came true, in that the Council of Basel issued a decree against Pope Eugenius which caused him great trouble. Some time before this Pope Gregory, a Venetian of the house of Coreri, a man with much influence, had been made Pope. Now he was uncle to Messer Antonio, the friend of Messer Gabriello ; and, having been chosen Pope, he at once determined that his nephew, Messer Antonio, who was at S. Giorgio d' Alga, should be made Cardinal, but when he sent his request Messer Antonio replied that he had no mind to accept the honour unless His Holiness should also raise to the Cardinalate Messer Gabriello, with whom he had been brought to enter the religious life. Pope Gregory agreed to this request, and so the two were made cardinals together. Pope Gregory did not hold the pontificate long after this, and was succeeded by Pope Alexander. Then came Pope John, who was followed by Martin, and in a short time Messer Gabriello was made Legate at Bologna, where he acted with great prudence.

men established a separate community, the Observantists, under the original rule of S. Francis.

After Pope Martin's death* it was necessary to elect a new Pope and Engenius was chosen, but dissension arose between him and the Romans, who are contentious people ; moreover, he was not the first Pope they had treated in such wise. So great was their violence that they were minded to lay hands on him and put him in prison ; but he, having learnt from his friends what was threatened, left the pontifical lodgings, clothed in a friar's mantle, and went to the port which is called Ripa, where he got into a boat and bade them cover him with leathern shields so that the Romans might not recognise him. His foes were roused to such a point of wickedness that they followed him and, not being able to lay hands on him as they willed, they shot arrows at the galley, and had he not been covered as described they would have killed him. His nephew, the vice-chancellor, wishing to follow him in flight, was captured and put in prison, where he lay some two years. Pope Eugenius in his vessel arrived at Porto Pisano with nothing but what he had about his person, but, on reaching Pisa, he reclothed himself and set things in order, and then proceeded to Florence, where, as he was received with the greatest honour, he determined to remain, the city commending itself to him as the seat of his court. This happened in the year fourteen hundred and thirty-three and he entered Florence in the month of June in the same year, all the leaders of the city going to meet him, some to Pisa and some to greet him on the road. While he was at Pisa he abode with Agnolo di Filippo Pandolfini, where he remained long enough to allow the ordering of the festival in his honour, which indeed was a thing marvellous to behold. All the chief citizens went on horseback to Signa and accompanied the Pope to Florence with full ecclesiastical pomp, according to the custom of the Popes, and with something more if that were possible. And at that time the city was crowded with citizens of worth and reputation.

When the Pope came to Florence he was sumptuously lodged in S. Maria Novella. He had lost a great part of the States of the Church, which were recovered soon after. He arrived in Florence in the year thirty-three, and on the eighth of September, thirty-four, the leaders of the city, suspecting

* 1431.

that the Signory then in office had a mind to alter the form of
the state, took up arms and seized the Piazza, whereupon Pope
Eugenius offered to compose the difference, having been
called upon to act both by the Signoria and by the other citizens
who were anxious for peace. On this business he sent Cardinal
Vitelleschi the Patriarch, who told the leaders that they should
repair to the Pope who would settle all their disputes. They,
trusting the Pope, went to him bearing arms, and these they
laid down and put themselves in his hands. While the Pope
was thus engaged, the new Signory, which had just come into
power, exiled Messer Rinaldo degli Albizzi and his sons, and
Messer Ridolfo Peruzzi and other citizens, recalling Cosimo dei
Medici who had been exiled a year ago. When he heard this
the Pope was greatly angered, for it seemed to him that these
men had been exiled through trusting his word. Nor could
anyone appease the mind of His Holiness in this matter, and
he would have done anything to procure their restitution
to their country, as may be seen from what he did subsequently.

While His Holiness was residing in Florence, he set himself
diligently to reform the Church, and to enact that the religious
orders should keep within their own bounds ; also, as far as
he could, he made the Conventuals accept the Observantist
rule. As to the other religious houses, he reformed S. Marco
at Florence, which was then occupied by Conventuals—not
of the order of S. Dominic but of the other orders—ten or
twelve in number. Pope Eugenius desired that Cosimo should
restore it for the Observantist friars of S. Dominic, to whom
he had assigned it. Cosimo promised His Holiness that he
would spend thereon ten thousand, but in the end spent forty
thousand ducats. And he reformed the Badia of Florence,
although it was already Observantist, but with an abbot
chosen for life, and His Holiness, fearing that the Badia, if
vacated in the reign of another Pope, might not come *in
commendam*, gave to the abbot, who was a Portuguese, an
abbey in Portugal and annexed the Badia of Florence to the
congregation of S. Giustina under the condition that there
should be an annual election of the abbot, which custom
continues to this day. He also put under the Observantists
the monastery of Santo Salvi of the order of S. Giovanni

Gualberto, with the same rule for the election of the abbot
as at the Badia, and brought from Mezzo a brother of Alamanno Salviati, a man of saintliest life, and also a brother
of Nicolini d' Arezzo, and by the agency of these two clerics
he reformed the monastery. The brother of Salviati had at
one time been a great merchant, and had returned to Florence
with a large fortune, but, being convinced of the vanity of this
world, he restored all of his wealth, which his conscience told
him was unjustly gained, and the residue of honest gain he
gave away for the love of God. Having done this he took
religious vows as the safest refuge.

To return to Pope Eugenius. Settimo, an abbey of great
antiquity of the order of S. Bernardo di Cestello, was partly
in commendam and partly in the hands of a certain abbot who
had let it fall to ruin and had sold the farms ; so that, in lieu
of the forty or fifty monks it formerly supported, it now held
but two. Seeing this Pope Eugenius gave it to the Cardinal
of Fermo, a very holy man, in order that he might reorganise
it and recover the lands from certain powerful neighbours,
under the authority of the Pope. After giving it to the
cardinal, he caused certain of the monks of the Badia of
Florence to enter this abbey, and to assume the habit of S.
Bernard, part of the income being assigned to the cardinal
himself and part to the monks ; and in this way he succeeded
in recovering the lands and setting the monastery in order,
the number of monks soon rising to forty. The cardinal
was set upon the recovery of the abbey estate, and during his
life he arranged that the abbey should be free after his death,
and when he died it came to the brethren. Pope Eugenius
gave to them Cestello, a monastery òf monks, and while he
was in Florence he sent to Cestello, at an unusual hour, the
Cardinals of Piacenza and Fermo, who, having entered bearing
certain apostolic directions, directed that those of the
brethren who were willing should repair to another monastery,
Santo Donato in Polverosa, and that those who were not,
should give up their house to the brethren they recommended.
He found much difficulty in reorganising Santo Donato, and
gave Cestello to the friars ; and all those monasteries in various
parts which he could not reform he abolished, such as S.
Maria della Neve, Santo Silvestro and many others. Whenever

he could, he brought them to decent ways of life, where he could not, their house ceased to be, in order to make an end of the unseemly spectacles they caused. The abbey of Fiesole was in the hands of an abbot who maintained there one or two chaplains, but Eugenius took it from him and sent thither some regular Augustinian canons. Afterwards Cosimo dei Medici built the wall there which still stands, and gave to the canons aforesaid Santa Maria della Neve, a monastery of monks which had been disestablished, so that, when they might come to Florence, they might have a resting-place. Eugenius put the Servites under the Observantist rule, to which they submitted for some time, but after the Pope's departure they cast it off. He imposed it in lieu of the Conventual rule wherever he could : indeed, he would say that, if God would give him grace enough, he would bring all religious persons under the Observantists.

The Conventuals held Alverina, and this place the Pope handed over to the brethren of the Observance of S. Francis. In order that their work should have free course, he selected, at S. Bernardino's request, an Observantist friar to direct the rest, this office lasting two or three years. He did the same in the case of the Friars of S. Dominic. Wherever it was possible in the States of the Church, he established the Observantist rule ; in Rome at S. Maria in Ara Cœli, and in the Franciscan convent. He paid a visit to Pope Nicolas, who was then apostolic subdeacon ; S. Giovanni Laterano, which belonged to the secular priests, he found had been for the last four hundred years in the hands of the regular canons of S. Augustine, wherefore he restored it to its owners and constructed near by a large building at his own expense for religious uses in which he installed fifty or sixty monks. He reorganised Scopeto, outside the gate of Santo Pietro Gatolini, and added thereto other houses and endowments, and a convent of women in order that it might be able to exist as a religious house as it exists to-day. The Paradiso was very poor, and in like manner he secured its future by adding to it an abbey and other houses to enable it to exist.

He possessed many praiseworthy qualities which shall be recorded to show he was not inferior to any of the Popes in the past. He consecrated with much pomp the Church of

Santa Maria del Fiore in Florence ; the bridge, which was
built from one church to the other, being hung with draperies
of blue and white, the colours of the Pope, and the woodwork
which supported these decked with myrtle, laurel, pine and
cypress. The hangings were stretched from one side to the
other and heavy curtains hung all the way between the
churches, carpets also and benches on both sides, a sight
marvellous to behold. Along this gallery came the Pope and
all the court of Rome, the Pope in full pontificals and mitre,
all the cardinals in their finest copes, the bishops, who were
also cardinals, in damask mitres ; the bishops in mitres of
calimanco with the cross borne before them according to
pontifical usage, the apostolic subdeacons in their regular
surplices, and the whole court of Rome duly arrayed. At this
time there was in Florence a splendid gathering of prelates
and ambassadors from all parts ; the Pope and all the court
of Rome went in procession along the gallery, and the people
on foot made up a great gathering of the citizens of Florence
from within and from without. When the Pope and his
court entered Santa Maria del Fiore they found the church
nobly adorned and filled with curtains and ornaments fitting
for such a solemn occasion. Round the altar had been contrived a fine level space, covered with carpet, where were
stationed the College of Cardinals and the prelates, the Pope's
seat was covered with damask of white and gold, and about
it were benches for the cardinals. The Pope's seat stood on
that side where they read the Gospel, and on the other side
were the singers ; the ambassadors according to rank and the
College of Cardinals were near the Pope, and on the other
side the bishops, archbishops and prelates. The Pope sang
the pontifical mass in due order, and the ceremony was of
the finest. Afterwards he consecrated Santo Marco at
Florence, where all the Roman court attended in the same
order.

After Pope Eugenius had stayed a certain time in Florence
he left it for Bologna, and from there went on to Ferrara. The
dissensions between the Roman and the Greek Churches had
lasted many years, wherefore Pope Eugenius expressed his
wish that certain of the Greeks should come to Italy at his
charges in order that they might secure union with the Roman

Church. The Emperor of Constantinople,* together with the Patriarch and all the chief prelates of the Greeks, crossed over into Italy and went to Ferrara, a vast number all at the expense of the Pope, but on the outbreak of plague they withdrew to Florence, where quarters and sustenance were provided for the Greeks, month by month. On their arrival in the city, by the advice of the many men of distinction in the Pope's court, S. Maria Novella was fitted with sumptuous seats and benches, and was called the council chamber of the Greeks. For at this time there was sitting at Basel another council, opposed to Pope Eugenius, which at first was well regarded, and cardinals and ambassadors from all parts went thither : but the cardinals began to withdraw, the most important loss being Santo Agnolo, the president of the council. As soon as the Council of the Greeks in Florence was constituted by the advice of the principal cardinals, led by the Cardinal of Piacenza, the Council of Basel was cited to appear. Indignant at this citation, the Council of Basel elected out of their own number a Pope of little weight, Pope Felix, formerly Duke of Savoy, who had retired from affairs of state and become a hermit ; but though he was made Pope, he commanded no obedience, save that of his own state, and after a short time he laid down his papal honours, and was content to be cardinal and legate in Savoy. The Council of Basel soon came to nothing on account of the action of the Council of the Greeks.

At this season certain Armenians, Jacobites and Ethiopians were sent by Prester John to the Roman Pontiff, who paid all their charges, and also summoned the learned men of Italy and other lands. And when His Holiness had assembled a great number of these, they all came together in the presence of the Pope and the court of Rome to discuss the differences between one Church and the other, the chief of which was whether the Holy Ghost might proceed from the Father and not from the Son. The Roman Church held that it proceeded from both, and in the end the Greeks assented to the Roman belief. There was at this time at the court of Rome, as I have said already in another place, Nicolo Secondino of Negropont, the interpreter between the Greeks and the Latins, and it

* John Palæologus.

was a wonderful experience to hear him transfer words from one language to another : from Greek to Latin when the Greeks might be speaking, and then from Latin to Greek. Finally, after long disputations, the Greeks assented to the Roman view in every point where there had been division ; as did the Jacobites and the Armenians and the subjects of Prester John.

And on a solemn day the Pope with all the court of Rome, the Emperor of the Greeks and all the bishops and prelates assembled in Santa Maria del Fiore, where had been made a goodly arrangement for placing and seating the prelates of either Church. The Pope was placed on the side where the Gospel is read, together with the cardinals and prelates of the Roman Church, and on the other side the Emperor of Constantinople with all the Greek bishops and archbishops. The Pope wore full pontifical vestments ; all the cardinals wore their copes ; the cardinal bishops mitres of white damask ; and all the bishops, Latin and Greek alike, copes ; the Greeks in their robes of silk in the Greek fashion had a more goodly and dignified appearance than the Latins. The Pope sang a solemn mass, after which all the prerogatives of the union with the Greeks were recited with the greatest solemnity. The Greeks promised never more to be in discord with the Roman Church, as in the past, and the Emperor and all the chief personages who were with him put their names to this, but the Patriarch was not one of these ; for, after having agreed with the rest and consented to the union, he fell sick and died a few days after, reconciled with the Roman Church.

During this ceremony the Emperor occupied the place where the Epistle is read by the high altar, in which same place, as I have already said, were all the Greek prelates. All Florence was there to witness this noble function. Opposite to the Pope's seat, on the other side, was a chair covered with a silken cloth on which sat the Emperor, clad in a rich robe of damask brocade and a cap in the Greek fashion, on the top of which was a magnificent jewel. He was a very handsome man with a beard of the Greek cut. Round about his chair were posted the many gentlemen of his retinue, clad in the richest silken robes made in Greek fashion ; their attire being most stately, as was that of the prelates and of the laymen also. It was a very wonderful thing to behold this goodly ceremony : the reading of the Gospel in both the Greek and Latin tongues as is done on Easter eve in Rome. I will not pass on without a word of special praise of the Greeks. For the last fifteen hundred years and more they have not altered the style of their dress ; their clothes are of the same fashion now as they were in the time indicated. This may be seen in Greece in a place called the fields of Philippi, where were found many records in marble in which may be seen men clothed in the manner still used by the Greeks.

To come back to the point we left, to the ceremony of the union with the Greeks ; on the same morning was also confirmed the union of the Armenians, the Jacobites, the people of Prester John and the others who had come in order to join the Church of God. And the records of all these solemnities were written in Florence by the decree of Cardinal Cesarini of S. Agnolo ; and, as memorials of such a noble achievement, the said cardinal commanded that these writings should be kept there, and he further ordained that all the original deeds referring to this union should be kept in the Palace of the Signory : *ad perpetuam rei memoriam.* As soon as the union was accomplished* Pope Eugenius made eighteen cardinals, and made known the names of all on the same day, two of them being Greeks, Niceno and Ruteno, also Pope Paul. Pope Eugenius, wishing to gratify the Florentines by creating two or three cardinals, set himself to decide the claims of those before him and ultimately approved only those of Nicolao degli Alberti, Bishop of Camerino, a man of the greatest worth and of good estate.

After Pope Eugenius had lived some years in Florence, a difference arose between him and the authorities, who felt some suspicion, when he announced his intention of going to Siena and thence to Rome, that he was ill-disposed towards the city. This suspicion arose from the intrigues of the Venetians. By letters, and by the action of their ambassador at Florence, the Venetians strengthened the resolve of the citizens to bar his leaving. Many citizens assembled for discussion, and the opinion of the wisest was that he should on no account

* Vespasiano never mentions the subsequent relapse of the Greeks and the failure of the Council.

be hindered, but allowed to depart of his own accord ; for the Venetians were counselling a policy they would never have adopted themselves. He who proposed to let the Pope go, and gave the fullest reason for this course, was Messer Lionardo d' Arezzo : all agreed in this opinion and sent word of their decision to the Pope by Messer Agnolo Acciaiuoli, who told the Pope that he might go wherever he wished, so he departed for Siena on the same day.

I will not conclude without giving certain particulars concerning Pope Eugenius and his worshipful personality. He was tall and handsome : spare, grave and reverend in appearance, so much so that no one could keep eyes fixed on him. He discharged the office of Pope with wonderful efficiency, and while he abode in Florence he never let himself be seen, or moved from his lodgings in Santa Maria Novella, except at Easter or on the solemn feasts of the year ; and the air of devotion which hung around him was such that few who looked on him could retain their tears. It happened one evening that one of the chief men came to consult him and kept his eyes cast down, and could not look upon the face of the Pope who, perceiving this, spoke to him and asked him the cause. The man replied that there was something in the aspect of the Pope which forbade him to raise his eyes to gaze upon it. Many times I beheld the Pope and the cardinals on a gallery beside the door of the cloisters of Santa Maria Novella, when the Piazza itself and all the streets leading thereto were crowded with people, and the reverence felt by them was so great that they stood astonished at the sight of him, silent and turning towards the spot where he stood. And when, according to pontifical usage, he began to recite the *adjutorium nostrum in nomine Domini*, the whole piazza seemed to be filled with wailing and lamentation, praying God for mercy on account of the great reverence they had for His Holiness : indeed, it was as if the people felt they looked upon the Divinity as well as upon the Vicar of Christ. The Pope and all the cardinals around him, men of the highest station, stood reverent and devout ; then, indeed, it seemed that he was in truth Christ's representative.

To come now to his daily life ; for a long time he drank no wine, nothing but water with sugar and a little cinnamon.

For his food he was content with one dish, always boiled, of which he ate according to his inclination, and for this end he caused one dish to be kept always ready in the kitchen that it might be got ready, so he was never behind time. He never ate before the appointed hour, and greatly relished fruit and vegetables. He gave audience to all who would see him as soon as his business might be despatched, especially to the servants of God and to those whom he knew to be good men. He gave alms most liberally to anyone who might ask, making no store of money, which he esteemed little, and being always in debt because he saved nothing. In his house were many gentlemen of the kingdom of Naples and of other countries, to whom he gave board and lodging for the love of God, and certain nephews of his own, laymen, in like manner. But he was careful that these should have no share in the Estate of the Church, for he felt he could not give away what did not belong to him. As to alms, these he gave, as I have said, to any who might ask for them.

One day a citizen of ours, one Felice Brancacci, a poor man and an exile, went to His Holiness and asked for succour. The Pope handed to him a purse full of florins and opened it, telling him to take therefrom whatever he might want. Felice in a shamefaced way, put out his hand timidly, where-upon the Pope, laughing, turned to him and said, "Help yourself liberally to what I give willingly, and take what you want without counting." He never kept store of money in his house ; as he got it, he spent it quickly. One day some-one brought him four or five thousand florins, and he bade Bartolomeo Rovarella, who was in the room with him, to put the money aside. Being busy at the time, Rovarella put the money under the mattress of the Pope's bed, where it remained several days. Soon after, when the Pope was in his chamber, a certain man came to whom he wished to give money, where-fore he told Bartolomeo to bring out the bag of money. Bartolomeo, knowing that the Pope would take it ill that the bag should have been put under the bed, hesitated to with-draw it. But as the Pope repeated his demand for it, he was forced to produce it and took it from the bed in the presence of the Pope, who at once showed his anger. He turned to Bartolomeo, and reproached him that he had concealed this thing in the bed, as if it were something of great value, and bade him for the future to make no more such mistakes, by way of showing him that too much store should not be set on money.

In his private lodgings he kept at his call four ecclesiastics, two of the order of S. Giustina, who occupied the Badia of Florence, and two of the Blue Friars—Pope Eugenius' own order—besides a secular priest. With these four he did the services day and night, and never failed to arise to say matins. He slept in a shirt of coarse serge and made a rule that two attendants should always watch in his chamber, changing duty every three hours. Whenever he might wake, he would find close to his bed books such as he wished to read, and he would call those who watched, and sit up, whereupon they would bring him in a pillow, a book and two lighted candles. He would read one hour or two according to his fancy, and when he had read enough he would again summon his attendants to take away the book and the lights. He had such dignity of presence that those who had to do with him were often reluctant to address him.

This wonderful gift was his by nature, and in addition there was the holiness of his life and the pontifical dignity. He kept undiminished the highest powers of the Church of God, in that no king or prince could ever make him yield in the least where the dignity of the Church was in question. The King of France was unwilling to keep certain engagements towards the Church of God,* and desired that the Pope should give way in this matter, threatening that, in case of refusal, he would withdraw his obedience, and ultimately he got his way. The Pope had disputes also with the Venetians because they desired to concern themselves with things which were no business of theirs, and to act against the dignity of the Church.

To return to the point we left, Pope Eugenius, when he quitted Florence, betook himself to Siena, for he was little inclined to return to Rome on account of the ill demeanour of the people towards the honour of God and the Church. He tarried some time at Siena before going on to Rome, as he desired to know from the Romans the conditions under which he might return. Through the absence of the Pope Rome had

* A reference to the Pragmatic sanction of Bourges.

become a mere cow-pasture, for the people kept cattle and cows in places which are now filled with seats of traders, and everyone went clad in peasant's cloaks and boots, because of the long absence of the court, and of the wars that had been prevalent. After the Pope had come back with a splendid court most of the people reclothed and re-established themselves, and showed greater respect for His Holiness than they had ever shown before. The Pope next despatched Messer Tomaso da Sarzana and Messer Giovanni Carvagialle, the auditor of the Rota, beyond the mountains, and, on account of their efficiency in the discharge of their mission, Pope Eugenius sent two red hats to Viterbo to meet them on their way back to Rome, and these were the last cardinals made during his pontificate. They entered Rome in great state, and when they went into the Pope's presence to inform him as to the outcome of their embassy Pope Eugenius said to Messer Tomaso, " You shall be my successor."

After he had been Pope for eighteen years, he arose one night to say matins and began to groan and laid down the breviary which he held in his hand. The four attendant monks did not dare to ask what ailed him, and Pope Eugenius, having recovered himself, turned to his attendants and said, " As soon as the office shall be finished, you may ask me what ails me and I will tell you." He then recommenced his praying, and when he had done the attendant clerics, wishing to know what was the matter with him, asked him why he had groaned. He replied, " The end of my life is drawing near, because the hermit told me in the monastery of Santo Giorgio, where I was a monk, that I should be made cardinal and afterwards Pope, that I should attain to the eighteenth year of my pontificate, and that I should then die. I am now come to this, little more of life will be mine, wherefore, if there be anyone who wants aught of me, let him ask it of me before I quit this life, which is near its end." After this they all began to weep. On the following day he caused the door of S. Peter's to be closed and went thither with three of his household, and when they had come to the third door which leads outside he saw a marble stone on which was inscribed *Eugenio papa terzo*, who had been a disciple of S. Bernard. Then he turned towards those who were with him and said, " I wish that my grave may be beside this with an inscription saying that it is the tomb of Eugenius the fourth." He then went back to his apartments and in a short time he fell sick, and knowing that death was near, he gave his mind to those matters which all faithful Christians, like himself, regard. When the prelates and the clerics who were usually about him came into his presence, he turned to them and said with a sigh, " O Gabriello (for this was his name) how much better it would have been for the health of thy soul if thou had'st never been Pope nor Cardinal, but had'st died a friar! Wretched are we all, that we only know ourselves when we are come to our end."* Then, having taken all the Sacraments of the Church, he yielded his soul to his Redeemer, dying just as he had lived in the most holy frame of mind. And this was the end of this worshipful Pope, light and ornament of the Church of God. I have not written this as his life, but only a brief commentary thereon. There will be found so many noteworthy matters concerning His Holiness that a book might well be written from them. Let this stand by way of a short record.

POPE NICOLAS V (1398–1455)

Maestro Tomaso da Serezana, who afterwards became Pope Nicolas V, was born at Pisa of humble parentage. In course of time, through civil strife, his father was banished and withdrew, at his own instance, to Serezana, where he let his son learn grammar as a child. He was an apt scholar, and when he was nine years old his father died leaving two boys, Tomaso, and Filippo who was afterwards Cardinal of Bologna. In the same year Tomaso fell ill, whereupon his widowed mother, perceiving that he was sick and having the highest hope in this son of hers, was in the greatest grief and anxiety. She offered constant prayers to God that He would deliver her son from danger, and while she was thus praying and fearing lest her son should die, she fell asleep about daybreak, but

---

* The Pope's closing years were troubled with disputes with the King of France and the Emperor and the electors with regard to ecclesiastical " obedience " The German legation and the cardinals wrangled by the sick man's bedside. Æneas Sylvius represented the Germans, and a conclusion favourable to the Papacy was reached.

somehow it did not seem to her that she was sleeping, as she was called by her name, " Andreola," by some one who said to her, " Have no fear of your son's recovery." Moreover, in this vision she saw her son clothed in pontifical vestments, and some one told her that he would be Pope, and bade her keep firm hope that all these things which were told her would come to pass. When she was awakened from sleep, she went forthwith to see her son and found him much better, and she told to all the household the vision she had seen.

When the boy had quite recovered his health his mother, firmly sustained by the hope given to her in the vision, urged him to apply himself to his studies ; but there was no need for this, seeing that he was by nature most anxious to learn. Thus, by the time he was sixteen, he had an excellent knowledge of grammar, had heard and read much in the Latin tongue : and had begun logic, philosophy and theology. Then he left Serezana for Bologna that he might there prosecute his studies. He made great progress in logic and philosophy, and in a short time he became learned in all seven of the liberal arts. He remained at Bologna till his eighteenth year, when he was made Master of Arts ; but through want of money, he found it necessary to go to Serezana to his mother, who had married again, in order to procure the wherewithal to pay his charges. The mother was poor and the husband not over-rich, moreover, Tomaso was to him not a son but a stepson, so no money was forthcoming. But being determined to continue his studies he went to Florence, at that time the mother of learning and of all merit, and soon after he met Messer Rinaldo degli Albizzi, a prominent citizen, who engaged him at a liberal salary, which he well deserved, as the tutor of his sons. After a year of this engagement Messer Rinaldo left Florence ; and, wishing to remain in the city, Messer Tomaso made an advantageous agreement with Messer Palla di Nofri Strozzi to act as tutor. In the house of Messer Palla the greatest honour was paid to his worth in order that the boys might treat him with respect. At the end of another year he had received from these two citizens enough money to allow him to return to his studies at Bologna, although in Florence he had lost no time.

So he quitted Florence and went to Bologna, where he was

fain to reside on account of the school of theology : and in a short time, being already learned in philosophy and a Master of Arts, he became a Doctor of Theology in his twenty-second year. Messer Nicolao degli Albergati, Bishop of Bologna, who was of the order of the Carthusian brothers, begged him to come and reside with him ; and after he had gone thither the bishop discovered his great merits, and gave over to him the entire ruling of his house. After he had taken up this governorship he did not lose an hour of time, and always attended the disputations in the assemblies. I heard from him that, being a Master in Theology, he overlooked the works of the Master* of the Sentences, and the works of all those who had written comments thereon, because in these it often happened that one writer would set down what another had omitted. He knew the works both of the modern and the ancient doctors, and there were few Greek and Latin writers whose works he had not studied. He knew the whole Bible by heart, and his citations thereof were always appropriate. During his pontificate these evidences of scriptural study, in the answers he was called upon to make, added greatly to his fame and honour. When he was twenty-five years old he was ordained priest by the hands of the Bishop of Bologna, and a short time afterwards Pope Martin, having heard of the good repute of the Bishop of Bologna, of his own accord made him cardinal with his title from Santa Croce in Jerusalem, this necessitating his transfer from Bologna to Rome. Messer Tomaso went with him to Rome, which was full of distinguished men, with whom he would hold disputations in theology or in philosophy whenever time permitted. And, not to leave unnoticed his proficiency in universal knowledge, I have heard him remark how he had ascertained from the records of divers authors that Italy had been in the hands of the barbarians, the Goths, the Vandals, the Getæ, the Huns, the Lombards and the Heruli, for four hundred and fifty years, and that it was a wonder to him that books or anything of worth should have survived.

While Messer Tomaso was thus settled in Rome, Pope Eugenius considered how peace might be made between the King of France and the King of England and the Duke of

* Peter Lombard.

Burgundy.* Bearing in mind the honesty and good faith of
the Cardinal of Santa Croce he resolved to send him as legate
to France and England, and to the court of the Duke of
Burgundy, where he was held in the highest esteem. Moreover,
he designated Maestro Tomaso as a member of this embassy,
largely because of the reputation he had acquired during his
sojourn at the court. The cardinal, through the good offices
and industry of Maestro Tomaso, played a most beneficent
part in settling the disputes between France, Burgundy and
England. He put an end to divers wars and discords which
were rife in these regions, and on his return to Rome, after the
conclusion of peace, the Pope, who was greatly pleased at
what he had done and confident in his fitness for another
mission of the same sort, despatched him to Germany on
account of the frequent quarrels between the princes of that
country. Here he remained for a year, and almost all the
disputes were brought to an end, partly through the benevo-
lence and good faith of the cardinal himself, and partly through
the promptitude and industry of Maestro Tomaso. They
suffered privately much pain and weariness from the roughness
of these people, who are still barbarians. After his return
to Rome the Pope sent the cardinal to Ferrara, where he
brought about a peace between Duke Filippo and the Venetians and the Florentines.† Here again the cardinal worked
hard for peace, and rested not till they had succeeded in
accomplishing this good work. Italy had long been harried
by armed bands and by war, and these troubles now ceased.
In all these missions the diligence of the cardinal was seconded
by that of Maestro Tomaso. The cardinal was troubled
with stone and other infirmities, and gave over to the care of
Maestro Tomaso the general management of his public and
private affairs.

On account of a conspiracy laid against him by the Romans,
Pope Eugenius fled from Rome to Florence,‡ and thither went

---

* " Eugenius prædictum Cardinalem ad sedandum quoquo modo
hujusmodi bellicos tumultus a Roma usque in Galliam, & Britanniam,
ac Burgundiam, e Latere, ut dicitur, Legatum misit. Quaquidem in
Legatione Thomas noster, ut antea erat, sic totius familiæ personæque
dominicæ gubernator accessit."—Muratori, *Rerum Italic. Script.*,
II, part 2, p. 914. B. Rymer, X, 530. Eugenius became Pope in 1431,
and this embassy was sent in 1432.

† 1433.   ‡ 1434.

also the Cardinal of Santa Croce and Messer Tomaso. There they found many distinguished men, and many also came with the papal court. For the reason that Lionardo d' Arezzo, Giannozzo Manetti, Poggio, Carlo d' Arezzo, Giovanni Aurispa, Gasparo da Bologna, a very learned man, and many others were accustomed to assemble every evening and every morning at the corner of the palace for discussion and conference on various matters, Maestro Tomaso, as soon as he had gone with the cardinal to the palace, would repair thither and join them. He rode on a mule with two servants on foot, and generally would wear a blue cloak, while the servants would be clad in long coats of *moscavoliere* with priests' caps on their heads. There was no such pomp in the papal court then as we see now. He would constantly be found in the place above named holding discussions, or about the Pope's court, conversing and arguing, for he was a very ardent dialectician. When Pope Engenius left Florence he went to Bologna, where the cardinal had his bishopric ; and, the episcopal residence being in very bad condition, the cardinal, as soon as Maestro Tomaso arrived in the city, began to confer with him as to the rebuilding of it. He gave him a commission to carry out the work, and in a very short time the bishop's home was rebuilt from the foundations.

After the Pope quitted Bologna he went to Ferrara, where he sought to bring the Greeks into communion with the Roman Church, and so arranged things that all the leaders of that people consented to repair to Ferrara. The Pope agreed, in order to bring them to the true Church, to pay all their charges, their lodging as well as all their necessary wants. The Emperor in person and the Patriarch of the Greeks, the two chiefs of that religion, came together with all the most learned men of Greece. After they had been some time in Ferrara the plague broke out, and it was necessary to leave that city and go to Florence, where they took possession of houses for the lodging of the Greeks, who numbered about five hundred bishops, archbishops and other prelates. Pope Eugenius had assembled in his court all the learned men he could find, friars and priests and seculars, and caused benches to be erected in Santa Maria Novella for the Council, which, by the advice of certain of the learned cardinals, was called

35

the Council of the Greeks. Moreover, the Council of Basel was summoned to appear at Florence, and by this action it was dissolved and its authority annulled. The doings of these learned men in this most momentous occasion are known to everybody; how in this Council every morning, before the Pope and the cardinals and all the court of Rome, the Latins disputed with the Greeks concerning their capital error, which was that the Holy Spirit proceeds from the Father alone, and not from the Son, while the Latins, by the true meaning of the Faith, maintain that it proceeds from the Father and the Son. Amongst those who were present was a certain Nicolo Secondino from Negroponte, who spoke in a fashion which was marvellous to hear, because, when the Greeks spoke and brought forward arguments to prove their opinions, as soon as they had ended Nicolo Secondino explained in Latin *de verbo ad verbum* everything they had said. Then the Latins spoke, making answer to the arguments of the Greeks, which answer Nicolo translated into Greek. In all these disputations Messer Tomaso found himself on the side of the Latins. He was amongst the leaders and the highest in esteem with both factions, through the universal knowledge he possessed of the Holy Scriptures, and of the doctors, ancient and modern. Pope Eugenius strove unceasingly to abolish heresy all over the world, and amongst those who had come to Florence were certain Ethiopians and Armenians and Jacobites, who are Christians with certain heretical opinions. To all of these they sent some learned man, skilled in the language, and amongst these were some friars of Santo Antonio, true friars, very roughly clad; they were unshod, wore hair cloth and ate neither flesh nor fish that had blood. Pope Eugenius handed over to Maestro Tomaso the duty of disputing with these three nations, the interpreter being a Venetian who was well versed in twenty languages, and twice every day, with the help of this interpreter, Messer Tomaso would hold discussions with them. After these disputations had gone on for some time, these Ethiopians and Armenians and Jacobites were brought into union with the Roman Church by Messer Tomaso's influence, and of this union there is public record in the Palazzo dei Signori, together with that of the Greeks, the greater part of whom also joined the Church. And Maestro

Tomaso had much to do in this affair of the Greeks, and of the
three other parties as well.

In all matters his merit made itself apparent, and, notwithstanding the high esteem of his position, his carriage towards all those who knew him was most amiable. He was
very witty, he had a pleasant word for everyone, and all those
who held converse with him were afterwards friendly to him,
by reason of his admirable manner and of his marvellous
natural gifts. His negotiations with the courts of all the nations
of the world gave him an honourable position, and in these
he had always met men of worth and worship. He behaved
most liberally to all, not regarding what he possessed as really
his own. He did not know what avarice was ; indeed, if he
retained anything of his own, it was simply because no one
had asked him for it. He spent money beyond his power, as
at that time he maintained a large number of clerks, the best
he could find, and never considered their wage. He had
full trust in his own ability, knowing that he would never
want, and he used to say that there were two things he would
do, if he had the money to spend, that is to say, buy books
and build houses. During his pontificate he did both. And
although at this time he was poor, he was determined that
all the books which were produced for him should be of the
finest in every respect. He had books in every branch of
learning, and amongst them the works of S. Augustine in
twelve fine volumes, all newly edited in the best style :
likewise the works of ancient and modern doctors, nearly all
of which he had read and annotated with his own hand ; for,
taking both the ancients and the moderns, he was one of the
finest scribes that ever lived, and in these books of his, where
he could find no notes, he added some of his own. And to-day
in Santo Spirito, in a library called after Boccaccio which
forms part of the library of the friars and was built by Nicolao
Nicoli, who placed therein certain of Boccaccio's books in
order that they might not be lost, there is a book which Maestro
Tomaso gave to the friars, the treatise by S. Augustine,
Contra Julianum pelagianistam and against other heretics,
which is throughout annotated by him. Whenever he went
with the cardinal out of Italy, he never returned without
bringing back some book hitherto unknown, such as the

POPES AND RULERS

Sermons of Pope Leo, the notes of S. Thomas on S. Matthew, a most excellent work, and many others. There was no Latin or Greek writers in any of the faculties with whom he was not acquainted ; and as to the arranging of a library there was no one to equal him, and for this reason Cosimo dei Medici, when he was about to set in order the library of S. Marco, wrote to Maestro Tomaso begging him to send direction as to how a library should be formed. And who is there who has not gone through this trouble before bringing some such a scheme into working order ? Maestro Tomaso wrote the instructions with his own hand, and sent them to Cosimo ; moreover, he did the same with the libraries of Santo Marco, of the Badia of Fiesole, of the Duke of Urbino and of Signor Alessandro Sforza.

All men of letters are under heavy obligation to Pope Nicolas for the favour he extended to them, and for the high estimation he gained for books and for writers everywhere. It often happened to Maestro Tomaso that he found himself without money, so he had to buy books on credit ; and, in order to pay his scribes and miniature painters, he borrowed as much as it seemed he could afterwards repay. He was by nature generous : this liberality of nature is indeed a blessing, and, on the other hand, avarice is accursed. It was said by S. John Chrysostom that if all the world, transmuted to gold, should be placed before a miser, his greed would be so great that he would still be unsatiated, and that a man could more easily fly through the air than a miser could become liberal. Avarice is expressly contrary to nature. Maestro Tomaso had the widest experience, and besides the seven liberal arts, was supremely gifted as a politician, as if he had never applied himself to anything else, but had been brought up in the administration of important matters of state, on which indeed his judgment was marvellously clear. All who might talk with him on any subject of learning, would imagine that he must have studied it exclusively. His natural talent had something of the Divine, as had also his mental impressions of what had befallen him.

He hated ceremony and flattery, and was familiar with everyone he met whether as bishop or ambassador, he treated with honour all who might visit him, and he willed that those

who had aught to say to him should sit down beside him, and
occupy the first place ; moreover, should anyone refuse to do
this he would take him by the arm and make him sit, whether
he would or not. Should his visitor be a man of worship he
would accompany him on his departure out of the room as
far as the staircase. It happened one day in Florence that
Giannozzo Manetti, who had gone as ambassador to France,
went to visit him and, as he held Manetti in great respect, he
did him all possible honour. After the visitor had stayed
some time, he rose to depart, whereupon Maestro Tomaso, in
spite of his protests, went with him into the hall, and then to
the staircase and ultimately to the ground floor. Manetti
stood still, not wishing that his host should go farther, but he
had need of much patience for, not only did Messer Tomaso
want to go with him all down the stairs, but, when he got out
of the house, he insisted on going as far as the door of the
Osteria del Leone, where the ambassador was staying. When
he had come to the hotel he turned to those people who were
passing, and highly praised Messer Giannozzo saying, amongst
other commendations, that he was a very worthy citizen, and
inferior to none of those whom the Roman republic had produced when it was in its greatest glory.

He was of the most modest disposition towards those of his
own household with whom he had dealings. It is true that
he expected to be understood by the beck, so assiduous was
he with regard to all the matter in hand, and he was fain that
all about him should be the same. He was by nature given
to anger, but his prudence led him to keep his wrath within
bounds. He employed no Italian servants, but all either
Germans or Frenchmen. Being questioned one day why he
employed no Italians he replied, "Because they were of a
spirit so high, that they would always get too big for their
station. Now whatever task you put on a Frenchman or a
German he only feels that he is doing what he ought to do ;
he remains contented and never wants to get into a higher
place, and even if you employ him on the vilest work, he will
serve you faithfully." For a long time he enjoyed no emolument, tor there was not then a salary for everyone as there is
to-day, and the first office he held was when Pope Eugenius,
who was then in Florence, made him apostolic subdeacon, that

is one of those who carry the cross before the Pope, and take part in the Mass, one of them reading the epistle at the Papal Masses. These subdeacons are of two classes, one numbered and the other not, and they have an emolument of three hundred ducats a year. Maestro Tomaso was of the numbered; he had already held an archidiaconate in France without care of souls, but he had no other benefice at this time.

After his departure from Florence Pope Eugenius went to Siena, taking the cardinal and Maestro Tomaso with him. Here the cardinal fell grievous ill with stone and died, having made a will by the Pope's grace by which much of his wealth went to pious uses. He gave the execution of his wishes into the hands of Maestro Tomaso, so great was his confidence in him after his twenty years of service. After the cardinal was dead they took from his body a stone as big as the egg of a goose, weighing eighteen ounces. Then Pope Eugenius, of his own accord, made Maestro Tomaso Bishop of Bologna; and, soon after his return to Rome, he sent him as ambassador to Florence to transact some important business. At this period Pope Eugenius was greatly irritated with the Florentines. Being present one evening with the Signoria, Maestro Tomaso spoke with regret about the differences existing between them and the Pope, going on to say that, by reason of this bad feeling, the Pope had more than once made alliances with King Alfonso and Duke Filippo.* After finishing his mission in Florence, he returned to Rome, whereupon the Pope sent him on another to King Alfonso with respect to the Pope's anger against the Florentines; and, this despatched, he went back to Rome. Having seen how well he had conducted these negotiations, the Pope sent him as ambassador to France and Germany on important matters, and in these he succeeded as well as in the two former missions.

Later on Eugenius sent him, together with Messer Giovanni Carvagialle, a Spaniard, the auditor of the Rota and a very distinguished man, to France and Germany; and on their way they passed through Florence. On his nomination as Bishop of Bologna, Maestro Tomaso had resigned his other two benefices, the subdiaconate and the archidiaconate, and was without income because Bologna then refused obedience

* Filippo Maria Visconti of Milan.

to the Church, and held back the revenues of the bishopric. On this account Pope Eugenius made him vice-chamberlain. The first words he said to me when I saw him in Florence were that Pope Eugenius was poor, and he himself of the poorest, for the reason that his only source of income was his bishopric, from which he received nothing ; that Pope Eugenius was most liberal, but was without cash and consequently unable to give him such a sum as would allow him to complete his task in France. Then, turning to me, he said, " You must go to Cosimo and beg him to place at my disposal a hundred ducats *per diem* until the date of my return and tell him the reason therefor." I went to Cosimo, who said to me, "I wish to do better even than he demands," and thereupon he sent to him Roberto Martelli, who told him that he had a commission from Cosimo dei Medici to issue a general letter to all the companies and correspondents of the house, who would pay over whatever sums Maestro Tomaso might want. This seemed to him even too great liberality, and he bade Roberto to thank Cosimo on his behalf. Roberto replied in a tone of courtesy, setting forth the good will of Cosimo towards his lordship.

I will here relate what happened one morning before he took his leave. He invited the envoy of Bologna, who was then in Florence, to dinner, and on that same morning I found myself in their company. It was the season of Advent, and Maestro Tomaso was fasting, though he was on a journey, and was keeping Lent. He prepared a fitting repast for the envoy, and when they were at table he took in hand the book of Santo Giovanni Cassiano, dealing with induction to benefices, and said, " It is always my habit wherever I may be, in travelling or otherwise, to read at the beginning of a meal." According to his wont he had upon the table two small bottles, holding about two glasses each, filled the one with red and the other with white wine, both well diluted with water, and these he would hardly finish. I have set this matter down here because certain malignant and envious people have slandered him in the matter of drink, without knowing anything about him, simply because, during his pontificate, he provided his house with good wine, not for himself but for the use of certain prelates and gentlemen of France, Germany and England with whom he had made close acquaintance when he was in their country. When any of these came to Rome he presented the wine to them, and for this reason it was bought. While he was at table this morning with the Bolognese envoy he turned to him and said, " It grieves me much that you have not given me the income of the Bishopric of Bologna ; you gave me the bishopric, but if I wish to live there, it will be necessary for me to sell my dearest possessions, my books ; but what offends me more than all is that you have turned the bishop's house, which is the house of God, into a haunt of thieves ; sending thither any vagabond who may come your way. Would to God that some day you will recognise how great your offences are."

Having quitted Florence the ambassadors travelled to France and Germany. And here I will relate what he told me concerning this embassy. He declared that, because they were apostolic legates, all the people went down on their knees when they passed along the roads in Germany ; and for the same reason the greatest honour was everywhere paid to them. Also that this honourable treatment lasted as far as Padua, where it fell off greatly from what it had been beyond the mountains. These two remarkable men, by their prudence and their uprightness, settled many disputes ; and the report of their success reached as far as Rome ; so that the Pope, realising the great and praiseworthy work of Maestro Tomaso, determined to reward him therefor. When the two legates had come back to Florence Maestro Tomaso went forthwith to the Signoria, and when he saw me he began to laugh and said, " I have drawn two hundred florins by these general letters of Cosimo, and now I must needs have a hundred more to pay the charges of my journey to Rome. Let us go to Santo Giovanni where the pardon is going on, and afterwards we can go to Cosimo's house." I told him there was no need to do this, and that I would settle the matter. But he went to the pardon, and when he came out of the church he came upon Cosimo in the piazza of Santo Giovanni, and spoke to him about the hundred florins he wanted over and above the two hundred he had already drawn by the general letters. Cosimo answered, " The hundred florins, and as many more as you will, shall be at your disposition." He went on, " Roberto Martelli will wait on you, and will hand over to you whatever sum you may want." Roberto came in due course, authorised to give him what money he required, but he would take no more than a hundred florins.

Having received this money he started the next morning on horseback for Rome, and when he reached Viterbo it appeared that Pope Eugenius, without letting it be known to any of the party, had sent thither two red hats for Tomaso da Serezana and for Giovanni Carvagialle, a Spaniard, who was named Cardinal of Santo Agnolo ; moreover, many men of consideration went to meet them, and they were likewise met near Rome by the whole of the College of Cardinals and the ambassadors, entering the city with the stateliest ceremony. Having entered Rome they went to the feet of His Holiness Pope Eugenius, where they explained the commission given to them, and everything they had done from the day of their departure till now. Afterwards Maestro Tomaso made a most appropriate speech to the Pope and thanked him for the grace he had conferred on him by the gift of the cardinal's hat, testifying his deep gratitude to His Holiness and to the College of Cardinals in the most eloquent words. When this was done the two cardinals quitted His Holiness, attended to their houses by all the cardinals and ambassadors who were there, as well as by those who had accompanied them in their entry into Rome.

It chanced that, in the course of a few months, Pope Eugenius fell sick of a grave distemper and passed away from this life, dying as virtuously as he had lived. The career of Pope Eugenius is an example of obedience to a salutary rule of life, and after his death it became necessary to order the funeral rites within nine days according to custom ; and, as on such occasions, a funeral oration was always made over the dead, this charge was now given to Maestro Tomaso. The oration was spoken with great dignity and eloquence, and gave such great satisfaction to all the College, and to the others present that it moved the cardinals to make him Pope, independent of his eminent merits, and in spite of his recent election to the College. I heard from the leaders of the College that the majority had chosen him, and that his reputation was greatly augmented by this noble oration. Everyone knows how great is the power wielded by talents like his. All the cardinals entered the conclave at the Minerva, each one going to his room without intrigue or news from without. At this time the College of Cardinals was a very worthy and holy one.

It happened on the first night of the conclave that a marvellous vision came to Maestro Tomaso as he slept in his chamber, dreaming of the election to the Papacy which lay before the cardinals. Amidst these sleeping fantasies, there appeared to him Pope Eugenius clad in full pontifical habit, and it seemed as if the Pope was minded to dress him in these garments, and that he refused. Maestro Tomaso, having asked him why he wanted to put upon him the pontifical vestments, the Pope replied, " Because you will be my successor ; put on all of them except the mitre." As soon as he awoke from sleep he began to laugh and turned to the two companions who were with him in the room, whereupon they asked him why he laughed, and he told them of the vision he had seen, never deeming that aught would come of it, as he was only nine months a cardinal, of low station, not conscious that anyone spoke of him, and never thinking to arrive at such honours. He could claim nought but his integrity and the success of his diplomacy.

Having come to the election of the Pontiff, without any communication from without, they unanimously made him Pope on the second day. After they had taken him and placed him in the chair, according to custom, he remained some time in bewilderment, this thing having come upon him unexpectedly. One might say that it had been brought about by miracle, for in eighteen months he had been made bishop, cardinal and Pope entirely from merit.

In his pontificate he made it plain that he had been elected by divine mercy to pacify Italy, vexed by war and violence for many years. Shortly after his election I, having gone to wait upon His Holiness, went one Friday evening to his weekly public audience. As he came into the audience chamber, about seven in the evening, he spied me at once and called to me in a loud voice that I was most welcome, that I must have patience, and that he wished to see me apart. Not long after, one came and bade me go to His Holiness, whereupon I went and, following usage, I kissed his foot, after which he bade me rise and dismissed all the rest, saying that the audience was at an end. He withdrew to a private apartment close to a doorway which led to a garden balcony. In it were some twenty candles lighted, four of them near to His Holiness. He made a sign that these should be taken away, and when they were removed he began to laugh and cried out to me, to the confusion of his puffed-up attendants, " Vespasiano, would the people of Florence have believed that a priest, fit for nothing better than to ring a bell, should have been made Sovereign Pontiff ?" I answered that Florence would believe that he had been chosen by reason of his many virtues, and in order to pacify Italy. To this he replied and said, " I pray God to give me grace to bring about what I have in my mind, and to do this same thing during my pontificate without using arms other than those which Christ has given me for my defence : that is to say, His Cross. And this will be my course as long as I shall rule."

Then he turned to me and said, " You know what great kindness Cosimo dei Medici has done me in my time of need : however, I am now going to reward him and to-morrow I shall make him my banker. One can never go wrong in liberality towards men of good heart. [There was a time, during the jubilee, when the Medici bank held in its hands more than a hundred thousand florins of the wealth of the Church : this I heard from a trustworthy person in their service.] He then went on, " I wish to pay high honour to the Florentines, and to-morrow I will give them audience in public consistory, as it is given to kings and emperors, to give them this preference and do them this honour." He added, " It will be well to recall from exile Ser Filippo."* I assured him that this would be done—as it was. Afterwards I commended to him Messer Piero degli Strozzi for some preferment, whereupon he said that he should have the first office that fell vacant. He kept his word, for shortly after, the parish of Ripoli being vacant, and the application duly brought before him, he remembered his promise, and gave it of his own accord to Messer Piero. Many times he told me to ask for whatever I might wish for, but I, inexperienced as I was, asked for naught. After I had been with him some time he said, " Stay here this evening," and

* Probably Filippo di Ser Ugolino.

45

then he called to Messer Piero da Noceto and said, " To-morrow you shall dine with us." Then he went into the chamber beside his own and said, " Stay here to-night," and because it was Lent he sent out for provisions. He grieved much that the house of Pope Eugenius had been pillaged, and that the household were forced to put up with borrowed beds : and he told me many things beside which I will leave untold because, as I am writing a commentary on his life, I would not seem to be speaking of myself while I ought to be speaking of Pope Nicolas.

He began his pontificate to the satisfaction of all those who knew him, and the apostolic seat gained great repute throughout the world on account of this happy election. All the learned men of the world flocked to Rome of their own free-will. Some Pope Nicolas sent for because he wished that they should reside at the court of Rome. He made assemble there a vast number of distinguished men, and he began to grant audiences in public consistory. At this time Florentines held all the chief offices in diplomacy and government in Italy ; and on the mornings when he gave audience to the Florentines in public consistory many foreigners attended, learned men and men of standing ; and many more came attracted by the fame of Messer Giannozzo Manetti, who was one of the six Florentine ambassadors, the others being Messer Agnolo Acciaiuoli, Messer Giannozzo Pitti, Messer Alessandro degli Alessandri, Neri di Gino and Piero dei Cosimo dei Medici. Giannozzo Manetti was not then a *cavaliere*. They arrived with a hundred and twenty horses, and made their entry with the greatest pomp, accompanied from outside by all the court of Rome and the cardinals. It was wonderful to see the ambassadors all clad in the same fashion : all six in garments of the richest crimson cut velvet with open sleeves lined with miniver, and with them twelve youths with garments of like fashion of crimson damask, lined with miniver. On the morning when audience was granted to them the hall was full of the most illustrious personages, and there was a gathering of cardinals, all of them men of distinction, and ambassadors from all parts. Messer Giannozzo made an excellent speech, lasting an hour and a quarter, in a new style of oratory which had been but a short time in use.

All listened most attentively and no one moved. The Pope was deeply absorbed, almost as if he were asleep, and one of those near him held his arm now and again to support him. When the oration, which was in two parts, was finished, it seemed that Pope Nicolas had it by heart, for he recapitulated it part by part in a wonderful manner. On this morning the sanctity of His Holiness waxed greatly as did the fame of the ambassador. In his reply the Pope won much approval and everyone departed well content.

In his new office he began at once to rid the Church of whatever offence he could deal with. The old Duke of Savoy, Amadeus, had been elected Pope by the Council of Basel (he lived in a hermitage he had built in Savoy), but now the Council had almost come to an end through the departure of its most important members in the time of Eugenius, this man found means to procure for himself election as Pope to the exclusion of Eugenius, but this deprivation had no authority or reason, and he commanded no obedience save that of his own land. On his election Nicolas, by way of abating this abuse and unifying the Church, made an offer to this Pope Felix that he should renounce his pontificate and become cardinal-legate with full authority in his own country. Felix consented and thus the schism in the Church came to an end. Nicolas could think of nothing but the restoration of peace in Italy, and in this he succeeded by forming a league between all the Italian States for twenty-five years, settled by an apostolic bull with penalties for any power which should disregard it, desiring also that he and all his successors should adjudicate in any dispute which might arise between the parties. He gave to the league and to those who held to it his blessing, and to those who broke it his curse. He worked so that Italy, which was vexed by war when he became Pope, was pacified. He abolished simony, and no one dare mention it in his presence.

The fame of his goodness was spread throughout the world, and many lands, on which the Church had lost its hold, came back to it voluntarily and without turmoil. At the first stage of the league King Alfonso had been left out by the Venetians and greatly angered therefor, as he claimed to take the first place, but now that all things were settled and the Venetians had evacuated the King's lands, Pope Nicolas sent to Naples the Cardinal of Fermo, and ambassadors to all the other Italian States, so that by the persuasions of the Pope and of the Cardinal the King consented to agree to the league, and Italy was pacified. It would seem that this must have been the work of the Holy Spirit, for the Pope kept truly to what he had professed at the beginning of his pontificate, that he was minded to find his protection in the Cross of Christ, and this he did continually.

He made eight cardinals, all of them distinguished men, save his half-brother on the mother's side, known as Messer Filippo, who became afterwards Cardinal of Bologna. After he had created seven cardinals, all men of mark, it did not seem meet to him to promote his brother, but when the College of Cardinals saw what he had done, they sent an urgent petition to him; and then it was with great difficulty that he was persuaded to give his brother the hat. Afterwards, when the cardinals' names were published, he spake to each one the customary words of praise, but to Messer Filippo he said, " At the request of certain of your brother cardinals we choose you, Filippo, as a cardinal," without praise or any other word spoken to him. The cardinals whom he created at the same time with his brother were nominated from the lowest order in the Church. Messer Latino Orsini, a courtier of some standing and of the highest family; Messer Antonio Cerdano, one of the greatest of philosophers and a theologian matched by few of his time; Messer Niccolo di Cusa, most learned in the seven liberal arts, a great theologian and a man of much power, German by nationality but not by habit; Messer Alano, Cardinal of Avignon, a man of general knowledge after the manner of his country; Messer John of York, a man of weight; Sbigneo of Cracow, a very remarkable personage, and another distinguished cardinal named Messer Giovanni Eduense, a Burgundian. All these were created on account of their personal worth, without which they would never have been made. Moreover, the Church of God possessed few prelates of merit who were unknown to His Holiness.

At this time came the year of jubilee, the true jubilee being at the end of every fifty years according to the regulation of the Church, and there was at Rome a crowd so great that no one could remember one greater. It was a marvel to witness the concourse of people which was gathered together. The roads from Florence to Rome were so full that, looking at the people who traversed them, it seemed that they must be ants : so much so that on the bridge of Santo Angelo there was a crowd of people of all ages, packed so close that they could move neither one way nor the other. For this reason when each one strove to go his own way, there arose so fierce a struggle between those who came and those who were there already, that more than two hundred men and women were killed. When Pope Nicolas heard of this most grievous accident he was greatly displeased, and provided that the like should never again happen ; moreover, he built at the foot of the bridge two chapels in memory of this slaughter, and he caused all the victims to be buried.

A vast amount was sent to the apostolic seat in Peter's pence, whereupon the Pope began to build, and searched for Latin and Greek books in all places where they might be found, never regarding the price. He collected many of the best scribes and gave them continual employ. He brought together a number of learned men and set them to produce new books, and also to translate others not in the libraries, rewarding them liberally ; and when the books were translated and brought to him he would hand over ample sums of money in order that the translators might go to their work with a good will. He spent much in supporting men of letters, and at his death it was found by inventory that since the time of Ptolemy, there had never been collected such a store of books. He caused copies to be made of all, not reckoning the cost ; indeed, if he could not procure a particular work, he would have it copied. After he had induced a great company of learned men to repair to Rome on liberal payment, he wrote to Messer Giannozzo Manetti at Florence to come also to practise as a writer and translator. Manetti left Florence for Rome, where he was received by the Pope with the highest honour. Nicolas granted to him, besides the office of secretary, six hundred ducats, exhorting him to undertake the translation of the books of the Bible and Aristotle, and to finish the books himself he had already begun, *Contra Judæos et gentes*, a wonderful work indeed, had it ever been finished ; but no more than ten books of it were written. He translated

49

the New Testament and the Psalter, *De Hebraica veritate*, with
five books of apologetics in defence of the Psalter afore-
mentioned, showing that in all the Scripture there is not a
syllable without a hidden meaning.

It was the design of Pope Nicolas to found a library at S.
Peter's for the general use of the Roman court, and this would
have been a wonderful work could he have accomplished it ;
but, forestalled by death, he left it unfinished. For the
elucidation of the Holy Scriptures he caused quantities of
books to be translated : likewise many pagan writings and
certain works of grammar necessary for the study of Latin.
The *Ortografia* of Messer Giovanni Tortello, whom His Holiness made his librarian, a valuable and useful book amongst
grammarians : the *Iliad* of Homer : *De Situ Orbis* of Strabo
were translated for him by Guarino, to whom he gave five
hundred florins for each part, Asia, Africa and Europe, making
one thousand five hundred florins in all. Herodotus and
Thucydides were translated by Messer Lorenzo Valla, whom
he paid most generously for his pains : Xenophon and Diodorus by Messer Poggio ; Polybius by Nicoli Perotto, to whom,
when he was presented to the Pope, Nicolas gave five hundred
papal ducats, newly minted, in a purse, and told him that this
was not the reward he merited, but that in due time he
should receive one which would content him. The works of
Philo, a Jew of the greatest merit, unknown in Latin. The
De Plantis of Theophrastus and the *Problemata Aristotelis* were
both translated by Theodore, a Greek of great learning and
eloquence. The *Republica* of Plato, together with the *Leges*,
the *Posteriora*, the *Ethica* and *Physica*, the *Magna Moralia*,
the *Metaphysica* and the *Rhetorica* were done by Trabizonda.
The *De Animalibus* of Aristotle, a very valuable work, by
Theodore. Amongst sacred writings the works of Dionisias
the Areopagite, a marvellous book, was translated by Fra
Ambrogio, the most of the translations hitherto made having
been very barbarous. I heard Pope Nicolas say that this
translation was excellent, and that he understood it better
in this simple text than in the others with the numberless
comments and notes they contained. The wonderful book, *De
preparatione evangelica*, of Eusebius Panfilus, a work of most
profound learning. Many works of S. Basil, of S. Gregory

Nazianzen, about eighty homilies of Chrysostom on S. Matthew, which had been lost five hundred years and more. Twenty-five of these had been translated by Orontius more than five hundred years ago, and this work was much in use, both by ancients and moderns, for it is on record that when S. Thomas Aquinas was on his way to Paris, and before he arrived there, he was shown these homilies, whereupon he exclaimed, " I would rather have S. John Chrysostom on S. Matthew, than the city of Paris," so highly did he esteem it. This was now translated by Trabizonda, as well as Cyril on Genesis and on S. John, works worthy of all praise. There were many others translated or written at the request of His Holiness of which I have no report. I have written only about those known to me.

Pope Nicolas was the ornament and the light of literature and of learned men, and if after him there had appeared another Pope following in his footsteps, letters would have achieved a position worthy of them, but after him they fell into evil case through want of bounty. The repeated liberality of Pope Nicolas caused many to come to him who would not otherwise have done so. He did honour to literature in every possible way. On his way to Naples Messer Francesco Filelfo chanced to pass through Rome, and he did not at once wait on the Pope who, when he heard of his presence, sent word that Filelfo should visit him, and when he saw him he said, " Messer Francesco, I wonder greatly that you should have come to Rome without coming to see me." To this Messer Francesco replied that he was taking certain works of his to King Alfonso at Naples, and that he had preferred to visit the Pope on his return. The Pope had in a purse at his side a sum of money which had been bequeathed to him, five hundred florins, and this he brought out of his purse and said, " Take this money for your charges on your journey." This is indeed liberality ! He carried by his side a purse containing always several hundred florins, and these he gave, for the love of God, to those deserving his bounty, bringing them out of his purse by handfuls. Liberality is natural to mankind, it does not come by nobility, nor by gentility of birth, for in all classes may be found men liberal and avaricious. Pope Nicolas did builder's work in several of the Roman churches, especially to be noted is the wonderful structure he erected in S. Peter's, which would hold the whole Roman court, and in all the churches of the country he did marvellous works, concerning which Messer Giannozzo Manetti has written in his life of the Pope.* The building which he carried out would have sufficed for the activity of one of those Roman Emperors who ruled the entire world : much more for that of a pope, and then he beautified the buildings with ornaments for Divine worship which cost a fortune. It was happiness to him to spend, and he never counted the cost as many others have done. In the year of jubilee he canonised Santo Bernardino da Massa with the solemn functions used for such ceremonies, and placed him in the catalogue of saints because of his numberless miracles, and of his marvellous life.

The Pope had risen to great fame and renown by reason of the mighty buildings which he had erected and of the many books which his scribes had produced in Rome and in other places ; wherefore, Almighty God, according to His way of sometimes chastising us to let us see that we are but men, sent upon Rome and upon all the country near a most destructive plague of which certain of the Pope's household fell sick and died, and the Pope himself began to be much afraid ; whereupon there occurred to him what S. Paul said to the Corinthians : how we should not exalt ourselves through glory and magnificence. " And there was given to me a thorn in the flesh," *Angelus Satanæ qui me colaphizet ; propter quod ter Dominum rogavi ut discederet a me : et dixit mihi, sufficit tibi gratia mea, nam virtus infirmitate perficitur.* The Pope, perceiving how the plague was increasing, quitted Rome for Fabriano. On the journey thither he fell sick at Tolentino so that Maestro Bavera, his physician, believed that he must die, so grave did his condition seem. But by night Pope Eugenius appeared to him and bade him fear not, for he would not die of this distemper, but would live till the eighth year of his pontificate. In the morning, when Maestro Bavera went to him, he was greatly better and he told the physician what had befallen him during the night. He recovered quickly and went on to Fabriano, where his apartment was never clear of the builders, and scribes, and translators who

* Muratori, *Rerum Italic. Script.*, XX, part 2.

followed him, and he was continually engaged on the works he had begun.

After the Pope's return to Rome there came ambassadors from the Emperor Frederic of Germany, newly elected to the Empire, to beg the favour of coronation by His Holiness. Nicolas consented that he should come to receive the crown, wherefore he quitted Germany and went to Italy with a great following of barons and gentlemen, men and horses being decked with wonderful ornaments. With him went the King of Hungary, fourteen years old, and the Duke of Bavaria and many other gentlemen. At the same time came his wife, Leonora, of the noble house of Portugal, and in her train many Portuguese gentlemen. When they met in Rome the retinue of the Emperor, it was a wonderful sight to see, such a crowd of gentlemen so marvellously adorned with everything fitting. When the Emperor and Empress, accompanied by the College of Cardinals and all the Roman court and numberless lords, spiritual and temporal, had entered Rome, the Pope assigned to them two apartments nobly furnished, one for the Emperor and one for the Empress. At that time ambassadors from almost all the world had come to Rome.

Of the coronation of an Emperor by a Pope, a rare occurrence, I will here say something I heard from one who was present. The Pope was seated on his chair, near which stood all the College of Cardinals and the Roman court and all the legates there present. The Pope being seated, the Emperor appeared before him and forthwith knelt down in front of the Pope and kissed his foot and his right hand. Afterwards the Pope bent down, kissing him on the right side of his face, whereupon the Emperor made a short speech of supplication to the Pope that the crown should be given to him. After this the Pope answered graciously according to the custom and then they departed, each one going to his own lodgings. The day after the Empress came and went through the same form of kissing the foot and the hand of the Pope. Several days having elapsed the Pope repaired to S. Peter's in the same state and, after he had taken his seat, the Emperor and the Empress came to receive the crown. After their coming a solemn mass and certain prayers were said for the Emperor, who knelt at the predella of the altar while the Pope girded him with a sword decorated with gold. Then he placed in the Emperor's right hand the regal sceptre, and a golden ball in his left, and put upon his head a sumptuous crown of gold full of jewels. Then he remained still for a space, and stretching out his hands offered to God the following prayer, " *Omnipotens sempiterne Deus, qui ad prædicandum æterni regni evangelium, romanum imperium præparasti, præsta, quæsimus huic Federico tertio novello imperatori, fideli famulo tuo, arma cælestia ut superatis barbaris et inhumanis gentibus ac catholicæ fidei inimicis pacis, secura et intrepida tibi serviat libertate.*" After he had made this prayer Frederic answered as follows, " *Exaudi, quæsumus, omnipotens et sempiterne Deus, pias et devotas preces Nicolai tui summi pontificis, ut cuncti ecclesiastici et sæculares populi, prælati, respublicæ, et principes, omnibus christiana fidei hostibus penitus abolitis, atque ad ultimum internecionem usque deletis, liberius servire atque efficacius famulari valeant, et per hunc certum ac securum omnium fidelium nostrarum gentium famulatum, cuncti christiani homines digna utriusque et præsentis et futuræ vitæ præmia consequi mereantur.*" The Emperor and the Empress were crowned merely by the placing of the crown on the head. After the coronation the Emperor and Empress quitted Rome and went to Naples to visit King Alfonso, who did them honour in such sumptuous fashion as had never been heard of in these times.

A short time after the Emperor and Empress had quitted Rome for Naples it came to pass that, notwithstanding all the benefits Pope Nicolas had done to Rome in general and to many citizens in particular, certain ribald spirits made conspiracy to kill the Pope and to seize Rome.* Almighty God, who forsakes not those who trust Him, willed that this evil should come to naught, and for this reason disclosed the conspiracy which had for leader Messer Stefano Porcari, a wicked man, who was taken and, having come before the ordinary judge, was hanged. Though many were in the plot, he alone died ; the Pope, being most merciful, pardoned all the rest. This Stefano Porcari, before he came into notice, appeared one night to Pope Nicolas in a dream and, from what he then said, he evidently meant to seize the state and take the Pope's life. God had great mercy towards Nicolas in

* 1454.

revealing to him all the accidents of his life, fortunate and unfortunate as well ; before they came to pass they were all shown to him in his visions. There is no such pleasure in this life for great men, when they awake, as to feel that all is well.

Pope Nicolas, having sent to the Certosa of Florence for a certain Don Nicolo di Cortona and for Don Lorenzo da Mantua, the prior of Pisa, both of them very saintly men, they came to Rome on the Pope's summons not long before his death. After they had arrived in Rome and had seen the Pope, he was minded to instal them in an apartment beside his own, so that he might be with them whenever he wished, for he held them in the greatest esteem, both for their holiness of life and for the great wisdom he had marked in both of them. And from Don Nicolo, the prior aforesaid, I heard how one evening the Pope came alone into their room where he found the friars seated and talking together. On the Pope's entry they prepared to get up, but he would not let them, and made them keep seated and sat down between them, asking them, as soon as he began to speak, if there was in the whole world a more unhappy man than himself. He went on to say that the sorrow which troubled him most was that of all the people who entered his apartments there was not one who told the truth about the matter he was considering : that he was so greatly troubled that, if fair dealing allowed, he would willingly renounce the Popedom and be once more Maestro Tomaso da Serezana ; and that he had formerly enjoyed more ease in a day than he now had in a year, pouring out his grief to them without cease till they all wept. Everyone knows there is often great misery where in common belief there must be great happiness. In the public eye Pope Nicolas was looked upon as the most fortunate Pope of the Church of God for many years ; nevertheless he spoke of himself as the most miserable and unhappy of men.

The Pope, continuing in this course, brought some fresh amendment every day into the government, and he gave to none of his relations or connections any estate or lordship : giving them nothing but those offices at ordinary stipends such as the pontifical authorities are wont to give. He made no fresh cardinals beyond those created at the beginning, holding this dignity in great respect, and resolute to maintain its reputation by conferring it on worthy men and on no others. His unceasing activity injured his robust health with gout and other infirmities so that, having brought into his house the two friars before named from the Certosa, Almighty God provided that, in the season of his great need, when the saving of his soul might be in question, he might have by him two fathers so worthy and holy as were these two. So great was the strength and constancy of his mind that, though he was plagued with the sharpest bodily pains, no one ever heard him either cry out or complain. He always showed the bravest spirit : he sang or caused to be sung to him psalms and hymns and prayers in the presence of God, and in these he prayed God for patience and for pardon of his sins. About His Holiness were the two holy friars of the Certosa and many others who gave him consolation in this great affliction, and he answered all most humbly. During his last illness he gave several answers worthy of note, and of all these I will name only that which he made to the Bishop of Arras who was leaning on the foot of the bed and weeping. This bishop was highly learned in theology and in the seven liberal arts and most eloquent, as he showed by his public speeches. The Pope with his eyes fixed and his face turned towards the bishop, observed that he was weeping and spake in the gentlest words, " My friend, may those tears of yours take their flight to Almighty God, and with devout and humble prayers beg Him to forgive my sins. And I will remind you that your true and good friend, Pope Nicolas, is dying." Then he bent his eyes on the bishop, and everyone felt that the time had come to weep, loving the Pope as they did. After he had finished speaking the sighs and lamentations of those present compelled them to quit the chamber.

The two friars from the Certosa were with him continuously and gave him the Sacraments, never leaving him day or night all through his illness. There happened to His Holiness a good fortune which happens to few, inasmuch as everything he wanted was done for him : he lacked nothing either for the body or for the spirit up to the end of his life. I once heard Pope Nicolas say in praise of Fra Nicolo da Cortona* that he had never known another such a priest as he was. For when

* See *Life of Nicolao degli Albergati*, p. 123.

he went with the Cardinal di Santo Croce into France and
England, the friar accompanied them for a year, and Nicolas
affirmed that he could never say whether he was made of soul
and body, that he never gave him the least trouble, that he
never perceived in him any variation, and that he looked upon
him as divine rather than human. On account of these unheard
of merits Nicolas held him in high affection, and would fain
have procured for him the cardinalate, but he would never
assent to this, declaring that he had no mind to incur so great a
danger, or to put in doubt that which was now so clear to him.

Perceiving that the hour of his death was drawing nigh ;
albeit his mind was sound, he bade them summon to him all
the College of Cardinals, and many other prelates likewise,
and began to speak in these terms which were written down
by Messer Giannozzo Manetti. He went on to say, " Being
assured, my well-loved brethren, that the hour of my death is
near, I wish now to speak some weighty and momentous
words for increasing the power and dignity of the apostolic
seat, not committed to writing or to parchment, and not
graven on tablets, but I would liefer tell them to you in my own
words, to give them greater force. I pray you listen to Pope
Nicolas, my brethren, while he, with his last words, pronounces
his testament before you all. First I give thanks to God in
the highest for all the immeasurable benefits which, in His
infinite mercy, He has given me from the day of my birth until
now. Next I commend to you this spouse of Christ, adorned
so fair, upon whose exaltation and magnificence I have spent
all my powers, as you all know well, being assured that the
honour of God is manifested by the majesty dwelling in her,
and by the privileges she exercises, so many and great and
worthy of their originator, the creator of the universe. I have
done what is required of every Christian, and especially of the
Shepherd of the Church ; I have made my confession when
sound in mind and intellect, I have eaten in penitence the
sacred body of Christ, and shared His table with both my
hands, praying of Almighty God pardon for my sins ; I have
partaken of these sacraments and now have come to extreme
unction, the last of all the sacraments for the healing of my
soul. And once again with all my powers I commend to you
the Roman Church, notwithstanding what I myself may have

wrought therein ; this question seeming to me to be one of those momentous ones which it is your duty to satisfy in the sight of God and man. This Church is the true spouse of Christ whom He redeemed with His own blood, desiring that by His merits the whole human race should be partakers therein, and because all the world perished by the sin of Adam, He was fain to redeem it by His most precious blood. This is that seamless robe which the impious Jews strove in vain to divide. This is that bark of S. Peter the Apostle the chief of them all, tossed about by varied accidents of the winds and not in the least discomfited : disturbed by vicissitudes of all kinds and neither submerged nor sunk, for Almighty God has held her up. Support and rule her with all the strength of your souls, and let this task be helped on by your good works, holding out a righteous example both in your life and in your habits. If with all your strength you watch over her and love her, God will reward you for the same in this present life, and in that to come you shall receive eternal rewards. As to this we beg you, with all our might, that you will do as we desire, brethren most beloved in Christ."

Having spoken in this wise he lifted his hand to heaven and said, " Almighty God, grant unto Holy Church and to these fathers a shepherd who will preserve and enlarge it : who will rule and govern Thy flock." Then turning to those around him, " And I pray and hearten and exhort you as strongly as I can that you will please to commend me to God in your prayers." When he had thus spoken he stretched out his arms and cried in generous spirit, " *Benedicat vos Deus Pater et Filius et Spiritus Sanctus.*" He spoke with high and solemn voice in pontifical manner. All the cardinals were standing with their eyes upon him, and shortly afterwards with the Cross and religious sentences before him his sanctified soul passed from this life amidst the prayers of those who were present. Up to the time of his passing these holy priests and cardinals and other prelates were always with him. Long time had elapsed since any pontiff had died after the fashion of Pope Nicolas, and it is a matter of wonder that, up to the last moment of his life, he never failed either in speech or in sanity of mind. Thus died Pope Nicolas, light and ornament of the Church of God and of his own time.

PLATE II

TOMB OF NICOLAS V

PLATE III

FEDERIGO, DUKE OF URBINO

PLATE IV

BARTOLOMEO COLLEONE

PLATE V

ROBERTO MALATESTA

PLATE VI

CARDINAL NICENO [BESSARION]

PLATE VII

TOMB OF THE CARDINAL OF PORTUGAL

PLATE VIII

MONUMENT TO S. BERNADINO

PLATE IX

COSIMO DE' MEDICI

PLATE X

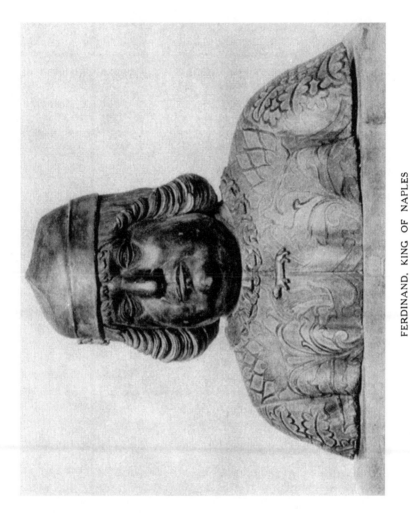

FERDINAND, KING OF NAPLES

PLATE XI

SIXTUS IV GIVING AUDIENCE

PLATE XII

SIGISMONDO PANDOLFO MALATESTA

PLATE XIII

MATTEO PALMIERI

ALFONSO, KING OF NAPLES

ALFONSO, KING OF NAPLES (1401–1458)

Neapolitan history is so closely interwoven with that of the other states that a brief summary of the chief events may be useful to the reader. When Vespasiano begins Ladislas, son of Charles III of the house of Anjou, was King. He died in 1414 and was succeeded by his sister, Joanna II. She had no issue, and adopted Louis of Anjou as her heir ; he died in 1470, and she then adopted René of Provence, his brother, the father of Margaret of England. Joanna died in 1435, whereupon Alfonso of Aragon, who was already King of Sicily, opposed and ultimately expelled the Angevins, and ruled prosperously till 1458. His son Ferdinand, a cruel and vicious tyrant, succeeded him, and the country again fell into anarchy through the revolt of the Angevin barons. This was finally quelled by the victory at Troja in 1463. *Vide Life of Alessandro Sforza.—Translator's Note.*

King Alfonso was a prince of the highest worth [the holder of seven kingdoms and born of the noblest Christian lineage, springing from Theodosius the Christian Emperor, a man of might and authority. This house has never varied from its family line after the manner of other royalties : like that of the kings of France which, on the failure of the line, has of necessity applied at divers times to the Popes, who have nominated other families worthy to rule. In this house, as it has been said, the line has never failed, and the house of King Alfonso has produced as many men of mark as any house in Christendom ; and especially many kings in Spain*], and although King Alfonso's life in ten books has been written by Messer Bartolomeo Fazi,† a very learned and eloquent writer, yet Fazi treats only of his martial deeds, beginning from the time of Pope Martin, and has told nothing of his private life and habits. For this reason I have written down these matters, which he has left unnoticed, seeing that he took note only of events of high moment. Nevertheless, having been well known to many of those who were about his person, I shall be able to tell you certain things which I have heard

* The portion of the text within brackets is only found in the *Codex Marucelliana.* Alfonso's seven kingdoms were Aragon, Catalonia, Valencia, The Balearic Isles, Sicily, Sardinia and Corsica, and Naples.

† Published in Lyons in 1560. Vespasiano carries out his intention of writing Alfonso's life in an anecdotic strain, for in none of the others is he so full of personal details. On the other hand, this life is very imperfect in historic events, few of which are noticed.

from trustworthy men in His Majesty's service. He was a lover of letters, taking much delight in the Holy Scriptures and especially in the Bible, which he knew by heart. Messer Giannozzo Manetti told me that His Majesty had a thorough knowledge of the Scriptures, and that he would always cite the Bible and the Commentaries of Niccolo di Lira. Messer Giannozzo was greatly astonished to find that he knew it almost by heart, and one day he questioned His Majesty, who answered that he had read the Bible through many times with Niccolo di Lira's exposition. His rule of life was that a man was bound to do everything which led to the making of a good Christian. He was most merciful to the poor, and devout in hearing Mass three times every day—two plain and one sung—and in this he never failed. It happened one day that he was hearing Mass at Christmas when word was brought, warning him that he should quit the place forthwith because Messer Giovanni Vitelleschi,* a cardinal, was approaching with an armed band, bent on treason and villainy. When he heard this the King cried out to all to keep their places till the Mass should be finished, and everyone remained still, being sure of the King's trust in God. When Mass was over the King departed, and they had scarcely cleared the altar when the Patriarch Vitelleschi appeared, and, not finding the King, withdrew to the seashore. There he found ships ready to embark him and his force, otherwise he would have fared ill, because he had previously made a treaty with the King under oath and was really his prisoner. Had the King laid hands on him he would have smarted for his treachery. Thus the King was delivered from danger through his faith in the Sacraments.

Messer Giannozzo Manetti,† who was Florentine ambassador at Naples, told me of the King's profound reverence for divine worship. The King invited him to the service on Christmas-eve,

---

* Vitelleschi was one of the most notorious soldier prelates. Eugenius IV had taken up the Angevin cause against Alfonso, and had sent Vitelleschi with an army into Naples. This episode, which occurred during a truce, is noticed by Fazi in his *Life of Alfonso*, by Panormita in *De dictis et factis Alphonsi regis*, and in Costanzo, *Storia di Napoli*.

† See *Life*, p. 372. Manetti was one of the most illustrious of the *Circolo* of S. Spirito and probably the finest Hebrew scholar of his time. Unlike Bruno and Marsuppini he remained an Orthodox Catholic.

and when he went into the King's chapel at one o'clock at night he found His Majesty kneeling and listening to the service which had already begun. He held before him an open Bible which he read without cease. So great was King Alfonso's power of endurance that he remained kneeling from the first hour of night till the fourteenth, with nothing on his head; indeed, not one of the lords or the ambassadors or anyone else would have put up with such discomfort. As an instance of his diligence in Divine worship, every Holy Thursday he would wash the feet of as many poor men as he had years of life, washing them in proper fashion : drying them afterwards and giving to each of the poor men a white garment, a pair of shoes, an Alfonsino, a Carlino and I know not what other money besides. Afterwards on the same day he caused a dinner to be spread, and made the poor men sit down thereto ; and, having directed the cook what viands should be sent up, the King stood at the table with a napkin round his neck and a girdle. As soon as the eatables came from the kitchen the King set them before the guests, together with wine and all else needful with most humble carriage. His Majesty, indeed, was unwilling that they should be served by any other hand than his own. Every day he repeated without fail the office of Our Lord with great devotion, and he never failed to rise during the night, remaining on his knees for some time : this custom he observed as long as he lived ; and it may be added that he kept all the due fasts, and the vigils of the feast days of Christ, and of the most glorious Virgin Mary, and fasted on bread and water every Friday. Even when he was gravely ill he refused to alter his habit. Whenever the body of Christ might be borne to the sick, past where the King happened to be, he would always leave the palace, as soon as he knew of it, and accompany it to its destination. On the festival of Corpus Christi His Majesty went to it, and bade all the ambassadors and the lords about the court to accompany him. He carried one of the staves of the canopy over the body of Christ, walking barefoot and bareheaded.

His kindly habit was to visit those who were sick. There was a youth of the noblest ancestry in the flower of his age, who was in the King's service and greatly beloved by him. When the King heard that he had been given up by the physicians he went to the house of the youth, who was named Gabrielletto,* and began to exhort him to meet his heavy infirmity with strength and patience, telling him that it was God's own will to call him to Himself, and that in the bitter suffering which afflicted him, his soul must needs bid farewell to his body, wherefore he should bow to the will of God, and humbly beg of Him pardon for all his sins. He urged Gabrielletto to submit to God's will, and realise that this wretched life of man is brief and unstable : that it would quickly pass away, and that we can have little hope in anything, seeing that all things are tottering to an end. Wherefore he ought to make up his mind and be patient even under such a cruel trial as was the giving up of life, wretched though it was. And according to what Messer Antonio Panormita,† who was present at this exhortation and has written thereanent, the words of His Majesty had such power that the young man found peace for his soul and was content to submit to God's will.

Cruelty of all sorts was foreign to his nature. It happened once that the Genoese fleet attacked the mole of Naples,‡ and caused His Majesty the greatest anxiety. At that time there was in Naples an engineer skilled in the making of fireworks, who explained to His Majesty that, if he would consent, the whole of the fleet and the men on board the same might be burnt. He, moreover, gave the King a sample of his powers

---

* He was Gabriello Curiale of Sorrento. See also Panormita, *op. cit.*, III, p. 52.

† Antonio Beccadelli was born in 1394 at Palermo and was called from his birthplace " Panormita." He was educated at Siena, where he met Æneas Sylvius as a fellow-student and ultimately became one of the leading humanists of the age. He was first professor of history at Milan, and afterwards secretary to King Alfonso and tutor to Prince Ferdinand. He died in 1471. Panormita was a voluminous writer of the polished Latin verse then fashionable, but he is chiefly remembered in connection with the " Hermaphroditus," a poem obscene enough to incur the censure even of Poggio. In his enthusiasm for the classics he is said to have sold a farm to buy a MS. of Livy. His books were forbidden by the Church ; nevertheless he enjoyed the patronage and friendship of the Emperor Sigismund, Alfonso the Magnanimous, Cosimo dei Medici and many scholars.

‡ This probably refers to the attack made by the Genoese fleet on Naples in 1457 ; *v.* Fazi, *Commentarii*, Lib. X, and Costo, *Annotazioni al Compendio di Storia di Napoli*, Lib. VI. (Vespasiano only makes bare mention of the defeat of Alfonso's fleet by the Genoese at Gaeta in 1435 and his subsequent captivity in Milan.) *Vide Life of Count Camerlingo*, p. 330.

which convinced him that the attempt would succeed, whereupon Alfonso turned to the engineer and to certain others who were standing by and said, " God forbid that such a host of men should perish by my will : sooner the state should fall than that I should be the cause of such an evil deed." He then sent away the engineer and, having armed certain ships, he bade the nobles embark thereon, but they hesitated to do this by reason of the danger, whereupon he turned to his son, Don Ferrante, and bade him go on board, and this he did straightway. As soon as the nobles saw Don Ferrante embark, they all followed him on board, one after the other. This may be taken as an instance of the King's pity and compassion.

He was very prompt to forgive injuries which others might work him. There lived in France a certain gentleman of the country who had always spoken ill of King Alfonso, and continued his slanders, so that no one, returning to Naples from France, could fail to tell the King what this Frenchman had said of him. A gentleman of King Alfonso's court was greatly angered at this Frenchman's presumption, so he determined to seek him out and punish him for his offences against the King. He quitted Naples for France with his horses and servants and, having come into the region where this Frenchman lived, he found a way of having dealings with him, and they often supped together. It happened that the Frenchman possessed a house some distance from his own, with land adjoining, and there he lodged this gentleman of King Alfonso's court, who, after he had tarried there some days, determined to avenge the ill which this man had wrought against the King. Having gone one day from his dwelling to that of the Frenchman, he commanded his servants to seize him and convey him to Naples. They took the Frenchman on board ship and bore him away out of the country to King Alfonso, and when this gentleman, bringing with him the Frenchman, entered King Alfonso's presence he spake thus, " Sacred Majesty, I made up my mind that I would not come again before you, except I should bring with me this Frenchman." When the King looked upon the Frenchman he said, " I give you free pardon ; but see that hereafter you speak not ill of great princes, because they have long arms and can make their power felt in all places ; wherefore in the future be more cautious than you have been in the past." Having thus spoken he let him go. The Frenchman was astonished, and could not believe that he had escaped punishment. When he realised the King's mercy he was so bewildered that he completely changed his tone, and could not say enough in praise and commendation of His Majesty.

He would give to everyone without counting the cost. Many stories are told about his boundless liberality. First he used to say—and it was quite true—that he never had money in his pocket, nor kept any under his own charge. It happened that one of his officers who collected the hearth tax* had received ten thousand florins, and laid the same on the table of the King's closet until the treasurer should come. There was in the closet with the King a youth of high family in attendance, and this youth cast greedy eyes on the money. The King, observing him, asked what he was looking at, whereupon the youth replied that he was looking at that heap of money, and that if he possessed it he would be happy indeed. As soon as King Alfonso heard this he turned to the youth and, putting his hand upon the money, he said, " Be happy and fortunate as I can make you," and he gave him the money to show him two things : one that he himself set no value on the money, and the other that if happiness lay in the possession of the money, it was he, Alfonso, who had conferred it. He kept around him so great a crowd of learned men that, in the year of his death, he spent twenty thousand ducats on their maintenance.

He gave to Messer Bartolomeo Fazi of Genoa five hundred ducats, while he devoted his time to writing his *History of King Alfonso*, over which work he spent many years, bringing it to an end in ten books. When it was finished the bounty he had received from the King was exhausted, and he then desired to have advanced to him some two or three hundred florins beyond his allowance. He spoke of this matter with Panormita and with Matteo Malferito, who arranged that, some morning, he should take his history to His Majesty the King, and that they themselves should be present when he should bring it. They presented the history to the King, and

---

* This tax was first levied in Naples by Alfonso.

he took it and read the account of the storming of a castle which pleased him greatly ; so much so that he felt he must have been present. Having read this description he turned to Antonio and Matteo, praising it greatly, and bade enter Messer Bartolomeo, who was waiting outside the door. Antonio and Matteo next turned towards the King and said that Messer Bartolomeo had a request to make of His Majesty, that he would give him the same which he had spent beyond his allowance. The King called his chamberlain, bidding him bring one thousand and five hundred florins in a purse, which he gave to Messer Bartolomeo and then thanked him for the work which he had done. Afterwards he said, " I give you these one thousand five hundred florins, not as a payment for the work which you have produced, for this indeed cannot be paid for by money, and even if I were to give you one of the finest estates I possess, I should not be able to recompense you, but in the course of time I will see that you be duly rewarded." Messer Bartolomeo, who had reckoned on receiving only two or three hundred florins, was dumb-founded when he saw one thousand five hundred, and hardly knew where he might be, being somewhat timid by nature, and Antonio and Matteo came to his aid in expressing gratitude to His Majesty the King.

It happened in the times of Pope Calixtus that a young Florentine, who had acquaintance with Giannozzo Man-etti, had several times taken gold out of the kingdom, in violation of an existing law, and had incurred the penalty of death and confiscation of his goods. He was accused by one of his own countrymen, the charge was proved, and everything he possessed, including his writings, was taken from him. As soon as this was told to Giannozzo, who was then in Rome, he went to the Pope and laid the case before him, whereupon the Pope straightway caused to be written a letter to King Alfonso, begging that the youth's goods might be restored. Bearing the letter Giannozzo went to Naples, where he forthwith sought audience with the King to whom he presented it. The King, as soon as he had read it, said, " Had you so little faith in me that you must needs get this letter written by Pope Calixtus ? " Giannozzo answered him quickly, saying, " It was not that I lacked faith in Your Majesty : it was that, when I went to ask leave of His Holiness and to put the case before him, he said, ' I am minded to write a letter to His Majesty and to recommend your petition.' And this was the reason of the letter, and not any doubt of Your Majesty's gracious disposition." Hearing this His Majesty turned to him and said, " Messer Giannozzo, do these goods belong to you ? " and the answer was, " Yes." Again the King put the same query, and again the answer was the same ; whereupon His Majesty, turning to Giannozzo, said, " I give you this youth of yours and all these goods which by right belong to me. The youth shall not lose his life, and it is my desire to treat you liberally in every respect." Then he summoned one of his attendants and bade him fetch the youth out of prison, and return all the goods in question.

At this period there came to Naples certain peasants of Barcelona who were at odds with the townsfolk, and on this account they had recourse to His Majesty. And because they must needs tarry in Naples while the King made himself acquainted with their claims, he gave them a thousand ducats to pay the cost of their maintenance. One of the courtiers thought that this sum was too great, so he, desiring a reduction, said, " Sacred Majesty, these people are only peasants." The King, to show this courtier his ignorance, answered in Catalan, " A thousand ducats is a small sum, give them fifteen hundred," and thus these peasants received more ducats than they had ever seen in the whole of their lives. Here His Majesty demonstrated his great liberality, and the ignorance of the courtier who was minded to teach him his duty and to answer for him. One day His Majesty went out of Naples and, as he was crossing a bridge over the river Garigliano, he saw a poor woman who was weeping. In his generous way he bade his people bring her to him, and then he asked what was the matter with her. She replied, " I had an ox and I joined in partnership with my neighbour, and we ploughed our land with our two oxen. Now, woe is me, my ox has fallen down from this bridge : he is dead, I can no longer cultivate my land, and I and all my children will die." The King, before he left the place, gave the poor woman two oxen in place of the one she had lost, and for her neighbour, who had one ox, he bought an additional one, so that, for the future, each one could plough the land without having to depend on the other. Two things may be remarked in these doings of his : one is his extraordinary compassion and kindness joined to exceeding liberality ; and the other the integrity and justice with which he treated all his subjects, small as well as great.

There was in Naples a young man of the royal house, greatly loved and esteemed by His Majesty on account of his kinship. He was a youth of most praiseworthy parts and was loved and well spoken of by all. By way of religious duty this youth went to the Holy Land, and on his return the King generously went several miles out of Naples to meet him. After his return he met one day as he was walking about the city, by some snare of the enemy of mankind, a young woman, very fair and lightminded, and she, who was some thirty years of age, began to ogle him, and he her, so that he often was wont to pass that way, as she would probably show herself. Her husband was in the King's service, and one evening she arranged with the wretched youth that he should come to her house during her husband's time of service at court. The youth came as it had been planned, but he remained with her too long, so that the husband, who carried a key of the door, met him as he was coming downstairs. When he saw him he called out, lamenting the shame that had been put upon him, and then, taking the knife he wore as his side, he dealt the young man a blow in the left breast and slew him outright. When this gentleman realised what he had done in his anger, and that this youth was a highly prized kinsman of the King, it seemed to him he was ruined, and as he went along, debating whether any deliverance might be possible, he remembered that the King was of a most merciful nature, and determined, as a last hope, to have recourse to His Majesty. Having made up his mind, that same night about the sixth hour this gentleman, pale with terror, set forth and went to the Castello, where the King was. He knocked at the door and an officer opened it and asked his business ; whereupon he replied that he urgently wanted speech with the King. When he was brought there he said that what he had to tell must be told secretly, so all others withdrew and then the gentleman told the King the trouble which had befallen him. When he had heard it, His Majesty

turned to him and said, " Now see that you tell me the truth,"
and the way the gentleman spoke convinced the King that
he spoke truly. Then he said to the gentleman, " Now go
and see that you act rightly, as you have acted up to this
moment, and have no fear of this youth's brothers or of anyone else ; mark that any violence done to you will likewise be
done to me, and do not doubt that what I promise shall be
duly performed." Later that same night he summoned the
young man's brothers, and told them what had occurred,
remarking that this gentleman had acted in a becoming
manner, and that they should send for the body and give it
burial. Also that they should be careful, under pain of
losing his favour, that no outrage should be done to this
gentleman. They duly observed all that the King had ordered,
and afterwards the gentleman abode in Naples unmolested.

His Majesty gave to Gerardo Gambacorti the right of
attachment and of reprisal over the goods of certain Florentines,* because this Gerardo had lost Bagno and other places
by his own doings, and much property as well. Now when the
King was away from Naples, Gerardo, together with certain
others of the court, intervened and laid hands on a great
quantity of Florentine cloths and stuffs, to the value of forty
thousand ducats, and, having seized them, put them up to
auction and sold them. The Florentine traders went to Messer
Giannozzo, who chanced to be in Naples, begging him to go
seek the King who was at Foggia in Apulia, and protect their
interest and property. He quickly mounted his horse, and
when he arrived at Foggia the King was absent, so he awaited
him in his apartments and walked up and down in the hall
till he returned. When the King came back he espied Messer
Giannozzo first, and, putting his hand on his shoulder, he
said, " Messer Giannozzo, what are you about, coming here
thus unexpectedly ? " Giannozzo made as if he would kneel
and kiss the King's hand, but he would not suffer him, and
asked him what he wanted, whereupon he told the King the

* It is difficult to understand Alfonso's subsequent action, praised
by Vespasiano, if this grant was meant to be operative, or how a man
of Alfonso's character could ever have made it. Gambacorti treacher-
ously conveyed to the Neapolitans in 1453 the fortress of Bagno, which
the Florentines had granted to him in exchange for his Pisan possessions, but his plans were discovered and he fled to Naples. See Macchiavelli, *Storia Fior.*, L. VI, p. 313. (London, 1905.)

whole story. His Majesty ordered that lodging should be found for him, saying that on the morrow the business should be arranged. However, on the following morning, before daybreak, the King went out without letting Messer Giannozzo know, but before he set forth he left in his apartment an officer with full authority to despatch the matter and see that all the goods seized should be restored. Now the one who had to write this letter of settlement was unwilling to write it entirely by himself, so they delayed until His Majesty should return in the evening, and when he came back he called upon Martorella by name, and bade him write a letter to the effect that everything, whether sold or not, should be restored to the lawful owners. Then Martorella and Giannozzo retired to prepare the letter, and while they were engaged over it Martorella said to Giannozzo, " His Majesty the King spoke in Spanish, and you did not rightly understand him." Giannozzo, who was of a very quick intelligence in affairs, replied, " I know Spanish, and I understood clearly what His Majesty said. If you are willing to write the letter according to His Majesty's directions—well and good—if not, I will go to His Majesty again about the business." Martorella, knowing Giannozzo's character and the affection the King had to him, said, " There is no need that you should seek the King again, for I will write the letter in whatever terms you may direct." And this he did in the completest manner possible, making restitution down to the merest trifles. These are some of the liberal actions of King Alfonso, and show what he did in reasonable service to his friends.

In all transactions the King's strength of mind and innate righteousness were apparent. He strongly condemned gaming, denouncing it as pernicious. He used to tell how, being then eighteen years old, he was at Barcelona during the feast of the Nativity and, happening to play one evening, he lost some five thousand florins. After he had lost them he called one of his chamberlains and bade him fetch some money. When it was brought he played again and began to win, so that in the end he won back all he had lost and likewise all the money of his fellow-gamesters. With this heap of florins before him, he bade everyone keep quiet, and then bade the chamberlain to fetch the little book of Our Lady, and this having been brought, he opened it and then and there made oath, with both his hands on it, swearing and promising to God and the Virgin Mary that he would never play again ; a promise he kept to the day of his death. Afterwards he turned to those who were present and said, " This to show you that what I have done, I have not done through greed," and then he took the florins in his hands and distributed them amongst those who had been playing with him until the heap was finished. After this most generous action, he addressed all those who were present and said, " I knew well that, if I should let myself be involved in this habit of gaming, it would prove a hindrance to my mind, and bar me from turning any thoughts upon worthy matters ; so strong would be its power of impediment, and for this reason no man shall ever again behold me at the gaming-table."

He had great liking for men of letters, as has been already stated, and while he resided in Naples he would let Signor Antonio Panormita read to him the Decades of Livy,* and to these readings came many gentlemen of the court ; there were readings likewise in the Holy Scriptures, in the works of Seneca and in philosophy ; indeed, few minutes of his time were unworthily spent.† When he invaded the Marches with his army, to restore to the Church this territory, which Duke Francesco‡ had seized in the time of Pope Eugenius, the troops of His Majesty, under his personal leading, met Niccolo Piccinino, who had been sent there as general by Duke Filippo, and in a short time the King won back this territory for the Church. As it was then summer, Panormita would read every day a portion of Livy, and all the gentlemen of the army would attend these readings ; it was indeed a sight worth seeing ; that of King Alfonso listening to this learned discourse in a place where many spent their time in

---

* Livy seems to have been his favourite author. There is the story of the arm bone of the historian, dug up by the Venetians and despatched to Alfonso, who received it as if it had been a holy relic ; and that of the magnificent Codex of Livy sent to the King by Cosimo dei Medici. The royal physicians feared treachery, suspecting it to be poisoned, but " Rex prima facie visus est medicis assentiri, illis animo illudens, nam cum Livius in medio constitutus esset, illum manibus accepit, legit, evolvit ; subinde medicos qui continue adversarentur, rogitans ut desinerent ineptire." Panormita, *De dictis et factis Alphonsi regis*, I, p. 36.

† 1443.   ‡ Francesco Sforza.

gaming. He had with him divers very learned masters in theology and philosophy, amongst whom were two men of great excellence ; one of them, named Maestro Sogliera, he made Bishop of Barcelona, and another called Messer Ferrando was a wonderfully learned theologian and philosopher. He was a man of holy life, greatly reverenced by the King ; indeed, he feared Messer Ferrando somewhat because, whenever Messer Ferrando might hear of any deed of the King which did not seem to him just and honest, he did not spare his reproaches. He was one of such power of character and of such holy life that when the King was minded to confer upon him divers bishoprics and other benefices, he would have none of them, being unwilling to lay this load upon his conscience. He was confessor to His Majesty and was, through his rectitude, the most potent influence for good, as will appear in the end. He often held debate with the Masters of Theology ; either to enquire as to doubts, or to dispute generally.

Alfonso, from his liking for scholars, supported many who were in want. After the death of Pope Nicolas, from whom Giannozzo Manetti drew a pension of six hundred ducats a year, Giannozzo went to Naples, to settle the affair of a certain youth, in the first year of Pope Calixtus, whereupon King Alfonso requested that he would reside at his court. The King thought highly of him from his acquaintance with him as ambassador ; also he wished to test him by making him engage in disputations in all the seven liberal arts. Giannozzo went away to settle certain of his affairs, and when he returned to Naples the King paid him the highest honour and offered preferment, even allowing him to choose his own special grant, which the King agreed to sign forthwith. There was assigned to Giannozzo a grant out of the salt dues, and when the grant had been made the King commanded them to bring it to him for his signature. When it was brought he signed a charge of nine hundred carlini to be paid out of the salt dues, appointing him a member of his council and president of the Sommaria. When it was all done he spoke graciously to Giannozzo, assuring him that this was a willing gift, and that if he had naught but one loaf of bread, it should be divided between them. Afterwards he said,

" Messer Giannozzo, men of your sort value time greatly, and much time is lost by those who wait about the court. As I wish you to keep your time for your studies, there is no need for you to frequent the court. When we wish to see you, we will send for you : enough honour and respect will be done to us, since we shall be conscious that you are near us." He assigned twenty thousand florins a year to the learned men about his court. In those times he and Nicholas V were the great benefactors to learning, and if patronage had gone on as it had been begun by these two extraordinary princes we should have had many more men of letters in our day than we have, and they would have lived in greater honour and esteem. If honours are wanting, men will also be wanting, because they see no prospect of reward for their labours. Many men were indebted to these two lights of learning ; men who made translations from other authors, and wrote works of their own worthy of all praise.

He loved not only scholars, but good men and those whom he knew to be virtuous in their carriage, and he was most benignant to all. And of a truth, gentlemen of noble blood and race are of a nature different from that of those who would usurp a nobility which is not theirs ; and their actions and their way of life show this plainly. It happened one day that the King went out hunting and greatly enjoyed the sport ; and while riding straight at a wild beast, he missed his attendants and got separated from them. As he went along he came upon a poor man whose ass, laden with flour, had fallen. The peasant, who knew not that it was the King, cried out : " Oh, sir, I beg you help me to get my ass on his legs again." The King straightway dismounted and helped the poor man with the sack of flour, and by the time they had got the ass on his legs, the gentlemen in attendance upon the King rode up, and made obeisance to him, whereupon the poor man, feeling that he was in fault, fell on his knees and asked pardon. The King began to laugh and, having bidden him to rise, ordered him to come to Naples, and afterwards gave him certain things of which he was in need.*

Sometimes the King would divert himself with some merry joke or sport. There was once in Naples a Sienese ambassador

* Panormita also tells this story. *Op. cit.*, I, p. 25.

who, after the way of this people, was very haughty, and as the King mostly wore black clothes with a buckle to his cap and a chain of gold round his neck—being seldom seen clad in silk or brocade—this ambassador when he had audience with the King would always wear garments of the richest gold brocade. The King often jested with those about him concerning this wearing of brocade, and one day he said, laughing, to one of his gentlemen, " Certes, I should like to alter the colour of that brocade." So he fixed that audience should be given in a very poor apartment and commanded that everybody should hustle the Sienese ambassador in his brocaded coat. On the morrow the poor man in his finery was pushed and hustled by the King himself, as well as by all the ambassadors, so that none of those who knew the story could keep from laughing when the court was over at seeing how this brocaded coat, which was crimson, trimmed with fur and with golden fringe, was marred and spoilt. When the King saw him go out of the room in this plight, he could not keep from laughing, and for several days he did nothing but laugh over this story of the Sienese ambassador, who never knew that the King had played this trick on him.

Another Sienese ambassador to the court of Naples had brought with him a horsecloth edged with long points, and the King, when he saw it, laughed heartily, and arranged, one day when he was going to the chase, to ride past the ambassador's house, and to summon him to come out in haste. The messenger having entered called to him, and bade him attend on His Majesty who desired to see him, whereupon the ambassador ordered his horses to be saddled straightway, and mounted his steed, adorned with the horsecloth aforesaid, wearing new-soled boots and a long cloak. In the course of the hunt that morning the King rode through every hedge he came to, and the ambassador, following him, left bits of his horsecloth here and there, so that, in the end, the greater part of it and its long points were left sticking in the hedges, and a good bit of his cloak as well. The morning was rainy and sudden showers fell continually, and His Majesty the King took off his cloak when he spoke with the ambassador, wherefore he himself got soaked to the skin in order that the ambassador might fare likewise. In the evening when he got back to Naples the ambassador was wet from head to foot, his new-soled boots were damp and cold ; the horsecloth had been left in shreds on the hedges, and what remained was no bigger than the saddle of his horse : and all its points and ornaments were lying about on the ground as if they had never been. The ambassador without his cloak, in hood and new-soled boots, and wet through, as you may imagine, was a strange object. The King had made merry over the affair of the brocaded coat, and this new adventure was for several days the joke of the court, where they did nothing but laugh over this new story which was known to all the gentlefolk and men of worship.* So great were the cares of state which beset him every day, that he would never have been able to play the part of a ruler had he not recreated himself now and then.

As I have narrated certain merry moods of His Majesty, I will now tell of some others of a different character, such as often assail those of high estate. One evening about the seventh hour, when His Majesty was preparing for bed, and had already retired to undress, his secretary came to him with a heap of letters which it was necessary that he should read through and sign before he retired for the night. When His Majesty saw these letters he turned to those who were about him and said, " Is there in the whole world a more wretched man than I am ? Is there a groom about the court who lacks time for sleep and repose, while I am forced to remain up and read and sign letters before I can go to my bed ? " Some of those present said, " Sacred Majesty, surely it is a fine thing to be a king like you, and to live as you live." The King turned to them and said that he knew well

---

* Alfonso had a grievance against the Sienese because, while they were fighting as his allies against Milan, they made peace without consulting him. Piccinino, who was then in his service, harried the Sienese territories so severely that they sent ambassadors to arrange a peace. These ambassadors were Galgano Borghesi, Leonardo Benvogliente and Æneas Sylvius. In the *Commentaries of Pius II* (1–26) we read, " Auditos Galganum et Leonardum Alphonsus divissima excepit oratione, multa de Senensibus questus est, nec oratores ipsos pacificis oculis itineri poterat. At cum accessisset Æneas, hilari vultu et honesto sermone receptus ; quem ut primum Rex intuitus est. Nunc, inquit, libet de pace loqui." Possibly these ungentlemanly tricks described may have been played on Galgano and Leonardo.

enough what manner of life his was, that no one could be more wretched and unhappy than he was, and that many of those whom others esteemed happy were miserable. With these he classed himself, declaring that those about him were no judges of things of which they knew nought. King Alfonso used to say that if the shirt he wore on his back knew his secrets and his inward thoughts, he would throw it upon the fire. He was very secretive in matters of importance which he had to handle, and was loth to take advice ; for him it was enough that he could take counsel with himself, a habit which many blamed, seeing that nobody, however exalted he may be, can dispense with advice.

After he had governed his many kingdoms for forty years with such great ability, and when the Church and all Italy enjoyed peace, in the time of Pope Nicolas, who had the greatest faith in King Alfonso, it happened that one of the Italian princes* was eager for war, and was minded that Pope Nicolas should be the one to break the peace, and for this reason he spread a report that he was about to send a force into the territory of Perugia. When he heard this, Pope Nicolas was greatly troubled, and quickly despatched Messer Giovanni Margheriti [a Catalan, who was afterwards Bishop of Girona and made cardinal by Pope Sixtus] to His Majesty the King at Naples with a request for two thousand horsemen, because he feared that war was like to break out at Perugia. As soon as the cardinal had received this commission, he went to the King and laid before him the request of His Holiness, whereupon the King was very angry and answered : " Go back and tell His Holiness that I will do nothing, because I have no mind that he should be the first to break the peace of Italy. Let him be advised too that, though this ruler may talk of sending an army against Perugia, he will do nothing of the kind ; he has only spread this report in order that His Holiness may send troops himself, and thus give him a pretext for breaking the peace†

---

* It is difficult to identify this personage. Muratori, *Annals*, IX, p. 256, writes that Pope Nicolas sent Cardinal Capranica to Naples in 1454, but does not mention the Cardinal of Girona.

† The peace referred to was that consequent on the Congress of Lodi, 1454. It was made between Florence, Venice, and Milan. It is noticed also in the *Life of Cardinal Capranica*, p. 133.

afterwards. This is the reason why I will not act." When Messer Giovanni had learnt the King's wishes, and the reasons which moved him, knowing them to be true, he took his leave and went back to Pope Nicolas, to whom he told all King Alfonso had said.

The Pope, who failed to understand both the wishes and the actions of the King, and being somewhat hasty by nature, was greatly upset, and declared that this was not what he had looked for from King Alfonso, that he hoped he might always, in his need, find support in the King's favour, and that the royal promises which had been made would be kept; seeing that he was disturbed and angry at this reply of the King, Messer Giovanni waited till he had recovered his temper and was no longer vexed, and then said: " Has your Holiness said all you are minded to say? " The Pope assented, and Messer Giovanni went on. " Listen now to the reasons for the King's refusal to act as you desired. First, he is loth for your Holiness to be the first to break the peace. Second, though this ruler may threaten to send troops to Perugia he will not send them; he said this merely to induce your Holiness to send a force thither, so that he himself may be able to justify his aggression later on. Then all will point to your Holiness as the breaker of the peace." When Pope Nicolas heard this plea he said, " I am not convinced by the reasons you have brought forward, nor have I changed my mind; but there is one consideration which leads me to have patience, which is that, having to deal with His Majesty the King, who has governed his state for more than forty years, I ought rather to trust to him with his long experience, than to myself who am new to rule." And thus he recovered his temper. Not a month passed without some confirmation of King Alfonso's words. Messer Giovanni duly brought this to the notice of the Pope, who remarked at his departure that he had been right, and that King Alfonso had perfectly understood the business.

The King had a sound judgment and a hatred of crooked dealing. He was upright and good, without guile or crooked dealing. He would often blame the Italians in that they deceived him by showing him one thing for another, a practice most repugnant to his royal and open nature. There are many remarkable things to be told about his expeditions against the infidels, of his acquisition of the kingdom and his siege of the city of Naples, and of his triumph when he entered it like a conqueror of old.* All these are given in the history of Bartolomeo Fazi. I will only tell of the visit of the Emperor† with a great train of nobles and a splendid equipage. Such doings as these we see no more in these days ; indeed, the splendour of King Alfonso's reception would not have been unworthy of one of the Emperors of old times. Anyone who reads of the same cannot be more amazed than was the Emperor himself over the supreme honours which were done to him. This feasting which King Alfonso provided cost more than a hundred and fifty thousand florins ; there was a hunt in which a vast number of noblemen and gentlemen took part ; and a banquet, such as even the largest cities of the country could not have matched, was spread. In every place—and there was an infinite number of them—men ate from silver dishes the most sumptuous meats. Not only could confetti be had for the asking, but all sorts were given free to be thrown away. All about the place were set up fountains which spouted here Greek, here Muscat, and here red wine of every kind, and wines of luxury as well. At all the fountains were silver cups, and anyone who would might drink, and the Germans took their due share. If it had not been described by Bartolomeo Fazi, Panormita and others, it would have been treated as a fable. His Majesty the King gave to the Emperor many gifts of great value, and presented to him the device of the Banda‡ that he might make him a Knight of the Virgin Mary, a title borne in respect to Our Lady. On the Saturday the Emperor entered Rome on his return from Naples, when, on his approach, all the cardinals and nobles of the court of Rome went out to meet him, and some one, by way of jest, cried out on seeing the new order : " He went to Naples an emperor and has come back a Knight of the Banda." Many things worthy of note might be told which have been set down by capable writers in flowery and elegant Latin, and not in the vulgar idiom

* The magnificent arch of Castel Nuovo still stands as a memorial of victory. † Frederic III.
‡ Members of this order wore a band of red silk across the breast.

with which it is impossible to display things in such seemly fashion as in Latin.

All the happiness men enjoy diminishes at the end of life. Before His Majesty was stricken with the illness which caused his death, many of those about him had died, so that it seemed to be the beginning of the end of his life, and every day he waited to see whether some adversity might not befall him, seeing that heretofore he had enjoyed such great happiness, and for a long season had known naught but good fortune. As it has been said already His Majesty was well versed in the Holy Scriptures and in all the sciences ; wherefore he knew well that happiness would never abide long with any man without yielding place to its adversary ; that is to say, ill-fortune. While he was perpetually thinking of and perpetually dreading the advent of some misfortune, either to the State or to his own person, it happened that he fell ill with an infirmity, called by physicians *diabetica passione*, in which there is an excessive flow of urine, more than is meet to pass, and being thus stricken with sickness he called to him the most distinguished physicians of Italy, both of the body and of the soul. Of the last were a very holy man named Maestro Sogliera, Bishop of Barcelona, a noted theologian, and likewise Maestro Ferrando, a Catalan, of whom I have already made mention, a most illustrious and devout man. He was resolute in dealing with the cares and attractions of the world, and, as the King's confessor, when he perceived any wrongdoing in him he lost patience and never failed to reprimand him. The King held him in great respect for many things he did : for the holiness of his life, and for his refusal to accept from the King's hands rich benefices. He would have none of them, but was content with a cure with a small income and with no souls to look after. He wished for nothing more, nor to incur the dangerous risk of a cure of souls, nor to bear this weight on his conscience, thus showing that he had read the Holy Scriptures to some purpose ; not as vast numbers of others read them, who read them only, and have no wish to understand them.

The King was now ill and confined to his room, as is the way with sick men ; but there was no sign that his ailment was mortal ; wherefore Maestro Ferrando desired to be informed as to its nature, whether it was fatal or not. The physicians told him that this distemper was irremediable, except God should work a miracle, and the longest the King could hope to live would be twenty or twenty-five days. Having been thus informed Maestro Ferrando and the Bishop of Barcelona considered together what they should do, and in the end they decided that it was not meet to deceive His Majesty the King, but rather to tell him plainly of his dangerous state. They agreed that Maestro Ferrando should be the one to tell him in such terms as seemed fitting, seeing that great men never wish to deceive themselves, even when they are brought face to face with such a tremendous matter as the laying down of their lives, and the rendering of an account of all the deeds—good as well as bad—which they may have wrought in this world. Having thus decided, they announced to His Majesty the danger of his condition, and Maestro Ferrando went into the King's chamber and saluted him, and then said, " Sacred Majesty, I have always known you to be a man of the highest courage, and now it is meet that your Majesty should show the same, if you should never have showed it before, when I speak to you about your illness. It now pleases Almighty God to call you to Himself, and for this reason it behoves your Majesty to accept your condition with a manly spirit, such as you have always shown in other matters up to this present day."

After this speech His Majesty turned to him and said, " I am quite content and bend myself to the will of God, and I accept this happening with a spirit as stout as I have felt in all others hitherto." Then quickly he called Messer Ferrando, his confessor, and said, " Let us now attend to what I would do ; first of all I must make confession," and he began by making a general confession, examining each circumstance by itself, and Messer Ferrando asked him the reasons which had prompted him to divers of his undertakings, and when it seemed to him that these reasons were unjust he said so. Then the King answered and put forward some justification, where any could be found, but where there was none he gave way to unbounded grief. And it was the same with everything he felt to be weighing on his conscience, and he spake thus in lamenting his sins to Almighty God, saying to his confessor : " I possess seven kingdoms, and I would give a hundred, if I had them, so that I had not fallen into error." And with his grief came tears and heavy sighs. When several more days had passed, during which they did all they could to cure him, he diligently examined himself, and as time went on he let his mind dwell on sacred things, and read the *Meditations of St. Anselm,* a very holy book. When he had completed his self-examination, he asked for the holy body of Christ, and all those about him marvelled to see the tears and mourning and devotion with which he took it, and the extraordinary grace which God granted to him to find out his sins, to recognise his Redeemer, and to sever himself from the love of this wretched and unhappy world. The Bishop of Barcelona and Messer Ferrando never left him, save to take food, and he remained in this state about twenty days.

By some working of the devil a strange thing happened ; for one day, when the Bishop of Barcelona and Messer Ferrando had gone to dinner, there came from Ferrara a hermit who, when he had come where the King was, announced that he would fain speak with His Majesty on God's behalf. When the King heard this, he ordered him to be brought in and, when he appeared, bade him say what he would. The first words of the hermit were, " Be of good courage, for you shall not die of this disease." The King naturally felt a certain hope, and ordered them to treat the hermit well, but when Messer Ferrando and the Bishop of Barcelona came back, they saw clearly the diabolical fraud and deceit of the hermit. Messer Ferrando told the King that this was some deceit wrought by suggestion of the devil. They sought out where the hermit lodged ; and, having gone thither, they found him and, losing all patience over his fraud and deceit, said to him, " The devil has made a great effort indeed to have sent you here from Ferrara to be the cause of so great a mischief. You know well with what great trouble a king or a man of worship can be brought to reconcile himself with death, and the devil has caused you to act so that you have persuaded the King that he will not die : while we have brought him to bow to the Will of God and to meet death, you have changed all this through your persuasions. However, you must look to your doings and see that, from this day forth, you be not found in these parts ; and that, after making one great mistake, you do not make a greater." The hermit, seeing that his trick was found out, quitted Naples forthwith, and returned to Ferrara.

Messer Ferrando and the Bishop of Barcelona went back to the King and pointed out to him that the hermit was a deceiver, and persuaded him to renew his exercises for the salvation of his soul. After he had confessed and communicated several times he desired to take the last sacraments while he should be conscious, and several days before he died asked that the holy oil might be given to him. They were unwilling that this should be done, whereupon he said that they ought to be satisfied with what satisfied him, and told the bishop to order it to be brought, which thing was done, His Majesty making all the responses, and offering all the places on his person for due anointment. When this had been done he called his son and bade him be a good son of the Church, and always cleave to her as a faithful Christian. Afterwards he commended to him this kingdom of his, which he had governed in the fear of God ; and had thought of God's honour only. He bespoke his bounty towards his servants, in that he himself had not recompensed them so fully as their labour deserved. Having thus spoken devoutly he raised his arms and gave to King Ferdinand his blessing, while of all the nobility of the realm and multitude of other gentlemen, there was not one who could restrain his tears. Although the room was filled with wailing and crying, he himself kept his undaunted courage. And God did him this great kindness, that he suffered no failure of intellect, but went on with his reading. Two holy men were always by his side, and left him not till the end : the last words he uttered before he expired were, *In manus tuas, Domine, commendo spiritum meum.* He died without a struggle and resigned his soul to his Redeemer.

Now it might be asked me, " Did this death scene happen exactly as it is here written ? " and to this I would reply that, soon after the death of King Alfonso, the Bishop of Barcelona and Messer Ferrando came to Florence, and one evening I called at Messer Ferrando's lodgings where I found him in bed through the fatigues of travel. He rose at once, and bade

me sit beside him ; and, after I had been made known to
him, I said, " Messer Ferrando, I beg you to tell me something
as to how King Alfonso met his death," and he told me what
I have here set down, and other matters beside which I omit.
After he had told me everything he said, " Great princes
commit great sins, and for this reason I do not want you to
judge whether the King may be saved or not, but one thing
I would say plainly, that of all the favours which can be given
to man in this life, the greatest is this, and I pray to Almighty
God that he will grant me so great a favour as to let my end
be just such another as King Alfonso's. And if anyone
should ask whence the King gathered this saving grace at
his latter end I would say that it came from the assiduity with
which he, from his youth onwards, kept the vigils of the feasts
of Our Lord and of Our Lady—taking naught but bread and
water—and heard every morning three Masses, never omitting
to say the office of Our Lady with divers prayers and exercises.
And in addition he would rise every night to say matins and
certain other prayers." Messer Ferrando went on to say,
" Moreover, it is well for every man to persevere in good works,
beginning as a child and going on to the end, in order to secure
for himself such grace as King Alfonso obtained."

Anyone looking upon Messer Ferrando as he spoke might
have quoted him an example of penitence. He was a man of
forty years, tall in stature, thin, wan and grave, averse from
all worldly pomps and feastings, free of speech, a foe of
dissimulation and falsehood, saying nothing of himself by
way of boasting or swaggering, as is the practice of many, and
hating ceremonies and superstitions. Moreover, anyone who
may have spoken with him, and realized what his life was,
would pronounce his words to be true as Gospel, as they are.
Whoever may ponder aright over this commentary of King
Alfonso's life, must surely agree that, as a rule, the example
of life which he has given is well worthy of imitation ; and all
that I have written I have heard from men worthy of belief
and of high station, having no respect for tricks of style,
but only for the truth. As his memoir has already been
published in Latin, I find it well that some note should be
made of his life in the vulgar tongue ; and if the exact order
of time has not been kept in what I have here written, let

no one be surprised, because I have set down these things just as they came into my memory, recording them irrespective of date.

FEDERIGO, DUKE OF URBINO (1422–1482)

PROEM

To the Commentary on the sayings and doings of the most invincible Federigo, Duke of Urbino.

To the most excellent Signor Duke Guido, his son.

Most illustrious prince, I have presented in this short Commentary certain things worth remembering concerning the most excellent Duke Federigo your father, stimulated thereto by his great worth, and also by the fact that I was his contemporary. Moreover, no other united as he did, in his own person the soldier and the man of letters, or knew how to make intellect augment the force of battalions. He followed Fabius Maximus who acted thus in his struggle with Hannibal, judiciously delaying his movements and thus saving the Roman republic. Now because your illustrious father did the like, in winning new territory and in other famous deeds of arms, we may say of him as the highest praise, that he never met defeat : praise which few great captains can claim. Nevertheless, he was brought to conclusions with the chief powers of Italy and with the shrewdest fighters, as will appear in the story of his life. And over and above military affairs, he showed himself one of the best and wisest of rulers, and not only did he govern his own state prudently, but the chief rulers of Italy were guided by his good sense and council in their own task as sovereigns. You will mark these things and many others, put briefly in this Commentary. Some of them I have seen, and some I have heard from men worthy of credit, and I have despatched them to your illustrious lordship, his worthy heir and successor in all his extraordinary virtues, to let you see my loyal service. I have written them in the Tuscan tongue in order that the renown of so great a prince may be made known to those who are ignorant of Latin, as well as to those who understand it. Therefore, most illustrious

POPES AND RULERS

Signore, accept this short Commentary from the hand of your faithful servant, Vespasiano, who, had he been able to send aught of greater value, would willingly have despatched the same to your illustrious lordship, to whom I especially commend myself.

FEDERIGO, DUKE OF URBINO

Concerning Messer Federigo of the house of Montefeltro, Duke of Urbino, though his life may have been written already, I will not refrain from recording certain matters worthy of remembrance, seeing that I have written commentaries on the most illustrious men of the age. Like Scipio Africanus he took arms early and served first under Nicolo Piccinino, a distinguished captain. Messer Federigo had many praiseworthy qualities, and such another character, virtuous in every respect, the age could not produce. In arms, his first profession, he was the most active leader of his time, combining strength with the most consummate prudence, and triumphing less by his sword than by his wit. The many places he captured, both in the kingdom* and throughout Italy, he captured by forethought and was never worsted. All who may study his life will read of many victorious battles, much territory conquered, and all with honour. I will say nought of the battle of S. Fabriano† when, the Duke being sick with fever, the fight began and lasted three hours, and all feared that the King's forces were overthrown. The Duke, seeing the danger and knowing that the peasant soldiers were the stronger, mounted his horse, fever stricken as he was, and rode into the field, and soon restored their courage which they had lost since the fight had gone against them. In this case, by his wonted skill and prudence, the battle proved a victory and not a defeat. Had it not been for his coming, they would have been irretrievably routed, in spite of the strenuous efforts of their leaders. Next I record the siege of Fano,‡ a

* Naples.
† Federigo and Alessandro Sforza defeated by the Angevin forces under Piccinino, 1460. In a tournament before the battle Federigo was disabled, and this accident may have affected the result of the fight itself.
‡ 1463. Sigismondo Pandolfo Malatesta was one of the chief free captains of the time and a lifelong foe of Federigo.

84

strong well-found town, held by Robert of Rimini, son of Signor Gismondo, equipped with artillery and other defensive engines and manned with Signor Gismondo's best soldiers, which by his strategy he took by assault, as well as other lands of Signor Gismondo, who himself was a leader of renown. Nevertheless, the Duke seized the greater part of his lands, these having been granted to him by Pope Pius and King Alfonso, who were Gismondo's foes.

I will note amongst his other eminent virtues his good faith, in which he never failed. All those to whom he gave his word bear witness that he never broke it. King Alfonso and King Ferdinand, in whose service he was for more than thirty-two years, and to whom he was faithful not only where he was bound by writing, but also where he had only given his word. At that time, when it seemed that the action of Bartolomeo of Bergamo must bring hurt to the Florentines, and when the Duke of Urbino had finished his term with King Ferdinand and was free to act as he wished without any question of bad faith, the Venetians, who always went straight to the point, decided to order the advance of Bartolomeo with the object of winning the leadership in Italy. They knew that everything rested with the Duke of Urbino, and that the side he supported would be the victor, wherefore they sent an envoy to the Duke, who then lay between Imola and Faenza, having with him the commissaries of His Majesty the King, of the the Milanese and of the Florentines. When the envoy arrived he said he would fain speak with the Duke of Urbino, knowing that he had finished his contract and was free to bargain as he would. When he was brought into the Duke's presence, he made clear his business and sought the Duke's services on the part of the Signory of Venice. The Duke answered that everything he had to say, he would say in the presence of the commissaries of the League ; that, though as a matter of fact his contract had come to an end, as a matter of faith it had not, and he was still bound to His Majesty the King. The envoy, seeing he could not get what he wanted, departed to Cervia and from there sent a letter by messenger to the Duke of Urbino, offering him a hundred thousand ducats in war and cixty thoucand in poaoo. Tho Duko would not read the letter, but handed it to the commissaries of the League, and then sent away the messenger without a reply, having told the commissaries, and the envoy as well, that he was fain to continue in the pay of His Majesty. Thus he showed that his faith was inviolable, whether under obligation or free.*

During the operations of Bartolomeo against the Florentines, the Duke of Urbino, commanding the forces of the League, acted like Fabius Maximus against Hannibal ; always hanging close about him, and never letting him take up any position : keeping two or three miles distant, and occupying any post his foe might vacate. He acted thus carefully, because the Venetian army was the flower of Italy, and Faenza had deserted the League and taken Venetian pay. Thus, having lost the troops of the Signor of Faenza† and the city itself, it behoved the Duke to be on his guard for the present, and for the future as well. The Signor Astorre Manfredi had commanded the troops of Faenza in the Duke's pay, and he was now most solicitous that the Duke and his officers should enter Faenza. As it was March, and country quarters very uncomfortable, all desired to go there, but the Duke would not consent , and, if he had, the Venetians would have won a great stroke, because it was planned that Astorre should not disclose his adhesion to Venice till the Duke and his officers should be inside Faenza, where they would have been taken. This danger was avoided by the Duke's prudence in refusing to enter Faenza, and when it was known everyone saw that he had saved the army and rescued the States of Florence and Romanga from the Venetians. Another danger—one amongst an infinite number—was avoided by his prudence ; and here again he delivered Italy from the Venetians, who never again had such a chance of success. They had prevailed upon the Lord of Imola to join them, and this he would have done if the Duke had not found a way to mend matters by sending to him some of his most trusted agents when he heard of the Lord's intention. He acted in such manner that the affair came to nothing, and to make things doubly sure he sent to Imola five hundred mercenaries of the King, who received ten ducats

---

* Vespasiano scarcely ever gives a date. This transaction seems to have happened in 1467.

† 1449. On account of this desertion Alfonso, when asked to sign the treaty of Lodi, refused unless he should be allowed to punish Count Astorre for his treachery.

per mensem on account of a terrible plague which was prevalent. Now if Imola had joined Venice—Faenza having already done so—Bologna would have been in such great danger that she would have been forced to do the same ; and in this case she would have had to advance into the Mugello, seeing that her camp had always been in the enemy's country.

The Duke escaped many dangers and won great fame. Once when the camp of the League was pitched about four leagues from Bartolomeo's at Molinella,* a place between Ferrara and Bologna, he learned from spies that Bartolomeo was about to attack him. Now his camp was on ground where footmen could fight far better than cavalry, and Bartolomeo had five thousand foot, and the League only fifteen hundred besides certain bands from other states. The Duke while he waited realised his danger and told the leaders under him that the fate of Italy was in their hands, and that if their army should be defeated the dominion would pass irrecoverably to the Venetians. The Duke thought over many projects by way of helping the cause of the League : he sent Piero dei Felici, his chancellor, to Bologna to ask the Sixteen for five hundred mercenaries. But the Bolognese perceived that the forces of the Venetians were stronger than those of the League ; and, fearing for their state, they refused his request and sent to tell the Duke their reasons, which were that, the position of the League being so vastly inferior to that of Bartolomeo, the Duke must needs come to terms with the Venetians. When the Duke received this reply he deemed it a strange one, and sought a way out of his troubles. Having failed in his application to the Bolognese, the Duke assembled the commissaries and the leaders of the army of the League to forecast the plans of the enemy, and what they themselves ought to do ; to await an assault or to attack the foe in his camp. In any case they were in pressing danger, and it was for him to determine which course might best safeguard the League. They must consider well whatever course they took ; for it might not follow that they, even as victors, would be able to disabuse the Venetians of the vain hope that they

---

* 1467. It was here that field artillery was first used. Bartolomeo Colleone's army was largely supported by Florentine exiles and the enemies of the Medici. The battle was indecisive.

might seize upon Florence and occupy the greater part of Italy, and by their conquest hold at their discretion, not only the League, but the whole of the country. Various counsels were given ; some for awaiting, and some for delivering an assault. The opinion of the Duke was that, in this case, it would be well to make a move to retrieve their fortunes, and not to stand still, that the danger of inaction was manifest, for, as it has been stated already, infantry could do much more on such ground than cavalry, and the Venetians had three thousand more footmen than the League, which had more horsemen ; that the way out of the difficulty was undoubtedly to seek the foe, and not to await him. But some maintained that they ought to send to the Sixteen at Bologna for footmen, not knowing that this the Duke had done already, whereupon he told them of it, and bade Piero dei Felici, who was present, tell all that had happened. This he did, stating that this help had been refused, and how he had been told that Bologna had need of the troops for its own defence ; that, considering their unfavourable position, they ought to come to terms with the Venetians, failing any better plan.

Then the Duke said, " Consider well the condition of the League which is now directed by your hands ; this matter is so weighty that every man ought to speak his mind fully. It must be plain to all that Bartolomeo is bound to await us in his camp ; and I, for reasons given, tell you that if we wish to save the League, a matter which is in your own hands, we ought to attack him and not to await him ; for, with a foe at such a strong advantage, our one hope is to assault his position. And even if it may seem to you that we attack at a disadvantage, we are choosing the lesser of two evils in assaulting ; and if you will second me, this is the only way to save our army, and the League of which we are soldiers. Wherefore, comrades, set yourselves now to accomplish the hopes of the League, and the fame of your valour will run throughout Italy ; how you have done the work before you in the honourable and seemly fashion which has always been your wont. I have never doubted, nor ever shall doubt, of your valour, of which you have given proof, or of your strength and courage ; and, with you, I am ready to risk my personal safety in this our need. I hope, with God's help, we may triumph fighting for justice and reason against those who fight against them. For all of the allied powers are content with their condition, and are striving their best to maintain it. Our adversaries, on the contrary, are dissatisfied with their government and trying to seize unjustly what is not their own. These considerations therefore ought to hearten us to attack them manfully, trusting in God who, for these reasons, will give us victory."

When the leaders saw what the Duke's will was, and listened to the weighty and unanswerable arguments he advanced, they replied that they were satisfied with his reasons, that they knew they would do well in following his advice, and that they were ready, like him, to devote their lives to the saving of the army of the League. When the Duke heard this he praised them highly, adding that, from the faith he had in them, he expected no other reply, and thanked them. He next drew up the troops for the assault on the foe, posted about four miles away, and when they moved off he addressed them as was his wont, impressing on them the danger they would incur by neglecting the necessary formation, and reminding them that by victory they would win the greatest glory that any soldiers had won for many years, fighting as they did under such disadvantages as were theirs to-day. Again he reminded them that if they did not observe his orders, as he trusted they would, they would put the League in imminent peril and cover themselves with irremediable shame and infamy.

He then let the squadrons advance towards the foe who expected no attack, deeming the conditions too disadvantageous. They neared the hostile camp about the nineteenth hour ;* they quickly got ready their arms and the Duke let the squadrons advance to the attack, both sides fighting shrewdly, for all the distinguished men of Italy were present, and now one party prevailed and now the other. The Duke had drawn up his line wonderfully well, forbidding anyone to break it under pain of death. On both sides many were stricken, but mostly of the enemy. The Duke of Ferrara bore himself valiantly, and would have given still farther taste of his quality had he not been forced to quit the field

* 1 p.m.

with a gunshot wound in his heel. So many wounded were borne into Ferrara that the city was full of them. Fighting like this from the nineteenth hour to the first hour of night, that is for six hours, every man on either side was half dead through fatigue. Bartolomeo Colleone that day also gave proof of his generalship, though they had come upon him unaware, with such great violence. He advanced to the front and cried out : " Valiant leaders, the hour is late and the men on either side have fought strenuously, thus it seems the time has come to stop the battle." The Duke agreed, and afterwards used to tell that the foe had begged leave to cease fighting ; but no one could fight any longer ; and, had it not been for shame, he himself would have done the like ; it was his particular good fortune that the foe had first cried halt. Then there was the trouble of the heat, and the quitting their own quarters to beat up the enemy's. After the fight it was settled that the League had the advantage, and that the Duke's decision had been a very wise one.

After the fight the troops returned to their quarters without let, the most dangerous military movement being the quitting and regaining of quarters scatheless, and this was done with sound judgment under the eye of the Duke. The result was that the Venetians, seeing the Duke's skill, had no further wish to meet him in arms. With a greatly inferior force he always maintained himself in the enemy's country, and outside the territories of the League, manœuvring in such wise that he kept the armies face to face.* Henceforth the Venetians lost courage, because, while they were stronger both in horse and foot, the Duke gained the victory. The Duke and the League reaped great renown by this feat of arms ; a proof of the value of an active chief in settling the plan of campaign, and how on him depends victory and the safety of the state. Though the history of this will be written in Latin, it has seemed good to me to make mention of it here, since I was informed thereanent by one who was present. No doubt it will be written in more elegant style, but here I have left out nothing of the truth.

* It would seem that this fighting must have occurred during Federigo's last campaign, the war of Ferrara in 1482. In the next pages Vespasiano shifts the narrative back to 1469.

As to the defence of Rimini. On the death of Signor Gismondo, the Church laid claim to that state. The Magnifico Roberto* was then in Rome, and he prudently left unknown for Rimini. Arrived there, he took possession first of the castle and then of the country around, whereupon Pope Paul, seeing that he had been tricked, made plans to seize on the territory, and engaged a large number of soldiers for that purpose. Roberto was at that time in the favour of the King, who determined to defend Rimini with all his forces, wherefore he requested his allies to aid him in this work, and they consented. Then the Duke of Urbino was directed to go to Rimini with his forces, and the King promised to send the Duke of Calabria† with all the troops available. It would be necessary to be in strength, seeing that they would have to traverse the states of the Church without holding the pass. Also he requested the States of Milan and Florence to send the troops they had promised, but not all those who promised kept faith ; for when the Duke of Calabria, riding day and night with his lance at his thigh through hostile country, came to Rimini and found that the troops promised had not been sent, it was necessary that he should leave more troops than had been allowed to guard his rear. This neglect in sending the promised forces came near putting the Duke of Calabria in peril ; and Rimini would have been lost had it not been for the prudence of the Duke of Urbino. The Duke of Calabria arrived in safety with his army, leaving a good part of his troops, as has been mentioned. His Majesty grieved much over the ill faith of certain of his allies, seeing the great peril his son incurred thereby, for he expected they would have done what they promised.

The Duke of Urbino, finding himself at the head of these forces, with the army of the Church fourteen squadrons stronger in front of him, was in no way alarmed at beholding their array ; and, having determined to join battle with them since there was no other way of saving Rimini, he turned to Don Alfonso and the other leaders and said to them, the day before the action, " To-morrow you shall reap the greatest

* Sigismondo died 1468. Roberto was his son.
† Son of King Ferdinand whom he succeeded as Alfonso II. He fled before Charles VIII in 1495 and abdicated without striking a blow.

honour you have ever known ; what though the army of the Church be fourteen squadrons stronger than our own, we will shatter them." The next day he drew up his forces for action according to his own plan, and then he formed a great squadron of five hundred picked men-at-arms. Next he sent one company after another to begin the action, charging everyone, under pain of death, to follow his instructions, and all obeyed. When the time had come, he let advance the great squadron of picked men into action, and the enemy, seeing no other course, began to flee on all sides, and soon the field was cleared of hostile troops, indeed they could have captured as many of them as they wished, every squadron having been broken up. All this the Duke carried out with his wonted skill, winning the battle more by science than by force.* If I were to relate all the deeds of arms wrought by him I could show him equal to any of the captains of old.

As to the acquisition of Volterra by the Signoria,† which was due entirely to his foresight ; because, on account of the nature of the site, it could never have been effected by force ot arms alone. At the time when the Duke was in the pay of the King and of the Florentines, the people of Volterra, through certain differences with the Florentines, had rebelled and taken the government into their own hands. When the King heard of this he wrote straightway to the Duke, charging him, at the request of the Florentines, to march with his own forces and those of the League ; and, if the troops in Romagna would not suffice, with twelve additional squadrons of Neapolitan soldiers, to whom he had sent word that they should obey the Duke as if he were the King. When the Duke received this letter he wrote at once, telling the Florentines of the King's commission ; and afterwards reminded them that it behoved them to go slowly about the business and take time ; that it was easy to begin, and difficult to abandon ; that failure in it might mean the ruin of the state. He got an answer that in due time they would call upon him, and after several days they determined to engage with Volterra ; advising the Duke, and sending Bongianni Gianfigliazzi

* Battle of Rimini, 1469.
† Macchiavelli, *Flor. Hist.*, B. VII, p. 362. The war originated through the finding of a mine of alum. 1472.

with money to bring him quickly to the city. When he understood from Bongianni what the Signoria willed, and saw the danger of his position through delay, he mounted with all the horsemen he could raise ; and before leaving he wrote to Piero dei Felici, who was acting for him in Florence, charging him to ask no pay from the Florentines during the war of Volterra, because he wished them to understand that he was serving them for goodwill and not for gold. The people of Volterra besought all the powers and princes of Italy for aid to keep them from falling into the hands of the Florentines, but they found no one to help them ; even the Pope had sent several squadrons of horse to help the Signoria. Every Italian power was concerned in this dispute.

When the Duke came before Volterra, he took up a position, apparently a weak one, but really strong, for it was invulnerable on all sides. He drew up his own and the papal forces in an order which gave the impression that it was vulnerable, whereas it was very difficult. From his camp he made all possible demonstrations of assault on the city, nevertheless he waited with his wonted shrewdness to come to some agreement. He often sent soldiers to talk with those of the enemy, also to see whether he might not be able to gather something from the soldiers of Volterra to help on a truce : making clear to them, that, being alone in this contest, they could not possibly withstand the Florentines. But while these negotiations went on, he prosecuted the siege without cease by all possible means by night and day. He continued his dealings with certain of the enemy's soldiers, inducing them to come over to him, and letting them see how he stood ; and the people of Volterra, despairing of better terms, began to listen to his overtures and negotiations began. At Florence the opinion was that there was no other solution possible, and they begged the Duke, in God's name, to free them from the danger they were in. He bade them not to fear, for he would soon disentangle them. The men-at-arms complained to the Signoria, saying that it would be a great loss for them to be kept there more than a year, that the Signoria should try to come to terms, in order to free themselves and send their soldiers to the hospital : to favour them, instead of slighting them. To the Duke every day seemed a thousand until this peace should be made.

The people of Volterra, finding themselves besieged on all sides and the city blockaded, though exit and entry were not entirely stopped, began to consider terms of peace. They sent negotiators into the camp, under safe conduct, and the Duke, conscious of his danger, at once came to business and the deliberations lasted several days. Finally the place was delivered over to the Florentines,* property and person being respected ; the privileges of electing a Podesta and a Signory were taken away, and the people placed under the rule of Florence. The Duke, in agreement with the Florentine Commissaries, Messer Bongianni Gianfigliazzi and Jacopo Guicciardini, entered the city and forbade everyone, under pain of the gallows, from touching anything ; but the Milanese mercenaries began to plunder, whereupon the Duke and the Commissaries hastened with arms in their hands to stop the pillage, but they could not prevent the mischief. Next the men-at-arms began, so that great disorders arose which could not be remedied. The Duke did all he could, but he was unable to save the place and he suffered much vexation on this account and even wept. Everything would have gone well, but for this riot, as the Commissaries and all those who were present could tell.

Volterra having been recovered, the Florentines recognised that he had done a deed which was almost impossible considering the difficulties of position and the evil disposition of the people ; they realised the danger better after than before the fall of Volterra ; also that the place had been taken by his skill and prudence. The Signoria of Volterra used to say that its five hundred footmen were enough to defend the city from the whole of Italy. After the victory the Duke entered Florence with the highest honours : all the citizens went to meet him ; he was lodged in the house of the Patriarch with all his following at free cost, and greater honour was never done to any man. They gave him two pieces of gold brocade, and two bowls belonging to the Signoria worth a thousand ducats or more. Afterwards, in memory of the victory, they gave him the Palace of Rusciano with all its

* 1472.

appurtenances, and all the chief citizens visited him there. For several days there was feasting in all the lands round Florence, and the Duke was escorted by the leading citizens through their estates. Having written thus about Volterra and of his prudence in capturing it, I will demonstrate how he alone liberated Italy from the Venetian sway. The Duke of Ferrara had joined the League of His Majesty the King, Milan and Florence, and all of these were bound to protect him, should be he attacked by any other Italian power.* Now the Venetians, under the pretext of some dispute, planned war against Ferrara and persuaded Pope Sixtus to join them in attacking the Duke. When the preparations necessary for this enterprise became known to Milan the Florentines and the Duke of Ferrara, they sent ambassadors to His Majesty the King, bidding him have a care that the Duke of Ferrara should not lose his dominions, because the Venetians were bent on the domination of Italy, and, if Ferrara, Bologna and Mantua should be lost, they would be able to act as they pleased. At Naples the ambassadors agreed that no defence was possible without the help of the skill and strength of the Duke of Urbino. And they were met by the fact that, Roberto Malatesta, because of his quarrel with Milan, had now gone over to the Venetians† and taken their pay, an event which encouraged them greatly in the enterprise.

When the ambassadors of the League had been several days at Naples, discussing with His Majesty what they should do, they agreed that they should go, accompanied by an envoy of the King, to Urbino in order to hear the Duke's opinion, and to engage him at the cost of the King, of Milan, and of Florence. An agreement was made, but the Pope was still set upon attacking the Duke of Ferrara and handing over his lands to the Venetians, while the Duke himself was ready to submit all the disputes he had with the Venetians to His Holiness, to be settled in the customary way, but the Pope refused this: indeed, all the allies begged him to consent,

---

* 1474. In 1471 the Duke of Ferrara, urged by Francesco, the son of Palla Strozzi, who had died an exile in Ferrara, had attacked Florence in alliance with Venice. The Duke was disappointed with the terms of the subsequent peace and joined the League against Venice.
† 1479.

but they could not alter his decision. Whereupon all the ambassadors of the League quitted Rome, to show their displeasure at the attitude of His Holiness towards their undertaking, and went to Urbino to make an agreement with the Duke as to the commando, and to arrange that all the parties should bear the charges, which at first had been laid on the King alone. When they came to Fossombrone they met the Duke, who gave them magnificent entertainment. Negotiations began and, as all the ambassadors had full powers, they came quickly to an agreement.

The Venetians knew that none but the Duke of Urbino could hinder their attempt on Ferrara, wherefore they sent word to him offering him eighty thousand ducats per annum if he would stay at home : it would be enough for him to recognise that he was in their pay.* While the Venetian messenger was at Urbino on this business, it chanced that one of the Duke's chief officers was in his closet, and after the Venetian had left, he turned to the Duke and said, " Eighty thousand ducats is a good price simply for staying at home " ; whereupon the Duke replied wisely, " To keep faith is still better, and is worth more than all the gold in the world." Having settled the terms, they deliberated as to the defence of Ferrara, and the ambassadors proposed various schemes for this, and for attacking the Venetians, in order to expel them from their lands on terra firma and break up their campaign in Lombardy. Also to let the Duke of Calabria attack the Pope, and hinder him from aiding the Venetians against Ferrara, and compel them to send troops to support the Pope. There was good prospect that these plans would succeed, if the preparations at Ferrara should be carried out as proposed. With the troops of Ferrara, Mantua and some from Lombardy, Ferrara might be defended and the Duke of Urbino might interrupt the campaign of the Venetians in Lombardy. This scheme of the Duke's was the best ever devised.

When he had prepared his force, and set all other things in order, the Duke, having ranged his army, opened one of the finest campaigns ever made in Italy.† He joined forces with the Florentines and took the field at Città di Castello in order to make the Pope withdraw his forces to guard his own

* 1482.   † 1482.

96

borders. His son Antonio advanced with a force to Forlì, in the hope of stirring up that state, while the Florentines, under Nicoli da Castello, who kept the inner line, advanced against Città di Castello. The Duke, having come to Florence with a part of his army, stayed there two days, and then begged leave for the route of Ferrara in order to see how things stood there, and then go into Lombardy, supposing that affairs were as favourable as he had been given to understand, and that the troops prepared there were sufficient for the defence of Ferrara. He moved quickly and found the whole country in such ill order that, but for his foresight, it must have fallen into the hands of the Venetians. When he arrived he was greatly angered at finding that nothing had been carried out as he had been informed, and that if he should depart for Lombardy and leave the country in this condition Ferrara must be lost, seeing that Signor Roberto,* who knew the country, had passed the swamps by bridges of fascines and gained a good part of the Polesine, and taken Chioggia and other places near. Soon afterwards he captured the Polesine of Rovigo, which was difficult to defend, and had got well in advance of his foes and the country clear before him. When the Duke of Urbino saw this move of Signor Roberto and what he had gained thereby, he realised that Ferrara must surely fall if he did not intervene, wherefore he went to Mantua and persuaded the Marquis to occupy a certain pass and hinder the foe from passing that way. He likewise wrote to Milan, bidding them send help quickly if they did not want Ferrara to be lost. Four hundred men-at-arms were sent, and the Duke, having posted the Marquis of Mantua in the pass, went himself to a place called La Stellata and faced Signor Roberto, who had frustrated a promising scheme, for if the Duke did not reach Ferrara all would be lost.

Signor Roberto made a move to capture Ficheruolo, a very important town, because it stood between the combatants. As soon as the Duke saw this he set about its defence, and threw into it all the best men he had ; men he knew and trusted. Roberto had brought thither bombards and kept up a fire day and night, knowing how greatly the possession

* Roberto Malatesta, in command of the papal forces.

97

of the town would help him to capture Ferrara. The Duke
of Ferrara stood on the defensive ; and what with the fights
that constantly took place, and the bombards and small
guns which went off day and night, and the constant changes
made by the Duke in the disposition of the garrison within
the place, Signor Roberto was hard set to hold his ground.
The assailants set about to build a bastion, and one day the
Count Antonio di Marciano, the next in command to Signor
Roberto, went to occupy it, but when the Duke was informed
of this he sent against him the best men-at-arms he had.
When the enemy set about making the bastion the forces of
the Duke of Urbino attacked them fiercely, and many on
either side were killed and wounded. Messer Piero degli
Ubaldini, one of the Duke's best men, was killed, and Count
Antonio di Marciano and many men-at-arms were captured,
so the bastion was not constructed.

Signor Roberto still remained before Ficheruolo, having
assaulted it shrewdly, but the men in the place made a brave
defence. Before he delivered his attack, certain of the
Venetians believed that it had succeeded and the place must
be theirs that day. The Commissaries wrote off to Venice
that it was taken, whereupon the Venetians made great
rejoicings over the victory. But those within the town
maintained their defence by the help of those without, and
for that day it was saved. There was chagrin in Venice
because they had celebrated the capture of the place pre-
maturely, and every day the Duke found new means to
harass the Venetians, letting the troops of the League ride
free as far as Padua, pillaging and slighting the country and
taking many prisoners and cattle. Signor Roberto lost heart
because every day the Duke fell upon him with some new
and successful scheme of offence. It was regarded as a
marvel that they should have held Ficheruolo so many days,
as it was not a strong place. At last, contrary to the expectation of the Duke, the foe made a fierce attack and contrived
at the same time to corrupt some of the garrison ; so, after a
long defence, the place fell ; but had there been no traitors
inside, it would have resisted another fifteen days.*

* Federigo died at Ferrara on September 11. The war was ended
by the peace of Bagnuolo in 1484. Roberto Malatesta, his antagonist,

FEDERIGO, DUKE OF URBINO

Hitherto I have written concerning some of the Duke's military exploits, leaving his greater deeds to be dealt with by those who will write his history ; and now it seems meet to say something of his knowledge of the Latin tongue, taken in connection with military affairs, for it is difficult for a leader to excel in arms unless he be, like the Duke, a man of letters, seeing that the past is a mirror of the present. A military leader who knows Latin has a great advantage over one who does not. The Duke wrought the greater part of his martial deeds by ancient and modern example ; from the ancients by the study of history, and from the moderns through nurture in warlike practices from early infancy under the discipline of Nicolo Piccinino, one of the worthiest captains of his age. But to return to letters, the Duke of Urbino was well versed therein, not only in history and in the Holy Scriptures, but also in philosophy, which he studied many years under a distinguished teacher, Maestro Lazzaro, afterwards for his merits made Bishop of Urbino. He was instructed by Maestro Lazzaro in the Ethics of Aristotle, with and without comments, and he would also dispute over the difficult passages. He began to study logic with the keenest understanding, and he argued with the most nimble wit that was ever seen. After he had heard the Ethics many times, comprehending them so thoroughly that his teachers found him hard to cope with in disputation, he studied the Politics assiduously, and during his stay in Florence, after the capture of Volterra, he requested Donato Acciaiuoli, who had already commented on the Ethics, to write comments also on the Politics. This he did and sent his work to the Duke who, having read these, wished next to read the Natural History and the Physics. Indeed, it may be said of him that he was the first of the Signori who took up philosophy and had knowledge of the same. He was ever careful to keep intellect and virtue to the front, and to learn some new thing every day.

died the same day at Rome. Girolamo, the Pope's nephew, was suspected of having poisoned him in order to seize Rimini. Pope Sixtus, either through gratitude, or to ward off suspicion, at once erected a sumptuous tomb in S. Peter's to Roberto's memory. He broke with the Venetians by joining the League, and also excommunicated them. *Vide Life of Bishop of Cologna*, p. 197.

After philosophy he was fain to study theology ; that learning on which every Christian ought to frame his life. He read the first part of S. Thomas, and certain other works of his, thus acquiring a strong predilection for S. Thomas' doctrine, which seemed to him very clear and able to defend itself. He rated S. Thomas as clearer than Scotus though less subtle. Nevertheless he wished to know the works of Scotus, and he read the first of them. He knew the Scriptures well and the early Doctors, Ambrose, Jerome, Augustine and Gregory, whose works he desired to possess ; likewise the works of the Greek Doctors, Basil, John Chrysostom, Gregory Nazianzen, Athanasius, Cyril and Ephrem, done into Latin, and works in poetry and history which he read and re-read ; also Livy, Sallust, Quintus Curtius, Justin, the Commentaries of Cæsar, which he praised beyond measure ; all the forty-eight lives of Plutarch, translated by various hands, Ælius Spartianus, together with certain other writers of the decadence of the Roman power. Æmilius Probus, Cornelius Tacitus, Suetonius, his lives of the Emperors, beginning with Cæsar and going on to other times. He read also Eusebius' *De Temporius* with the additions of Girolamo Prospero and Matteo Palmieri.

As to architecture it may be said that no one of his age, high or low, knew it so thoroughly. We may see in the buildings he constructed, the grand style and the due measurement and proportion, especially in his palace, which has no superior amongst the buildings of the time, none so well considered, or so full of fine things. Though he had his architects about him, he always first realised the design and then explained the proportions and all else ; indeed, to hear him discourse thereanent, it would seem that his chief talent lay in this art ; so well he knew how to expound and carry out its principles. He built not only palaces and the like, but many fortresses in his dominions of construction much stronger than those of old time ; for some, which were built too high, the Duke made much lower, knowing that the fire of the bombards would not then hurt them. He was a skilled geometrician and arithmetician, and a German, Master Paul,* a great philosopher and astrologer, with whom, just before his death, he read books on mathematics, dis-

* *Vide Life of Cosimo de' Medici*, also of *Master Pagolo*.

coursing thereon like one learned in them. He delighted greatly in music, understanding vocal and instrumental alike, and maintained a fine choir with skilled musicians and many singing boys. He had every sort of instrument in his palace and delighted in their sound, also the most skilful players. He preferred delicate to loud instruments, caring little for trombones and the like.

As to sculpture he had great knowledge, and he took much thought as to the work which he had made for his palace, employing the first masters of the time. To hear him talk of sculpture you would deem it was his own art. He was much interested in painting, and because he could not find in Italy painters in oil to suit his taste he sent to Flanders and brought thence a master* who did at Urbino many very stately pictures, especially in Federigo's study, where were represented philosophers, poets, and doctors of the Church, rendered with wondrous art. He painted from life a portrait of the Duke which only wanted breath. He also brought in Flemish tapestry weavers who wrought a noble set for an apartment, worked with gold and silk mixed with woollen thread, in such fashion as no brush could have rendered. He also caused other decorations to be wrought by these masters, and all the doors were enriched with works as fine as those within. One of his cabinets was adorned in a fashion so wonderful that no one could say whether it was done with a brush, or in silver, or in relief.

Reverting to the study of letters, from the times of Pope Nicolas and King Alfonso onward, letters and learned men were never better honoured and rewarded than by the Duke of Urbino, who spared no expense. There were few *literati* of that age who did not receive from him generous gifts. He gave Campano, a learned man fallen into poverty, a thousand ducats or more. Many fine works were sent to him, and when he was in Florence he bestowed upon men of letters more than fifteen hundred ducats, and I can say naught of his gifts in Rome, Naples, and other places, for they are unknown to me. No one ever was such a defender of learned men, and when Pope Sixtus persecuted the Bishop of Sipontino† the bishop

---

* Justus von Ghent.
† See the bishop's Life, p. 181.

would have fared badly if the Duke had not protected him. He was always fain to have in his palace some learned man, and none ever came to Urbino who was not honoured or received at the palace.

We come now to consider in what high esteem the Duke held all Greek and Latin writers, sacred as well as secular. He alone had a mind to do what no one had done for a thousand years or more ; that is, to create the finest library since ancient times. He spared neither cost nor labour, and when he knew of a fine book, whether in Italy or not, he would send for it. It is now fourteen or more years ago since he began the library, and he always employed, in Urbino, in Florence and in other places, thirty or forty scribes in his service. He took the only way to make a fine library like this : by beginning with the Latin poets, with any comments on the same which might seem merited ; next the orators, with the works of Tully and all Latin writers and grammarians of merit ; so that not one of the leading writers in this faculty should be wanted. He sought also all the known works on history in Latin, and not only those, but likewise the histories of Greek writers done into Latin, and the orators as well. The Duke also desired to have every work on moral and natural philosophy in Latin, or in Latin translations from Greek.

As to the sacred Doctors in Latin, he had the works of all four, and what a noble set of letters and writings we have here ; bought without regard of cost. After the four Doctors, he was set on having the works of S. Bernard and of all the Doctors of old, without exception, Tertullian, Hilarius, Remigius, Hugh de S. Victor, Isidore, Anselm, Rabanus and all the rest. After Latin works came Greek writings done into Latin, Dionysius the Areopagite, Basil, Cyril, Gregory Nazianzen, John of Damascus, John Chrysostom, Gregory of Nicea, all the works of Eusebius, of Ephrem the monk, and of Origen, an excellent writer. Coming to the Latin Doctors in philosophy and theology, all the works of Thomas Aquinas, and of Albertus Magnus ; of Alexander ab Alexandro, of Scotus, of Bonaventura, of Richard of Mediavilla, of the Archbishop of Antoninus and of all the recognised modern Doctors, down to the Conformità of S. Francis : all the works on civil law in the finest text, the lectures of Bartolo written on goat-skin. He had an edition of the Bible made in two most beautiful volumes, illustrated in the finest possible manner and bound in gold brocade with rich silver fittings. It was given this rich form as the chief of all writings. With it are all the commentaries of the Master of the Sentences, of Nicolao di Lira, and of all the Greek and Latin Doctors, together with the literal glossary of Nicolao di Lira. Likewise all the writers on astrology, geometry, arithmetic, architecture and *De re Militari ;* books on painting, sculpture, music and canon law, and all the texts and lectures on the *Summa* of Ostiensis and other works in the same faculty. In medicine all the works of Avicenna, Hippocrates, Galen, the *Continenti* of Almansor and the complete works of Averroes in logic and natural philosophy. A volume of all the Councils, held since ancient times, and the logical, philosophical and musical works of Boethius.

There were all the works of modern writers beginning with Pope Pius ; of Petrarch and Dante in Latin and in the vulgar tongue, of Boccaccio in Latin ; of Coluccio and of Lionardo d' Arezzo, original and translations ; of Fra Ambrogio, of Giannozzo Manetti and Guerrino ; the prose and poetical works of Panormita, and Francesco Filelfo, and Campano ; as well as everything written by Perrotto, Maffeo Vegio, Nicolo Secondino (who was interpreter of Greek and Latin at the Council of the Greeks in Florence), Pontano, Bartolomeo Fazi, Gasparino, Pietro Paolo Vergerio, Giovanni Argiropolo (which includes the Philosophy and Logic of Aristotle and the Politics besides), Francesco Barbaro, Lionardo Giustiniano, Donato Acciaiuoli, Alamanno, Rinuccini, Cristofano da Prato, Vecchio, Poggio, Giovanni Tortello, Francesco d' Arezzo and Lorenzo Valla.

He added to the books written by ancient and modern doctors on all the faculties all the books known in Greek, also the complete works of Aristotle and Plato (written on the finest goat-skin) ; of Homer in one volume, the *Iliad*, the *Odyssey*, and the *Batrachomiomachia ;* of Sophocles, Pindar and Menander, and all the other Greek poets ; a fine volume of Plutarch's lives and his moral works, the *Cosmography* of Ptolemy illustrated in Greek, and the writings of Herodotus,

Pausanius, Thucydides, Polybius, Demosthenes, Æschines and Plotinus. All the Greek comments, such as those upon Aristotle, the *Physica de Plantis* and Theophrastus ; all the Greek vocabulists—Greek into Latin ; the works of Hippocrates, Galen, Xenophon, S. Basil, S. John Chrysostom, S. Athanasius, S. John Damascenas, S. Gregory Nazianzen, S. Gregory of Nicea, Origen, Dionysius the Areopagite, John Climacus, S. Ephrem the monk, Æneas the Sophist, the Collations of John Cassianus, the book of Paradise, *Vitæ sanctorum patrum ex Ægypto*, the Life of Barlaam and Josaphat, a wonderful psalter in Hebrew, Greek and Latin, verse by verse, and all the Greek works on geometry, arithmetic, and astrology. Finding that he lacked a vast number of Greek books by various writers, he sent to seek them so that nothing in that tongue which could be found should be lacking ; also whatever books which were to be had in Hebrew, beginning with the Bible and all those dealt with by the Rabbi Moses and other commentators. And besides the Holy Scriptures, there are books in Hebrew on medicine, philosophy and the other faculties.

The Duke, having completed this noble work at the great cost of thirty thousand ducats, beside the many other excellent provisions that he made, determined to give every writer a worthy finish by binding his work in scarlet and silver. Beginning with the Bible, as the chief, he had it covered with gold brocade, and then he bound in scarlet and silver the Greek and Latin doctors and philosophers, the histories, the books on medicine and the modern doctors, a rich and magnificent sight. In this library all the books are superlatively good, and written with the pen, and had there been one printed volume it would have been ashamed in such company. They were beautifully illuminated and written on parchment. This library is remarkable amongst all others in that, taking the works of all writers, sacred and profane, original and translated, there will be found not a single imperfect folio. No other library can show the like, for in all of them the works of certain authors will be wanting in places. A short time before the Duke went to Ferrara it chanced that I was in Urbino with His Lordship, and I had with me the catalogues of the principal Italian libraries : of the papal library, of those of S. Marco at Florence, of Pavia, and even of that of the University of Oxford, which I had procured from England. On comparing them with that of the Duke I remarked how they all failed in one respect ; to wit, they possessed the same work in many examples, but lacked the other writings of the author ; nor had they writers in all the faculties like this library.

I began by treating of his warlike deeds, then of his martial and literary merits combined ; wishing to show that if any-one should be fain to produce so skilful a captain as the Duke without the aid of letters, the attempt to produce a man of such excellence must be vain without the conjunction of these two elements. I now bring forward a third quality, the faculty of wisely governing States and Lordships, a faculty rarely possessed by those endowed as richly as he was with the qualities I have already specified. In the ruling of his states and of his house, his age saw not his peer. First, in order that his rule might be conjoined with religion, he was before all things most devout and observant in his religious duties ; for without this, and without a good example to others by his life, his rule would never have endured. Every morning he heard mass kneeling ; he fasted on the vigils ordered by the Church, and throughout Lent, and the year before he died the Signor Ottaviano,* who loved him greatly and perceived that Lenten fast was hurtful to him, got a dis-pensation for him from Rome. One morning during Lent this dispensation was laid before him at table, whereupon he turned towards Ottaviano, laughing, and thanked him and said : " If I am able to fast, why should you wish me to keep from so doing ? What an example I should be giving to my own people ! " And he continued from that day to fast as heretofore. Every morning with his household, and with whatever townsfolk might wish, he heard the sermon, and after this the mass ; and on fast days he would cause to be read to him some holy book or work of S. Leo. When the reader came to a weighty passage he would bid him stop in order that it might be thoroughly considered, and every day he made Maestro Lazzaro read to him some passage of Holy Writ.

* The son of Bernardo Ubaldini and of Federigo's sister Anna.

POPES AND RULERS

As to works of alms and piety he was most observant. He distributed in his house every day a good quantity of bread and wine without fail, and he gave freely to learned men and gentlefolk, to holy places, and to poor folk ashamed of their case, and he never forgot anyone of his subjects who might come to ask. Wherever he could he established Observant Friars in his dominions, allowing them alms to set the country in order at his charges. He introduced the friars of Monte Oliveto and the Jesuates* and the friars of Scopeto, and was as a father to all. The Duke never let a religious person approach him without doing him reverence, and taking him by the hand, and in conversation would always sit down beside him. He honoured these persons more than any man I ever saw. There was in Urbino a holy convent of nuns with some sixty inmates, and the Duke did much to the convent to make it suitable for their well-being. Once every week he would betake himself alone into the church, and sit by a grating that was therein. The Superior, a lady of years and authority, would speak to him, and he would ask if the nuns lacked anything. Indeed, he provided this convent and the Observant Friars with all they needed.

As to the ruling of his own palace, it was just the same as that of a religious society; for although he was called on to feed at his own expense five hundred mouths or more, there was nothing of the barrack about his establishment, which was as well ordered as any monastery. Here there was no romping or wrangling, but everyone spoke with becoming modesty. Certain noblemen committed their sons to the Duke for instruction in military science, and they would remain with him till they were efficient. These youths were under the charge of a gentleman of Lombardy of excellent character who had been trained by the Duke long time since, and now governed these youths as if they had been his own sons. They paid him the highest respect, keeping their actions well under restraint, as pupils in a school of good manners. The Duke had a legitimate son of singular worth, Count Guido, and other legitimate children born of Madonna Battista, the daughter of Signor

* Founded by S. Jan Colombin in 1367. Montaigne in his *Travels* writes: " They are not priests, neither do they say mass nor preach, but they are skilful distillers of citron and other waters."

FEDERIGO, DUKE OF URBINO

Alessandro of Pesaro, an illustrious lady. At her death she left her children very young, and to his son the Duke assigned, as tutors, two gentlemen of due age to teach him the course he ought to follow. Afterwards he put him under a learned young man who taught him Greek and Latin, and was expressly charged by the Duke to let him have no traffic with young folk, in order that he might at once assume the grave temperament which nature had given him. He had a marvellous memory, of which I can give numerous examples ; for once, when Signor Ottaviano put Ptolemy before him, he knew how to point out all the regions of the earth so that, when he was asked for any place or district, he found it at once and knew the distance of one place from another. The Duke possessed a Bible with historical comments, the events of each book being narrated, and there was no name or place which the young prince did not know, even the unfamiliar names in Hebrew. He was educated to be worthy to follow his father, and the same training is still pursued. Another son of his, Signor Antonio, born to him when he was a young unmarried man, devoted himself to arms and was of excellent carriage. His daughters, attended by many noble and worthy ladies, occupied a wing of the palace whither went no one but the Signor Ottaviano and the young prince. When the prince came to the door of their apartments, those in attendance remained outside, going to the waiting-room till he should return. In his carriage he was most observant of what was becoming.

Having spoken of the governance of his house, let us now tell of that of his subjects. His treatment of them suggested that they were rather his children. He liked not that anyone should ever address him on behalf of any of them, seeing that everyone could speak to him at any hour of the day, when he would listen to all with the utmost kindness, remarking that this gave him no trouble. If there was anything he could do for them, he would see to it, so there might be no need for them to return, and there were few whose business could not be despatched on the same day, in order that no time might be lost. And should he mark that anyone amongst those who desired to address him might be shamefaced, he would call him up, and encourage him to say what he would. His sub-

jects loved him so greatly for the kindness he showed to them
that when he went through Urbino they would kneel and say,
" God keep you, my Lord," and he would often go afoot
through his lands, entering now one shop and now another,
and asking the workmen what their calling was, and whether
they were, in need of aught. So kind was he, that they all
loved him as children love their parents. The country he
ruled was a wondrous sight : all his subjects were well-to-do
and waxed rich through labour at the works he had instituted,
and a beggar was never seen. If it happened that anyone,
through misbehaviour or neglect of the laws, should be condemned, the Duke in clemency would intervene and settle
the matter to the content of all. For all offences he showed
a merciful spirit save one, to wit : blasphemy of God, or of the
Madonna, or of His saints. For this he had no grace or forgiveness.

He was as benevolent to strangers as to those of his own
state. Once I saw him go to the piazza on a market day, and
ask of the men and women who were there, how much they
wanted for the wares they were selling. Then, by way of
joking, he added, " I am the Lord and never carry any money :
I know you will not trust me for fear you should not be paid."
Thus he pleased everybody, small and great, by his good-
humour. The peasants he had spoken to went away so
delighted that he could have done with them whatever he
wished, and when he rode out he met none who did not
salute him and ask how he did. He went about with few
attendants ; none of them armed. In summer he would ride
out from Urbino at dawn with four or six horsemen and one or
two servants, unarmed, at his stirrup and go forth three or
four miles, returning when other folk were rising from bed.
When they dismounted it would be the hour of Mass, which the
Duke would hear, and afterwards go into a garden with the
doors open and give audience to all who wished, till the hour
of repast. When the Duke had sat down the doors would be
left open, so that all might enter, and he never ate except the
hall were full. Some one would always read to him ; during
Lent a spiritual work, and at other times the Histories of
Livy, all in Latin. He ate plain food and no sweetmeats, and
drank no wine save that made from such fruits as cherries,

pomegranates or apples. Anyone who wished to address him might do so either between the courses or after the repasts, and a judge of appeal, a very distinguished man, would lay before him, one by one, the causes before the court which he would determine, speaking in Latin. This judge told me that the decisions of the Duke could not have been bettered if they had come before Bartolo or Baldo.* I saw a letter written on behalf of a physician who sought an appointment at Ancona. The Duke said, "Put in this clause: that if they want a doctor they had better take him; if they do not, let them please themselves, for I have no mind that they should do what they do not wish, because of my letter."

In summer, after rising from table and giving audience to all who desired, he went into his closet to attend to his affairs and to listen to readings, according to the season. At vespers he went forth again to give audience; and then, if he had time, to visit the nuns at S. Chiara in the monastery he had built, or to the convent of S. Francis, where there was a large meadow with a very fine view. There he would sit while thirty or forty of his young men, after stripping to their doublets, would throw the lance either at the apple or at the twigs in marvellous fashion; and the Duke, when he marked a want of dexterity in running or catching, would reprove them, in order that they might do better. During these exercises anyone might address him; indeed he was there for this end as well as for any other. About the hour of supper the Duke would bid the youths put on their clothes. On returning to the palace it would be time for supper, and they would sup as I have already described. The Duke would remain for a time to see if anyone had aught to say, and if not he would go with the leading nobles and gentlemen into his closet and talk freely with them. Sometimes he would say, "To-morrow we ought all to rise early and walk in the cool. You are a set of boys and prone to lie a-bed. You say you will come, but you will do nothing of the kind, and now good night."

One day he remarked to me how every man, great or small, who might be at the head of any state ought to be generous, and he censured all those who acted otherwise; and, as to those who would apologise for their want of humanity through

* Two noted jurists.

some defect of nature, it behoved all such persons to right themselves by strong measures, seeing that great men ought to cultivate humanity as an attribute before all others. Humanity can make foes into friends. It is long since Italy had known a prince so worthy of imitation in every respect as the Duke of Urbino. He showed the greatest discretion towards those who had pleased him. Once it happened that, having had large dealings with a certain merchant, one of his household came and told him that this merchant was making vast sums out of him, and that the goods he supplied were not worth the price charged. The Duke smiled and said he was quite content that the merchant should make his profit, and that he would not have made it had he not been highly deserving. He went on to say that he was greatly obliged to this merchant who had trusted him, when he was poor and just come into his possessions, with five or six thousand florins when no one else would have lent him a single one. On this account he was glad that the merchant should win what seemed to him a just profit. He thus silenced the servant, who went away shamefaced. One day when he was at Milan, he was discussing various matters with Duke Galeazzo, who said to him, " Signor, I would fain be always at war, with you to back me, then I should never be worsted." The Duke replied, " What I know of warfare, I learned from His Excellency Duke Francesco your father." Duke Galeazzo said nothing in reply, unable apparently to find a word. Some blamed the Duke for over-much clemency, but this quality is much to be praised, and few suppliants went away unforgiven, whatever their offence. He hated cruelty of every kind.

One admirable quality he possessed : to speak ill of no one. He praised rather than blamed, and he took it ill if one spoke evil of another before him, deeming such an action to be shameful. He loved not to hear those who praised their own deeds : indeed, on this score he was most modest, and he always preferred that others and not himself should speak of what he had done. Nature had given him a choleric temper, but he knew well how to moderate it, and he softened his temperament with the utmost prudence. He gave himself entirely to his state that the people might be content, and one of the greatest of his merits was that when he heard of a quarrel he would send for the parties, and give his wits no rest till peace should be made. Amongst his many kind actions in mitigating dissension was the case of one of his subjects of honest birth who chose as wife a girl of a station similar to his own with numerous kinsfolk, betwixt whom and the husband arose bad feeling, so that he was in no way inclined towards the wife whom he had taken. The affair came to the point at which he might have to defend his honour, which meant that he would probably be cut in pieces by one or other of the kinsfolk. The Duke, knowing the scandal which would follow, by way of avoiding it ordered the parties to settle their quarrel on a certain day; and when they had come before him he began with those who had the girl in charge; and, speaking in kindly eloquent words, gave them many and good reasons for what he advised them to do. As is the case with ignorant people, the more he said the more firmly they resisted. When he saw their disposition he turned to the young man and said, " If I desired you to become a relative of mine, would you not consent, having regard for my station? Would it not seem to you a desirable relationship? " The young man replied that in this case it would not be fitting, between so great a man as the Duke and one like himself. Then the Duke said, " But will you not pay regard to something which satisfies me? " The young man, persuaded by the Duke, affirmed that he was content, whereupon the Duke said, " I think very highly of this young woman for her virtue and goodness, as if she were my own daughter; so you are becoming a relative of me, and not of her family." By these words the Duke bound him, so that he was forced to consent, and he took her with the good wishes of all. The Duke took them both by the hand, wishing them good luck, and saying that their relationship with him began from that hour, that he wished them always to bear this in mind, and in all their needs to make use of him. He gave them a noble marriage-feast and they both went away highly pleased, and hereafter the husband and wife maintained an admirable carriage one towards the other. Acts like these, the bringing of peace to his subjects, are worthy of a prince.

What steadfastness the Duke showed in withstanding the loss of Ferrara! He had tarried there long in order to beat off the Venetian leaguer, knowing how important this would be for the rest of Italy, and by his prudence he had hitherto held the Venetians within their bounds, but now that they had advanced their camp as far as the park, he knew that he would be in great danger if he did not keep sharp watch within the walls. His Excellency, through immense discomfort and bad air, fell sick with fever and though, by reason of his temperate habits, the fever left him after a few days, he was very weak, and all his friends and the physicians advised him to go to Bologna where the air was better. The Duke, aware of the danger threatening the land, took more heed of the general welfare than of his own particular case, perceiving that, as soon as he should be gone, Ferrara would fall for want of necessary precautions, which had been neglected by the man who had been charged to execute them. He was earnestly persuaded by those of his own house and by his friends, as well as by messengers from Signor Ottaviano and Count Guido, that he should quit that malarious air ; but, though he knew his life was in danger, he was deaf to their prayers, having lost all zest for life, as is common in marsh sickness. His reply was always that, though he was conscious of his risk, he would do nothing to imperil the city, bearing in mind what this would mean for the rest of Italy, and for the faith the League had placed in him. If the Venetians should win Ferrara, the last obstacle to their power in Italy would be gone and the peril overhanging Mantua and Bologna would be obvious. Bologna taken, the state of Florence, near and conterminous therewith, would lie at the mercy of Venice. Likewise Faenza and the rest of Romagna, about which there had been no contest, save with Giovanni Galeazzo and Filippo Maria Visconti, to prevent these territories from falling under Milanese sway. It would be much worse were they to fall to Venice to-day. As to the other districts on the confines of Lucca, which they might attack by this approach, and the harassing of Pisa, all this would mean a great danger to the Florentines.

Now the Duke, who was one of the wisest and most pious of men, being moved by the considerations above written, resolved to consider first the public weal and refused to retire from the defence of the place, though he was putting his life in peril. Having firmly taken his stand, no one could move him to leave Ferrara. Knowing that he must die, he was fain to remain there and save the city, rather than to depart and let it be captured, merely to save his own life. Then there would be the loss of honour, for men might say that his doings brought Italy under Venetian dominion. After he had made up his mind, his distemper began to increase in the bad air of the country, which was not suited to his case. When he saw that he got worse every day he considered the welfare of his soul, and arranged the affairs of his state, that no future trouble might arise. In temporal and in spiritual things alike he directed that everything should be done down to the minutest detail, as it was provided in his testament. He ordered that the monastery of S. Donato, occupied by Franciscan Observantists, about a mile outside Urbino, should once more be made a church, with everything that was needful, as was afterwards done, and he wished to be buried therein beside Count Guido. There was no need for him to make any provisions in his will in the interests of Divine worship, or as to the governance of his house. Had he failed in this there might have been regrets as to his doings, but as experience has since shown, no hurt of any kind was done either to his own house or to his subjects. When he had provided for the future of his sons he began to consider his own soul and many times made confession like a good and faithful Christian, and set in order everything necessary for salvation, and took the sacraments of the Church in due seasons. And God gave him grace so that he was able to carry out all these matters with sober judgment, carefully considering everything he had to do, and omitting naught that was due. He was most pious and merciful in all his dealings, wherefore he might well claim to be called the father and protector of the wretched and afflicted.

After his death his body was borne with the highest possible honours to the Church of S. Donato, served by the Franciscan Observantists, according to the directions of his will. The greater part of what he left was at the disposition of Signor Ottaviano, his nephew, who had his full confidence, by reason of the great affection which subsisted between them ; to him also he trusted the management of state affairs, as far as they concerned his son, indeed he had such love for Ottaviano that he desired him to succeed to the government of the state, if the Count Guido should die without heirs. There are many things worthy of note concerning the Duke, but these will be set down by those who write his life. As far as I have gone, I have written a brief commentary, in order that the vulgar may know something of the Duke as well as those who read Latin. Of all the things written here, the greater part are from my own experience, having been at the court; and those which I have not seen, I have heard of from men of good repute who were about His Lordship.

ALESSANDRO SFORZA (1404–1466), LORD OF PESARO

Alessandro Sforza was the brother of Duke Francis of Milan and Lord of Pesaro. He was a man of remarkable parts and skilled in the art of war, having given abundant proof of his valour in divers places in Lombardy and Tuscany. He fought also in the service of King Ferdinand of Naples in the wars he waged for the recovery of his kingdom. Besides being a master of military discipline, he was well-lettered, a friend of men of learning, always having about him learned theologians, especially those who excelled in the speculative tenets of S. Thomas Aquinas, for he was much inclined to this doctrine. When time allowed, he would cause these to be read to him, or he would hold disputation with some theologian or with Gasparino, a most eminent philosopher. On his accession he gathered together a noble library. He sent word to Florence ordering the purchase of all the books which were available, and that others should be transcribed regardless of cost. He demanded all the works of the four Latin doctors, many Latin translations from the Greek, all the works of S. Thomas, of Bonaventura, of Alexander and of Scotus: likewise all works of poetry, history, astrology, medicine, cosmography of the very finest. They were produced for him at Milan, Venice, Bologna and all over Italy in a fashion which did not seem fitting for a ruler of so narrow a revenue, but fitting rather for a king. The Bibles and breviaries were very fine. Amongst his other good qualities was great diligence. A learned man with a liberal salary cared for the library and nothing was spent to waste. He managed this library until his death, adding a great number of books in every faculty.

He was very religious and a lover of the poor, especially of the members of the Observant order. He built a suitable monastery at Pesaro for the Franciscan Observantists and called it after Girolamo. He was unwilling that it should lack anything necessary for Divine service, either in books or in the ornaments of the Church: wherefore this monastery was made worthy of any Italian state. It now has twenty-five or thirty inmates. Afterwards he transferred to S. Gostanza the Observantists of S. Domenico in Pesaro, and now they have a fine house. He was most liberal to all the gentlefolk who passed that way, and he always was anxious to entertain persons of quality in his own house, paying them the most distinguished honour. He was not daunted at the prospect of having to entertain the Emperor and all his train, some in his house and some about his lands. He did the highest honour to his guests and was most exact in all his doings. And as a return for all this courtesy a free grant of a coat-of-arms with many other privileges was made to all his house. About him he always kept a number of men distinguished in military affairs and in letters. He had a high reputation as a ruler, and was just in all his doings. He set the best example in his own household and in his general life and habits, because all his deeds sprang from the desire to honour God, and for the maintenance of holy religion. When others spake he was always a ready listener, especially to his own dependents, who loved him greatly. He beautified his own country, keeping it in good order as anyone may see.

As I have said he was a consummate commander, highly esteemed by his forces in divers parts of Italy where he had fought: in the recovery of the kingdom* and in the rout which he inflicted on Duke Giovanni† at Troia. Count Jacopo‡ in command of a fine army was also his opponent on that day. The beating he gave these commanders was one of the greatest feats of arms Italy had seen for a long time. Alessandro saw Duke Giovanni advancing—together with the army of Jacopo, a very skilful leader—and he knew that

* Naples.　　　　† Jean d'Anjou, son of René.
‡ Son of Niccolo Piccinino.

the forces of Duke Giovanni were more numerous and better drilled than those of the King,* who had lost a good part of his dominions, was short of money and had to face the revolt of nearly all the Neapolitan barons†—wherefore he determined that this day should see the loss or the winning of this kingdom. He drew up his forces and, having decided how he should open the battle, he came suddenly to grips with the enemy who were occupying a certain hill. The chief aim of Alessandro was to drive them from this. Having set the attack so as to capture it he pressed it strenuously on both sides and finally took it. Whereupon Alessandro, feeling that he had accomplished enough by this operation, approached His Majesty the King, knowing that he would incur dangerous risk by continuing the fight. He proposed to the King that operations should cease for that day. But the King was persuaded that this day would either make him or mar him, and answered that the battle must go on. All the forces were now on level ground, but the army of Duke Giovanni was still the stronger, nevertheless the King said, " To-day I will be King or nothing " Alessandro now renewed the fight, which for several hours went on fiercely and the King's troops began to gain an advantage over those of Duke Giovanni, and Count Jacopo had but little stomach for the fight that day, perceiving that there was no chance of victory. Nevertheless, Duke Giovanni saw plainly that, if he should put the King's army to rout, the kingdom would be his. So it happened that his forces were defeated.‡ That day the King and Alessandro gave fine proofs of their valour, and the rout which followed restored to King Ferdinand the realm he had lost—taking it from Duke Giovanni who held the greater part of it ; and surely Alessandro must have known that he himself had given the kingdom back to Ferdinand who had lost it. He defeated the army of Duke Giovanni and in a short time restored the whole realm to the King. Duke Giovanni was well pleased to depart and went back to France.

Signor Alessandro deserved high praise in every respect,

---

* Ferdinand I.
† Porzio, *La Congiura dei Baroni*, Florence, 1884.
‡ Sismondi, *Histoire des Français*, xiv–118. This was in 1462.

and was the second great captain produced by his age* who combined military skill with the love of learning, the first being the Duke of Urbino. Our age had only these two who thus cultivated literature together with the practice of arms. In his time he did great deeds in battle and commanded many armies. In his last engagement at Molinella with Bartolomeo of Bergamo, who was in the Venetian service, he bore himself valiantly. This passage of arms lasted from the nineteenth hour to the first hour of the night,† and each army bore itself most creditably. As it has been said he was illustrious in military governance, in affairs of state and in his own household. As wise men do he withdrew from the practice of arms when there was no occasion for it, and with respect to his age, taking up a quiet way of life and learning to know himself. All these things Signor Alessandro did ; he gave up the active exercise of war and confined himself to the ordering of his state, spent his time with divers distinguished men of letters he had about him in his house, ever reading, especially sacred books, and letting them read to him every day certain lessons and repeat the office. He had two breviaries and heard mass daily. He gave himself up entirely to Divine worship and to visiting the convent of S. Girolamo, which he had built for the order of the Observantists, conversing often with religious persons and giving alms liberally. He occupied all his time in promoting the honour of God and in the salvation of his own soul. He was so richly gifted with virtue that whoever may write his life will gain great honour therefrom. I have made this brief record in order that the memory of such a worthy man should not perish, and I am confident that his life will be written by some other.

GOSTANZO SFORZA, LORD OF PESARO

Messer Gostanzo Sforza, the son of Signor Alessandro, was a man of letters and an expert captain as well ; a gentleman in conduct, of a religious disposition and a friend of all good

---

* Vespasiano says nothing of the disastrous defeat suffered by Alessandro at Sarno in 1460 at the hands of Niccolo Piccinino.

† 1 p.m. to 6.

men. He lived in the State which his father left to him, a good ruler and beloved by his people. He reformed certain of the monasteries, notably the Franciscan Observantist house in Pesaro, which he put under the rule of S. Domenico as well, being also a generous friend of the religious persons who led good lives. He set Pesaro in order and built several new streets, giving to divers citizens sites for building in order that they might use them at their own will. He planned a very fine castle and laid the foundations, a wonderful work all constructed according to his own notions in a very noble design. His father left him a library which he increased by many books which he caused to be written. He was greatly devoted to literary men and made provision for some of them. He was very liberal in giving, and would bid every man of condition, who might enter the state, to visit him at his house. His habit of life was splendid in attire, in horses and in everything about him. He was handsome in person and well qualified in the art of war, indeed, had he not died so young he would have won distinction in arms, in letters and in all worthy ways. As it was he was on the road to fame at the time of his early death. It seems to me that I may set down certain notes of which I have knowledge in this commentary. Men with a reputation often make mistakes, which are caused by the acts of those about them whom they are bound to believe. Wherefore the saying of Pope Nicholas was a true one : that the greatest evil rulers had to suffer was that no one ever came into their presence who would tell the truth about what he had in mind, and Pope Pius said that all went willingly to Piacenza or Lodi, but no one would go to Verona.

Cardinal Branda (1341-1433)

MESSER BRANDA, Cardinal of Piacenza, was of the Milanese family of Castiglione. He was resident at the court of Rome for many years, and in the time of Cardinal Acciaiuoli lived in his house. He was well versed in all state affairs, and few matters of importance were settled without his advice. I remember that, at the time of the Council of Basel, when Pope Eugenius was trying to disperse it, it was found necessary to send an answer to certain bulls censuring the Pope, which had been sent to Florence. When it was written Pope Eugenius committed it to certain cardinals for examination and subsequent despatch to the Cardinal of Piacenza. When they had done with it, as the cardinal was ailing, they took it to his house and read it to him, and he desired they should leave it. As it did not satisfy him he re-wrote it. From what I heard later his script needed no addition or curtailment. It was sent to Basel where it puzzled the heads of the doctors, as it was based on the Canon Law in which the cardinal was profoundly learned.

At this time he was ninety years old or more, and still so robust in body that he would often go afoot to the palace of the Popes. His home life was of the simplest. His establishment numbered thirty persons; two of them nephews, whom he had brought up under the care of a very excellent preceptor. There was a common life for all the household according to the requirements of a prelate of his condition. One of his nephews was a very learned bishop, and he kept about him in the palace his auditors and other men of condition. The Cardinal Cesarini was advanced by him and became such a worthy member of the Church of God that the Cardinal of Piacenza used to say that if the Church possessed no other than the Cardinal of S. Agnolo, he would be qualified to reform it from the foundations. He kept a few mules, but no horses, wherefore the prelates and the servitors of the house besought him to find out a more polite style of living. In those days the servants wore no liveries, nor were lighted torches used. They wore blue or dark-coloured cloth ; on the head a sort of priest's cap, and hoods on the shoulders. The bishop sat at table with the cardinal, also bishops or persons of quality who might be invited, and the auditors and chaplains ate at another table opposite to that of the cardinal, and beside it was one for his nephews, standing with napkins over their shoulders. At table some one read aloud according to the habit of the friars. At the close, after grace was said, some question of theology, or of conscience, or of Canon Law would be started. The cardinal proposed and joined in the disputation, which always lasted two or three hours every morning ; and at supper the cardinal, on account of his age, took no food beyond a spoonful of soft bread with chicken broth seasoned with pepper ; also two half glasses of wine. The furniture of his room were ordinary, a plain bed with a cover of arras cloth and the bedstead merely plain wood. The curtain at the door was a piece of blue cloth with his arms stitched thereon.

I remember how one evening that I had with me a book of Piero di Candia (afterwards Pope),* a member of the Franciscan order, with comment by the Master of the Sentences,† and that the cardinal was sitting on his truckle bed in his chamber lighted only by one wax candle. So strong was his constitution that, though he was now over ninety years of age, he only used spectacles at night (he kept them in a case in his room). Taking up this book he asked me to give him his spectacles which he only used at night. The cardinal was greatly occupied in duties as legate of the Church and in all of these he acquitted himself with honour, thinking it no detriment to his dignity to preach in public in any of the places to which he was sent. He was greatly inclined to show favour to men of learning. In Lombardy he founded a library free to all those who desired information on literature. All vice he hated, especially lying, for one day when one of his nephews told a lie the cardinal sent at once for the master

* Alexander V.   † Peter Lombard.

who had him in charge and bade him strip the boy naked in his presence and beat him soundly in order that he might not become a liar. In all his departments were to be found some of the wise and prudent men who were about the court of Rome in his time. He restored many churches, mostly those of the benefices he had held, furnishing them with fittings and with books for the singing choir. I will not enlarge on his other praiseworthy qualities lest I become prolix, and I believe that writers of credit have already supplied details dealing with his remarkable virtues. One thing I will not leave unsaid, that he exercised such great influence in the court of Rome and throughout the Church of God, on the Pope himself and on all the cardinals, that any matter which had passed his judgment never failed to win approval.

CARDINAL ANTONIO DE' CORERI

Messer Antonio, of the Venetian family of Coreri and a nephew of Pope Gregory, was a pious youth who became a friar together with Pope Eugenius at S. Giorgio d' Alga in Venice. After a time his uncle was made Pope and at once proposed to nominate Messer Antonio as cardinal, but Antonio had no wish to quit the religious life for the cardinalate. Urged by the Pope, he consented, with the condition that Messer Gabriello, who afterwards became Eugenius IV, should also receive the hat, and to this the Pope agreed. Henceforth Messer Antonio gave a good example by his holy life. When the Council of Basel became hostile to Pope Eugenius divers cardinals repaired thither, amongst whom was Messer Antonio, now known as Cardinal of Bologna. He took with him his nephew Gregorio, a gentle and learned youth.

At the Council Gregorio, not yet twenty years old, delivered a speech to the council which contained certain censures of Pope Eugenius. It was hailed as a marvellous effort, both on account of its matter and the method of delivery. So great was the reputation Gregorio won thereby that, had the Council possessed the power of making cardinals, they would assuredly have nominated him. After a time Cardinal

CARDINALS

Antonio returned to Rome, having gained greatly in honour. While Pope Eugenius was at Florence the cardinal went there and tried to persuade the Pope to make Gregorio a cardinal—he even offered to resign his own hat for its transfer to his nephew—but the Pope, for some reason I do not know, refused. But Gregorio was certainly worthy both by life and attainments. The cardinal enjoyed the revenues of two abbeys, one in Padua and one in Verona. He gave over both to the Observantists, and assigned one-half of the revenue to the monks and the other for himself as sustenance. He also provided that at his death the abbeys should be free for the monks. Up to the age of eighty-two his health was perfect. When Pope Eugenius left Florence for Rome, the cardinal determined to leave the court for the abbey at Pavia, where he spent his time in prayer. After two months he resolved to dispose of all his goods. He took account of all the revenue of the abbeys and summoned the procurators of the abbeys to confer with him. He then reckoned from his accounts his revenues, also the value of his plate, books, furniture and raiment, even the clothes he wore, and bade the valuers let him know their total worth. Having ascertained this, he divided the same between the two abbeys, reserving only a cup, a chasuble, and two silver tazzas.

After he had divided all these articles between the monasteries he assembled the two Fathers and said to them: "I have given you a certain sum of money, and also the money I have received from these houses. If I had possessed more I would have given you more. Have patience and remember me in your prayers." The two Fathers were amazed, and thanked him heartily. Afterwards the cardinal thanked God for what he had done. Let all great men and prelates learn to act as this cardinal acted, who was minded to bequeath his estate thus rather than leave it to an heir. He lived about four months after his disposal of his goods, concerning which I heard from Messer Gregorio Corero, his nephew, who was present when it was made.

CARDINAL ALBERGATI (SANTA CROCE), 1395–1443

Messer Nicolao was of the Albergati family and took his title from the Church of Santa Croce di Jerusalem in Rome. Sprung from Bologna, he became a Carthusian and was made cardinal by Pope Martin V without knowing anything about his promotion. He was of saintly life, wearing always the Carthusian habit, sleeping undressed on a straw mattress and eating no meat, either in health or sickness. After he had been made cardinal he was summoned to Bologna by Pope Eugenius, who had gone thither with Thomas of Sanzana, one of Albergati's pupils—and every one knows his fame, and how he took the name of Nicolas out of respect for the cardinal. When he returned to Rome he became well known through the holiness of his life and his learning and knowledge of Canon Law, and the Pope, who was striving to make peace between the Kings of France and England and the Duke of Burgundy,* could find no man more fitting for the office of ambassador, so he sent Albergati to settle the terms. By his rectitude he won the respect of noble and simple, and he laboured hard for peace, but the English were so stubborn that he could not sway them ; with the French and the Burgundians he succeeded better. His fame grew at Rome and throughout France and Burgundy because he had abolished so many daily abuses which were the ruin of the country, and this peace which he carried back to Rome added greatly to his reputation. The Pope, recognising his ability, sent him to Germany to settle the quarrels between some of the princes, a task he executed successfully. After he had finished his mission he returned with honour to Rome, and the Pope then desired that he who had brought peace to France, Burgundy and Germany should pacify Italy as well. War had been going on for years between Duke Filippo and the Venetians, wherefore the Pope named Ferrara as the place to which these powers should send their envoys and submit their quarrels to him, and sent Cardinal Albergati as agent. After

* This embassy is noticed in the life of Nicolas V; a truce was signed in 1431 between France and Burgundy.

both parties had argued the differences between them, the cardinal brought about an agreement to the great profit of all and to the increase of his own reputation. In his mission to France he took with him for company Don Nicolo da Cortona, a saintly man who is much praised in the life of Pope Nicolas. His health suffered greatly from long journeys, through fastings, through lack of meat, and the hair cloth he wore, besides the discomfort of various infirmities which he bore most patiently. At Rome many disputes arose over religious matters which, being referred to the cardinal, were settled by him on account of his high reputation. Pope Eugenius went to Bologna, where he stayed some time, but the bishop's palace was in ruins so the cardinal bade Maestro Tomaso to have it put in repair ; not with any splendour, but to make it a fitting house for the bishop, as it is to-day.

After the Pope had tarried some time in Bologna he went to Ferrara and arranged for the coming of the Greeks, and for the union of the Churches. On leaving Ferrara he went by way of Florence to Siena, where he found the water unwholesome, turbid and chalky. There he fell sick with a bad attack of stone, whereupon he at once set his affairs in order ; not that he had much to leave, as he gave to God almost all he had. He left many books to the Certosa of Florence, one a Bible which had cost five hundred ducats, and wished to be buried there. Being gravely ill, the physicians could only think of one remedy for him—a dangerous one—which was to drink a beaker of the blood of a he-goat, but when he heard of it he refused it, saying that he had long been a monk of the Certosa and had never broken one of its rules, and that, knowing the nature of his illness, he was sure there was no remedy for it. Pope Nicolas never showed such constancy as did this cardinal who shed no tear. Having thus decided he turned to the holy men who were about him and, after the lapse of some days, he gave up his soul to his Redeemer, as saintly in death as in life. After he was dead Thomas of Sanzana wished to have him opened, and, this done, they found in him a stone, as big as the egg of a goose, weighing eighteen ounces, and when Thomas returned to Florence he brought it with him and placed it in my hand to show what agony the cardinal must have suffered, declaring that the physicians had erred, for it would have been impossible to crush it. Let those who blame prelates of all kinds remark what worthy men the Church has produced under all conditions.

CARDINAL CESARINI (SANTO AGNOLO), 1398–1444

Messer Giuliano Cesarini, Cardinal of S. Agnolo, was a distinguished member of the College. A poor man's son, he was sent to study at Perugia, which was then ruled by Braccio, a famous Mantuan captain, who had as deputy Bindaccio da Ricasoli, a gentleman, a scholar and the friend of scholars. From his people Giuliano got no more than would keep him shod and clothed. He frequented Bindaccio's house, bringing much credit thereto from his brilliancy as a civil lawyer. In the humanities he wrote well both in prose and verse : some of his poetry he presented to Bindaccio, who rewarded him with a ducat or two to help his needs. At night he lacked light for his writing, and when the candles were removed he would scrape together fragments of tallow and make it serve to illuminate his working. Extraordinary men like him will employ many devices which rich men would never think of. He had to borrow books for study, and he deemed it ill to make notes in other men's volumes, so he would buy cheap legal texts, one of which, the Pandects without gloss, he showed to me annotated in his own hand with beautiful writing.

He left Perugia after taking the doctorate and repaired to Rome, where he lived in the house of the Cardinal of Piacenza. He soon made his mark amongst the most eminent scholars, and in due course was created cardinal. On the assembly of the Council of Basel he went there and met the most illustrious men of Christendom. By general consent he was elected president and, after much debate, it became clear that the Council favoured the deposition of Pope Eugenius and the election of S. Agnolo in his place. This proposal he put aside, and devoted all his energy to the reform of abuses. Perceiving that affairs were thus greatly prejudiced, and being unable to effect his reforms, he determined to quit Basel, knowing that the Council must needs be dissolved. But he felt that he, as president, could have no hand in this, wherefore he withdrew to join Pope Eugenius at Florence. Here the Pope, the cardinals and all the chiefs of Italy besought him to reconsider his action, for it was no light matter for a man of his eminence to take such a step as this withdrawal. Here we will refer to his virtues. It was believed in Rome and wherever he had lived that he had never known woman; he slept always in a shirt of serge, and fasted on all Fridays, vigils and throughout Lent. He said the office each morning; and during the night, after awakening the chaplain to say it with him. At times he would say it in the adjoining Servite Church. He built a stairway by which he could pass above the cloisters into the presence of the Host, and say matins and prime and tierce. He confessed every morning to a very discreet German priest who lived in his house. He was bountiful by nature, and spent for the sake of God all he had. No suppliant ever left him without getting what he sought. One day some Observantist friars who had been begging went away while I happened to be talking with the chamberlain. " If you ever see Monsignore without his cloak," he said, " don't be amazed, for he gives away for God's sake all he has, and what he has not as well."

Having himself been a student, and suffered the want already named, he felt pity for poor scholars; so, whilst he was in Florence, he enquired if there was in Rome or in Florence an efficient faculty, for he knew of a youth of talent who could not follow his studies on account of poverty. He bade the young man come to his house and entertained him two months to see whether he was apt to learn, and how he bore himself. He found the youth to be worthy, so he taught him the whole corpus of the Civil Law. Then at Perugia, or Bologna, or Siera, places affected by scholars, he paid to the Sapienza his accustomed fees for seven years, and gave him texts of the Civil and Canon Law, and money for his expenses, and outfit of raiment for the Sapienza whither he finally went. Then he said to the youth, " My son, I have done for you what no one ever did for me so that you may make a good man, fearing and loving God above all. In this case you will prosper, and while I live you will never lack anything needful." He treated several youths in the same fashion. This is true bounty, such as everyone who has means therefor ought to practice. To all who may read this life it should be noted that he had no other income than the cardinalate and the bishopric of Grossetto.

His house was sparingly kept without luxury or sideboard display. At meals he only ate of one dish. Sometimes he would eat alone in his chamber, having brought food with him. After he was at table he would retain only two or three to serve him, and let the rest go to their supper. His house was the best appointed in all the court. It happened that, during the first summer he spent in Florence, the greater part of his household fell sick. His beneficence was unbounded. First he gave orders to those who had control that the physician should visit the sick morning and evening, and that the druggist should send them all they might want. He also was careful about their souls, and ordered that anyone falling sick should be confessed at once. The helper of the stableman, the humblest member of the household, fell sick and the cardinal visited him like the rest.

And with those nearing their end and in need of help at the last extremity! I saw the cardinal at the death-bed of Battiferro, his secretary. At the last moment he sat on the bed, with his face close to that of the dying man, comforting him at the last. I have known many men of worth, but never one equal to the Cardinal of S. Agnolo. The Cardinal of Piacenza used to say that if all the Church perished except the Cardinal of S. Agnolo he alone would be able to recreate it.

At this time there was in Florence a Jewish physician, and the cardinal, who was displeased that he should be a Hebrew, made constant efforts to make him a Christian. This man was learned in the law and Spanish by nationality, and the cardinal would urge him every day to embrace the Christian faith. Finally he, with the aid of Giannozzo Manetti, persuaded the Hebrew to be baptised. As soon as the man was converted the cardinal desired that there should be a solemn rite in S. Giovanni with Agnolo Acciaiuoli and Giannozzo Manetti and himself as sponsors. Baptism was celebrated at the great font covered with fair cloth. After the ceremony the cardinal caused the convert to be clad in a new suit of red, and the whole company partook of a fine feast at the Servi to celebrate the bringing of this man into the true light of our faith. The cardinal desired that the convert should share his house and table, treating him with the greatest respect, and allotting to him a servant and two horses.

He loved especially all those of godly life. In the hospital of Lemmo was a company of pious men—the Company of S. Girolamo—which met every Saturday evening for prayer and discipline, and the cardinal often attended their meetings with divers of his household. He entered the oratory, sat at the table, prayed and submitted to discipline like the others. One day, when I was still a youth, he asked me whether I belonged to any society in Florence. I answered that I did not, whereupon he said, " I wish you would join that of Ser Antonio di Mariano. I will go to him about the matter," and this, I write this to show that he thought of small and great alike. Later he asked me whether I would like to be a priest, in which case he would help me in my studies and to a benefice. I asked for fifteen days to decide, and at the end of these he enquired again, whereupon I declined. Then he added, " If there should be any other service I can do for you, it shall be done." The cardinal was always active in rectifying usages which had gone astray, especially those which concerned God's honour. It seemed to him that the Servites no longer lived in the fear of God, or in such fashion as would have pleased Pope Eugenius, who desired that all friars should become Observantists. Wherefore, with the Pope's countenance, he reformed this house and made it Observantist. All the friars were sent away and replaced by a goodly brotherhood of the same order, so that the house became a house of true religion. While he remained in Florence this house and S. Marco were religious houses worthy of the name.

He was always alert to do all he could for the health of the souls of those under his immediate charge. He would often visit unexpectedly the rooms of his household to ask them how they were occupied. One day he found his secretary reading the *Ermafrodito of Panormita*.* As soon as the secretary saw the cardinal in the room he quickly threw the book into a chest, but not quickly enough to escape the eye of the cardinal, who forthwith asked him what he was reading. Struck with shame, the secretary stood speechless. The cardinal, who was of a jocular nature, said, " You have thrown

* One of the most licentious books of the age.

it into the chest and thus confessed the truth." Then he fetched it out and, much ashamed, showed it to the cardinal, who took it, discreetly remarking that it was not fit to read, seeing that Pope Eugenius had directed papal excommunication against all who should read it. Then he made the secretary tear it up and, when this was done, he said, laughing, " If you had known how to give me the right sort of answer, perhaps the book need not have been destroyed. You should have told me you were searching for a jewel in a mass of dung." He spake thus gently, so that the young man should not be terrified and fearful that he had incurred the cardinal's anger. One day a servant lost a favourite mule of the cardinal. On his return the cardinal questioned him and, after hearing the story, was greatly angered. He turned to the man and bade him go and search for it. If he could find it, well and good : if not, he must have patience and search again. Then he dismissed the fellow.

He loved all good and honourable men, especially those free from concealment or hypocrisy, such as Lorenzo di Giovanni de' Medici, the brother of Cosimo, a prominent citizen. Lorenzo went frequently to visit him and chatted with him in familiar strain. And when Lorenzo fell sick with the infirmity of which he died, the cardinal, with his wonted kindness, would often go to him and encourage him to be patient and submit to the will of God, especially counselling him to have care for his soul, like a good and true friend. When it pleased God to release him the cardinal took part in the obsequies at S. Lorenzo. He also sent his household with his banner and more than thirty torches. The cardinal was also greatly attached to Pope Eugenius.

He was urgent to lead all men to Divine worship; especially those who were misled by error. He worked hard to crush the Bohemian heresy, and went thither to confute their arguments and to meet the leading Bohemians, wielding his authority to the best of his ability, for, in addition to his other learning, he was a great theologian. But he did not wish to stand alone. He requested that all the doctors in theology who were then sitting in the Council of Basel should intervene also. He had already seen in his palace three volumes—rather a script than a Bible—by a Carmelite friar against the Bohemians, a wonderful work which drew out the Bohemian arguments and overthrew them by the authority of the Latin and Greek doctors. The cardinal did all he could to turn them, but in vain. They could not be more obstinate than they were, for, after having enjoyed all the benefits of the Church so long, they had no mind to divest themselves of them. Pope Eugenius had done all he could to unite the Greek and Roman Churches, and now he willed that the Patriarch, the Emperor and the chief men of the country should cross over into Italy and go to Ferrara at his charges in order to make good the union. In this undertaking the Cardinal of S. Agnolo was very active and played a good part with his diligence and benignity and good faith.

After a time in Ferrara the plague broke out and they withdrew to Florence, whither also the Pope bade the Greeks adjourn. By the advice of S. Agnolo and other cardinals the Council of Basel was summoned to join that of Florence, for there was no better way to settle this important question without the risk of fresh schism. At Florence the chief theologians of the Greek and Latin Churches met, and the Cardinal of S. Agnolo would always argue in favour of the Roman Church. There were also Jacobites and Ethiopians who had come for reconciliation with the Church. The cardinal accompanied by Thomas of Sarzana met these, whom they freed from their errors. Afterwards he disputed with the Greeks, who yielded at the end and joined the Roman Church. The privileges of the Greeks having been read and confirmed and authenticated in public by the consent of the parties, the same was done in the case of the Armenians, the Jacobites and the Ethiopians, but I do not know whether the deeds of these were written in their several languages. All these documents passed through the cardinal's hands, and he wished to retain the originals and give copies to the other parties. All these came into possession of the Signoria. And besides these privileges the Latin and Greek prelates testified under their hand that they agreed to this union, which was then confirmed by all. This act would not have been passed but for S. Agnolo's prudent handling ; moreover, out of his slender estate he gave as much as he could to the Greeks on account of their poverty and transported them into Greece at his own expense. When the union of the two Churches was completed everyone returned to his own land, and Pope Eugenius made two Greek cardinals, a distinguished monk of S. Basil named Bessarion, and the Archbishop of Russia, who became Cardinal Ruteneo, a most worthy prelate. These were created *in perpetuam memoriam* of the union, and on account of their merits.

After Pope Eugenius had carried out this union of those who had divided the Christian religion, he set to work against the foes of the Cross of Christ and came to an understanding with that noble prince the King of Hungary,* to whom he lent a large sum to help in the war against the Turks. The King had lured the Turkish commander into a dangerous position, but certain unworthy Christians, calling themselves traders, conveyed a large body of Turks across a narrow strait, for the sake of gain alone—which proved a great detriment to the Christian army, as will presently appear. Pope Eugenius sent thither friar Giovanni di Capistrano, a very saintly man, to preach to the people and to arouse in them the love of Christ against the infidels, and they achieved wonderful success, the people coming in of their own will. After this great beginning against the infidels, Pope Eugenius determined to send an Apostolic legate with greater powers, and selected the cardinal for this post. He accepted the Pope's offer, saying that he would be well content should it be necessary for him to die for the Christian religion. On leaving Florence he bade farewell to all his friends, begging them remember him in their prayers and entreat God to use him for the best end. He journeyed by way of Hungary into all parts of the land, following his habit of saying mass and making confession every day. In the camp of the Christians in Hungary he preached to all the people around. He went one day to a place several miles from the camp to hold a pardon, he and all the soldiers with him walking devoutly barefoot. He never went against the Turks without first having preached and said mass, and the consecrated body of Christ and a hundred tapers were carried before him. I have heard from trustworthy witnesses that, by his good example, he turned to religion all the soldiers, who afterwards were

* Uladislas VI.

chaste in camp, going to mass and confession and walking barefoot as they had done with the cardinal. Pursuing this enterprise, through the grace of God and through the presence of so many good men in the army, they conquered a great part of the Turkish territory and went from this camp five days' journey towards Adrianople. They prospered thus through the skill and wisdom of the King and the cardinal. The campaign would have succeeded completely but for the obstacles put up by the Turks, who crossed the sea from one side to the other. The King and the cardinal learned that the Turks had occupied a certain site, and planned an attack upon him, as they had great advantage of position and hoped for complete victory. The cardinal thought little of life or of death, being prepared to submit entirely to the will of God. One day, as is reported by those who were present, he pronounced, by way of a testament, what he wished to have done. Then he turned to those of his household and spoke to them, exhorting them to carry themselves righteously and to pray to God for him, that though he himself was going into danger, he wished none of them to follow him. Then he took them, one by one by the hand, and kissed them with tears, exhorting them to live well. By this action it seems as if he foresaw what was to happen; that he would join the martyrs of Christ who died for His name. Having said all he had to say, he bade his household farewell, not wishing that they should incur any danger. He then joined the King and the others, and they moved on to the appointed place, which the Christians had mastered. Then certain false Christians,* passing as traders, transported over the water a vast force of Turks at the price of a few ducats per head. And so vast was the force they carried over that, when the battle was joined, unexpected by the Christians, the King, the cardinal and all the nobles of the province were killed, no one was left to tell the true story of the fight.† Considering the treachery of the Christians, it is reckoned that after the Hungarians had begun the battle, many thousands of Turks who had not been reckoned for joined in and surrounded them, whereupon followed the slaughter in which the King and the cardinal fell. The result of this reverse caused the loss of Constantinople and much territory.

* In Venetian Service.   † This was the Battle of Varna, 1444.

DOMENICO CAPRANICA

CARDINAL CAPRANICA (FERMO), (1400–1458)

Messer Dominico, Cardinal of Fermo, was a man of distinction and of holy life, born at Rome of humble parentage. He was nominated cardinal by Pope Martin, on account of his great gifts, towards the end of the Pope's life, but received the hat afterwards. He went to the Council of Basel, not as a cardinal but as Bishop of Fermo, with several of the leading cardinals of the College, and gained there considerable reputation, wherefore the Council, on account of his merits, made him cardinal. The court was now at Florence and Pope Eugenius invited him to attend ; and he arrived in Florence wearing the hat as a cardinal, although Pope Eugenius had wished him to come without it, so that he might present it himself, but to this Capranica demurred.* He was learned in the Canon Law, and after much dispute as to whether he should come with the hat or without, Pope Eugenius consented to his wishes, seeing that he could not persuade him otherwise. He entered Florence accompanied by the whole College of Cardinals in great state, and won high approval. He hated ostentation and pomp, he kept a frugal house and he took a high position in the Church, and was made Penitentiary-in-Chief. He lived an ascetic life, sleeping fully dressed, wearing a hair shirt, and scorning all court ceremonies. Those who came to speak to him, ignorant of his habits, would take off their caps and kneel to him, saying, " I have come to your most reverend Lordship " ; when they began thus he would say, " Let us drop all these titles, come and tell me what you want of me." And if the visitor began again in the same fashion the cardinal would leave the room saying, " You have no need of me." There were others who would say to him, " We want such and such a thing from Your Eminence," and to these he would say, " I have understood you," and if the thing could be done he answered that he would do it, and if not he would cut the matter short and say, " It cannot be done for certain good reasons."

He was Chief Penitentiary to Pope Nicolas at the Jubilee, and the whole world came together to discuss various pontifical

* The Pope's objection was that Capranica had been made cardinal by the Council, and it was probably a valid one.

matters ; and every morning the cardinal gave audience to those who demanded it. He noted down their petitions to the Pope, and those which he could not commend he marked with a cross, and every morning and evening he would be obliged to hear numberless pontifical cases. Then when he went before Pope Nicolas, the Pope, as soon as he saw him, would laugh, and turn to whoever might be with him, and say, " Here comes Monsignor of Fermo with the Litanies in his hand." Then he would read the petitions to the Pope, who would give his assent to those he wished to grant, and make a mark against those he refused. The next morning the petitioners would come for their answer, and when those whose requests had not been granted asked the reason why, the cardinal would answer, " Because it did not suit him." Then, if the petitioner importuned him further, the cardinal would become deeply engaged and reply, " If I had to make answer to everyone and give my reasons for refusal, time would not avail me, even if I lived as long as Methusalem, and even then none would be satisfied." He administered justice with wonderful efficiency, and none ever went before him who did not receive due consideration and justice. Both popes employed him on several embassies, and everywhere he was greatly honoured on account of his integrity and his legal knowledge. His servants were as well-mannered and as honest as any at the court of Rome, and amongst them were worthy men of various nationality. Messer Jacopo of Lucca, through the mediation of Messer Agnolo Acciaiuoli, joined the household of His Eminence, and as the cardinal knew him to be a man of somewhat haughty spirit, he wished to read him a lesson, so, having made him his secretary, he gave him certain letters to write. Jacopo was a dextrous scribe and wrote excellent letters, but when he brought one to the cardinal, however good it might be, the cardinal would censure it and tear it up and tell him to go and re-write it. This he did merely for the sake of discipline. After he had been with His Eminence for some time his proud manners were greatly changed, at the same time he could not endure the yoke of obedience, and he took leave of His Eminence and went to live by himself. His sojourn with the Cardinal of Fermo was so useful to him that without it and the friendship of other cardinals, gained by his association with Capranica, and his own changed demeanour, he would never have been made Cardinal of Pavia by Pope Pius.

The Venetians had made peace with Duke Francesco and with the Florentines, and while they were still in league with King Alfonso they evacuated their positions, thus giving great offence to the King. It appeared to Pope Nicolas and to the other powers desirable that the affairs of Italy should be set in order, and that, if a powerful sovereign like the King should stand aloof, nothing could come of the League of twenty-five years, and for this reason the powers concerned sent ambassadors to Rome to beg the help of the Pope, as the friend and guardian of the peace, not only in Italy but throughout the world, that he also should despatch to Naples an Apostolic legate with due authority to treat with the King. Having judged the capabilities of all the cardinals, it was decided that the Cardinal of Fermo was the most influential and the best fitted to grapple with the situation, so they begged His Holiness to let him accompany their ambassadors to Naples. The Pope, who wished to settle Italy, sent for the Cardinal of Fermo and commanded him to go with the ambassadors to Naples to treat with King Alfonso and to induce him to join in settling this peace, and a league for twenty-five years. The cardinal went to Naples, together with all the other ambassadors of Italy.*

Arrived at Naples, the cardinal-legate *de latere*, on account of his great reputation, his saintly life and his courtly ways, was received by the King with more honour than any of the others ; His Majesty and the lords of the kingdom and the ambassadors went out to meet him, and the King provided lodging for all of them, and paid all their expenses, according to his wont. The cardinal at once endeavoured to persuade the King to join the League, but His Majesty was very unwilling to consent, for it seemed to him that the Venetians, in concluding the peace with Milan and in evacuating their position without consulting him, had shown him scant courtesy, as it was only reasonable that he should have been put in the first place. The cardinal began by showing him the benefits that would follow, and how nothing would be

* 1455. This peace is referred to in many other of the " Lives."

more pleasing to Pope Nicolas. None of the other ambassadors spoke of the matter, knowing that if the cardinal failed no other means would avail. After a long discussion with the King, Capranica at last persuaded him to join the League, but with these conditions, that he might wage war with the Genoese, with Signor Gismondo* and anyone who might hinder the allies. The cardinal at once wrote to Rome and all the other ambassadors to their respective states as to the wishes of the King, and they all received a full mandate to assent to the treaty under these conditions. And they would have done more if necessary, so greatly did they approve of the cardinal's action, and none of them objected. All lauded the straightforwardness of the cardinal, who by his powerful arguments convinced the King. Thus peace and the alliance were settled for twenty-five years under these conditions, and the aim of Signor Gismondo would have ensued and the Genoese would have been in evil case but for the death of King Alfonso.† The Pope at once gave his assent and blessing to the peace. He intervened as the head of Christendom, and wished that all disputes that might arise amongst the nations should be judged by himself and his successors. Furthermore, he gave his blessing to all those who should observe it, and the contrary to those who would not, and desired they should all swear by the authorisation of their governments to observe it, and this they did. All this the Cardinal of Fermo forwarded greatly by his judgment and wisdom and he thus ensured the peace of Italy for many years. Not long after this Pope Nicolas died,‡ and having come to the election of a new Pope many of the cardinals gave their votes to the Cardinal of Fermo for several reasons: for his virtues, his learning, not only in matters of the law which he had studied from his youth, but also for the immense knowledge he had gathered in a life's experience and through his wide reading. They deemed that no man in the College was worthier of it than he. But it often happens that an old man is elected so that another election may soon follow, and now the Conclave chose a Catalan, a man of eighty who called himself Pope Calixtus, but

* Sigismondo Pandolfo Malatesta. Alfonso never ratified the Peace of Lodi. † 1458.
‡ March 24, 1455.

they were much censured for not having elected Fermo, the Italian, instead of a Catalan of eighty. Yet, at Constance, when the Church had to be restored to unity and the Italians were only a third part, that is in a minority at the Council, they were so powerful that Pope Martin, an Italian, was elected. The Cardinal of Fermo was a humorous man ; one day when he was passing over the bridge of S. Agnolo towards the palace, a poor man who had escaped from the Catalans begged alms of him, and asked him to give him a carlino for the love of God, as he had escaped out of the hands of the Catalans. The cardinal laughed and said, " Rather give me one, for my case is worse than yours ; for you have escaped, and I am still in their hands." Although Pope Calixtus was a worthy man, he could not rule the Church, as, on account of his age, he spent nearly all his time in bed. Anyone who may wish to write the life of the Cardinal of Fermo will find ample material.

CARDINAL NICENO—A GREEK (d. 1472)

Messer Bessarion, a Greek, was a cardinal-bishop and a man of much weight in the Church of God. He was a monk of the order of S. Basil who came to Italy in the train of the Emperor of the East, being the first of the distinguished Greeks to visit this country. Afterwards, on the union with the Greeks, he was made cardinal by Pope Eugenius on account of his remarkable merits, together with eighteen others. There was, moreover, one more, the Cardinal-Archbishop of Russia, who was styled the Cardinal Ruteno. Bessarion's reputation was great, and in all the difficult questions which then arose, men always referred to him. He was Bishop of Tusculum and went as legate to many places, reaping much credit wherever he went on account of his justice and praiseworthy carriage. He spent much time in Bologna, where his administration was wonderfully successful, and in France, where he won universal reputation. He was well versed in Greek and Latin, a lover of letters and of literary men and much taken up with the doctrines of Plato and with those of Aristotle as well. He defended the Platonic doctrines against certain opponents* and wrote a defence of Plato, a work of great merit and authority. He also translated a work which he called *De factis et dictis memorabilitus Sacratis.*

He stood so high in the estimation of the cardinals that, after the death of Pope Pius,† he was really Pope for one night ; for, after he had been elected Pope in conclave at the second voting, his opponents said, " He is Pope : the matter does not concern us farther, and to-morrow, at the first voting, he can be proclaimed." But they made an agreement together, and all the night they worked persistently to prevent his election, saying that those who had elected him would suffer for it later, and going from one cardinal to another declaring that a few years ago Niceno was a heretic. " Can we allow men to say we have made a Pope who is a heretic ; that will indeed be shameful ? " And they spoke thus to such good purpose that in the end they elected the Pope they wished for. On the day following they chose Paolo, a good election, without any secret understanding and in canonical form. Like a wise man he made no demonstration, and let things run their course. By his worth this Pope maintained the good name he had hitherto enjoyed, and in due course he died and Sixtus succeeded.

While he lived at the court of Rome, Niceno caused transcripts to be made of many Greek and Latin books, dealing with all the faculties, and besides these he bought all the books he did not possess, spending the greater part of his income in the praiseworthy practice of book-buying, and after he had bought a vast number, Greek and Latin, sacred and secular, he resolved to find a place worthy of them, especially the volumes in Greek. And in case this luckless state should come to an end, and all the books therein be in danger of destruction,

---

* Trapezuntios published a book condemning Plato in 1458. He accused him of having ruined Greece and maintained that Mahomet was a far greater philosopher. Others, notably Theodore Gaza, joined in the long and acrimonious dispute, which at least had the effect of rousing an interest in Greek letters in Italy.

† Vespasiano has completely mistaken the course of events. It was after the death of Nicolas V that Bessarion was put forward ; he was never elected even for one night, and the cardinals ultimately chose Alfonso Borgia, an aged Spaniard, as Calixtus III. Again in 1741, Bessarion was proposed and rejected in favour of Sixtus IV. In both cases he was refused the Papacy on account of his Greek origin.

he deemed they ought to be bestowed in some fitting place, and he could think of no place in Italy better than Venice to which, being a seaport, travellers would naturally betake themselves. Wherefore, as he was on most friendly terms with the Venetians, he resolved to found a public library in their city, free to all who wished to use it. It was agreed between him and the Signory and the Doge, after serious debate, that a public library should be built where two custodians should always be present, so that all who wished might go there; and so it was arranged. There were six hundred or more books in Greek and Latin which were sent to Venice during his lifetime, the cost of which was immense. In all the Sacred College there was not another cardinal so generous as was the founder of this library. In doing this he did not consider only his own convenience: he thought rather of the service he might render to those who were literary workers, by providing books for their needs.*

He always showed favour to literary men, and gave them advancement. Messer Lauro Quirino, a Venetian gentleman, learned in Greek and Latin and an excellent philosopher, lived for some time in the house of Niceno. Messer Nicolo Perotto, Bishop of Sipontino, who had come to Rome with Master William Gray, the proctor of the King of England, was very anxious to learn Greek, and begged his patron to arrange for his instruction by the cardinal. This was done, and Perotto became a learned Greek scholar; moreover, the cardinal made him bishop and the governor of his household, and conferred offices in the Church on his father and kinsfolk. Beside the learning he acquired, and the dignity he enjoyed in the cardinal's house, Perotto grew rich in the many offices he held, and his father was made a knight. Men of learning and worth were under great obligation to him, and when Messer Francesco da Savoia,† who afterwards became Pope Sixtus, came to court, Niceno took him into his house and

---

* Bessarion gave his books to Venice in 1468, but the proposed library was not built for nearly a century later. *Vide Tiraboschi*, Vol. VI, Book I, Chap. 3.

† He was the son of a fisherman of Savona and had nothing to do with Savoy. He was a youth of talent and was taken into the service of a member of the della Rovere family, whose name he subsequently took. Macchiavelli, *Flor. Hist.*, p. 354, calls him " a man of base and vile condition," *vide* also Gregorovius, vii, p. 242.

caused him to give lectures on Scotus, for he was a great Scotist. Pope Paul recognised his learning and made him a cardinal, so that he might always reckon on his assistance. But afterwards it came about that he regretted much what he had done ; for the event did not prove to be what he had reckoned.

After the death of Pope Paul, Messer Francesco da Savoia was chosen his successor—by what means I do not wish to judge—and in this election Bessarion, deeming Francesco unworthy of the papacy, abstained from voting. After his election Sixtus took little notice of him. One day the Pope went to the Castello to see the jewels of Pope Paul and there he met two Venetian cardinals, nephews of the late Pope, who had voted for Sixtus in the conclave under certain promises. They now fell on their knees before Sixtus and asked for the grant of their tassels which he had promised to them, whereupon the Pope turned to Niceno—somewhat awed before him as a man of great name—and said : " What these men ask for is the property of the Church." The cardinal replied, " It is indeed the property of the Church, and it is your duty to keep it intact and not to throw it away." Whereupon the Pope dismissed the cardinals without giving them aught, entirely on account of Niceno's decision. Now Niceno being a cardinal and a man of high character, the Pope was embarrassed and ill at ease in his presence, so to get rid of him he made him legate in France ; but Niceno was an old man, infirm and cruelly afflicted with stone, consequently he nearly died on the journey. He set out for France, not too well pleased with his mission, and when he arrived he met with an unsatisfactory reception on account of the hostile disposition of the King and his wayward humours ; so he felt he must needs depart, having added nothing to his reputation.* Recognising the claims of honour, and valuing it above all, he returned to Italy, old and sick and troubled, and died shortly afterwards.

All human affairs are wont to end in this wise, and especially those which rest on honour, wherefore it behoves us to turn to God in all our doings. Many worthy deeds were done

* Sismondi, *Histoire des Français I*, XIV, p. 419. Louis XI treated him with marked disrespect. He died in 1472.

by the Cardinal of Niceno of which I have no personal knowledge, and anyone who is acquainted with them will do well
to write his life.

Cardinal Roverella (Ravenna) (d. 1461)

Messer Bartolomeo Roverella was a Ferrarese and Archbishop of Ravenna. He went to Florence in the time of Pope
Eugenius and, being of humble estate, he studied with Bishop
Scipione, a man learned in polite letters. After his studies he
became a priest and bishop's chaplain. The Patriarch at this
time was Cardinal Luigi, and Messer Scipione frequented his
house assiduously, the cardinal being the chief at the court.
Messer Bartolomeo often accompanied him, and, as a well-
lettered man, won the consideration of the Patriarch. At
this time Pope Eugenius had in his office two monks of San
Giustina and two others of the Azzurini order, to which the
Pope also belonged when he was made cardinal. Likewise,
as private secretary, Messer Andrea da Palenzago who, at his
death, was replaced by Messer Bartolomeo on the Patriarch's
recommendation, and whoever wished to see the Pope would
approach him through Bartolomeo.

He gained the goodwill of all the cardinals and of the
court, which advantage was not diminished by the death of
Pope Eugenius, and when Pope Nicolas succeeded he became
Bishop of Ravenna, although he already held other preferment. The Pope sent him on divers missions on behalf of the
Apostolic See in which he always won high favour. Afterwards Pope Pius sent him into the kingdom with full power
to support His Majesty in the wars, when Duke Giovanni*
held part of the King's territory which he had seized. He won
the good opinion of the King, and was made cardinal by
Pope Pius. His conscience was pure. He loved and served
God, hating all pomp and superstition, simple in his way of
life, and averse from all pride and ostentation. While at
Rome he would receive any guest he might invite without
ceremony. He won the good opinion of the Pope and of all
the court. On the death of Pope Pius they elected Pope

* Jean d'Anjou.

CARDINALS

Paul, who continued to favour the cardinal, maintained equal rights, and abolished simony altogether. In these matters the cardinal agreed with him entirely.

On the death of Pope Paul public opinion favoured him strongly, and before the Conclave everyone gave him the papacy. In the first poll of the Conclave he received the largest number of votes; and he would certainly have been elected had not some of the cardinals asked him to support certain proposals which they favoured. But Ravenna was entirely honest, and believed it to be simony to promise anything for the sake of support, wherefore he answered that he could not give them promises, or say more than that he would support any proposal which seemed just and honourable and nothing which did not. When they saw that he would not give rash promises they withdrew their votes. By God's will it happened that the men concerned in this affair fell into trouble; some were ruined and some lost their lives. I will not omit a remarkable saying of Giannozzo Manetti, who was wont to say he had noticed throughout his life that men who commit crimes against their fellows are always punished in this world, giving numerous examples, one of which I will relate. When Pope Eugenius was in Florence there were rumours of war and he wished to leave the city. The Florentines were in league with the Venetians, and were waiting instructions from them as to whether he should be allowed to depart, and word came that he should be detained, if necessary, by force. This request the Florentines refused, but the four Venetians who proposed it all died by violent deaths within the year, as Messer Giannozzo testifies—one, Messer Amoro Donato, was cut to pieces; another, whose name I do not know, was bitten, when about to mount his horse, by a little French dog, which had become mad, and died; the other two also died violent deaths shortly after. These instances show how dangerous it is to do any injuries to popes or cardinals or other ecclesiastics.

Soon after this the cardinal died after a useful and virtuous life, with the same disregard of pomp and worldly honour which he had always shown.

JACOPO DI PORTOGALLO

Messer Jacopo of Portugal, titular of Santo Eustachio and cardinal-deacon, descended both on his father's and his mother's side from the most distinguished houses in Christendom. From his father's side he was born of the royal house of Portugal. His father's sister was of the house of Burgundy. It would take long to tell of his progeny, but it is so well known that further mention of it is needless. From his earliest youth Messer Jacopo was devoted to literature, which he studied in Portugal under the best teachers. Not only did he study Latin letters, but he planned his life on the lines of virtue, and determined to live in chastity, although he was better favoured than any other youth of his age. He was actively interested in everything that did not run counter to his vows, he avoided all unseemly conversation, he shunned the society of women, and he held in detestation dancing, music and singing. Having been thus educated in Portugal his parents devoted him to the priesthood, and sent him to study the Canon Law in Italy. At seventeen years of age he went to Perugia, accompanied by a retinue suitable to his condition.

Here he followed the same course of life, and every day became more confirmed in his opinions. Sometimes it happened that there was singing and dancing in the neighbouring houses; as soon as he heard this he would go to some other room where he could not hear it. On the first day of Lent he joined the friars at Monte Oliveto near Perugia, eating with them in the refectory, sleeping in his clothes, and frequenting the church at all hours of the day and night, until the end of Lent when he returned to his home. At this time, when he was about eighteen years of age, he was made proctor; he often said the office, and heard mass every day, and fasted, and slept fully clothed, and let his life be an example to all good men. He went nearly every day for prayer to Santo Oliveto. The King of France, the Emperor, the King of Portugal and the Duke of Burgundy urged the Pope to make him a cardinal, but, following the usual order, he was first made a proctor.

CARDINALS

Shortly after this promotion he was created cardinal, but he made no change in his manner of life or conduct. It was a marvel to everybody that a youth of only twenty years of age, very handsome in person, of noble birth and the mirror of good manners should have chosen such an austere life. Let not anyone excuse himself by saying that he has not the gift of continence, if this noble youth, rich, seemly in person above all others of his age, with all the liberty he could wish for, and free of restraint, was able to control himself. He was a diligent student, said mass, read many holy books and was continually occupied. He would never suffer unseemly speech in his presence. He never conversed with women, nor went where they might be. I once saw a Commentary with a marginal note in the cardinal's handwriting telling how S. Jerome had said that no woman should enter any room unaccompanied, and the cardinal added another, that no woman should enter a room where men are, either accompanied or unaccompanied.

He remained a short time in Rome and then went to Tuscany, where, when he was twenty two years old, he ruptured a vein in his chest. When his state became dangerous he was advised to go to the baths, but this proved of little service. On arriving at Florence he found that it suited both his mind and his body as a residence, alternately with Monte Oliveto near the city; when he was at Florence he wished to consult various physicians concerning his illness, but in the case of a man of such distinction they were diffident as to whatever they should propose, but he told them to do whatever might seem to them the best for his soul and body. He was assiduous in making confession and communicating and in everything necessary for the welfare of his soul. In the course of the cure, which seemed to make little progress, a curious accident happened owing to a strange blunder of a physician. One day this man came and tried to induce him, as an extraordinary experiment, to submit to a remedy, revolting to him, and hurtful to his spiritual welfare. According to what this man said it would be advantageous to the cardinal's health if he slept with a young girl, and that no better remedy than this could be found. When he heard these words, the cardinal lost all patience with the physician that he should have made such an abominable proposition, knowing what his manner of life was. He rebuked the physician as he deserved, asking him what had become of his conscience that he should prefer the welfare of the body to that of the soul. Then he forbade him to enter his chamber, or to take any further part in his cure. I heard this from the Bishop of Algarve, and from others who were present at the time.

The cardinal remained with the monks of Oliveto, and the Bishop of Algarve, the head of the community, remained with him. The cardinal now knew that his disease was incurable, and set to work to clear his conscience of whatever might be hurtful. He was most humane by nature, liberal in helping the poor for the sake of God, careful of the welfare of those who served him, most modest in his household, the enemy of pomp and superfluity, holding to the middle way of life, which is the way of the happy. His household wished in all things to follow his example. In due time he settled his Will in Apostolic form, providing that he should be buried in the Church of San Miniato at Florence, of the Order of Monte Oliveto. He directed that a chapel should be endowed for daily mass, and also provided everything necessary for the services. He desired that all those in his service and the poor should profit by the residue. He had collected few treasures, and the few articles, his books, his clothing, his chattels would not have amounted to more than three thousand florins, so that there was not enough left out of his estate to endow the chapel, but the Bishop Silvense saw to everything, and the Duchess of Burgundy paid most of the cost.

His end was most holy as his life had been, for when we consider that this youth of twenty-two, of noble birth, with the means of doing whatever he pleased, willingly abjured all worldly delights, we cannot help thinking this was by the grace of Christ, and that the purity of his life was so acceptable to God, that he was numbered amongst the elect. On the tomb which is now in San Miniato* the hands were modelled from his own, the face is an excellent likeness because it was taken immediately after death ; in beauty of body and mind he was unsurpassable, and I, the writer, who

* This tomb by Antonio Rossellino is one of the most beautiful in the world.

saw and heard these things from worthy witnesses, who were perpetually about His Eminence, am overcome with astonishment when I think of them.

Let all who read this life learn that it is in the power of all to tread the path followed by the cardinal, of their own free will, in the same manner. For holiness of life and conduct and for all the virtues, the cardinal is worthy to be compared with any of the men of old. If his life should ever be written in terms commensurate to its dignity it will be rated as a wonder ; and still more if it should be written in Latin so that all nations may know him as he lived.

THE CARDINAL OF GIRONA

Messer Giovanni de' Margheriti was made Bishop of Girona in the time of Pope Nicolas and afterwards cardinal by Pope Sixtus. The Pope wished to give the bishopric to Messer Cosimo de' Ricco, but the King of Aragon was determined that Messer Giovanni should have it. On account of this dispute, Messer Cosimo, being a man of considerable influence, went to Barcelona and excited a rebellion against the King, but he never became Bishop of Girona. Messer Giovanni was a young man when he was promoted, and stood high in the estimation of Pope Nicolas who made him Clerk of the Camera Numeraria, and directed him to go to the Camera Apostolica to take up the office. At this time Messer Luigi was chief chamberlain and, when Giovanni appeared at the Camera, Luigi straightway tore off his cloak and refused to admit him. Giovanni prudently said nothing, but went at once to the Pope and said to him : " Holy Father, if you had not deemed that I was fitted for the office you have given me you would not have sent me to the Camera Apostolica, nor would you have wished that the Patriarch should tear the clothes off my back and insult me in this fashion." His Holiness was deeply offended when he heard of this outrage, and at once ordered the chamberlain into his presence. As soon as he came the Pope said : " Monsignore, as you know well I hesitated for some time whether I should give you the office of chamberlain, knowing your temper ; now the first thing you do, after I have made Messer Giovanni Clerk of the Camera on account of his merits, is to tear off his clothes and refuse him admission, and if it were not that I am unwilling to punish you as you deserve, I would show you your mistake and do everything that a Pope can do at such a juncture." Messer Luigi then realised that he had made a great mistake and asked the Pope's pardon, and when Giovanni came again to the office he at once admitted him and perceived that he had done well by carrying out the Pope's wishes. Giovanni behaved with great prudence in this matter ; according to him Pope Nicolas used to say that he never wittingly used his pontifical authority except in conjunction with the patriarchal, in order to restrain his own hasty humour. All the cardinals who attended him, except the Patriarch, were forced to stand while he was seated.

After the death of Pope Nicolas, the bishop lived with King Juan of Navarre, where he educated the present King* and his brothers ; he was greatly beloved by all these, especially by the young King, who besides being sober in his life and habits was just and religious, hearing mass every morning and confessing once a week. In his household he maintained certain Dominican brothers, learned in theology and philosophy, with whom at table he would often hold discussions. His kingdom had long been in a disturbed state, seeing that there was no one able to quell the disturbances ; moreover, the King had only recently succeeded to Spain and Catalonia by his marriage with the young Queen Isabella— in these kingdoms females succeed equally with males. Wishing to pacify his dominions so that he might be able to traverse them in peace, he began to punish the crowd of rebels who swarmed everywhere, and so well did he succeed that a man could travel anywhere with gold in his hands, and the nobles who were accustomed to govern their lands after their own will, without regarding the King, were brought by prudent policy into their right station, and all this was brought about by the strict justice which King Ferdinand used, without respect to persons and by treating everywhere lords and peasants on the same lines.†

* Ferdinand the Catholic.
† *Vide Life of Alvaro de Luna*, p. 338.

CARDINALS

The bishop tells of certain cases of justice which happened in his times. It happened that His Majesty was in a certain part of Spain where it is the custom of princes to move from one place to another, and as usual, wherever the King might go, there would be a great concourse of people who had affairs to settle. A certain gentleman came to meet the King and went to lodge in an inn which, as usual in these countries, was very mean, and left with the host all his belongings, amongst which was a wallet containing money and writings. He told the host to keep it carefully whilst he went to speak with the King on certain business. Having finished with the King, he returned to the inn and asked the host for the articles he had left with him, especially for the wallet with the money and papers. The host then declared that he had not the wallet, and pretended to be astonished ; whereupon the gentleman again asked for it and said that if it were not produced at once he would go and report the matter to the King. The host denied that he had got anything belonging to the gentleman and told him to go where he liked. The gentleman then sought the King and told the whole story. The King, judging from the gentleman's demeanour, felt sure that he had given these articles to the host, and believed him, so at once he sent for the host and with requests and threats bade him return the wallet to the gentleman ; but, even to the King, the fellow denied it, saying that he knew nothing about it, and had never had the wallet. The King was still convinced of the gentleman's honesty, and, following God's example, determined that truth should prevail. He thought out a method, and once more summoned the host and urged him to make restitution, but the man was still obstinate. His Majesty then snatched his cap off his head, and commanded certain of his followers to guard the fellow, and not to let him go till he should return. His Majesty then went into his own room and having called one of his servants he bade him take this cap to the inn, and give it to the host's wife, saying, on the part of her husband, that she should hand over to him the wallet which he had left in his charge. She at once gave the wallet to the servant, and he bore it back to the King. When the wallet was opened it was found that nothing of its contents was missing. The King then went again to the host, who had been under restraint, and bade him tell the truth of which the King himself was now assured, adding that if he found he was guilty his head should be struck off. As he still remained obstinate the King brought out the wallet and asked him if he recognised it. As soon as the host saw it he cried out for pardon to the King, who answered that this was not the time for mercy, but for justice. When the money was counted and found intact, he gave it back to the gentleman, and bade him go his ways, and then condemned the thief to the gallows. The host appealed earnestly for mercy, but the King replied: " You know how often I asked you to tell the truth, this is no time for mercy." Then he bade him settle his spiritual concerns before he should be hanged. This sentence was a wise and prudent one.

The bishop told me another story. A gentleman passing by Zamora was attacked on the road and robbed of two hundred and fifty ducats and of six finger rings. When the gentleman arrived at Zamora he recognised there the man who had robbed him. He went to the governor of the town and stated his case, whereupon the governor ordered the arrest of the thief, who, on being brought in, confessed his crime and handed over his plunder to the governor. This done the governor called in a stranger to give bail for the thief in order that he himself might defraud the gentleman, who, seeing himself wronged, went to the King and stated his case. The King summoned the governor of Zamora before him and demanded why he had liberated this thief who had in his possession the money and the rings of the gentleman. The governor replied that he was entitled by right to give bail and release. The King said, " Who is this thief whom you have bailed, and what bribe did he give you ? " The governor answered that he knew nothing about him. The King, seeing the deceitfulness of this man, called in a doctor of laws and bade him declare whether the governor was right or not. Meantime the gentleman was clamouring for restitution, so the King had the governor and the doctor of laws brought before him in public aud ence, at which Messer Giovanni Margheriti was present. The King then demanded a reply from the doctor of laws, who declared that, having considered the case, he found that the governor had

the right to act as he did. The King was much chagrined at
this answer, deeming that the doctor was in league with the
fraud, and in an access of anger he bade the governor of
Zamora give back to the gentleman everything that he had
lost, and all the expenses he had incurred while he was waiting
for justice to be done; he then condemned the governor to
the gallows. Then he turned to that doctor to whom he had
submitted the case and said, " I will punish you so that you
shall in future understand how to do justice." Everything
was given back to the gentleman and the governor was hanged
by the neck. After this sentence was given the Bishop of Elva
turned to the King and said : " Neither Bartolo nor Baldo
could have decided otherwise."

The cardinal was sent on several diplomatic missions by
the Pope and by King Juan. He went as ambassador to
Florence at the time when Duke Giovanni* had occupied a
good part of the kingdom,† being sent by King Juan to
demand of the Florentines due observance of the agreement
which they had with King Ferdinand and with King Alfonso
and his heirs and successors. They were thus bound to King
Ferdinand as his heir. I was with him when he went to state
his case before the commission, and I made bold to ask him
whether he wished to state it in Latin, or in the vulgar tongue.
He told me he proposed to make it in Latin. I replied that,
seeing there were few who understood Latin, it would be more
effective if he delivered it in the Tuscan dialect. He went to
the palace, where were assembled the Signoria and many
others who had been convoked, and spoke fluently in the
vulgar tongue and was greatly praised, both for his elocution
and for his able statement. He did all that he could to
persuade the Signoria and the citizens to observe the treaties
which obliged them to support King Ferdinand. Then he
went to Rome, and on to Naples, thence to Catalonia, where,
after the loss of Barcelona, he worked zealously to bring about
those agreements which later on proved so advantageous.
Finally he returned to Naples just after the King had lost
Otranto;‡ he then went on to Rome as ambassador of the

* Jean d'Anjou.   † Naples.
‡ The Turks captured Otranto in 1480 with assistance of the
Venetians. King Ferdinand suspected the complicity of the Pope as

Spanish king to urge the Pope to support King Ferdinand against the infidels. This His Holiness did by sending an Apostolic legate and doing all that was necessary for safety. Then the bishop left Rome to exhort the Venetians, as the greatest sea power, that it might please them to lend their aid in this time of danger to King Ferdinand through the occupation of Otranto by the Turks, and of the outrage on Christendom, and of the loss and scandal to the holy name of God, lest the evils which had already begun should come to a full head. But the Venetians were not to be moved. Would to God that their help had not been less than their hindrance! The bishop was indignant at the unheard of barbarity of the Venetians who seemed to be acting without fear or honour of God. Neither by exhortations nor any other means could he persuade them. The ambassador of France, that most Christian power, supported him, but neither one nor the other could prevail. But it was not the will of God that the Christians should perish. Suddenly aid came by a great slaughter of the Turks, and, if God had not given this help, there would have been none other, seeing that many unworthy Christians, who might have helped in such a good work, remained neutral or even gave secret help to the enemy. Oh, wicked race, oh, unheard of iniquity! The bishop, like a true and good Christian, could do nothing more with the Doge and the Signoria than hearten them on to this good action, but all his prayers and all his threats came to nothing. He even offered them forty armed galleys at the charges of the King of Spain, until the war with the Turk should end, and that any gain should go to the Venetians. To secure this he produced the bonds of the King, and of the Queen, and of the principal nobles of the land, but they would agree to nothing, and only gave a general answer, and all along there was constant intercourse of their ships with the Turkish fleet. The bishop lost all patience at this bad faith and ingratitude, but, as before said, God intervened. On hearing of the defeat of the Turks the French ambassador and the bishop went to the Doge, and to the Signoria, to testify to them their gratitude

well. The Cardinal of Girona terrified Sixtus by the picture he drew of the danger to Christendom so that he broke with the Venetians. Otranto was recovered a year later on account of an attack by the Persians on the Turks. *Vide Histoire de Venise.* Daru, III, p. 216.

to Almighty God for having delivered the country from the impious and cruel Turkish tyranny. They went in solemn procession to thank God for so great a blessing, but the Doge and the Senate remained obdurate and would hear nothing. The ambassadors spake in terms which should have put them to shame, but the only concession they would make was to join the procession in the honour of God. The ambassadors wished to have the bells rung, as was reasonable, and fireworks, but this request was refused.

All this happened on the morning of the Ascension, and on that very night, as is the custom, the Piazza was filled with wooden booths covered with canvas, when, by the grace of God, one booth caught fire which spread and burnt everything that was there. Then all the bells of the city began to ring, and rang through the night; the front of San Marco, where there was a statue of Our Lady, caught fire, and God wrought this miracle that all the ornaments about it were consumed, and Our Lady herself was uninjured. The next morning the ambassadors having heard bells ringing all the night, and seeing a great fire, went before the Doge, and the bishop addressed him: " Most serene Prince, although your Highness was unwilling to ring the bells or to allow fireworks on account of the Turkish defeat, God provided bell-ringing and fireworks all through the night." No answer was given, but the Signory took great umbrage at these words. The French ambassador supported the bishop, for everyone was outraged at the conduct of the Venetians.

While these negotiations were going on the Venetians sent ambassadors to the new Turkish commander to confirm the agreement which had been made with his predecessor.* When the bishop heard this he lost all patience and spoke his mind, reiterating all the arguments which he had held with them, and then departed in great anger, saying, that wherever he might find himself, he would make it clear to everyone their attitude towards Christianity. When he arrived at Florence he told the results of his mission to the ambassadors, and all whom it might concern; thence to Rome where he disclosed the policy of the Venetians to all who did not know of it, thence to Naples where he abode

* *Vide Histoire de Venise.* Daru, III, p. 122.

sometime. Meantime the Venetians had arranged a league with the Pope* to occupy Ferrara, wherefore King Ferdinand sent the Bishop of Girona to negotiate with the Pope and to induce him to ally himself with His Majesty, the Duke of Milan and the Florentines against the Venetians to prevent them from seizing Ferrara. The bishop conferred with the Pope at Rome, showing him by powerful arguments how necessary it was to His Holiness that Ferrara as a part of the pontifical dominions should be defended, disclosing the ill-faith of the Venetians and what was their object in this undertaking. His speech had great effect both upon His Holiness and upon all the cardinals, so that the affair began to move ; the weight of his reasoning procured the conclusion of peace, and of a league between the Pope, the King, the Milanese state, and the Florentines for the defence of Ferrara against Venice. It is well known that the troops which the Pope had sent to aid the Venetians were now ordered to act against them. The Pope, recognising his many virtues, now made the Bishop of Girona a cardinal with the assent of the College. He was most learned both in the Canon and the Civil Law, also in theology, in philosophy, in humane letters, in history and in cosmography. He wrote a book, the *Corona del Principe*, a wonderful work, indeed, a crown for the King, for all precious stones are in it, and every stone is an illustration of some kingly function. He wrote the *History of Spain*, a trustworthy record of events down to his own time. He died at Rome, and his end was worthy of his life. There is now a great scarcity of such distinguished men, they have disappeared, and there are none to take their place. Had he lived he would have done still greater things, but he died at Rome of an attack of stone.

CARDINAL OF RIETI

Cardinal Angelo di Rieti was the brother of the Cardinal of Fermo, a very learned man in theology and doctrine. He was highly conscientious and led a life as righteous as his brother's, seeing that he followed his footsteps. He maintained in his

* Sixtus IV.

CARDINALS

house Fra Mariano of Rome, an Augustinian Observantist, who by his bounty was instructed in theology and became an impressive preacher. The friar prayed for him in all his sermons, for by means of his good example he (the friar) had found religion and learnt what doctrine he knew, from which such good fruit had sprung and would still spring should Almighty God spare his life. Much praise could be bestowed upon this cardinal for his universal worth, but it must suffice to give it briefly.

CARDINAL OF SPOLETO

Messer Bernardo Eruli da Narni was Cardinal of Spoleto and was long time an auditor of the Rota. He was a great jurist and canonist and a just and upright man. By these merits alone he became cardinal, and not from reasons of friendship or nationality. He long enjoyed this dignity, ruling his life with strictest rectitude. Many causes came before him for decision, and there was no need for any of the parties to fear injustice, for neither emperor nor pope could have changed his notion of right. This innate goodness guided him all through life ; he was ever constant, and no higher praise can be given. He was cultured and impatient of all display within and without his house. His household was after the same pattern, for nothing else would have served him.

CARDINAL OF S. MARCELLO

Messer Antonio Casini, Cardinal of S. Marcello, was a Sienese, a great jurist and canonist, well versed in letters and in the affairs of Holy Church. He was highly esteemed by Pope Eugenius when the College was a most worthy one, each member having been added for his virtues and for no other reason. Amongst these was Messer Antonio, made cardinal by Pope Martin, that worthy pontiff who ruled the Church of God so well. All the cardinals he made were men of distinction, and amongst them was Messer Antonio. It has seemed right to add him to this catalogue of men of mark on account of his merit.

THE CARDINAL DI MENDOZA

CARDINAL DI S. SISTO—A CATALAN

In the time of Pope Eugenius lived the Cardinal di S. Sisto—
Turrecremata—a Catalan learned in philosophy and theology,
and one of great weight in the Church. He wrote many
books on theology. At the Council of Basel there was much
discussion whether the power of the Pope or that of the Council
were the greater, concerning which he wrote a valuable work
on the papal power. He was very loyal, and when Pope
Eugenius fled from Rome to Pisa and thence to Florence,
S. Sisto was the only one who accompanied him. He was a
Dominican and wore the habit after he was made cardinal.
He showed himself a gentleman in all his actions and disliked
pomp and display. He wrote many books, but I know naught
concerning them.

CARDINAL DE MELLA—A SPANIARD

Messer Giovanni de Mella, a great canonist and legist, was
of Spanish birth. After he went to Italy he was mostly in
Rome, and on account of his acquirements was made auditor
of the Rota, which office he held a long time and so efficiently
that when a cardinal had to be made he was chosen as one of
the first of the jurisconsults and *juris pontifici* entirely on
account of his sagacity. I know nothing of anything he
wrote, but considering his worth he is deserving of a place
among men of distinction.

CARDINAL DI MENDOZA—A SPANIARD*

Messer Piero di Mendoza, of noble Spanish birth, was made
cardinal by Pope Sixtus by reason of his merit. He had a
thorough knowledge of the Canon Law; also of the humanities
and of theology, and during his stay in Rome won great
honour and esteem. He caused many books to be transcribed, both in sacred and secular learning, in view of
forming a library. His father was one of the chief gentlemen

---

* He was made cardinal in 1473 and died in 1495. This cardinal
evidently outlived Vespasiano.

of Spain who, though not given to letters, understood the Tuscan speech. On this account the cardinal, while he was in Florence, caused a number of books to be written out in Tuscan so that he might render them into Spanish. In his Spanish house he collected a library of books in Tuscan for the use of all who might wish to use them. Messer Piero and all those of his house are of the noblest of the land. Since he has been cardinal he has never returned to Rome. Of the books he has written I know nothing, so I do not name them.

Cardinal Cusano*—a German (1401–1464)

Messer Nicolo di Cusa, of German nationality, was a man of worship, a great philosopher, theologian and platonist. He was of holy life, well lettered, especially in Greek. He travelled all through France and Germany, collecting a great store of books in every faculty; also he wrote copiously in theology. He was a shrewd dialectician and advanced his propositions by the most subtle arguments, wherefore his works were rated as high authorities. He cared nothing for state or for possessions, and was one of the most needy of the cardinals, thus giving an excellent example in all his doings. By his virtues he deserves to be put in the ranks of illustrious men. His death was fitting to his life, as he made a most holy end. Up to this point I have described, in form of comment, all those cardinals of whom I have had personal knowledge.

* He was made cardinal in 1448. He was chiefly distinguished as a mathematician and propounded an ingenious hypothesis as to the earth's motion. He was in advance of his age in his appreciation of the value of experiment, but his deductions were not always happy. Vespasiano seems to have been ignorant as to this side of his learning, but when he found a man to be a canonist and a theologian he deemed he had gone far enough.

IV: *ARCHBISHOPS AND BISHOPS*

HE was a Florentine, born of honest parents, and became an Observantist monk. Afterwards, with S. Bernadino, he settled the rules of the Order as they now are. This branch became quite independent of the General when it obtained the right of electing their Vicar. He was a learned theologian, especially in cases of conscience, as will afterwards appear. Confession and preaching were the exercises he specially favoured, and so great was his reputation in cases of conscience that a vast number were submitted to him for decision. He passed some time at Naples, where he wrote a treatise on confession, and at this time the Archbishopric of Florence fell vacant, whereupon the Signoria wrote to the Pope begging him to nominate to the see some one who would be agreeable to the citizens, and Cosimo de' Medici wrote to the same effect. Pope Eugenius replied that he would send a man of worth, and straightway nominated Fra Antonino. But news of this having come to the friars' ears, he and another friar withdrew to a spot where they could not be found, a lonely wood near Corneto. The official who bore the brief of appointment heard of this, and searched the wood. He looked for a rich *buona mano*, not realising that Fra Antonino was bent on refusing the see and a good salary. When at last he found Fra Antonino he presented the brief, and after the friar had read it no *buona mano* was offered. The official then asked for it, whereupon Antonino replied, " I won't give anything in return for bad news, and worse you could not bring. We have no money ; nothing but these capes." The official saw he had been deceived, and marked the confusion of Antonino when he opened the brief and read that he must accept the see on pain of excommunication.

ARCHBISHOPS AND BISHOPS

I will relate what I heard from Pope Nicolas about the matter. Pope Eugenius told him he had only made three prelates with an easy conscience. The Patriarch of Venice, the Bishop of Ferrara and Fra Antonino. Eugenius was full of praise of Antonino, having known him long. Pope Nicolas was the same. After his election he went to S. Domenico at Fiesole, from whence he again wrote to Pope Eugenius begging to be relieved, but the Pope stood firm ; also many Florentines went to entreat him and to show him how great a blessing his acceptance would be. As to his vestments he found many advisers ; some suggested a long cloak with a train, but he would have none of it, and said it must be of woollen stuff and touching the ground and no longer. As they made it two finger-lengths longer than a friar's robe, he cut it short, because once he had met a friar in a ragged gown which he tore off his back and gave the friar his own and got a new one. He wore a friar's habit and slept in a friar's bed in a linen shirt. He would have no arras cloths nor screens at the doors, which he wished to be open to whoever would see him. He bade the servants keep the benches clean so that those who sat thereon should not soil their garments. He engaged a vicar of a disposition like his own : no better man in all Italy. He kept no more servants than he wanted, and no saddle-horses but one little mule, which he borrowed from S. Maria Nuova. He also kept some horses for service and the mule with gilded bosses.

The income of his see was fifteen hundred scudi, but he spent on himself only five hundred florins. The rest he gave to the poor. He abolished even the shadow of simony and conferred orders on only those who were worthy, and reformed those clerical bodies which were greatly in need of discipline. He forbade soled shoes and made all priests wear sandals, and shear their long hair. Every priest was obliged to carry a breviary, duly signed and registered to prevent the sale of it. He expelled divers dissolute priests and those who were contumacious, and deprived them of their benefices when they proved incorrigible. He made no distinction between rich and poor, and always gave equal justice. One day Cosimo de' Medici came to him asking him to favour a case he had in hand, and he replied that, if Cosimo had right on his side, he wanted no help from anyone.

ARCHBISHOP ANTONINO

At this time there was scarcity in Florence, and town and country alike suffered great want. He caused a vast quantity of bread to be baked and instructed the officials to give it, not only to the manifest poor, but also to those who were ashamed to let their distress be known. He founded the society of *poveri vergognosi*, which still exists. For this work his own revenues did not suffice, and he obtained funds from Pope Eugenius and from the citizens. He did so many charitable works privately that all seemed well provided for in spiritual and temporal needs. People came to consult him about contracts, as to whether they were lawful or not, and one day when certain cases were brought before him for decision, he directed that they should be read to him, and during the reading he sat with head bowed as if asleep. The reader suggested that he should arouse himself and listen, and the archbishop bade him go on. Then, when he had heard all, he decided at once which contracts were lawful, showing he had been wideawake. He condemned dowries given to young girls in such wise that the parents should have the capital if the girl died. He advised those who had money at the Monte to leave it ultimately to the Comune, and Donato Acciaiuoli followed this counsel.

What leisure he had he spent in saying the office or in giving audience to those who asked for it, and always rose before sunrise. He worked at his *Summa*, a book which proved so useful and beneficial to the Christian faith. In spite of his heavy task of office he wrote the greater part of it while he was archbishop, by his prudent use of his time. He attended all the services at the cathedral and always remained till the end. One afternoon, after officiating at the Church of S. Stefano, he passed by the loggia of Buondelmonte, where he overthrew the tables at which some gamesters were playing, and there was not one of those fellows who did not bend the knee to him and look ashamed at having been caught gambling. When he was leaving S. Maria del Fiore, after preaching, he passed some benches filled with women and noisy ribald youths, who all got up and left when he turned towards them, so great was the reverence he inspired. His fame spread through Italy and all the Christian world, which was full of error, especially in coveting the goods of others ; and this *Summa* of his, referring to corrupt dealing and contracts in all countries, specialising as to certain regions, has brought light to all the world and spread the fame of his good works, and also laid down many valuable rules for right government.

On the death of Pope Eugenius, Pope Nicolas succeeded, and he, wishing to rule with justice, sent to bid the archbishop come to Rome to advise him in divers weighty matters. When in Rome he disproved the statement that prelates display extravagant luxury in order to win the popular favour. He wore a friar's habit, rode upon a sorry mule and had a scanty following ; still, wherever he went, the people knelt to do him honour and showed far more reverence to him than to the prelates riding on richly adorned horses and mules with troops of servants. Everyone in Rome held him in the greatest respect, and several of the cardinals, being perplexed over certain cases of conscience, consulted him and were at once enlightened by his elucidations. There was a general desire that he should be made a cardinal, but he let everyone know that he would refuse the honour, declaring that, by accepting it, he would be jeopardising the welfare of his soul : rather than become a cardinal, he would prefer to return to the state of a mere friar. Hearing these statements they left him in peace. No one could have honoured him more than did Pope Nicolas, moved not only by his holy life, but by what he had heard from Pope Eugenius. Antonino was specially fortunate in that he aroused more reverence in Rome than had been paid to any other prelate, through the integrity of his life.

On the death of Pope Nicolas, Pope Calixtus was elected and, according to custom, ambassadors were sent from Florence to carry the obedience, the archbishop being chosen as the leader. It was ordered by the Pope that he should be received in public consistory in order to do honour to Florence. He went in his ordinary habit, though urged by others to wear bishop's robes. The consistory was largely attended, and the archbishop delivered a remarkable speech which was highly praised by the Pope and all who heard it. It brought much credit to the speaker and to the city which had sent him.

After the duties of the ambassadors were finished they went, according to custom, to visit the cardinals, by whom the archbishop was graciously received, and when these visits were done they returned to Florence.

Nothing could move him from the ways of strict justice. At this time there was an influential citizen in Florence who had a case concerning one of his sons before the archbishop. The man was in the wrong about it, and gave constant annoyance and used improper speech when the archbishop was trying to show him that he was wrong. The fellow became unendurable in his abuse, but the archbishop always answered him with patience ; at last one evening he became enraged and laid hands on the archbishop, who still kept his patience. God, however, will not allow His servants to be molested, and on this account sent serious trouble on this man. He was banished from the city and afterwards declared a rebel : he fell from prosperity into calamity : he lost all his worldly goods and had barely enough to find food. The ill-conduct of this man and of his son, who had received many favours, was the cause of their downfall. They died in poverty and exile, so the sins of the fathers were visited on the children, according to the Scriptures. He strongly denounced the Florentine practice of taking an oath without any intention of keeping it, and he often admonished the Signoria thereanent, as well as condemning it to the citizens and preaching against it, condemning also the public use of the ballot beans after having sworn the oath of secrecy. In 1458, seeing that the breaking of the oath was generally overlooked and the vote rendered public, he proposed as a remedy to put up notices in all the churches that every vote should be given secretly, under pain of excommunication. Certain of the leaders were much perturbed when they saw these notices, and set themselves to throw obstacles in the archbishop's way. They chose the shortest course, believing it would prove the most effectual, which was to send some prominent citizens to threaten him. Five of these waited on him and began to denounce him for what he had done, whereupon he replied that he had only played the part of a good pastor by saving their souls from damnation for perjury. This made them more furious than ever, though the archbishop spake gently and with humility. Then they threatened to deprive him of his see, and he at once began to laugh. " For God's sake, I beg you, do this at once. You will do me a great favour and lift a great burden from my shoulders. I will go to my cell in S. Marco, of which I have the key beside me, and rest there in peace. Such a deed would please me beyond anything." His persecutors believed that this was said to baffle them and were vexed that this remedy of theirs should prove no remedy at all. Seeing that neither prayers nor threats could move the archbishop they returned to the palace to report to the Signoria what they had done.

On that same evening a friend called to see him, when the archbishop, laughing, told of what had happened, whereupon the friend laughed heartily, saying that there was one at the door who desired to speak with the archbishop, adding that he was one of the chiefs of the government. The archbishop bade his friend join the vicar in an inner room, and wait his return. He did this from a premonition of what was going to happen, for this visitor at once demanded to know what company he had in the house. He refused to say, suspecting that some outrage was contemplated.

The visitor departed and caused a watch to be set to see who might quit the house. Thereupon the archbishop, to save his friends, let them depart through the Church of S. Salvatore, bidding them go on past S. Maria Novella. This they did and got safely away. On the election of Pius II he was again chosen as Florentine ambassador, and this second mission brought him yet greater honour than the first. He was now old and greatly weakened by fasting and vigils. The six ambassadors were honourably received by the Pope, and when the archbishop rose to announce his mission he fell, being overcome by age, the fatigue of the journey and the long waiting. It seemed to the court and the other ambassadors that he was in serious case, but after he had been revived by rubbing and a cup of malmsey in an adjoining room, he returned to the consistory and delivered a speech even finer than that which he had spoken before Pope Calixtus. After the consistory he visited the cardinals according to custom, and then returned to Florence.

In all his dealings he was the humblest of men. By his holy life and carriage he won favour everywhere especially at the Roman court, and at one of the Papal elections received three votes. Had he been elected he would assuredly have reformed the Church. Through the weariness of mind and body, which follows long and continuous labour, he went to live in a house outside the Porta S. Gallo, but God had now determined to deliver him from his many troubles and gather him to Himself. A slight attack of fever prostrated him in his weakened state, and with a clear conscience he tranquilly awaited the end. He sent back the little mule which had been lent to him by the governor of S. Maria Nuova, whom he thanked for the use of it. He had no books of his own, not even a breviary, and he wrote all his digests on old waste paper. The books he needed he borrowed from S. Marco or S. Domenico, and at his death all his chattels were valued at 120 lire. Happy the man who could live in such fashion ! Of him may be said what S. Jerome writes of S. Antonio, the first of the hermits, who declared that he would rather possess S. Paul's garment of palms than all the wealth of Darius. As his kinsfolk were well-to-do, he gave them nought from the archbishopric, saying that these goods were not his, but belonged to the poor. At his request he was buried in S. Marco, which he loved, without any pomp. He lay for two days on a bier covered with a plain cloak, and all the people and many strangers who happened to be in Florence came to kiss his hands and his feet. I believe that many things worthy of record concerning him have been set down in the life of him written by Francesco da Castiglione.

S. BERNARDINO DA MASSA (1380–1444)

He was born at Massa of worthy parents. In his eighth year he was sent to learn grammar at Siena, and his parents then decided that he should study the Canon Law, which he read for three years ; but all this time was wasted as he did not take to the law, but to theology as necessary for his salvation, wherefore he studied it day and night. He cared only for the means by which Almighty God desired to extirpate the evils of the world, and was most generous to the poor, and thoughtful of the infirm. Being of this mind, and conscious of the snares of the world, he hated the secular life more and more, deeming that in it salvation would be hard to gain, and that worldlings lived in a sea full of shipwrecks. He meditated constantly on eternal life and death, and after living many years in this mood a great fear fell upon him ; then, on turning these things over in his mind, he came to hate the pomps and vanities of the world, and cast aside all these things and turned to the religious life. He debated whether he should follow S. Francis or S. Dominic, and in his twenty-second year he put this question to himself, and sold all that he had by way of detaching himself entirely from the world.

After much communing he decided to enter the Order of S. Francis, and began at once to perfect himself in the spiritual life and took the cowl. He saw that the life of the preaching friar was the greatest help to salvation, and this he adopted, and after practice in the same he became a marvellous preacher on account of his voice, his methods, his detestation of vice and his exhortations to virtue. In no other man was there to be found such a wonderful concourse of talents ; it would appear that these gifts did not all come by the way of nature, but that Almighty God had specially conferred them. He was skilled in everything, but more particularly in preaching, by which he spread light through the whole world, which was at this time blinded and darkened, especially Italy, where all rules of righteous life had been abandoned and where men no longer recognised God. So completely were they submerged and buried in abominable and accursed vices, to which they had become so inured that they feared neither God nor the honour of the world. Accursed blindness ! Everything had come to such a pass that no one censured these wicked and unbounded vices on account of their universal prevalence.

In his time a certain city of Italy was given over to every vice and especially to the hateful and accursed sin of sodomy. The people had rushed into this infatuation, wherefore it needed that God should rain down upon them fire and brimstone as upon the folk of Sodom and Gomorra. S. Bernardino, perceiving the excess of crime, began to curse these workers of iniquity, and by his preaching and by his curses and denunciations of this abominable sin and of all other vices, he purged this city and all the rest of Italy of the iniquities which in-

S. BERNARDINO DA MASSA

fected them. When he went to Florence he found it greatly
corrupted and at once set to work as he had worked in other
cities, condemning vice and showing his detestation of it, so
that the Florentines, who by nature are well-inclined towards
well-doing, altered their lives, so that the Saint may be said
to have given the city a new birth. To make the women give
up their vanities and amusements and their false hair, he
caused a bonfire to be made in the piazza of S. Croce, and
then commanded those who possessed any of these things to
bring them to him. He then burned them all ; a wonderful
change indeed in the minds of those who had been infatuated
by these pomps. S. Chrysostom says that it is easier for God
in His powerful working to create a new heaven and earth,
than to change the mind of man who has received the gift of
free will.

For forty years S. Bernardino preached, visiting every
village in the country : and bringing to the knowledge of
God parts of Italy in which He had hitherto been a stranger.
He redeemed the souls of men and stirred them so powerfully
that many now confessed who had never confessed before ; also
he restored to the rightful owners the goods of which they had
been wrongfully deprived and cleared many from unjust
slander, and made peace where there had been mortal enmity.
He pacified rulers, and cities, and peoples. He thought of
nothing else than the restoration of good will. Many dissolute and wicked men changed their lives, and entered the
religious orders of S. Francis and of the Osservanza. He
raised the character of Divine worship and built many houses
for the Observantist Order, whereby its power and fame was
much increased. It may be said that S. Bernardino established
this Order in its present form because, as everyone knows, the
Generals of this Order are now Conventuals, whereas before
S. Bernardino, all friars, whether Observantist or not, were
under the General's rule.

After this good work and extension of religious influences
S. Bernardino considered how he might make it secure, and
keep everyone to his own sphere. To carry this out he prevailed upon Pope Eugenius to appoint a Vicar, who was called
the Vicar-General, but this office was not to be perpetual,
and this Vicar was to be appointed by the Observantists

alone. Each year he had to go to their chapter, when the friars might reappoint him annually, but only for a term of three years in all, and could discharge him at the end of the year, and elect another. The Vicar-General had power only over the Observantists, a power which was equal to that of the General. The General could not interfere with the friars, nor had he any authority over them except through the Vicar, who was subordinated to the General with certain conditions.

When the fame of S. Bernardino had spread widely the Bishop of Siena died, whereupon the Sienese begged that, of his grace, he would become their bishop. Pope Eugenius chose him, and he went for election to Venice, where he preached during Lent. Many citizens were present to support him, and to urge him to accept the see, amongst whom was a man of great worth, Michele di Messer Piero Bennini, a man of letters, who argued strongly in favour of acceptance by S. Bernardino, showing how great would be the consequent benefit. When Michele had finished, S. Bernardino turned to him and said, "If ever you see me in any other habit than that of S. Francesco on my back, say, 'This is not Fra Bernardino.' This is my resolve which, please God, I will keep." He brought forward many other arguments which Michele could not answer, wherefore he wrote to Pope Eugenius that he would please to appoint some other to the see and to leave Bernardino to his work as preacher which he had hitherto followed. The Pope, recognising his desire and also the fruit of his preaching, had no wish to compel him. He was afterwards elected to two other bishoprics with the same result, thus showing his integrity and his unchangeable resolution. He condemned all vices, especially the cursed gulf of usury, the destroyer of the city, the province and the cottage. One morning he had been preaching in the cathedral of Florence concerning contracts, restitution, the bank and girls' dowries. That same evening, as was his habit, he went to his stationer's shop where he met Giannozzi Manetti, who addressed him, "You have sent us all to damnation." He replied, "I have damned no one : damnation comes from man's sin and wickedness." Manetti then began to discuss contracts for dowries where the capital is fixed, but S. Bernardino proved by clear reasoning that these contracts were illicit and that contracts for dowries, where the capital is fixed, were worse than contracts made by a Jew on red parchment.

Thus with great humility he solved every doubt, so that Messer Giannozzo and all the rest were well satisfied. Many people came to him every day for advice or about contracts or restitutions or other matters, and he gave reasonable explanations. Finally, that all might understand the matter, he wrote a book, *De restitutione*, which treats of all contracts, lawful and unlawful, dealing with these matters even more thoroughly than did Archbishop Antonino.

S. Bernardino adopted a form of preaching which was serviceable and appropriate to his hearers, condemning vice as much as possible and praising virtue. And in order that after his death others might enjoy the benefit of them, he wrote two books of sermons, one called the *Vangelo Eterno*, which treats chiefly of virtue and of the abominable nature of vice, so that all men might avoid it, the other volume he called *Sermoni*. In these two books he has put together as many sermons as can be preached in one year, and they attracted so much notice that nearly all the Observantist friars adopted his style. In his time vice was so widespread that neither S. Thomas nor Bonaventura any longer sufficed; new writers like S. Bernardino and Bishop Antonino were wanted, who by their writings might deliver the world from the blindness which had fallen upon it.

After S. Bernardino had preached for forty-four years in all the towns and villages, so that the word of God should be known, although he was a strong man, on account of the unendurable fatigues he underwent he was seized with gout and tormented by pain in the side and also afflicted with piles. Although he was troubled with these three heavy afflictions he only gave way when he was in acute pain, and as soon as he recovered he resumed his preaching and writing and counselling to all those who desired it. While any one of these infirmities might have made a man irritable and peevish, they affected him not at all, and he bore them patiently. In his seventy-fourth year, while he was preaching in Milan, he was ordered by his vicar to go to Aquila, then vexed by riot and sedition, in order that he might abate these troubles, but before he reached the city he fell ill of fever, and in a few days, being weakened by his many ailments, he made an end as holy as his life had been. Aquila profited greatly on account of the many miracles which were wrought after his death, and by the pacification of the country. The sacred body was taken to Aquila, where it remained three days before burial; a great crowd came from all the country round, and many miracles were then wrought, and also at the time of his canonisation, which was granted after a solemn investigation. Then the authorities wanted to know the place of his birth, the name of his father, the disease which caused his death, so that it might be clear to everybody. When the fame of all these miracles was spread abroad, pilgrims came from all parts to his shrine,* wherefore Pope Nicolas, after a diligent examination before the College of Cardinals and other distinguished men, solemnly canonised him in S. Peter's in 1450. Those who wish to read his life at length will find it written in Latin by Maffeo Vegio, and by Giannozzo Manetti in his book, *Contra Judæos et gentes.*

ORLANDO BONARLI—ARCHBISHOP OF FLORENCE

He was of an ancient Florentine family, a great legist and canonist, upright in every respect and careful in his advice. He taught for many years at Bologna at a high salary. Afterwards he was appointed to teach in the class-rooms at Florence, where for some time he lectured to large audiences. The court of Rome recognised his ability and made him auditor of the Ruota, an office only given to men of great distinction. At Rome, in the exercise of his duties, he won the confidence of all by his rectitude and was specially beloved by the Pope and cardinals. During his sojourn there Archbishop Antonino died, whereupon the Pope elected him to the vacant see for two reasons : one, that he would prove a worthy successor to Antonino, and the other that he was a Florentine of good birth and reputation. In order that he might tread in Antonino's footsteps, the Pope desired that all subordinates should continue in their offices. When Orlando became

* A vast tomb in the cathedral at Aquila by Silvestro, a pupil of Desiderio di Settignano.

archbishop he was most careful in his administration; nevertheless some of the citizens opposed him, for all men are prone to resist the application of the law. He always did his duty, having no respect for persons in the eye of the law and of justice. He ruled his see most worthily, and left it in excellent order. Would to God that his successors had always done the same! It seemed to me necessary to give a short notice of this eminent man.

THE BISHOP OF FERRARA

Messer Francesco da Padua held a high office under Pope Eugenius, and, but for his youth (in those days the dignity was not given to everyone), he would have been made cardinal. It was on this account that the Pope passed him over, but when the see of Ferrara fell vacant he was appointed to it. He was well read, with a good knowledge of letters both sacred and profane, and took great pleasure therein. It may be that as a youth he went astray from the straight path,* nevertheless he always kept in the ways of religion and never entirely fell from righteousness. After Pope Eugenius died he decided to quit Rome. The Pope's death had prejudiced his standing at the court, so he now took thought of the bishopric, and realised that he had no responsibility, either to God or to man, so pressing was the cure of this benefice. Arrived at Ferrara, he took up the care of the bishopric, and soon learned that no man can do his duty unless he shall amend his life and live as it becomes the bishop of a see so important as was his own. So after he went to Ferrara he embraced the spiritual life. He shook off all other cares, and with fasting, assiduous prayer and reading of the sacred doctors, he followed a holy life, for it is for one of right feeling and judgment to make a change when disposed thereto.

In the early days of his conversion he sent to Florence for a little book written by Messer Francesco Petrarca, called *De conflictu curarum suarum*, which shows, in the form of a

* Bartoli in a note shows that Vespasiano has here softened down his original opinion of Francesco. Ughelli writes, quoting a MS. of Vespasiano, "This man (Francesco), by the evidence of Vespasian the Florentine, lived for some time in Rome steeped in all manner of vice."

dialogue, the author confessing his sins to Almighty God and receiving a reply from S. Augustine, who grieves over the sins confessed. Thus, with abundant tears, Petrarca confesses his sins to Almighty God and prays pardon. By the help of this book Messer Francesco turned to God, so that there was no one who knew him who was not wonder stricken at the vast change which had come over his life and habits in so brief a time. What time he had to spare he spent in reading or praying or repeating the office or conferring with any who might want his advice. He persevered in this course to the end of his days, giving an example which anyone might follow ; so great was the change in his deeds and words and way of life. He gave most liberally everything he had to spare to the poor for the love of God. At the court of Rome, at Ferrara and in every place where he was known he won renown so great that in his day men talked of nothing else but his praiseworthy carriage. He made a most holy end after the pattern of his life. And anyone who may write of this with diligence will find that it must have been shaped by miraculous rather than by natural agency. I have deemed it fitting, as an example to all those who are minded to honour God, to write this brief record of his life.

THE BISHOP OF VERONA (1410–1471)

Messer Ermolao Barbaro was a Venetian who was made bishop by Pope Eugenius. He knew something of Canon and Civil Law, had a wide knowledge of theology, and afterwards studied the humanities. He wrote an excellent style. He was a man of good life, and under Pope Eugenius he administered his diocese of Verona with diligence and spread largely the Divine worship. He was most courteous to all and brought his bishopric into excellent order, temporal and spiritual. He maintained in his house a number of learned men with whom he would constantly engage in literary discussion, and his house was ruled in a manner befitting a dignified prelate. If he wrote any work (as I believe he did) I have no knowledge of it. As he was a very worthy man it seems to me that his name should be added to this record.

THE BISHOP OF PADUA

BISHOP OF PADUA (DONATI) (1380-1447)

Messer Piero Donati was a Venetian gentleman learned in Canon and Civil Law, a sound theologian and well versed in Greek and in the humanities. He was much in favour at the Roman court, with wide knowledge in all subjects which are dealt with in Rome. Pope Eugenius, recognising his merits, made him bishop of Padua, where he lived in the liberal state to which he was inclined both by his natural disposition and his Venetian birth. When the Council of Basel met, in opposition to Pope Eugenius, it was found necessary to send thither a president to represent him, and to justify him with respect to the charges which were brought against him ; and for this office Bishop Donati, as one of the ablest men then of the court, was chosen. Here he played his part well and won considerable honour ; and in the opinion of many he ought to have been made cardinal, but why he missed the honour I do not know. When the Pope left Florence the bishop returned to his diocese, which is an important one with a fine income. He remained there some time engaged in study, also in the collection of a number of books of which he intended to make a library, but I know not if he did this.

Several miles outside the city the bishop possessed a fine house, whither he would often betake himself for exercise. When the plague came to Padua he sent to this house much of his property and great store of fine silver. While he was there it was God's pleasure that he should catch the plague. Certain of his kinsfolk, when they heard this, went thither, and, finding him in serious plight, they seized all the valuables, especially the silver plate. They feared catching the disease, so they departed and the greater part of the household did the same. No one was left but a chaplain, a faithful old man. As the bishop was burnt up with fever he asked for drink, wherefore the chaplain, when he found that all the silver vessels were gone, brought him some wine in an earthen cup. The bishop, when he saw it, cried: "Why have you not given me a silver cup ? " The chaplain, who was a simple creature, said : " Monsignore, there is neither cup nor tazza left, for your kinsfolk have carried them all off." When the bishop heard this, he neither drunk the wine nor spoke, but turned to the wall and so great was the grief which fell upon him that in a short time he died without having spoken a word. This fatal grief sprang from a defect in his nature, which was not a liberal one, and led him to set too much store on his goods. What I write here concerning the bishop's death I write from the report of one of his household who was present. Let the avaricious consider their end, and may no one come to their bedside to steal their goods, and let them trust no one, either friend or kinsman. I fear, moreover, that the bishop may have lost both his goods and his soul as well ; he was surely in sore peril thereof. It is well to learn wisdom by example rather than by experience, and as to the event I have not written to censure, but by way of warning to others, whether they be bishops, or lords or private citizens. I believe this bishop wrote certain books, but I will pass them by as I have never seen them.

Bishop of Padua

Messer Jacopo Zeno was a Venetian who became Bishop of Padua. When young he made a great name in Rome under Eugenius IV. He was learned in theology and in the humanities, and wrote an excellent style as may be seen in his works. The privilege of preaching before the Pope and cardinals was often granted to him on solemn occasions : at Advent, at Christmas, on Sundays and during Lent. He made many speeches in public which won approval for two reasons : for their elegance and from his perfect method of delivery ; indeed, it was owing to the reputation gained hereby that the bishopric of Padua, in his own country, was given to him. As he had always been devoted to literature, both in reading and writing, he now wrote the history of Carlo Zeno, an illustrious member of his own family, who in his life performed many valorous deeds of war by sea and land. Concerning these, Messer Jacopo wrote ten books which, according to the judgment of those who have read them, are written in an elegant and flowery style beyond the powers of most of our present writers. He gained great fame from this work.

He also wrote the lives of the popes down to his own time, a copious work and highly valued, and many treatises which I have never read. He is highly to be praised for having reached so high a place ; one to which few attain. I was loth to omit his name from this commentary, although one event of his life may shock those who read of it. He was over-devoted to the vanities of the world, and he died suddenly while walking in his palace, which may cause the reader to have fears for him, after reflecting thereupon.

BISHOP OF BRESCIA

Messer Piero da Monte was a Venetian and Bishop of Brescia, a man of worth and wide learning, a Doctor of Civil and Canon Law and versed in all the liberal arts. He laid aside the law and held to theology. As he desired to form a library, he bought all the suitable books he could find, and always had in his service scribes who copied various others. In Florence he caused to be copied for him many literary treasures in all the faculties, and especially in theology. He was in Constance when the schism was ended by the reformation of the Church and worked well for this reunion, so that amongst the illustrious men who were present he won much renown. Pope Eugenius sent him to England, where he officiated several years as collector,* and returned with much credit. Besides the bishopric, he held many appointments and offices in the Church of God. He was governor of Perugia, a post he held several years with general approval. He was a handsome man and eloquent in speech.

He wrote copiously, and one of his books, a repertory of Canon and Civil Law, is famous, and called after the author, *Brixiense.* It became widely known at once, and his fame still rests on it. He was several times named for the cardinalate, but was barred, once through intrigue, and once by death, which seized him when he might have succeeded. This is the way of the world, when a man deems that he may gather some fruit for all his labour death intervenes, and, if his work shall have been done for the honour of the world,

* Of Peter's pence.

rather than for that of God, it will be in vain. For most men are blind, as Messer Piero was in a measure ; he thought over-much of the world's honour and not enough of God's. For this reason most men are paid in the coin they long for ; that of this world and of its vanity. His end would have been better had he turned more to Almighty God. He died suddenly, and to die thus is dangerous.

BISHOP OF BRESCIA

Messer Domenico, who succeeded the last bishop, was a Venetian, brought up under the care of the Cardinal of Bologna, Pope Gregory's nephew and a very holy man. Messer Domenico was learned in all the liberal arts and the most wonderful theologian of the time ; so much so that during the time of Pope Nicolas, of Pope Calixtus, of Pope Pius and Pope Paul he was in great request when doubt was stirred up by rash spirits within the Church of God. On account of his great reputation he was always trusted to settle these affairs. His influence in the court increased rapidly, and he had strong desire to become a cardinal, but, just as the hat was ready for him, he, like so many others, was seized by death when the prize he longed for was within his reach, and all his hopes were overthrown. Messer Domenico was Bishop of Brescia for many years, when death ruined all the plans he had made. But we must commit all things to the disposition of God and take whatever befalls us as coming from Him, and recognise that, whatever He does, is done for the best.

PATRIARCH OF JERUSALEM

Messer Biagio di Mulino, a Venetian gentleman and Patriarch of Jerusalem, was given to the study of the sacred scriptures in which he was well read. On account of his virtuous life Pope Eugenius esteemed him highly, as he regulated the court and the chancery, and caused many sacred books to be copied and bought others, all of which he

sent to the various benefices which had been under his charge ;
bibles, homilies, books on the passion, and the morals of
S. Gregory. He kept his own house well, and educated several
nephews with the aim of settling them in the Church, and did
all in his power to bring them pure-minded to the service of
God and free from all vice. He hoped to be made cardinal
and the dignity was promised to him several times, but his
death prevented the fruition of his desire.

BISHOP OF RAUGIA (1437–1510)

Don Timoteo de' Maffei was a Veronese, one of the regular
canons of S. Agostino. He was a weighty preacher, and his
preaching brought good fruit to the Church. From his
twenty-fifth year he preached throughout Italy and made
many converts. Many preachers went to him for instruction,
and he worked hard of his own will for the love of God. It
was by his influence that Cosimo de' Medici built the Badia
at Fiesole, and adopted his architectural plan and disposition.
His influence with Cosimo could hardly have been greater,
seeing that his methods had the sobriety and strength which
especially commended themselves to Cosimo and to all those
who associated with him. He used a good style in writing,
as may be seen in his composition, and his preaching was
sound ; vastly different from much we hear to-day which
stirs up doubts and does not stick to absolute statements
without suggesting questioning in the form of disputation.
He preached as a man ought to preach, without doubt of any
sort and concerning matters already determined by the
authority of Jerome or Augustine ; indeed, he was a great
Augustinian and knew his doctrines thoroughly. If he did
not treat of modern doctrines he did not assail them with
doubts, after the fashion of those who argue in circles, and he
was strong and convincing in his denunciation of vice. He
was of fine presence and authoritative manner, which tells
for much. Wherever he went he won respect, and he visited
Rome many times. He won the special favour of the Cardinal
of Spoleto, a man of great influence, and when the bishopric
of Raugia fell vacant he was asked to accept it and to reside

there, so that the benefit of his preaching might be felt and the affairs of the diocese properly conducted. When he reached Raugia he found life there vastly different from what he had anticipated, and that he had taken upon his shoulders too heavy a burden by going to foregather with men of a nature entirely alien to his own. Try as he might, his efforts were always frustrated, for nothing availed to change the aims and customs of the people. He saw how he had changed a life of perfect peace for one of turmoil, and that no remedy was at hand. He had with him a monk of his order with whom he often grieved that he should have abandoned the peace and quiet of a religious life for a disorder like the one in which he now lived without benefit of any kind. Day and night he grieved over the misfortune that he should have taken this bishopric and thereby cut himself off from all spiritual consolation. After suffering long grief and anxiety, he fell gravely ill, his chief regret being that he was not back in the Badia of Fiesole living in charity and peace with the monks, where he would enjoy in a single hour greater peace than he had known since his first coming to this bishopric. In his sorrow he would shed floods of tears and lament to his companions. After his illness—which was *dolor lateris* and fever —had lasted several days it was aggravated by regret that he was deprived of the society of his monks, and he made an end as holy as his life had been. It is to be hoped that, after the rich reward of his preaching which has brought so many to religion, and his own forty years' service, that Almighty God had mercy on his soul. Wherefore, let all those who are in the order of the Osservanza abide there, and let power and place alone.

BISHOP OF FIESOLE

Maestro Guglielmo Bechi was a Florentine who in early youth joined the Augustinian order. He studied grammar, philosophy and theology, and by his talent became a good scholar. He studied at Paris, where he excelled in the seven liberal arts and in theology, which he handled with great subtlety in disputation. He preached at Florence and elsewhere and attracted large audiences of the learned and others, because he had the gift of pleasing all. He lectured on Aristotle, logic and philosophy, and on feast days he was appointed to read the Epistle of S. Paul. He was naturally eloquent and spent his time in reading, composing and preaching. He became general of the Augustinian Order, and in France, in Germany and in England he showed the value of his teaching, and throughout Italy as well. On his return to Rome, where he was highly esteemed, he was appointed to the vacant see of Fiesole, and after he was appointed and relieved of the care of the Order he had leisure to write his Commentary on Aristotle's Ethics, a work highly esteemed, and also one on the Economics. He wrote many sermons of various sorts, some for Lent and some for festivals, all of which won the approval of the learned. He wrote and bought many volumes to form a library, which is now in the Convent of S. Spirito at Florence ; also he gave certain volumes to the library of S. Maria del Fiore, where his name is written to preserve his memory. In this praiseworthy manner he spent his time. He died in Florence and an honourable funeral was granted to him, at which a sermon was given by Friar Marino of Rome, a brother of the Osservanza. His life was a virtuous one, and many citizens attended his funeral to honour his memory.

Bishop of Corone

Maestro Bartolomeo Lapacci of the Order of S. Dominic was born of poor parentage in Florence. He knew Greek and Latin and the liberal arts, and had such a wonderful gift of preaching that great crowds would go to listen to his sermons. He was famed for his learning, which few friars of his time could equal, and men of all classes went to hear him. He stood high in the favour of the court, and in the city or in the country he was always well received. He possessed a good store of Greek and Latin books and wrote many excellent sermons. He died in Florence, where he was honourably buried, having left some books to the Convent of S. Maria Novella, where he was a friar. His see was a very meagre one, so he spent his life in poverty and in righteousness. He made a name in the disputations during the Council of the Greeks in Florence.

ARCHBISHOPS AND BISHOPS

BISHOP OF CAPACCIO

He was Francesco Bertini of Lucca and Bishop of Capaccio in the Kingdom of Naples. He was associated with the Cardinal of Portugal, a most saintly man, who was greatly devoted to him, and after the death of this cardinal he went to the Cardinal of Ravenna, who, when he went to Naples, took with him Francesco Bertini. His good qualities induced the King to give him the vacant bishopric of Capaccio, and to send him as envoy to the King of England, where he remained some time in high favour with the court. Afterwards King Ferdinand sent him as ambassador to the Duke of Burgundy, who received him graciously, and during the terrible siege of Nuits the bishop was in camp with the Duke. One day a number of men were condemned to be hanged, whereupon the bishop, who was most humane in temper addressed the Duke, saying : " Sire, it is a barbarous act to put these poor men to death," and the Duke gave him a strange answer · " The Italians have a saying that dead men cannot fight." Said the bishop, " This is a ribald jest and not the speech of wise men." In a few days more than a hundred men were hanged without reason given. The Duke of Burgundy had some virtues ; he was abstemious and thus gave a good example, but he had the great vice of cruelty, and for this reason God willed that he should be killed by an unknown hand in battle, and left naked on the field. He would never have been recognised had it not been for a youth who had been in his service and remembered a mark he had under one arm. While the bishop was at the court with the Duke he underwent much discomfort and fell sick and died in Burgundy while still a young man. He was a shrewd and noble politician, and superior to most writers of his age. As he was always moving from place to place he left few writings. Had he lived longer he would have taken a high place.

BISHOP OF IMOLA

Messer Gasparre of Bologna belonged to the Observantist Order of Dominicans and was Bishop of Imola. In the time when Pope Eugenius was in Florence he was famed for his learning, especially the moral philosophy of Aristotle's Ethics. A great gathering of learned men and of the court and of the citizens as well attended his lectures daily at the university, and at the palace of the Podestà gatherings for disputation were held. Messer Gasparre, being a man of subtle and powerful intellect, was always the victor in these contests. At this time there was excellent teaching in every faculty on account of the great number of learned men who were assembled. The Abbot of Cicilia and Messer Ludovico from Rome were the chief lecturers. Also Maestro Gasparre, Nicolao Nicoli, Giannozzo Manetti and Messer Carlo d' Arezzo, and all the learned men of the age. Besides his learning he was a man of the gentlest life. He wrote certain books, but as I have no knowledge of them I will make no comment. This I will leave to those who may know them better than myself.

BISHOP OF VOLTERRA (CAVALCANTI) (*d.* 1449)

Messer Roberto Cavalcanti, a remarkable man of good descent, was a legist and canonist : famous in all the universities of Italy where he had studied and taught. He had attained such a high standing, apart from his worth and learning that, when it was necessary at Rome to appoint an auditor in the Ruota, they chose Messer Roberto Cavalcanti out of the great crowd of distinguished men of the faculty ; and in these elections they do not merely look a man in the face, but choose him for what he is worth. He discharged his duties so well that he won great approval and, had he not died early, he would, by public report, have become cardinal.

BISHOP OF VOLTERRA

Messer Antonio degli Agli was learned in Greek and Latin and a man of saintly life. He was governor for Pope Paul when Pope Eugenius was in Florence, for Eugenius, before he became cardinal, had recommended him as a learned and upright man. As soon as Paul became Pope he summoned Antonio to Rome, where he gained great power. When the bishopric of Fiesole became vacant the Pope gave it to him, and afterwards offered him Raugia, which he declined because, situated as he was, he could not reside there. This roused the Pope's anger, for he deemed Antonio was pusillanimous, and it was believed that but for this matter of Raugia he would have been made a cardinal. When the bishopric of Volterra was vacant the Pope gave it to him and also reserved for him S. Maria in Pruneta, because it might be said that he had restored it. He cared nothing for state and spent most of his time there, going occasionally to visit his bishopric of Volterra. He lived with great simplicity and spent his time between the Divine offices and reading and writing.

His income was expended in helping the poor to the honour of God, and few went away without succour. He spent not only the stipend of S. Maria, but also whatever remained of the income of his see. He wished to act justly and righteously. The revenues of S. Maria in Pruneta were large. He was doubtful of his own power to conserve them wholly now, and fearful that after his death the benefice might go *in commendam* and the Church lose her dues, wherefore in his lifetime he appointed nine chaplains, each with a suitable income and residence provided out of the parish revenues ; the wages of those who served the office were also to be paid. He endowed a canonry in S. Maria del Fiore to be filled by a member of the house of Buondelmonti, and at his death nine hundred florins to maidens of the same house who might wish to enter a monastery. He left an excellent name, both in life and habit, for he had lived as a good prelate ought to live ; no one was more studious and efficient. He was an excellent preacher and often spoke from his own pulpit. I have seen a Life of the Saints by him in which each saint is placed in order for the whole year. This book he dedicated and presented to Pope Nicolas.

THE BISHOP OF MASSA (DATI) (*d.* 1471)

Messer Lionardo Dati was a Florentine of good family who in his youth studied letters and produced some excellent

THE BISHOP OF SIPONTINO

work. He had fine taste and wrote well both in verse and in prose, and had good general knowledge of things. He was gentle by disposition and loved by all his fellows, specially Messer Antonio degli Agli. He held many benefices, the last of which was the bishopric of Massa. He was secretary to Pope Paul and was greatly liked as the head of the Segnatúra of letters, all of which passed through his hands. He had come to Rome in the time of Pope Pius, who highly esteemed him. Pope Paul discouraged simony and decided that all about him should do likewise. Messer Lionardo won the Pope's favour through his sincerity and diligence in secretarial duties. He was patient and won the favour of the Pope and cardinals so fully that had Pope Paul lived he would have become a cardinal. He showed much kindness to his household and to all Florentines.

I will now relate an anecdote. One day he went, according to custom, with a lapful of letters for signature by the Pope, who was sitting by the fire. The Pope asked him what he wanted, whereupon he answered that he had letters for signature. The Pope for some unknown reason took all the letters and threw them into the fire. Lionardo, seeing what had been done, put on his spectacles and stared at the fire. The Pope asked him what he was doing. " I am just looking at these letters blazing." The Pope laughed at this and seemed quite easy in his mind. Of Messer Lionardo's works I have only seen one, *De bello Etrusco*, a very elegant composition. He wrote epigrams and was a clever versifier. He left a modest patrimony which he had earned by zealous work at the court, where he was secretary during the whole pontificate of Pope Paul. He was an experienced courtier, who filled a high position during two pontificates, but it was Pope Paul who raised him to fame in recognition of the guidance he gave in affairs of weight which came before him.

BISHOP OF SIPONTINO (PEROTTO) (*d.* 1430)

Messer Nicolò Perotto, born of poor parentage, was learned in Greek and Latin, having been sent in his youth to study under Guerino at Ferrara, where by his ready intellect he

ARCHBISHOPS AND BISHOPS

soon became a fine scholar and master of an elegant style in writing. While he was at Ferrara, William Gray, Bishop of Ely, and of royal descent, was also a student there, and, having been told of the good qualities of Messer Nicolò, he asked him to lodge with him. He was so conscious of the virtues of Nicolò that he gave him as much as he needed for the purchase of books. After several years of assiduous study had passed, the King of England wrote to Gray and directed him to go to Rome as his proctor, whereupon he took Nicolò in his train. Here Gray was fully occupied with his duties, and Nicolò, being anxious to go on with his Greek studies, although he was already well versed in the language, begged his patron to arrange with Cardinal Niceno* that he might acquire still fuller knowledge of it. When he learned Nicolò's wishes Gray procured his admission to the cardinal's house when he was twenty years old. Here he studied Greek day and night till he became a profound scholar, and the cardinal, who was greatly attached to men of worth, showed him much favour and affection. He ultimately determined to become a priest, and by the cardinal's aid he got a benefice. His father was very poor, but Nicolò, who enjoyed certain emoluments and was able to live well, managed to have him made a *cavaliere* whereby he obtained an income from the state. Thus he was able to do good service to his family.

Messer Nicolò won great honour at the court for his writings, and the beauty of his style. Pope Nicolas, having seen some of his compositions, begged him to translate *Polibio Megalopolitano* from Greek into Latin, which work he executed with such skill that all who read it were astonished, declaring that no writer during the present pontificate had written with such elegance and erudition.† He then presented it to the Pope, who, when he saw it, was so greatly pleased that he gave Nicolò a purse of six hundred ducats. This work was of such excellence that, when it appeared in Florence, Messer Poggio and other scholars of the time praised it highly. It happened that, before this, Messer Poggio had differed sharply with Messer Nicolò, but now—so great is the power of truth—he was constrained to praise it unreservedly, saying he had

* *Vide Life of Cardinal Niceno*, p. 137.
† He also wrote the *Cornucopia*, a commentary on Martial.

never read a finer or more coherent style. This work brought him fame at the court of Rome and throughout Italy. He spent several years in Rome and had charge of the household of the Cardinal of Niceno. Nevertheless, he still found time for study, and when the bishopric of Sipontino became vacant the Pope gave it to him. Then, when he had established a suitable household for himself, he found posts for his father and all his brothers. He translated several works of S. Basil, *De Odio et Invidia*, Plutarch's *De fortuna populi Romani et Virtute Alexandri*, and others. He wrote a book on the rules of verse, and a grammar for the use of Latin students. Last, he wrote a great and intricate work on all the Latin and Greek authors which, though he called it the *Commento di Marziale*, is really an alphabetical list of all Latin writers, and much longer than the ten books of Livy, a work which he was able to complete without grammar or vocabulary so great was his knowledge of Latin. He wrote it at the request of the Duke of Urbino, who afterwards preserved him from disaster. Up to the time of Pope Sixtus Nicolò was very prosperous, and was nominated to several state offices, but this Pope at once began to persecute him ; to lay hands on him, to rob him of all he had and even worse. And if the Duke of Urbino had not remembered him favourably and had not come to his rescue—like a protector of all men of merit—he would have fared badly. As it was Nicolò was only saved because the Duke had a strong hold over the Pope. Nicolò was in no respect culpable, he was only attacked through envy and jealousy. He lost heavily through this molestation and, finding himself debarred from all enjoyment of the fruit of his labour, he fell ill of grief and died. He left a number of writings which are not mentioned here.

It happened that Nicolò Perotto had been with Sixtus in the household of Cardinal Niceno, and from this Perotto's misfortunes arose. Sixtus had been made cardinal through Niceno's influence, and in the course of his intercourse with Perotto, who was the head of the establishment, it is almost certain that ill will was generated which led to the subsequent persecution by Sixtus after he became Pope. While Sixtus was with Niceno he was a friar and a master in theology and reader to the cardinal.

ARCHBISHOPS AND BISHOPS

Heretofore notice has only been given to popes, rulers, cardinals and bishops who have been concerned with Italy. Now we will deal with certain foreign bishops worthy of commemoration who have lived in our time.

THE BISHOP OF ELY (GRAY) (1408–1478)

Master William Gray, an Englishman of the royal house,* was sent by his parents to study logic, philosophy and theology at Cologne, where there is excellent teaching in all these faculties. Here he remained several years, studying most diligently ; and, being of royal descent, he kept a fine retinue of servants and horses. Having spent some time there and acquired a good knowledge of logic, philosophy and theology, he felt a desire to learn something of the humanities, which he knew he could only gain by going to Italy. When the time came for him to leave Cologne it was necessary for him to order his departure with the greatest caution, because he was reputed to be a very rich man, and one who might pay a very high ransom ; moreover, there were many in Cologne who were on the watch for his leaving, designing to attack him somewhere on the road. Also the country was full of minor barons, and travel was dangerous. From the reports which were brought to him he decided on a plan by which he might travel in safety. It seemed best to him that he should feign illness, and should call the physician to visit him every day and then unknown, with a single companion, should steal away in the garb of Irish pilgrims. Meantime he arranged that the physician for the next seven or eight days should visit his apartment regularly. Thus the plan was settled with his physician that, as he was a foreigner, it was important that these doings should be kept secret. Having thus agreed with the physician and the people of the house, he chose a companion, and the two, carrying staves and clad in cloaks such as the Irish wear, left Cologne unknown. The physician followed up his visits for eight days, until they should have passed the regions where danger awaited them, and by this prudent stratagem he escaped peril.

* There is no evidence that Gray was connected with the royal line.

THE BISHOP OF ELY

When he arrived in Florence he sent for me and told me about this adventure. He ordered many books, which were transcribed for him, and then left for Padua to carry out his studies in the humanities. After he had been some time in Padua he was advised to go to Ferrara, where Guerino, a most learned man, was then teaching, and thither he accordingly went. After he had settled himself there he attended Guerino's lectures as a pupil, and there met a certain Nicolò Perotto, a young man twenty years of age and very learned. As Gray wished to have in his house some young man of letters he offered to receive Messer Nicolò, who, being very poor, willingly assented and rendered excellent service to his patron. During Gray's residence in Ferrara he caused to be transcribed for him a great number of books in the classics, in philosophy and in theology. At Padua, at Cologne and at every other place he visited he did the same, and his large collection of fine ancient books, and those others which he caused to be copied for him in divers places, were the origin of a noble library which he afterwards founded in England.*

After he had spent several years over his studies at Ferrara they wrote to him from England bidding him go to Rome as King's proctor, and as he had now finished his studies in the humanities and had shown the fine fruit of his scholarship he repaired to Rome, taking with him Messer Nicolò Perotto, who was anxious to continue his studies, especially in Greek. Perotto begged his patron to arrange for his reception into the establishment of Cardinal Niceno (Bessarion) so that he might satisfy his love of Greek letters. Gray was willing to further his advancement and so arranged matters with the cardinal that Perotto should be received into his house. From this arrangement sprang the rich harvest of Greek scholarship which Perotto produced, and likewise the subsequent rise of his family—as I have noted in my commentary on his life.

He gained much fame and popularity during his sojourn in Rome because, being a kinsman of King Henry who then ruled England, he was in high favour. It happened that the bishopric of Ely in England fell vacant, and the King having besought the Pope on his account, he was named bishop of

* At Balliol College, *vide* Introduction, p. 4.

that noble diocese. For several years he remained at the court of Rome enjoying the good opinion of all men, and when afterwards, on a summons from his own land, he returned to England, he was given the post of counsellor near the King. So great indeed was his reputation that he became one of the King's most trusted advisers, and held his post several years. When the discords broke out between the two parties he retired to his bishopric in order to stand aloof from either side, as became a bishop. After King Henry's death and the depression of his party, Master William Gray kept close to his studies and to the governance of his diocese, which he ruled in such wise that the peace was always kept, and his life was passed in honour and respect. There he founded a very noble library of all the faculties, which soon before his death he bequeathed to his successors with whom it remains to the present day.

THE BISHOP OF VICO

Messer Cosimo, Bishop of Vico, was datary of Pope Calixtus and, as he was a very able man, had almost entire control of the pontificate. He was jurist and canonist with a great knowledge of theology and the other faculties. I was one day with the bishop when we discussed certain matters, and especially the mistakes made by great men, mistakes which are not corrected because no one has the courage to speak of them. I then heard that when Calixtus became Pope he knew nothing but the Civil and the Canon Law; moreover, being an old man, he had not the solid judgment necessary for one who has to bear the burden of the pontificate. He succeeded to Pope Nicolas of happy memory, who was such a lover of letters that he collected books of every branch of learning, both Latin and Greek, from all parts of the world. When Calixtus became Pope, and saw such a wealth of fine books, many of them bound in crimson and silver, he was astonished, for he had never seen books bound except in canvas. Well might it be said of him, as is said of the legists, that a mere legist or canonist, without any other learning, is a man quite deficient of general knowledge. When he saw these noble books, instead of praising the wisdom of this

THE BISHOP OF VICO

worthy Pope, he simply said, " I now see how he has lavished the substance of the Church of God." He then began to throw away the Greek books, and gave several hundred volumes to Cardinal Ruteno, who was old and mentally deficient. Many of these books fell into the hands of servants and fared badly, and some which had cost many florins were sold for a few carlines. He also gave away many of the Latin books as of no value. This is the fate of precious things when they fall into the hands of those who do not appreciate them, and it was the same with the precious stones and pearls and jewels which Pope Nicolas had collected, many of them of great value. One day Messer Borges, the Pope's nephew, visited the Pope who was foolishly fond of him ; the Pope sent for the bishop and bade him bring out some pearls which he gave to Messer Borges. Later on the bishop saw these pearls sewn on the hose of Messer Borges. However, after the death of the Pope, Borges fared as badly as he deserved.

When the bishopric of Girona became vacant Pope Calixtus gave it to Cosimo, against the wishes of King Giovanni,* who desired it for Messer Giovanni de' Margheriti. The bishop, although he was otherwise an easy-going man, in this matter stood firm ; he would not renounce his rights and the King would not grant possession. Cosimo was a gentleman of Barcelona, where he had many relations and friends, and he was partly responsible for the revolt of Barcelona against the King, with whom he would never come to an agreement. This quarrel was the cause of much misery and misfortune to the country, and the people of Barcelona had other differences with the King, because he would not observe their privileges. When Pope Calixtus died the bishop went to Barcelona to take up his bishopric, but the King was still obdurate, and on account of this insult Cosimo, being in Barcelona, used all the influence he possessed to bar any agreement between the King and the people. The King was determined that Messer Giovanni Margheriti should be bishop, and he prevailed, because the Pope on whom Messer Cosimo depended was dead, and the new Pope was obliged to seek the favour of the King. Cosimo was a worthy man, but over-obstinate. He wrote many books in Italy, which he took with

* John, King of Aragon and Navarre.

him to Spain : and many of the books of Pope Nicolas, which had been given to Catalan gentlemen by Pope Calixtus, were also taken to Barcelona. On the death of the bishop the bishopric, as it has been said, remained with Messer Giovanni Margheriti.

THE ARCHBISHOP OF STRIGONIA

Messer Giovanni, Archbishop of Strigonia, by birth a Slavonian, was learned in all the liberal arts and a great theologian, acquainted both with the ancient and the speculative schools. Before he became archbishop he was so highly esteemed by the people of his country that he could do as he pleased in the state. While King Ladislas* was in Bohemia in 1457 a quarrel arose between the Count of Cilia and Ladislas, one of the sons of the Vayvode John Huniades ; they came to fighting and the Count of Cilia was slain by his opponent. The King, when he heard it, was greatly enraged and caused Ladislas to be beheaded in public, and imprisoned Mathias his younger brother, who is now King. When King Ladislas died of poison in Bohemia in 1458, Mathias was released from prison, and passed into Hungary, where, by the influence of the archbishop, and of the spiritual and temporal lords, he was proclaimed King. It was commonly reported that the archbishop, by the power he wielded, was the cause of this movement. How different was the fate of the two brothers, one was beheaded, the other was made King by the archbishop's help. Great services are usually repaid by ingratitude. When the King had attained this unexpected dignity he, knowing the archbishop to be a wise man, committed the whole government of the country to his hands, so that nothing should be done without his judgment and advice ; the King had so much faith in him, that a day rarely

* Ladislas Postumus, son of the Emperor Albert IV. He was born in 1439, and, though he was under the guardianship of the Emperor, Uladislas of Poland, seized Hungary, which was further divided by the factions of Corvinus and Cili. Corvinus died in 1455, and soon after his son Ladislas killed Count Cili in a brawl. King Ladislas then ordered Ladislas Corvinus to be beheaded and imprisoned Mathias his brother. In 1458 the young King went to Prague for his marriage, but died suddenly with some suspicion of poison. *Vide* Comines' *History*, B. vi, Chap. 13.

passed when he did not visit the archbishop, or the archbishop the King.

The archbishop was a God-fearing conscientious man, and zealous for well-doing in all things. One of the first of his acts was to collect a magnificent library, for which he gathered books from Italy and all other countries, and many which he failed to find he caused to be transcribed in Florence regardless of cost, provided they were fine and carefully revised. He enriched his country by bringing thither all the books he could find either original or translated, and there were few Latin books which he did not possess. But this was not all; he sent many youths to Italy for study at his own charges, furnishing them with books, money and all they wanted. He was as eager for Greek learning as for Latin, for amongst others he sent to Ferrara, to study under Guerino, Messer Giovanni, Bishop of Fünfkirchen, a good Greek and Latin scholar, and apt both in prose and in verse composition. Giovanni was one of the most estimable men this country ever produced, as will appear in his Life. Next the archbishop founded a faculty at Buda and brought thither the most learned men of Italy, rewarding them munificently. He also introduced many painters, sculptors, wood-carvers and men of every art, thereby elevating his country, which up to his time had been in a backward condition. Having initiated all these good works and filled his house with men of distinction, he took care that his establishment should be well ordered, civilised and religious. He encouraged virtue and fought against vice everywhere, his name was well known throughout the kingdom and Italy as well, especially in the court of Rome, and, on account of his high reputation, he would certainly have been made a cardinal had he lived.

Let all those who trust in good fortune beware of calamity. The King, like most other rulers, altered his system of government. He disregarded the advice of the archbishop, and followed that of a German ecclesiastic who had been one of the archbishop's underlings. He was, however, a man of little weight, and, according to public opinion, unfit for such duties. When the archbishop found himself superseded by a subordinate, he was ill-pleased, and felt that he did not deserve such treatment. Nevertheless, he temporised the best he could, but his former influence declined day by day, chiefly because he often censured this man's doings before the King with good reason, seeing that he was obnoxious, not only to the archbishop himself, but to all men of condition in the land. When he found that he had lost the King's favour, and that everything was in the hands of this bishop, he could bear it no longer, that such ingratitude should be shown to him by a king who owed to him his throne. He determined that the King should know he was still of some account, and began to have dealings with the King of Poland* by way of making him King of Hungary as well. The King of Poland was a powerful monarch, and seated on the Hungarian frontier might become a very dangerous foe. Thus the archbishop persuaded him to set a large army in motion, whereupon Mathias perceived that his kingdom was in jeopardy, and no remedy forthcoming. When he realised his peril, he tried to make peace with the archbishop, and put himself entirely in his hands, declaring that, if the King of Poland would retire he would give every possible satisfaction. But the Bishop of Fünfkirchen, who had been brought up in Italy and knew the treachery of men better than the archbishop, who was somewhat credulous by nature, sent word several times to him, begging him not to trust Mathias or he would be deceived, and affirming that, as soon as the King of Poland should have retired, he would find himself in evil case. And this warning he sent not once but several times. In his danger and perplexity Mathias could think of nothing else than to beseech the archbishop with oaths and promises to persuade the King of Poland to retire, and in this he ultimately succeeded. Now Mathias was aware that the Bishop of Fünfkirchen had urged the archbishop not to intervene in these negotiations, and this unfortunate young man, foreseeing what would happen to him through the anger of Mathias, fled the kingdom although he was ill with fever at the time.

Mathias, finding himself freed from immediate danger through the retreat of the Polish army, began to consider how he might once more persecute the archbishop, who foolishly had let the King of Poland depart without taking any other guarantee for his own safety than the word of Mathias, who

* Ladislas III, King of Poland, 1440.

delayed not the execution of his purpose for, while he was at
Buda, he summoned the archbishop thither, promising him
a safe conduct, but, as this did not satisfy Messer Giovanni,
he proposed further stipulations. These were sent by a special
messenger and the archbishop at once set out for Buda.
The King, as soon as he heard of his arrival, caused his house to
be surrounded and ordered his arrest, not considering that
he was an archbishop and a most worthy priest, nor his
promised word, nor that he owed his kingdom to him, nor his
royal faith, nor the safe conduct which he had given and
violated. The unfortunate archbishop was seized and taken
before the King. When he saw how he had fallen from good
to evil fortune and was now a prisoner, he began to despair.
Now most bishops possess well-guarded castles where a watch
is kept for their safety, and the castle of the Archbishop of
Strigonia was one of the finest in the world. He had built
it himself for security, and had fitted it with fine apartments,
one of which was a magnificent library, and in this castle all his
possessions were collected. The King caused him to be sent
a prisoner to Strigonia, and went thither himself to seize upon
his castle. The archbishop bade the castellan deliver up the
place, but this man scornfully refused. The King then made
a feint that he would kill the archbishop if the castle were not
surrendered, but the castellan remained obdurate. We may
imagine the archbishop's state. The castellan, a practical
man, refused to surrender the house unless the archbishop
should be freed. When the King saw that the castle was
very strong and only to be captured by negotiation, he
determined to win it by letting the archbishop go free, with
a few attendants and well guarded. The archbishop then
entered the castle which he delivered to the King. Although
he was allowed to live on in his own house under guard, he
only survived a few days, through this stroke of evil fortune,
the ill-faith of the King and through mental distress. He died
in great sorrow, and all his possessions came to the King.
Woe to them who trust the multitude ! The archbishop has
always been the friend and protector of all people, and in his
extreme necessity found no one to help him.

Let all men learn from his fate, and recognise in him a victim
of the caprice of fortune.

ARCHBISHOPS AND BISHOPS

THE BISHOP OF FÜNFKIRCHEN

Messer Giovanni, a Slavonian, was Bishop of Fünfkirchen and a nephew of the Archbishop of Strigonia, who, as he was needy, sent him at his charges to study under Guerino at Ferrara. He was a goodly youth of virtuous disposition, and during his sojourn at Ferrara won the goodwill of all who knew him. Men were astonished because he seemed to possess all the virtues and no faults. It might be said, not only that such an ultramontane had never come to Italy, but that no Italian of his age was his equal. By common opinion he had never known woman. In his studies of Greek and Latin he arranged his time so well that he never lost a moment, and was brilliantly clever both in Latin and Greek composition. He was famous not only in the university but throughout Italy. Many Slavonians have but slender wits, but this one outdid all his fellows and all Italians as well.

After mastering Greek and Latin and philosophy at Ferrara, the archbishop recalled him to Hungary to confer on him some favour adequate to his merits. He readily assented, but he determined first to visit Florence, which he only knew by report, and to make acquaintance with the many illustrious men who lived there in those days. After his arrival at Florence with horses and servants, the first person he wished to address was myself, because through me he could have introductions to the learned men of the city. He wore a purple mantle and was a distinguished figure, and as soon as I saw him I said, "Are you indeed the Hungarian? This is indeed a welcome moment. I feel that you must be, because from what I have heard of you, I seem to know you already." He then embraced me, and addressed me in the most gracious and apt words I have ever heard, saying that I had guessed aright. He then said that, for many reasons, he wished to visit Florence before returning to Hungary, especially in order to see Messer Giovanni Argiropolo, Cosimo de' Medici, Messer Poggio, Donato Acciaiuoli and all the other learned men. First he wished to see Cosimo, but as Cosimo was then at Careggi, I took Messer Giovanni with me and said that this Hungarian youth wished to have speech with one whom he already knew by fame. Cosimo immediately bade him enter his room and be seated. He then let all others retire, and after they had been together for a long time Messer Giovanni took leave of Cosimo and came out, and I entered. Cosimo told me that it had been a great pleasure to have spoken to this youth, who showed more good sense than any other ultramontane he had ever met, and that on no account would he have missed the chance of knowing him. Then he bade me do all that I could for him, adding that he would willingly second all my efforts. On the same day the youth went to see Messer Giovanni Argiropolo at his house, where were collected many of his scholars who were waiting for their daily lecture on logic. After they had exchanged greetings Messer Giovanni said he would like to hear this lecture on logic, and the lecture on philosophy the next day. He thought highly of Argiropolo's teaching and of the scholars (the fine flower of Florence) whom he saw around him. He spent much time with these as long as he remained in the city. On the following day he went to see Messer Poggio, and took with him forty verses which he had written the evening before ; these verses were much praised by Poggio and by all who read them, for he wrote in verse as well as he wrote in prose. He visited all the libraries in the city, and having bought many books, and transacted all the business he had in hand, he left with the good wishes not only of those who had spoken with him, but of all who had seen him.

From Florence he went to Ferrara to prepare for his return to Hungary, being urged thereto by the Archbishop of Strigonia. When he reached Hungary, he found the habits of these people very strange compared with those of the Italians, amongst whom he had sojourned, and although he was well received by the King, by the archbishop and by the notables, though his reputation could scarcely have been greater, he seemed ill satisfied with his position. He had, indeed, all the tastes and moods of a wanderer, and if it had not been for the persuasions of the archbishop he would have gone to settle in another place to which he had been invited on account of his reputation, but he yielded to the requests of the archbishop and remained in Hungary. At this time the bishopric of Fünfkirchen became vacant, an office of great importance. The King wrote in his favour to the court of Rome, the bishopric was bestowed upon him and he devoted himself to his duties with the greatest assiduity; nevertheless, all his spare time was devoted to literature. At this time the King of Hungary made several campaigns against the Turk, and in these the bishop always accompanied him, regardless of fatigue and discomfort in God's service. I have heard him say that when he was in camp with the King in December, it was necessary before leaving the tents to shovel away the snow. He busied himself to the utmost in good works, and thereby he gained the esteem of all men of worth, but the evil disposed viewed him with dislike and envy. One morning there was sent to his table a dish of roasted liver as a present by a certain prelate. Now Messer Giovanni was of a cautious nature, and at once suspected that it might be poisoned. He took a bit of the liver and threw it to a dog who swallowed it hastily ; then it began to swell and afterwards died. The bishop feigned to take no notice of this incident and threw the rest of the liver away, and kept silent in order to cause no scandal.

On the death of Pope Pius, Paul was elected, and on hearing this the King, who had only lately come to the throne, was obliged to send a mission to make his obedience. He was also anxious to send a distinguished envoy, so as to make a good impression in Italy and especially in the court of Rome, wherefore he chose the Bishop of Fünfkirchen, and the highest noblemen of his kingdom, and provided them with three hundred horses ; indeed, for many years there had not been seen in Italy so grand a train as this ; with such wealth of horses, or with such pomp, although many grand missions had been sent from all parts of the world. And for greater pomp the King saw that they took with them twenty thousand golden ducats packed upon two horses, all newly minted in Hungary and Venice, the finest money that was ever seen. They came here to Florence and were lodged in all the inns, to rest themselves and see the country. On leaving Florence they went to Rome and were met by the cardinals outside, and their entry to Rome was a wonderful sight. As the bishop was well known throughout Italy, the Pope gave him audience in public consistory, as is the custom, and then all the court

194

assembled to hear his oration. It was most worthy of the occasion, and never had the court heard one so well recited. All through his stay the bishop maintained his reputation for uprightness and ability. He then began negotiations with the Pope, requesting a subsidy for the King against the Turks and pointing out what the result of this would be, and what would happen if it were not granted. The King could offer no resistance without the help of His Holiness and other Christian powers. It happened that the papal chancellor, who had exercised strong influence over Pope Eugenius, had lately died and consequently there was a large sum of money available, wherefore the Pope was able to send to the King of Hungary some eighty thousand ducats. The Pope also agreed with the ambassadors to give a certain sum every year. The bishop won so much favour with the Pope and cardinals that whatever he asked for was granted at once.

He determined to collect a fine library, therefore he bought at Rome all the books in Greek and Latin he could find, in every faculty, and when he came to Florence he made further large purchases and was most liberal in his payments. When he departed he left several hundred florins for the transcription of those Greek and Latin books which he still lacked. Even when he was journeying, after having said the office, he would always be found with a book in his hand reading diligently. One day after he had dined with me he took a volume of Plotinus and went into the study and began to read. He became absorbed, as the matter was difficult to comprehend, and sat over it for three hours without stirring, and never lifted his eyes from the book ; not like other ultramontanes, who as a rule have no tastes for close study, but more like one of Athenian nurture, who had been brought under the discipline of Socrates. When he had shaken off his abstraction he turned to me and said, " If you wish to know how the Bishop of Fünfkirchen occupies himself, say that he does nothing besides translating Plotinus and attending to his bishopric." Having left directions in Florence as to what he wished to be done, he went to Ferrara, where he bought many more books, and did the same at Venice. He spent all his time most profitably either in study or in the society of learned men ; he cared nothing for fine clothes, nor for frivolous conversation. On his return to Hungary he was greatly honoured by the King and all the nobles on account of what he had done in Rome for the honour and profit of the King and for the interests of the Christian religion. Whenever it was necessary to send an ambassador to the Emperor, or to any other ruler on the King's behalf, he was chosen, and in any action against the Turk he would be amongst the first to take service. In Hungary he founded a fine library of Greek and Latin books of all kinds which he had purchased.

As in worldly matters, which are always unstable, differences arose between the Archbishop of Strigonia and the King, and the archbishop then encouraged the King of Poland to invade Hungary, only with the view of letting Mathias realise his error and folly. Mathias now found himself in great difficulties through this invasion and did his utmost to bring about the retreat of the Polish army through the influence of the archbishop, but when the Bishop of Fünfkirchen ascertained what was going on he bade the archbishop to beware what he did for the King, otherwise he would find himself deceived. The bishop was a very prudent man and saw plainly the end which he had to seek, but the archbishop, under bad advice, listened to the King's persuasions. At this time the bishop was ill with tertian fever, and could not confer with the archbishop and persuade him to alter his policy, but even before the King of Poland had retired he foresaw, beyond doubt, what would happen. The archbishop procured the retreat of the Poles, and this was the cause of his ruin. When the bishop saw what had happened he had great fears for the future. He was aware that the King knew of his intervention and advice given to the archbishop, so, ill as he was with fever, he left Hungary for Slavonia, and through the discomforts of the journey and fever the unhappy bishop died on the way. Thus in a short space of time both archbishop and bishop died miserably. These two had been the chief ornaments of the kingdom, and had drawn thither many men illustrious in every branch of learning,* who, now that they were dead, took their departure,

* The libraries of the Archbishop of Strigonia and of the Bishop of Fünfkirchen fell into the hands of King Mathias. This famous library was afterwards dispersed, many of the finest books going to the Vatican.

as the King would not grant them adequate remuneration
for their works.

BISHOP OF COLOGNA—A HUNGARIAN

Messer Giorgio, Bishop of Cologna, was brought up by the
Archbishop of Strigonia, who sent him to study the Civil and
Canon Law at Padua. Here he won great distinction and
gained the doctorate, and then, having mastered learning in
all its branches, returned to Hungary to reside in the house
of the archbishop, who esteemed him so highly that when the
Bishop of Fünfkirchen went as ambassador to Rome, Messer
Giorgio was one of his suite. During his residence with the
archbishop the times were troublous, and Messer Giorgio
showed such prudence and good sense that the King,* who
at first had been suspicious of him, realised that there was no
abler man about the court and found him indispensable.

He was sent as ambassador to the Emperor and other
princes, and later on to Italy when the Florentines were
attacked by Bartolomeo of Bergamo, wherefore he went to
Venice on behalf of the King to urge the Venetians to cease
this warfare, and when he was told that this war was not their
affair, but Bartolomeo's, he argued that such a costly enterprise was beyond Bartolomeo's ability and that, as he was
notoriously in their pay, he would not have acted against
their will. Moreover, the Venetian state required its commanders to obey closely all instructions given. He also
demonstrated that they had provoked this unjust war, that the
forces they could have used against the enemies of the faith
of Christ had been used against the Christians. Whether this
policy was just and honest he left them to decide. Moreover,
to make their intentions clear to all the world, they had sent
two commissaries into their camp.† And that before God and
the world there was never a more unjust undertaking than
this ; to have broken the peace which Pope Nicolas made
with such strong denunciations against those who should
violate it, saying, " You have been the first to break it." He

* Mathias Corvinus, 1458–1490.
† Manifestly the Turkish camp. This refers to the war of 1467
instigated by the Florentine exiles of 1434 and 1466.

proved all this by arguments which they could not answer, adding, as has already been said, that, if they had worked as strongly against the Turks as against the Christians, affairs would not have come to their present pass, and that their indifference in this Turkish war had given the foe new courage. They were compelled in the first place as Christians, in the second place because they had taken this obligation upon themselves at Mantua* and had offered to carry it out. He made every effort to avert this dishonour, but with little effect, as the Venetians were firmly set upon this enterprise. Seeing that he could do no good in Venice he went to their camp, but with no better result. He then went to Florence and told the Signoria of the mission sent by the King of Hungary to the Venetians, in favour of Florence, also of the obstinacy of the Venetians, and how it was useless to waste more time with them.

On leaving Florence he went to Rome in the time of Pope Paul, to encourage His Holiness to give support to the King in maintaining his army against the Turk, but the Pope was not in a position to take action ; he could only make promises, and finally they came to no decision. The King asked from Christendom one hundred thousand florins a year, offering to maintain an army against the Turk so strong that there need be no fear of him. After much time had been spent over this affair the bishop, like a wise man, saw that all these words led to no conclusion and urged the Pope to allow him to speak in the public consistory. This was granted, and one morning he went thither well furnished with arguments, showing that the Christians had never understood how to attack the Turk. That their attacks had always been made in such fashion which only gave the Turks fresh daring in assaults on the Christians, for if these necessary military preparations were made the Turk would no longer show such boldness. But all the attacks made hitherto by the Christians had been lukewarm, and of a nature to increase the stubborn valour of the foe. He went on : " The King of Hungary, my master, has many times been engaged with him ; with no more than twenty thousand men, he has always either broken his army, or put him to flight. Therefore, in order that your

---

* The Congress called by Pius II, 1459.

THE BISHOP OF COLOGNA

Holiness may understand what these Turkish forces really are, when we hear that he has a hundred thousand men in the field, we must remember that, of this hundred thousand, only twenty thousand or so are really fighting men ; the others, without firearms, carrying nothing but shields and bows and scimitars, are useless. So whenever the King of Hungary shall have twenty thousand Hungarians under arms, these hundred thousands of Turks, for the reasons I have stated, need not be reckoned." Messer Giorgio proved to the Pope and to the cardinals that if they would furnish one hundred thousand florins per annum there would be no need to bring the Venetians or any other power into the war.* He stayed in Rome for some time, endeavouring to obtain the cardinalate for the Archbishop of Strigonia, and to raise some of the money needed for the Turkish war. He was in full agreement with the Pope and the cardinals as to the elevation of the Archbishop of Strigonia, which would have occurred but for unforeseen accidents.

While he was in Rome he received letters from the King bidding him go to Naples to negotiate a marriage between King Ferdinand's daughter and the King of Hungary. This matter took little time, for with his prudence and dexterity he soon concluded this betrothal. He returned by the way of Florence, where he bought books to the value of three thousand florins for a library he was collecting for his provost-ship at Fünfkirchen. The King had already given him the chancellorship, and as all things passed through his hands he did what few men in his position have ever done. To the church of which he was provost he added a very noble chapel with four entrances, and four masses were said there every morning. He established certain festivals there every year, and provided that no one need be excluded therefrom. He gave a very fine library to the same church, in which were books of every faculty, three hundred volumes or more, and arranged them suitably. He put this library under the charge

* Pope Paul as a Venetian was probably lukewarm at this juncture. He was certainly more keen in attacking the Bohemian heretics than in beating back the Turkish advance, for, while Mathias was fighting victoriously on the Danube, the Pope directed him to transfer his army to Bohemia to punish Georg Poidebrad, who refused to extirpate his heretic subjects.

of a priest with a good salary, and saw that the church was well supplied with sacerdotal ornaments, psalters, bibles, homilies, books of martyrs and all others necessary for a church, and he desired that whatever dues were payable to him from this church might be remitted, and he did more than this; for all the money he received when he was Privy Seal he devoted to this library. When he returned to Hungary he found that his journey had cost him more than ten thousand florins. He had ordered cash to be sent to him from Hungary, but as this did not reach him in time he was short of funds. He was not in the habit of asking favours of anyone, but now he applied to certain people whom he had often helped for the loan of a good sum. For the loan of two hundred ducats they demanded a number of pledges, bonds and silver plate, but their conditions irritated and confused him so much that he refused to consent. Now I happened to know of a priest who had money and I asked him to lend the two hundred ducats on Messer Giorgio's good faith, so that he might understand that worthy and grateful men were still to be found in Florence, whereupon the priest put two hundred ducats into a purse and we went to the inn of Messer Giorgio, who was very uneasy in his mind. When we found him, I said : " I am loth that your reverence should be under obligation to anyone for two hundred ducats ; see here this worthy priest who will make the loan on your good faith." He seemed more pleased than he could say, and after he had despatched his books and other goods he started for Venice, where he found two of his servants with a good sum of money and at once sent it through a bank to Florence. Thus within fifteen days the priest's money was repaid.

When he got back to Hungary the King reappointed him Privy Seal, an office second only to that of the King. Whilst he held this office the bishopric of Cologna became vacant. The King immediately wrote to Rome and secured it for him. He was a liberal and high-minded man and his worth came to be proved, for he enjoyed the favour of the King, although he had been nurtured and formed by the Archbishop of Strigonia whom King Mathias persecuted ; and this was not to be wondered at, for of all his contemporaries whom the King might have employed not one was his equal. He had

the highest opinion of the bishop and he gave him his full
confidence.

THE BISHOP OF MILETUS

Messer Narciso was in high favour with King Alfonso. He
was of good Catalan family, and had an extensive knowledge
of philosophy and theology and was learned in all subjects.
He had besides a marvellous memory, for he could recall
everything that he read, quoting the right texts and where
they were to be found. He was a great talker, a man frank
and large-minded and one free of all deceit. After King
Alfonso's death he kept the favour of King Ferdinand and
could get from His Majesty anything he asked for. To a Diet
which was held in Germany and was attended by many men
of distinction, His Majesty sent Narciso, one of the best men
of his court, together with Messer Antonio Cincinello, a
polished courtier of gentle manners and fitted to deal with
the most important affairs. They passed through Florence
and remained there several days, as they wished to visit the
libraries and meet all the learned men who might be there.
As I have said before, Narciso's memory was miraculous.
As he went through the Florentine churches he condemned
the burials therein, saying that as the church of God was
pure and clean, it should not be defiled by dead corpses. He
declared that the regulars were the first who had adopted
this custom, and that the primitive Church discouraged this
indiscriminate sepulture, and even disapproved of the burial
of the saints. He proved this by a text from a decretal ; the
case of a bishop who asked leave of a Pope to inter the bodies
of two martyrs in his church, and was told that he might bury
them in the church porch, but nowhere else. But to-day
things are so much abused that they are ready to bury public
usurers anywhere, having respect to nothing, and making no
distinction between good and bad. I once heard him say
that he had known a man of such rare intelligence that he
could read the thoughts of others simply by looking at them,
adding that this was no new thing, but one well known to the
ancients. Hereupon he showed me a text of S. Augustine
taken from his book on Academics, in which he treated of

the providence of God, saying how one day when he was walking with two companions, they went to the house of one named Albicerio, their friend. This Albicerio had the faculty of prediction. To make trial whether his powers had been truly described to them, Augustine asked him if he could tell them what he had been doing this day. He said, "Yes," and began by telling one of them : " You have this day bought a piece of land and signed a contract for it," and other things which he had done, and so with all of them. Then, turning to one of them, he said : " Can you tell me what I am thinking of ? " The answer came that he was thinking of the beginning of the Æneid, "*Arma virumque cano.*" He divined everything, greatly to their wonder. Augustine asked one of his companions whether this was God's Providence or not, and he knew not what to answer. This is the faculty of reading a man's thoughts by his aspect.

When Messer Giovanni Argiropolo heard of Narciso's fame he went to see him at S. Jacopo in Campo Corbolino, where they held a long disputation chiefly on Platonic ideas. Narciso was at this time a licentiate, a most ardent and acute dialectician, and I do not believe that his age produced a more learned man than he was. After they had argued for a long time they went away together, and afterwards, when I was at Argiropolo's house, I asked his opinion of this licentiate, whereupon he replied : " He is the most learned man I ever met. No one ever understood Plato so clearly, especially that wonderful conception of ideas ; certainly none of the Latins approaches him." Narciso left Florence for Germany, where he had a mission to the Diet, and there he found assembled all the most learned Germans. He held daily disputations with these and won much credit both from the King and from his learned opponents. From the Diet he repaired to Naples, and the King gave him the bishopric of Miletus soon afterwards.

ALFONSO DI PORTOGALLO—BISHOP

Messer Alfonso was appointed governor to the Cardinal of Portugal, one of the royal house. He was chosen on account of his worth, his prudence and his great knowledge of the Civil and Canon Law, and had charge of his pupil from his tender years, so that by his judicious handling he might check the natural impetuosity of youth, but the pious disposition of his pupil gave him little trouble on this score. Messer Alfonso managed the household of the young cardinal, and no house in Rome was better kept or frequented by personages of higher merit. He remained with the cardinal until his death in Florence and saw to all his needs, temporal as well as spiritual. As it is written in his Life, the cardinal was a very Job in the matter of patience; he never complained, but bent to the will of God in everything. Much of his extraordinary merit came from the beauty of his character, but the bishop, by his good example and his righteous precepts, must have done much to lead him to live so virtuous a life. At his death the cardinal left the bishop his executor, charging him to carry out sundry pious works, though the property which he left—as he had enjoyed the benefit of it for so brief a time—came to very little. The cardinal desired that part of it should be given to God, and part to his servants as a reward for their trouble. He left equal sums for the payment of his debts and for the benefit of his household.

When the bishop had disposed matters after the cardinal's wishes he set about the erection of a chapel in the Church of S. Miniato, worthy of the cardinal's tomb. As there was no fund for this purpose the bishop spent some money of his own which he held in Portugal, and a handsome gift from the Duchess of Burgundy,* the aunt of the cardinal. He caused to be built the very noble chapel which may be now seen, and furnished it with fittings and missals and everything appropriate. He also endowed it with forty florins per annum, having secured the endowment on the rent of a house which can only be spent for payment of the friars who serve the chapel. But on any day when mass shall not be said at least twice, no money shall be paid to the friars. Thus the bishop has here set in order something the like of which is not to be found elsewhere. He was most careful in everything which concerned the soul of the cardinal, and his honour as well; and he was quite as zealous after as before his death. He was indeed a most excellent man. He remained in Florence until

* Isabel, wife of Philip the Good.

ARCHBISHOPS AND BISHOPS

he had settled the cardinal's affairs, and then, in the time of Pope Pius, went to Rome, where, through his merit and great knowledge as a legist and a canonist, he was made a regent in the Chancery, which office, one of great importance, he filled admirably.

GREGORIO, PRONOTAIO APOSTOLICO

Messer Gregorio, of the noble Venetian house of Corero, was nephew of the Cardinal of Bologna, also a nephew of Pope Gregory, a Blue Friar of Venice, who was made cardinal together with Pope Eugenius. This youth was a mirror of his age, in his tender years he was a pupil of Vittorino da Feltre, and reared in his house. He was handsome in person above all other youths, well versed in all knowledge, especially in philosophy, which he studied assiduously. In all his doings he gave a wonderful example, and with all his physical beauty and his courteous manners it was the firm belief of all who knew him that he remained continent. He always slept in a shirt of stuff with collar and cuffs of lawn. He gave a good example to the court of Rome, and he was likewise somewhat of an enigma to all who knew him. He wrote a wonderful style in prose as in verse, as may be seen in the works he left, especially in two addresses, one to Madonna Cecilia, the daughter of the Marquis of Mantua, one of the most beautiful ladies of her time, and still more beautiful in mind and disposition. Madonna Cecilia was betrothed to the young Duke of Urbino,* the predecessor of Duke Federigo. One day this young lady fled from her father's house to a convent of women, and disregarded all the prayers of her father and of Madonna Pagola, her mother, to return, remaining steadfast in her resolution. Messer Gregorio exhorted her to stand firm in her good resolve. His appeal was so noble that it was greatly praised by all; it seemed indeed that it might have been written by S. Jerome himself. This exhortation was so persuasive that, added to her own pious wishes, it confirmed her in her decision, a decision which she

---

* Oddantonio, the first Duke, whose death by assassination has never been explained. His illegitimate brother, the great Federigo, succeeded him in 1444. This marriage never took place.

maintained to her end, to her blessing and happiness. He wrote another exhortation to a youth who had been brought up in the house with him and had afterwards become a Carthusian monk. He composed many elegant verses. He was a great friend of Nicolao Nicoli, and loved him for his uncommon virtues, often saying, when talking of him, that whenever he went to visit him Nicolao would meet him with a book in his hand, and this he would give to him to read, and he behaved in the same way to many other distinguished young men who might visit him, for at this time there were many of these about the court of Rome and at Florence as well. When any young man might enter he would straight-way hand him a book and bid him occupy himself with it for a time. Then he would question him as to what he had been reading, and thus the youth would spend his time profitably.

Amongst the many cardinals who went from Rome in the time of Pope Eugenius, to the Council which had met at Basel for reformation of the Church, was the Cardinal of Bologna, an intimate friend of the Pope, and with him went as proctor Messer Gregorio, a young man of twenty. For this occasion he wrote an address, and when the Council had met he delivered it ; all who heard it praised it and he gained considerable credit therefrom. His way of life showed his virtuous disposition. He held *in commendam* the abbey of San Zenone, and in this abbey he established the Observantist rule, taking part of the income for himself and leaving the rest for the friars. When he found the ways of the court were not to his taste, he retired to this abbey and thus lived a holy life, and arranged that after his death the abbey should no longer be *in commendam*. Giving much to God, he spent very little on his own needs. His uncle, the cardinal, loved him very dearly for his good qualities, but as long as Pope Eugenius lived he could never gain for him the car-dinalate, although he was willing to resign his own hat if one should be given to his nephew. Pope Eugenius had taken a dislike to him, because he had gone to the Council of Basel, and would never change his belief that Gregorio had not gone there for the reasons he alleged. After the death of his uncle, the cardinal, the Bishop of Padua died, and the clergy unanimously sent a despatch to Rome asking for Gregorio's

ARCHBISHOPS AND BISHOPS

election, but the Signoria of Venice put forward Messer Fantino Dandolo, and wrote six letters in his favour, so that, as Messer Gregorio took no trouble in the matter and wished to possess his soul in peace, Pope Nicolas very unwillingly decided in favour of the candidate of the Signoria. Thus he lost the bishopric. Another benefice became vacant and was assigned to him, but whilst the documents were on their way, he passed out of this life, unburdened by any spiritual cares. We hope that he is now in a state of bliss, his life having been praiseworthy in all respects.

THE ENGLISH PROTONOTARY APOSTOLIC *

Messer Andrea Ols was an Englishman, and for a long time King's proctor. He was a man of the highest repute, both on account of his great learning and of his holy life ; indeed, I have known few foreigners who were like him in their habits and way of living. He was acolyte to the Pope and was well liked by all on account of his goodness. He spent the time in worthy fashion ; in saying the office, after which he would remain in his chamber with locked doors, on his knees in prayer for two or three hours. The rest of his time he would spend in reading holy books, and he kept by him a vast number of scribes who copied for him many books which he intended to take back to his church in England. After Pope Eugenius quitted Florence, Messer Andrea remained there entirely for the sake of the books on which his heart was set. Moreover, he was fain to have done with the court of Rome and to devote himself to the saving of his soul. Messer Andrea went counter to the ordinary ways of men in flying from fame and honours and in looking after his own affairs : for with his worth and goodness and with his widespread reputation, he might not only have been made a bishop but might have become cardinal. But he always avoided pomp and dignities, especially the bishop's office with its care of souls.

* " Orator quidam Britannici Procutorque Regis, nomine Andreas, Florentiæ relictus est. In quo multa quidem egregia laudeque dignissima esse discerentur ; multæ doctrinæ vir, et qui ante illa tempora diu in Gymnasio Britanniæ fuisset." Muratori, *Rerum Italic. Script.*, XX, p. 546. His name was Andrew Hollis. *Vide* Introduction.

THE ENGLISH PROTONOTARY APOSTOLIC

Amongst his other qualities was pity towards those in want, and he gave alms freely in public and privately. His house was so well ordered that all who stayed there had to look carefully to their carriage, for its ordering was a very religion of life, and in manners, an example of modesty and temperance, Messer Andrea having given up the English custom of sitting four hours at table. He lived in the Italian fashion, taking only one dish, and he and his household fared very soberly. He greatly favoured men of learning, especially those of good lives.* One morning during his stay in Florence he made a feast and he invited thereto Messer Giannozzo Manetti, Messer Carlo d' Arezzo, Matteo Palmieri and other learned men, as well as certain merchants his friends, amongst whom were Roberto Martelli. They debated many questions, and Messer Giannozzo was bent on maintaining the following proposition, " that all things which stand in the canon of the scriptures are the same as the truth, just as a triangle is a triangle ; that is to say, two straight lines and one drawn across." He met with much opposition, backed by the most subtle reasoning, but he always held firm to his conclusion, and after long argument his opponents found they could not resist his contention. The English envoy and all those who were present were amazed at what they heard, and when the disputation was finished he thanked Messer Giannozzo most courteously and bade him join his party at supper. From what I gathered from him later he regarded Messer Giannozzo as an extraordinary man with a wonderful knowledge of the scriptures and of all other matters besides a great skill in debate. In taking leave Messer Carlo d' Arezzo said to Messer Andrea that he need not wonder that Matteo Palmieri had not spoken, for he had kept silent out of respect for those who had.†

Messer Andrea lived in Florence more than a year and a half, during which time he bought, and caused to be written for him, a vast number of books in order to carry out his

---

* " Is quum in hanc incideret cupiditatem, ut doctis omnibus convivium pararet, qui sedes suas Florentiæ posuere, præter ceteros Jannotium invitavit una cum multis aliis apud se cænaturum," *et seq.* Muratori, *Rerum Italic. Script.*, XX, p. 546.

† Palmieri was suspected of heresy on account of a passage in his book, *Città di Vita. Vide Life,* p. 418.

worthy aims. His books being too numerous to be sent by land, he waited the sailing of a ship, and by this means he despatched them to England and then, his task being finished, he went also. On his return he withdrew at once from all secular affairs and betook himself with his books to a benefice which he possessed, putting aside all temporal cares as one who wishes to be dead to the world for the love of God. He was careful in his devotions, prayers and fasting, and in the remembrance of all who were in want, and in repairing such churches as needed. But many who should have praised him were ready to censure him, for in their eyes he had been placed where he worked in opposition to their opinions.

FRIAR AMBROGIO

He was a friar of Camaldoli, born of poor parents at Portico in Romagna. He entered the Order of the Agnoli in his early years and remained for a long time in the seclusion of this observance. He first studied Latin and then Greek under the tutelage of Emanuel Grisolora, who had come from Greece by the assistance of Messer Palla Strozzi, Antonio Corbinelli and of other distinguished men. Having gained a good knowledge of both these languages, he began upon Hebrew and acquired it also. With this stock of learning he took to translating in a style which was equal to the best of that age. Also his life was holy, for in this monastery dwelt forty monks, most saintly men who were the mirror of Florence. Everybody held him to be virgin, through his having gone into this monastery pure and undefiled at an early age, and having lived for forty years in this cloister.

He gained fame by the sanctity of his life and by his learning ; indeed, no person of quality would visit Florence without going to see him at the Agnoli, because they would consider they had seen nothing if they had not seen Friar Ambrogio. He was humble by nature, small of stature, with a face of much charm. Nearly all the great citizens of that time would go to visit him daily, and at that time Florence blossomed with distinguished men, such as Nicolao Nicoli, Cosimo de' Medici, Lorenzo his brother, Carlo d' Arezzo, Giannozzo

FRIAR AMBROGIO

Manetti, Messer Paolo, Ser Ugolino and Ser Filippo. One day Cosimo de' Medici spoke to me in praise of Friar Ambrogio, and of his great knowledge of Greek letters, how once Nicolao and himself were with him when he was translating S. John Chrysostom on the Epistles of S. Paul, and, while he was translating, Nicolao, who was a very rapid writer, wrote it down in current script, but he could not keep up with the highly ornate translation which the friar was making without any emendations. Nicolao often said, " Go more slowly, for I cannot keep up with you." Two of these translations, written by Nicolao with scarcely any alterations, are now in San Marco, and Friar Ambrogio would have translated many more if he had not been hindered. In Florence he read Greek with many pupils, and Latin with the friars in the monastery. Also he read Greek with the friars Jacopo Tornaquinci and Michele, with the seculars and with Messer Giannozzo Manetti.

When Pope Eugenius came to Florence in 1433 he, having heard of the great learning of Ambrogio, made him General of the Order of Camaldoli, which was then vacant, and removed him from the Agnoli. This was much to the detriment of his studies, for it was more to his taste to devote his time to letters than to government, to which he was not inclined. At this time the Council of Basel showed itself hostile to the Pope, who, recognising the great abilities of Friar Ambrose, determined to send him as ambassador to the Emperor Sigismund, and to the Council of Basel, where he was received with due honour. Strange things often happen to men of mark, for even they are subject to error like the rest. When he asked to be allowed to address the assembled Council, a public audience was granted to him. At the Council there were many learned men, the greater part of whom had been drawn thither by the fame of this distinguished scholar. When he had come to the middle of his speech, he lost the thread of it. Finding himself in this predicament before so distinguished a gathering, he drew the written speech from his sleeve, found the place where he had erred, corrected himself and finished the oration without further impediment. Friar Ambrogio realised how full of risk these public appearances were to a learned man like himself, and how easily he might be defamed amongst so august a company, and how he might lose in one

ARCHBISHOPS AND BISHOPS

day what had cost him years of labour to gain. He was highly commended for the course he had taken in correcting his speech. After he left the Council he went to the court of Sigismund, where he expounded the object of his mission in an admirable discourse.

Afterwards he rejoined the Pope, who was greatly impressed both by his worth and his literary excellence, especially in translation. Ambrogio would never have translated works other than sacred, had it not been for his obligations to Cosimo de' Medici for the many benefits which he had received from him in the course of the work he had done at Cosimo's request. It may be said that Nicolao Nicoli and Cosimo de' Medici had a great part in bringing Friar Ambrogio to the position which he had attained. Nicolao aided him greatly by lending him Greek and Latin books, and by inducing Cosimo and Lorenzo his brother to help him in his needs. Friar Ambrogio, had it not been for Nicolao, would never have asked for anything because he was by nature timid. In the course of his sacred translations he did one of the sermons of S. Ephrem, which he sent to Cosimo, who then wished to have *De vita et moribus philosophorum* by Diogenes Laertius translated from Greek into Latin. As he knew that Friar Ambrogio only cared to translate sacred works, he enquired of Nicolao whether he thought the friar would undertake it. On being asked he demurred somewhat, as he did not think that it was a work suitable for him, but at last consented. While he was translating it (which he did in a very short time), one of his pupils told me that he complained on having to do such work. When he finished it it proved to be a fine translation, highly esteemed both then and now. He wrote a proem to it and sent it to Cosimo. After Pope Eugenius had left Florence and gone to Ferrara, he summoned thither the Greeks who had crossed over into Italy, in order that the errors of their Church might be corrected. They lived at Ferrara at the charges of the Pope, who required that they should join the Roman Church. After the outbreak of the plague at Ferrara, the Pope and the Greeks also withdrew to Florence and disputations were held in Santa Maria Novella, the Greeks on one part and the Latins on the other. A great number of distinguished men were present, amongst whom was Friar Ambrogio. There was also

an interpreter named Nicolo Secondino, a native of Negroponte, who had formerly been in the Venetian service and gone
as ambassador to King Alfonso. Sometimes when Nicolo
could not be present Friar Ambrogio acted in his place, for
there were no other two who had sufficient knowledge in both
languages for the task.

On account of his saintly life and learning he won great
reputation. Learned letters gathered new strength through
his studies ; it was firmly held by all men of learning that
Friar Ambrogio and Messer Lionardo had revived the Latin
tongue which had been dead and buried for a thousand
years or more. At that time there was no other writer who
could approach the friar and Lionardo ; although Petrarch
did much to revive Latin he never approached these two.
But the attitude of the two men was quite different ; Lionardo
of Arezzo always held himself to be the sole restorer of Latin,
but when he saw how rapidly Friar Ambrogio gathered fame
he took it badly and became jealous of the friar, especially as
Nicolao Nicoli, Cosimo and Lorenzo de' Medici and many
scholars showed favour to him, although this patronage was
against his wish and alien to his nature. He won so high a
place in Florence that no one of condition came thither without visiting him, introduced either by Cosimo, or Lorenzo, or
Nicolao. Lionardo heard of all this, wherefore afterwards,
although he and Nicolao had always been on most friendly
terms, though he had dedicated to him his *Lives of Tully* and of
Demosthenes and many of his translations, though he had
named him on account of his learning and as the censor of the
Latin tongue, now from the envy which he felt in the matter of
Friar Ambrose, he was roused to such anger against Nicolao,
that he was led to write anonymously an abusive attack upon
him. This was the greatest mistake that Lionardo ever made,
and one for which he was deservedly censured. In the court
of Rome there were many men of weight, friends of Nicolao,
who were indignant and became violently hostile towards
Lionardo on this account. Some tell of an invective by Lorenzo
di Marco Benvenuti against Lionardo. I know not whether
copies were made of it. I have never seen one. Lorenzo was
learned and eloquent, but this was not enough for Messer
Lionardo, who fell into another error just as bad, by making

ARCHBISHOPS AND BISHOPS

a speech called *Contra hypocritas*, which everybody believed was made against Friar Ambrogio, who, however, was no hypocrite, for neither fame nor glory were ever sought by him. He had more care for the health of his soul than for anything else, as appears in all his doings.

Much more could be said of Friar Ambrogio.* He lived and died in holiness. Some years after his death I heard from persons worthy of credit how his body had been interred at a hermitage and planks laid over it by reason of the great cold, and when these were removed the public report was that miraculous flowers had blossomed though it was winter, and no air could have come to the earth over the grave because it had been covered by the planks. Here was a sign how God honoured his great merit.

---

* *Vide Epistles of Ambrogio Camaldolese* (Friar Ambrogio), with an introduction by the Abbate Mehus, 1759.

V : *STATESMEN*

Cosimo de' Medici (1389–1464)

COSIMO DI GIOVANNI DE' MEDICI was of most honourable descent, a very prominent citizen and one of great weight in the republic. He was well versed in Latin letters, both sacred and secular, of capable judgment in all matters and able to argue thereupon. His teacher was Roberto dei Rossi, a good Greek and Latin scholar and of excellent carriage. At this time many other youths of good station were his fellow-pupils : Domenico di Lionardo Buoninsegni, Bartolo Tebaldi, Luca di Messer Maso degli Albizzi, Messer Alessandro degli Alessandri and many others who came together regularly for instruction. Roberto lived in his own house, unmarried, and when he went out he was usually accompanied by the above-named, who were held in much esteem both for their good conduct and learning : moreover, Roberto would often entertain his pupils at table. He made a most excellent will which divided his large library of books written by his own hand—and he was one of the finest of scribes—amongst his pupils.

Returning to Cosimo, he had a knowledge of Latin which would scarcely have been looked for in one occupying the station of a leading citizen engrossed with affairs. He was grave in temperament, prone to associate with men of high station who disliked frivolity, and averse from all buffoons and actors and those who spent time unprofitably. He had a great liking for men of letters and sought their society, chiefly conversing with the Fra Ambrogio degli Agnoli, Messer Lionardo d' Arezzo, Nicolao Nicoli, Messer Carlo d' Arezzo and Messer Poggio. His natural bent was to discuss matters of importance ; and, although at this time the city was full of men of distinction, his worth was recognised on account of his praiseworthy qualities, and he began to find employment in affairs of every kind. By his twenty-fifth year he had gained

213

great reputation in the city, and, as it was recognised that he was aiming at a high position, feeling ran strong against him, and the report of those who knew roused a fear that he would win success. The Council of Constance, gathered from all parts of the world, was then sitting ; and Cosimo, who was well acquainted with foreign affairs as well as those of the city, went thither with two objects : one to allay the ill-feeling against him, and the other to see the Council which had in hand the reform of the Church, now greatly vexed by divisions. After staying some time at Constance, and witnessing the procedure of the Council, he visited almost all 'parts of Germany and France, spending some two years in travel. He hoped thus to let cool the ill-feeling against him which had greatly increased. He understood his own disposition which made him discontented with low estate, and made him seek to rise out of the crowd of men of small account. Many people remarked this tendency, and warned him that it might lead him into danger of death or exile. By way of lessening this resentment he began to absent himself from the palace, and to consort with men of low estate without either money or position, all by way of temporising; but his foes took this in bad part, affirming that what he did was a mere pretence to abate the suspicions of others.

While matters stood thus, about two years before he was exiled, there came to Florence Fra Francesco da Pietrapane, a man of the saintliest life, who, being well known to Nicolao Nicoli as a good man and a student of Greek and Latin, became also a friend of Cosimo. He called on Cosimo, and during his visit warned him to be watchful, for he would soon be in danger of death or of exile.* Cosimo, knowing the holiness of Fra Francesco, took good heed of this saying, and began to be greatly in fear. For he knew the character of the Florentines, and on this account he withdrew, as has been already noted, from frequenting the palace. But his foes knew in what high esteem he was held, both within and without the city, and how his fame increased every day. Wherefore they made a plan which proved the ruin of the city. The

* The charge subsequently made against Cosimo was one of embezzlement during the war with Lucca. During the operation against the city Filippo Brunelleschi was employed as an engineer to inundate the country around. Macchiavelli, *Flor. Hist.*, p. 205.

*borse** were closed and very few names were put in them for the gonfaloniers of justice ; indeed, in the quarter of S. Giovanni only two citizens were qualified for the office, Bernardo Guadagni and another. But Bernardo was on the *Specchio*,† wherefore some of his faction paid his debts in order to remove his disability, so that, by this means, they might bring about a revolution in the state and take off Cosimo's head. Bernardo consented to act as they desired. When the names were drawn, Bernardo was chosen, and when the Pratica‡ was held he followed up the plot and agreed with his associates to send for Cosimo and take his life.

On the eighth day of September, 1433, they sent to bid Cosimo come at once to the Signoria. On his way thither he met at Or San Michele his kinsman and friend Alamanno Salviati, who bade him not go, or he would lose his life ; whereupon Cosimo answered, "However that may be, I must obey the Signori," not suspecting their attitude towards him. When he arrived at the palace, without further parley, he was taken into a prison in the bell tower called the Berghettina ;˙ the Signori were still bent on making an end of him, believing that by no other means could they hold the government, so great was his power, within the city and without. While he was thus imprisoned, he learned the intention of his foes and feared greatly for his life, so he refused to eat any of the food that was brought to him, in order that they should not poison him.. While things were in suspense, some of Cosimo's friends tried to induce the gonfaloniere to spare his life and banish him, and they promised five hundred ducats if he would do this. The heads of the faction who had elected the gonfaloniere clamoured for the execution of Cosimo, pointing out that, if through kindness he should be spared, he would soon be recalled from exile and would prove their ruin ; but the gonfaloniere prevailed with his associates to spare Cosimo's life, and let him be exiled to Venice. Thus it came about that Cosimo and Lorenzo with-

---

* The bags in which were placed the names of those qualified.

† This was the book in which were inscribed the names of those in debt to the state. They were ineligible for all office. Cf. Macchiavelli, *Flor. Hist.*, p. 211. London, 1905. Sismondi, *Republiques Italiennes*, IX, p. 58. The money was found by Rinaldo degli Albizzi.

‡ *Vide* Appendix.

drew to Venice ; and certain other citizens, including Puccio and his brother, to Aquila. In this year, 1433, on the eighth day of September, they altered the form of the state. They proposed a Balia* and held a scrutiny, keeping the *borse* open for several months. Then they set up the Balia and closed the *borse*.

Now Cosimo being exiled his enemies in Florence used every means to ruin his credit both in Rome and in the city. But his wealth was so great that he was able to send to Rome enough money to re-establish his position. In fact, his credit increased vastly everywhere, and in Rome many who had withdrawn their money brought it back to his bank. In Venice Cosimo was held in the highest esteem, and those who had banished him—men of no reputation and with no idea of order in the state—did not realise that they would have to deal with such a powerful foe. They were new to the art of government, having had no practice in the same, and knew not how to rule. When trouble arose they soon changed their course, desiring to return to peaceful ways and let the city resume its tranquil and comfortable life in which no one citizen had more power than another, except those who had been placed by lot in posts of dignity. And though they had established a Balia and closed the ballot, they now ordered another scrutiny which deprived no citizen of his privileges, but gave them to all who had a right thereto. While Cosimo tarried at Venice, he was greatly esteemed by all the Venetians, who determined to despatch an ambassador to encourage the Signoria and those in power to recall him from exile. They began to favour him in divers ways, secretly, and to arrange for his return ; and as many in Florence were on his side, before a year had passed they made a plan to procure his recall by the help of the Prioratot which was friendly to

* After the restoration of the Guelfs in 1382 the dominant party found it necessary to set up occasionally what came to be known as a Balia. It was the temporary delegation of sovereignty to an assembly of citizens of varying number and elected by open voting. It could be elected for any period. The last Balia was called in 1466. *Vide* Appendix.

† When Rinaldo degli Albizzi found that this election had gone in Cosimo's favour he tried to annul it and make another Balia, but Palla Strozzi and other moderate men refused to support him. After the appeal to the Pope a new Balia was made which recalled Cosimo and exiled his enemies. Macchiavelli, *Flor. Hist.*, pp. 215–19.

him. At the end of the year his adversaries took up arms, being suspicious as to what might be the results of his return, whereupon Pope Eugenius, like a good pastor, appeared as a mediator to arrange a peace between the two parties of citizens. Those of the government of 1433, who had taken up arms, laid them down and submitted themselves to the good faith of the Pope. But though they were under the Papal guarantee, they were exiled after Cosimo's return. In this matter Pope Eugenius was deceived, for he believed that good faith would be kept on both sides and the city pacified.

Cosimo having come back to Florence, to the great satisfaction of the citizens and of his own party, his friends procured the banishment of divers of those who had opposed his recall, and of those who were neutral ; at the same time bringing forward new people. He rewarded those who had brought him back, lending to one a good sum of money, and making a gift to another to help marry his daughter or buy lands, while great numbers were banished as rebels. He and his party took every step to strengthen their own position, following the example of those of the government of 1433. In Florence there were many citizens who were men of weight in the state ; and, as they were friendly to Cosimo and had helped to recall him, they retained their influence. Cosimo found that he must be careful to keep their support by temporising and making believe that he was fain they should enjoy power equal to his own. Meantime he kept concealed the source of his influence in the city as well as he could. I have no wish to set down here everything that I could tell, for what I write is only by way of memorandum. I leave the rest to anyone who may write his life. But I say that anyone who may be fain to bring new forms into the state, that those who wrought the changes in 1433, brought ruin to themselves and to the state also. Many leading citizens, men of weight, never wished for these changes, declaring they had no wish to dig their own graves.*

Cosimo, after he had settled the government, called for a

* Macchiavelli, *Flor. Hist.*, p. 215. At this time, 1434, Duke Filippo broke the league with Florence by attacking Imola, and in 1436 Rinaldo degli Albizzi went to Milan to urge the Duke to war with Florence. Ultimately a peace for ten years was made between Venice, Florence and Milan.

Balia which banished many citizens. At this time Duke Francesco was in command of the allied forces of Florence and Venice near Lucca ; the two republics having agreed to share the cost of the soldiers' pay, but now the Venetians refused to contribute their part. Whereupon, after several letters had been sent in vain, Cosimo, as one highly esteemed in Venice, was sent to request the Venetians to hold to their promise and to pay the sum due to Duke Francesco.

On Cosimo's arrival all the citizens deemed that the Signory should take a new line and observe the promise they had made. Cosimo pressed his claims with the strongest arguments, but the Venetians kept obstinately to their view, for they were determined that the Florentines should not get Lucca without paying for it. When Cosimo perceived that they were set on this policy, and that they declined to recognise the benefits they had received, he grew to hate them on account of their bad faith ; so he wrote to Florence asking leave to withdraw and return by way of Ferrara, where Pope Eugenius had gone with all his court. When he arrived, he waited upon the Pope according to his commission and made complaint of the ingratitude of the Venetians. But Eugenius made light of this, knowing their character, and the College of Cardinals was of the same mind. From the way in which the Venetians bore themselves towards the Pope, they greatly roused his anger, as it appeared from what happened later. Cosimo went on several embassies and brought back great honour to the city.

Now Cosimo, having applied himself to the temporal affairs of the state, the conduct of which was bound to leave him with certain matters on his conscience—as is the case with all those who are fain to govern states and take the leading place—awoke to a sense of his condition, and was anxious that God might pardon him, and secure to him the possession of his earthly goods. Wherefore he felt he must needs turn to pious ways, otherwise his riches would be lost to him. He had prickings of conscience that certain portions of his wealth—where it came from I cannot say—had not been righteously gained, and to remove this weight from his shoulders he held conference with Pope Eugenius, who was then in Florence, as to the load which lay on his conscience.

Pope Eugenius had settled the Observantist Order in S. Marco ; but, as their lodging there was inadequate, he remarked to Cosimo that, if he was bent on unburdening his soul, he might build a monastery. After he had spent ten thousand without providing all that was wanted, he afterwards completed the monastery, spending more than forty thousand florins over the work. Beyond building the house he fitted it with everything necessary for residence. He gave all the musical books for the church and the greater part of those are now in the library, and furthermore provided the sacristy with everything needful for Divine worship. And because the Dominican brothers may not hold goods of their own, he paid all the charges of their life in common in order that they might enjoy their fine convent during their lives. For the daily outlay he settled with his bank what weekly sum should be paid to them, thus providing all they wanted. To save personal application to himself, much occupied with affairs, he gave orders to the bank that whatever sum of money might be marked on the bill should be paid and charged to his account.

As soon as he had completed the convent he wished to begin the church ; but he was anxious to demolish certain chapels with the full consent of those to whom they belonged, but in this he was frustrated, and accordingly he suspended the building. Cosimo did not possess books enough to furnish the library as it deserved, so the executors of the will of Nicolao Nicoli agreed to transfer to S. Marco all his books by way of carrying out the wishes of the testator, and letting the books be at the general service of all those who might like to use them. Moreover, in every book there was a note telling that the book was part of the estate of Nicolao Nicoli. Out of these books Nicolao left forty to the executors of his will, Cosimo and Lorenzo his brother. As soon as Cosimo got possession of Nicolao's library he went through the catalogue to see what books were missing. He searched everywhere for them and wherever he found them be bought them back, and in addition caused many more to be transcribed. All these charges for the library were defrayed by the bank on the order of Fra Giuliano Lapacino. When the library was finished as it now stands it did not satisfy him, so he was fain to add thereto all the books it lacked, but, being overtaken by death, he could not do this.

Having completed S. Marco he began to build at Mugello al Bosco a house of Observantist Franciscans, spending more than fifteen thousand florins over the convent and part of the church ; and, during this work, there came to him certain friars of Jerusalem who told him that their house, Il Santissimo Spirito, was in ruins and wanted rebuilding. Cosimo agreed to do the whole work, and he arranged through his house at Venice that the money should be paid according to the needs of the friars by a draft on his bank. They built there a vault over their church which they decorated, and anyone who may go to the Holy Land may see it with Cosimo's arms sculptured thereon. There is in Paris a college, called Florentine after a cardinal of our city who built it, standing beside the house of Bernardetto dei Medici. This college was almost in ruins, many repairs being needed, and likewise a well, so those in care of it applied to Cosimo, begging him to undertake these charges, to which he consented and did all the necessary work, which still remains.

Lorenzo, his brother, began to build S. Lorenzo, and in his lifetime completed the sacristy, a noble work, but left his task unfinished at his death. When Cosimo took up the work the first thing he did was to demolish the priests' lodgings, wretched hovels unworthy even of a country village, and to build new ones, which still exist. When he was questioned why he had began with the houses rather than with the church, he replied that, if he had not built them they would never have been done, whereas many would have undertaken the church for the sake of the honour to be gained thereby. He next set about the church and completed a good part of it before he died. At the same time he was engaged on the Badia of Fiesole, and while he was carrying out these two buildings one of his officials in the bank at Florence, in closing the accounts for the year, found that there had been spent on the Badia seven thousand florins, and on S. Lorenzo five thousand. He made this reckoning in order to alarm Cosimo and to induce him to hold his hand. He went to Cosimo and told him this, whereupon Cosimo answered, " I understand what you say. Those in charge at S. Lorenzo deserve blame

because they have done so little work, and those at the Badia
deserve praise because they have done more than the others."
Knowing that this official was ignorant and avaricious, he
wished to reprove him on both counts. Just then it chanced
that some of his friends went to visit him, for he was tied to
the house by gout, and he was full of complaints about this
official to whom he had just given a lesson in spending.
Cosimo was liberal in all respects. Over the lodgings at
S. Lorenzo and part of the church he spent more than sixty
thousand ducats, and then came the Badia, where he completed the lodgings, and a good part of the church which he
enlarged and decorated. He used all possible haste to complete this, but was always in fear that his time would be too
short.

He next considered how he might best gather together in
these lodgings a company of worthy and learned men. First,
he determined to collect a suitable lot of books, and one day,
when I was with him, he said : " What plan can you suggest
for the formation of this library ? " I replied that if the
books were to be bought, it would be impossible, for the
reason that they could not be found. Then he went on, " Then
tell me what you would do in the matter." I said it would
be necessary to have the books transcribed, whereupon he
wanted to know whether I would undertake the task. I said
that I would, whereupon he replied that I might begin when
I liked, that he left everything to me, and that, as for the
money for daily costs, he would order Don Archangelo, the
prior, to present the cheques at the bank where they would
be duly paid. He was anxious I should use all possible
despatch, and, after the library was begun, as there was no
lack of money, I engaged forty-five scribes and completed
two hundred volumes in twenty-two months, taking as a
model the library of Pope Nicolas and following directions
written by his own hand, which Pope Nicolas had given to
Cosimo.

First came the Bibles and Concordances with comments
ancient and modern. The first of the commentators was
Origen, who showed the way to all his followers. He wrote in
Greek, and a portion of his work, " On the five books of Moses,"
was translated by S. Jerome. There were the works of

STATESMEN

S. Ignatius the martyr, who also wrote in Greek, and was a pupil of S. John the Evangelist, most zealous for Christianity as a writer and as a preacher; those of S. Basil of Cappadocia, a Greek; those of S. Gregory Nazianzen, of Gregory of Nice his brother, of S. John Chrysostom, of S. Athanasius of Alexandria, of S. Ephrem the monk, of Giovanni Climaco, a Greek, and of all the Greek doctors which are translated into Latin, and after these came all the sacred works of the Latin doctors beginning with Lactantius.

As soon as the library was finished he provided the church with fitting books for the choir, and a fine psalter in many volumes. He gave hangings, missals, and chalices for the sacristy and all necessary utensils. The whole cost from what I have heard was seventy thousand ducats. At S. Croce he built the Noviciate with a chapel and a choir close to the sacristy at a cost of eight thousand florins or more, and he built his palace in the city from the foundations, spending sixty thousand ducats. At Careggi he built the greater part of what we now see and the same at Cafaggiuolo in Mugello at a cost of fifteen thousand ducats These works maintained many poor men who laboured thereon. There was not a year when he did not expend on building from fifteen to eighteen thousand florins, all of which went to the state. He was most particular as to his payment. He gave the contract for the building of Careggi to a master surveyor; and, by the time it was half done, Cosimo saw that before it should be finished the man would lose several thousand florins. So he said to the contractor, "Lorenzo, you have taken this work in hand, and I know that in the end you will be a loser of several thousands of florins. That was never my intention, but rather that you should make a profit. Go on with your work. You shall not lose, and whatever may be right I will give you." And he did what he had promised. Most men would have held that after the master surveyor had made the contract he should have kept it, but Cosimo with rare liberality thought otherwise. In all his dealings he never wished that those who worked for him should lose, but that they should be paid for their trouble.

I once heard Cosimo say that the great mistake of his life was that he did not begin to spend his wealth ten years earlier ; because, knowing well the disposition of his fellow-citizens, he was sure that, in the lapse of fifty years, no memory would remain of his personality or of his house save the few fabrics he might have built. He went on, " I know that after my death my children will be in worse case than those of any other Florentine who has died for many years past ; moreover, I know I shall not wear the crown of laurel more than any other citizen." He spake thus because he knew the difficulty of ruling a state as he had ruled Florence, through the opposition of influential citizens who had rated themselves his equals in former times. He acted privately with the greatest discretion in order to safeguard himself, and whenever he sought to attain an object he contrived to let it appear that the matter had been set in motion by some-one other than himself and thus he escaped envy and un-popularity. His manner was admirable ; he never spoke ill of anyone, and it angered him greatly to hear slander spoken by others. He was kind and patient to all who sought speech with him : he was more a man of deeds than of words : he always performed what he promised, and when this had been done he sent to let the petitioner know that his wishes had been granted. His replies were brief and sometimes obscure, so that they might be made to bear a double sense.

He had a very long memory which retained everything. One evening at home, when he wished for the love of God to give some more books to S. Marco—which books had lain for a long time in a press—he recalled all the books by name, and noted especially one of them, the *Digesto vecchio*, and said : " Make a note mentally that there is thereon the singular name of a certain German who formerly possessed it," remembering thus both the name of the book and of the German. When he came upon it he said, " I once owned it forty years ago and I have never seen it since." So great was his knowledge of all things, that he could find some matter of discussion with men of all sorts ; he would talk literature with a man of letters and theology with a theologian, being well versed therein through his natural liking, and for the reading of the Holy Scripture. With philosophy it was just the same, also with astrology, of which he had complete knowledge from having practised it with Maestro Pagolo and other astrologers. Indeed, he put faith in it, and always made use of it in his affairs. He took kindly notice of all musicians, and delighted greatly in their art. He had dealings with painters and sculptors and had in his house works of divers masters. He was especially inclined towards sculpture and showed great favour to all worthy craftsmen, being a good friend to Donatello and all sculptors and painters ; and because in his time the sculptors found scanty employment, Cosimo, in order that Donatello's chisel might not be idle, commissioned him to make the pulpits of bronze in S. Lorenzo and the doors of the sacristy. He ordered the bank to pay every week enough money to Donatello for his work and for that of his four assistants. And because Donatello was wont to go clad in a fashion not to Cosimo's taste, Cosimo gave him a red mantle and a cowl, with a cloak to go under the mantle, all new, and one festal day in the morning he sent them in order that Donatello might wear them. After a day or two of wear he put them aside, saying that he would not wear them again as they were too fine for him. Cosimo was thus liberal to all men of worth through his great liking for them. He had good knowledge of architecture, as may be seen from the buildings he left, none of which were built without con-sulting him ; moreover, all those who were about to build would go to him for advice.

Of agriculture he had the most intimate knowledge, and he would discourse thereupon as if he had never followed any other calling. At S. Marco the garden, which was a most beautiful one, was laid out after his instructions. Hitherto it had been a vacant field belonging to some friars who had held it before the reformation of the order by Pope Eugenius. In all his possessions there were few farming operations which were not directed by him. He did much fruit planting and grafting ; and, wonderful as it may seem, he knew about every graft that was made on his estates ; moreover, when the peasants came into Florence, he would ask them about the fruit trees and where they were planted. He loved to do grafting and lopping with his own hand. One day I had some talk with him when, being then a young man, he had gone from Florence—where there was sickness—to Careggi. It was then February, when they prune the vines, and I found him engaged in two most excellent tasks. One was to prune the vines every morning for two hours as soon as he rose (in this he imitated Pope Boniface IX, who would prune certain vines in the vineyard of the papal palace at Rome every year in due season. Moreover, at Naples they have preserved till this day his pruning-knife with two silver rings, in memory of Pope Boniface). Cosimo's other employment, when he had done with pruning, was to read the *Moralia* of S. Gregory, an excellent work in thirty-five books, which task occupied him for six months. Both at his villa and in Florence he spent his time well; taking pleasure in no game, save chess, of which he would occasionally play a game or two after supper by way of pastime. He knew Magnolino, who was the best chess player of his age.

It happened once that one of the chief citizens, having taken offence with Cosimo, complained of him to divers others. This, and much else which had not been said, was brought back to him ; but he held his tongue, and answered nothing to those who had repeated to him the slander which had been spoken of him. Because he was one of his greatest friends, he treated this citizen as he had never treated anyone else, for he sent for him and assured him that he was wrongfully aggrieved. And because he was a man of much weight, Cosimo addressed him thus : " You concern yourself with infinite, I with finite affairs. You raise your ladder to the heavens, while I rest mine upon earth lest I should mount so high that I may fall. Now it seems to me only just and honest that I should prefer the good name and honour of my house to you : that I should work for my own interest rather than for yours. So you and I will act like two big dogs who, when they meet, smell one another and then, because they both have teeth, go their ways. Wherefore now you can attend to your affairs and I to mine." On this occasion Cosimo spake more openly than ever before ; and the offence which this citizen took proved his total ruin through his ill-carriage, and his belief in evil advisers, wherefore the effect of Cosimo's plain speaking was not what he had intended, which was to silence this man and have no further speech with him. Certain rivals of Cosimo informed him that this citizen was still speaking against him, thinking to stir up enmity, and in this

STATESMEN

they succeeded. After Cosimo's death these same men set to work to injure the fame of Piero his son, now that the field was clear, as they would not have dared to do during Cosimo's life. Having made their attempt against Piero after his father's death, the whole affair came down about their ears. Had they gone to work more temperately it might have had a different ending and the city would not have been injured as it was by the parliament of 1466. But as to what then happened I leave others to write.*

Cosimo used the greatest caution in his answers, the mark of a prudent man. One day, when I was in his room, there entered one who had some dispute with another citizen who had offered him violence and had occupied certain of his lands. He complained vehemently to Cosimo who listened, keeping silence the while, but asked how recently he had visited these lands. He answered that he had just been there, whereon Cosimo said, " Go there often, take good care of them, and manage them well, and see that they want nothing." This cautious answer of his really meant that he knew nothing about the matter : but the petitioner replied, " See how honestly he has spoken in maligning no one. In saying you should go often to visit these lands which another has occupied, is to say that they are your own, and that you should defend your possession of them." All his answers were seasoned with wit. Many citizens came to consult him on their affairs, and one day came a man who had taken a wife and had been sworn to her several months. Meantime the dame's honesty came under suspicion, and the husband told the story to Cosimo and asked what he should do. Cosimo waited a little, and then said, " As to that horn which seems to you to be growing on your head, you had better swallow it, and then take a walk by the town wall. Then halt at the first ditch you come to, and, having brought up the horn, throw it into the ditch and bury it so that no one may see it." The man at once took Cosimo's meaning and, seeing that he had erred in talking about the business, kept silence afterwards and took the lady as an honest woman.

---

* The writer here refers to the attempt of Diotisalvi, Luca Pitti, Soderini, Agnolo Acciaiuolo and others against Piero in 1466. *Vide* Macchiavelli, p. 339 ; also Muratori, *Annals*, IX, p. 296.

COSIMO DE' MEDICI

While Fra Roberto was preaching to great crowds at the Osservanza, Cosimo showed him much favour, giving him liberal alms and denying him nought he asked, according to his practice towards all worthy churchmen. Fra Roberto had preached some time in Milan, where Duke Francesco had greatly honoured him and given him rich offerings. After this he changed his habits: he left the Observantists and took up a freer way of life. Duke Francisco gave him some Flemish cloth, very rich and costly, out of which he had made a fine cope and, having quitted Milan, he went to Florence, where he put aside spiritual things and lived in fine style as a layman. He waited on Cosimo, not knowing his humour, and Cosimo, having heard of his changed habits, no longer had the same feeling for him. He made Fra Roberto sit down beside him and, marking his sumptuous array, he put his hand on the fine cope which looked like silk and enquired, " Fra Roberto, what is this fabric ? " Fra Roberto answered that Duke Francesco had given it to him, whereupon Cosimo said, " I asked not who gave it to you, but what it was." Fra Roberto wrapped himself up and could not answer. After Cosimo had been minded to reprove him becomingly for the changed manner of his life, he drew near and, whispering in Cosimo's ear, begged of him the loan of two hundred ducats, but Cosimo, speaking fairly, told him he could not do this on account of the change in his ways. What he had formerly given was by way of alms : what he now withheld was by way of reminding Fra Roberto of his error. This reproof was given in such seemly wise that none of those present perceived it. But when Fra Roberto was gone he explained, becomingly, how obnoxious his present carriage was.

Cosimo was always liberal, especially to men of merit. The majority of men who affect letters, without any other profitable employ, are poor in goods ; men like Friar Ambrogio degli Agnoli, a man of religion, very holy and devoted to his order. Cosimo helped his monastery in all its needs, and a day seldom passed when he did not repair to the Agnoli, where he would find Nicolao Nicoli and Lorenzo his own brother, and would spend several hours with them. While Friar Ambrogio would translate S. John Chrysostom on the Epistles of S. Paul— as is told in his life—Nicolao wrote down what Fra Ambrogio translated, and, rapidly as Nicolao could write, he could not write fast enough for Fra Ambrogio's dictation and often was forced to beg him to go slower. This I heard from Cosimo who was present.

Nicolao had spent most of his substance in books and wanted for necessaries—as we may read in his Life. Cosimo, hearing of this, bade him not stint himself and told him that the bank had been ordered to advance him what he wanted, which the cashier would pay on receiving his bill. Nicolao duly took advantage of Cosimo's liberality ; most praiseworthy because it served the needs of so illustrious a man as Nicolao. During his life he drew from the bank five hundred ducats, thus making a good show before the world, which he could hardly have done but for Cosimo, who, when he went to Verona to avoid the plague, took with him no buffoons or heralds but Nicolao Nicoli and Messer Carlo d' Arezzo with whom he could discuss literature. Cosimo made no demand on Nicolao for the five hundred ducats, having always treated this loan as a gift, and in this fashion he succoured all good and learned men in their need. They are indeed good men who practise liberality like Cosimo.

I must not forbear to tell of his great generosity to Maestro Tomaso da Serezana, afterwards Pope Nicolas, while he was Bishop of Bologna, without income, seeing that Bologna had rebelled against the Church. Pope Eugenius sent him, together with Messer Giovanni Carvagialle, on an embassy into France, but being short of funds he could give them but little for the journey. Messer Tomaso being in Florence, I, as a scribe, went to see him, whereupon he desired me to wait upon Cosimo on his behalf to beg for a loan of a hundred ducats, because Pope Eugenius had not given him money enough for so long a journey. When I had done this errand Cosimo, without much consideration, said, " Tell him I will send to him Roberto Martelli, and will let him have what money he wants." I had only just returned to him when Roberto appeared with a general letter of credit to all Cosimo's agents, instructing them to pay to Maestro Tomaso whatever sum he might want and without limit. When Maestro Tomaso read of this unheard-of liberality—for he was only known to Cosimo by his good name—he expressed to Roberto his unbounded gratitude, in that more had been done for him than he had asked for, whereupon Roberto said that it was but a trifle granted on account of Cosimo's goodwill.

On his travels he drew two hundred ducats on his letter of credit ; and, on his return to Florence, found himself still in want of money to go on to Rome. There was a pardon at S. Giovanni and there Messer Tomaso met Cosimo coming out of church and thanked him for all he had done. He went on to tell him that he wanted another hundred ducats to take him to Rome, whereupon Cosimo said he would send Roberto with a commission for whatever he might want, and when he came Tomaso would accept no more than a hundred ducats. While he was at Viterbo a cardinal's hat was sent to him, and also one for his companion Giovanni Carvagialle, a Spaniard. Before the year was out he was made Pope, taking his title, Nicolas, from the Cardinal of S. Croce who had advanced him. After his election one of his first acts was to make Cosimo his banker in acknowledgment of the benefits he had received. In the year of Jubilee some hundred thousand ducats came to the Church, and Cosimo was well repaid for his generous accommodation. Cosimo had a beneficent eye, always friendly to men of merit, and knowing how to estimate their worth and to serve them. He was always ready to do what was asked of him, and besides he did much of his own accord.

When he was at Careggi he went to visit a very learned preaching friar, an Observantist Franciscan. He was much pleased with the friar's discourse and, at parting, asked him whether he had a Bible in which he could consult the texts which men brought out therefrom, to which the friar answered " No," whereupon Cosimo added that he would have more to say later. Meantime he bought a beautiful hand-Bible which he sent to the friar, begging for his prayers. This the friar accepted with much gratitude. It was through Cosimo's instrumentality that Giovanni Argiropolo came to lecture at Florence to the great profit of the citizens. He showed him much favour, and Giovanni often went to see him, because he did not then go abroad ; and on feast days, when he was free, Messer Giovanni and certain of his scholars would visit him. Cosimo questioned him on various matters : on the immortality of the soul and other questions of theology and

philosophy. Through long practice with men of letters
Cosimo possessed a sound judgment and his answers were
very satisfactory; but a man who could satisfy Cosimo
needed to be very skilful and discreet. One day, when Messer
Giovanni and Messer Otto Niccolini were with him, he asked
the first whether the writings of the jurisconsults were in
accordance with moral philosophy, or by what philosophy
they were inspired. Messer Giovanni replied that the writings
of the jurisconsults were to be put beneath those of the moral
philosophers, since they possessed nothing of the essence of
philosophy, but Messer Otto maintained the contrary, and
there was angry argument between the two. Cosimo was satisfied himself that jurisprudence must yield to moral philosophy,
but he was minded to hear Messer Otto's defence, which was
difficult to set forth, as it had to be proved by reasonable
argument. Finally the dispute was left in indecision; but
Cosimo was greatly pleased therewith and with the various
pleas employed.

He also befriended Marsiglio, son of Ficino, a man of good
talent and carriage and learned in Greek and Latin His means
were small, and to keep him from poverty Cosimo bought
for him a house in Florence and a farm at Careggi, giving him
thus income sufficient to allow him to live with one or two
companions, and generally to serve his need. A servant
of his had worked hard for many years at a wage agreed upon
of so much a month; and when incapacitated he paid the
man just the same, whereas many others would have just
given him house-room, or handed him over to some guild to
support. Cosimo was fain to support his servant out of his
own purse, not out of that of others, so he gave him a house
and farm out of which he might gain a living for himself and
his wife as a recompense for his labour.

Having spoken of the praiseworthy way of life followed by
Cosimo, specially in his management of things spiritual and
temporal as well as of those appertaining to the honour of
God, I will add that his fame was known throughout the world
so that all men of worship passing that way desired to visit
him. There was at Ferrara a bishop of Fünfkirchen,* a
Hungarian, a man of great learning and high station, who,

* *Vide Life*, p. 192.

having finished his studies, was recalled to his country, but was unwilling to depart till he should first have visited Florence and seen the three illustrious men who then dwelt there, Cosimo de' Medici, Messer Giovanni Argiropolo and Messer Poggio. When he arrived in Florence he told me he desired to see all three before leaving, and as Cosimo was then at Careggi I accompanied him thither. I told Cosimo of his wish, and introduced him, and the two conversed a long time. After the bishop had left, Cosimo told me he was the most remarkable ultramontane he had ever met. The bishop was greatly struck with Cosimo's marvellous presence and ready wit, saying that in all his life he had never conversed with a more extraordinary man. The presence of Cosimo took nothing away from his fame, which greatly increased, and numberless men of worship sought him through his world-wide reputation.

In his time lived many men of mark, both lay and cleric, and in literature of all sorts. They were to be met, not only in Florence, but in every part of Italy and foreign lands. First of all in his day lived Pope Martin, who reformed the Church of God which had long been vexed by schism and discord. Then came Pope Eugenius, and Pope Nicolas not inferior to either of these two. Outside Italy reigned the Emperor Sigismond, who held, besides the imperial dominion, the kingdom of Hungary, a valiant foe of the impious Turk, as is plainly manifest, because in his reign they were kept within their own limits and not suffered to oppress Christian people as in former days. Then there was King Alfonso, the paragon of the rulers of his time through the noble qualities which graced him, and Duke Filippo of Milan, who, though certain faults were blended with his undoubted merits, wielded such power that, when he was engaged with the Florentines and the Venetians at the same time, he gave them plenty to think about. To him succeeded Duke Francesco, a master of the art of war, who by his own strength made himself master of Milan. The Doge of Venice was Francesco Foscari, by whose valour and skilful policy the Venetians acquired almost all their territories on the mainland. Cosimo de' Medici was inferior to no one of those distinguished men in his remarkable qualities and outstanding merits.

STATESMEN

Fortune favoured him in all his undertakings. He had to deal with King Alfonso, who advanced with a powerful army against the Florentines ; and with the Venetians who were allied with Duke Francesco. Cosimo was always apprehensive of the effect of any further aggrandisement of Venice which would place Florence in peril ; so he did his utmost to prevent it. Duke Francesco saw clearly what the result would be if the Milanese failed to support him with supplies—as they afterwards did fail—because the Venetians had offered to Giannozzo Manetti at Rome, by the hand of their ambassador, Pasquale Malapieri, a blank treaty which they agreed to ratify, after it should have been set in order by the Florentines. After the business had been in hand some six months, Cosimo realised the situation and, because the Venetians had retreated into their own country, he felt he need not trouble further about them, and he was right in his endeavour to break their power. While Duke Francesco was fighting with the Venetians, Florence waged a successful war with King Alfonso and drove his army back over his borders.* At the end of this war there was peace for twelve years through Cosimo's skilful policy in bringing the Italian powers—especially in the case of Venice— to an equality of strength. Peace lasted as long as he lived, but as soon as he died† Venice again declared war on Florence, a step she would never have taken had he been alive. They despatched Bartolomeo of Bergamo with a strong army, so strong that His Majesty King Ferdinand and Duke Galeazzo and the Florentines with their combined forces had difficulty in resisting it. And as the Venetians realised that they were the victors in this expedition, they broke all their oaths and promises made by the mediation of Pope Nicolas : they also disregarded all his ecclesiastical censures, and paid no regard to any of these things. Having thus narrated these deeds of Cosimo by way of record, I have not been able to keep the same order I should have followed, had I been writing his Life, and on this account the details are set down irregularly ; but this record will suffice for future biographers, and will give them much information.

To return to Cosimo. It happened that a certain of his kinsmen—who indeed was very rich—never met him without

* 1448.　　　　　† 1464.

pouring out grievances, declaring that he was poverty-stricken, and every day he would tell the same tale. Cosimo made up his mind not to answer him so as to escape this worry, but one day, in the Piazza de' Signori, he met this kinsman who straightway began to repeat the same old tale. When he had come to an end Cosimo called him by name and said to him, " You are my kinsman, and nothing is more displeasing to me than your constant cry of poverty ; because the man who proclaims himself a pauper always suffers hurt thereby. Otherwhere than in Florence everyone makes himself out to be richer than he really is, but in Florence the custom is the opposite: so that a man gains in one respect and loses in all the rest, which is a grave matter. Reverting to your own case, can a man be called poor who has sixty thousand florins with the Lombards : who is concerned with trade in Rome, in Florence and in divers other places : who holds possessions, like you, on all sides, which you have bought regardless of price, outbidding all the rest : who builds sumptuous town and country houses : who lives in the state you and your family maintain with your horses and fine attire, the handsomest in Florence ? " Thus Cosimo laid the situation before him : he could make no reply as it was all true. This natural medicine cured him completely and he never grumbled again.

It happened that the surveyor of his building works cheated him of a large sum of money. Having investigated the business, Cosimo, like the wise man he was, did not fly into a rage, but simply withdrew the commission from the surveyor, and told him that he had no further need of his services, and that he had advanced to him as his agent a sum of money amounting to a hundred thousand florins. The story of this man and what he had done was soon spread all about the city ; men talked of little else, and wherever he went he met with blame. One day he met Cosimo, whom he had robbed and in my presence thus addressed him: " Cosimo, all over Florence men are saying that I robbed you and that on this account you dismissed me from the surveyorship of your buildings." Cosimo in his reply did not repeat that this man had robbed him (as indeed he had), but said, "What would you have me do ? " Said the other, " I would that should anyone ask you whether

STATESMEN

I had robbed you, you should answer, ' No.' " Then said Cosimo, "Get some one to ask me this question and I will tell the whole story." Some others, who were by, when they heard him began to laugh and said nothing about the matter, nor was anyone bold enough to comment on anything a man of worship like Cosimo might say. No other would have shown such great patience.

Cosimo used to say that in most gardens there grew a weed which should never be watered but left to dry up. Most men, however, watered it instead of letting it die of drought. This weed was that worst of all weeds, Envy, and that there were few except the truly wise who did not make shipwreck through it. In his latter days Cosimo fell into irresolute mood, and would often sit for hours without speaking, sunk in thought. In reply to his wife who remarked on his taciturnity he said, " When you propose to go into the country, you trouble yourself for fifteen days in settling what you will do when you get there. Now that the time has come for me to quit this world and pass into another, does it not occur to you that I ought to think about it ? " For about a year before he died his humour was to have Aristotle's Ethics read to him by Messer Bartolomeo da Colle, the chancellor of the palace, and he brought Donato Acciaiuoli to arrange in order the writings on the Ethics which he had collected under Messer Giovanni,* and when these came to Cosimo, Messer Bartolomeo read them to him, after emendation by Donato, and this emended text of the Ethics is the one now in use. Many other things might be told of Cosimo by one who purposed to write his Life, but I am not set on this task. I have only set down matters concerning him which I myself have seen or heard from trustworthy witnesses. I leave all the rest to anyone who may undertake the work of writing the Life of so worthy a citizen, the ornament of his age. What I have written is the actual truth according to what I have heard and seen, neither adding nor omitting anything. Whoever may put together this Life may be vastly more lengthy than I have been, and let things be more clearly portrayed.

* Giovanni Argiropolo.

PALLA DI NOFERI DEGLI STROZZI

PALLA DI NOFERI DEGLI STROZZI (1372–1462)

Messer Palla di Noferi degli Strozzi, of a noble family which has produced many illustrious scions, was notable for his high qualities and his knowledge of Greek and Latin letters. Devoted to literature he held it in the highest esteem and raised it to a position in Florence it had never before attained. Latin was far better known than Greek, which he determined to encourage and raise to an equal level. Wherefore he brought into Italy Manuello Grisolora, a Greek, and paid the greater part of his charges. As Grisolora had no books Messer Palla bought a number of Greek texts for him ; the *Cosmographia di Tolomeo* with illustrations, the Lives of Plutarch, the works of Plato and many more. Messer Lionardo made his translation of Aristotle's politics from Messer Palla's copy. Through Palla's introduction of Manuello Lionardo d' Arezzo, Guerino of Verona, Friar Ambrogio, Antonio Corbinegli, Roberto dei Rossi, Lionardo Gustini, Francesco Barbero, Piero Pagolo Vergerio, and Ser Filippo di Ser Ugolino, one of the finest Latin scholars of the time, became Manuello's pupils. Nicolao Nicoli also studied under him, especially in letters This was the rich harvest which sprang from Manuello's coming ; one which is being reaped to-day, which we owe to Messer Palla's generosity and noble mind. Messer Lionardo d' Arezzo said in praise of him : " In all the gifts, mental and physical, which made for human happiness he was more richly endowed than any other man of his time." He was a fine scholar in Greek and Latin ; he had marvellous ability and great personal beauty, so that if anyone, who did not know him, chanced to meet him, he would straightway exclaim : " This must be Messer Palla." He had a family of sons and daughters, the most seemly in Florence ; the girls having been educated by Madonna Marietta, the most accomplished woman of her time. They intermarried with the highest families as will appear from their pedigree. Neri di Donato Acciaiuoli, Francesco Soderini and Tomaso Sacchetti all men of high rank. Palla was highly esteemed in the city from which he received all possible honour. He was sent as ambassador on all the most important missions, and everywhere did well for the honour and benefit of the state. Beyond this he was scrupulously upright, and he ardently desired that his children might be the same. On this account he put them under the care of Messer Giovanni da Imola, and when the young people went about the city they were known to all from their distinguished carriage. When it was found necessary to improve the teaching classes in Florence, Messer Palla, from his well-known love of letters, was put in charge of the reforms which might give the city a good school of instruction. He at once set up classes for the study of the highest subjects, and the fame of the teachers he engaged attracted students from all parts of the world. From 1422 to 1433 Florence flourished greatly, rich in schools of learning and in illustrious citizens who strove to outdo one another in good works, and her good government made her feared and respected universally.

Messer Palla had always kept in his house learned and worthy tutors to teach his children; he set even more store on good manners and conduct than on learning. Besides Giovanni da Imola he engaged Messer Tomaso da Sarzana, afterwards Pope Nicolas V who had come from Bologna to Florence through poverty. Florence was a true *Alma Mater*, and he lived for two years in the houses of two generous citizens, M. Rinaldo degli Albizzi and M. Palla Strozzi. During this time he earned enough to enable him to return to Bologna and complete his studies ; and after he became Pope he was able to befriend the sons of his Florentine benefactors. Maso, the son of Rinaldo, was involved in a charge of rebellion, not altogether through his own fault, whereupon Pope Nicolas found for him an honourable office ; and Carlo, the son of Messer Palla, became the Pope's private chamberlain and shortly afterwards was made cardinal on account of his high qualities.

To return to Messer Palla. As a citizen he was habitually modest, and in all his dealings and in his public administration his chief care was to avoid envy, knowing how pernicious it might prove to be in a city like Florence, especially when incurred by men in high public position. He always avoided publicity. He never went into the Piazza except when he was sent for, nor into the Mercato Nuovo. In going to the Piazza, so as to avoid observation, he would go by S. Trinità and turn into the Santo Apostolo as far as the Via Messer Bivigliano. Then he would reach the Piazza and enter the Palazzo without delay. He never wasted time by loitering, but returned home after business and spent his time in studying Greek and Latin, Being greatly devoted to letters he bought a fine collection of books which he housed in a handsome building in S. Trinità for the use of the public. He wished to furnish it with books on all subjects, but this project came to nothing on account of the misfortunes which befell him.

Messer Palla's position in Florence was a fortunate one. His son Bartolomeo was one of the most charming youths in the city. His father held him dearer than any other of his children on account of his gentle manners and virtuous disposition. He profited rapidly from the teaching of the professors his father kept in the house, and soon showed a real taste for letters. But in his early youth he was stricken with illness and died in spite of all the efforts made to save his life. On account of the universal love and regard felt for him his death was greatly lamented in the city. All may realise how deep was the grief felt by Messer Palla at the loss of his beloved son, and all Florence knew that no heavier stroke could have fallen upon him. But being a wise man he saw that he needs must fight against his natural grief and show that he was indeed the man the Florentines deemed him to be. Having pondered this matter as a stricken father he determined to compose his soul in peace, seeing that there was no remedy, and that this stroke was the will of God towards some good end. He resolutely put his grief behind him, and would say to any who came to console him that he had taken leave of Bartolomeo, and that he had rather they should speak of him no more ; that what had pleased Almighty God must also please him. Thus he indulged in no vain repining, showing the greatness of his soul in this as in other matters.

Another trouble assailed him. He was so heavily taxed that his income did not suffice to meet his expenditure, wherefore he was forced to borrow money from divers citizens. His debts were eight hundred florins or more, and on this sum he repaid three *per mensem*, which was not enough. Therefore he did what every good citizen would have done. He went as ambassador to give his city the fruit of his judgment and to secure the payment of his debts.

He was the intimate friend of Giovanni de' Medici, with whom he went as ambassador to Venice, also with Cosimo— Giovanni's son. They met at Lucca in 1420 when they fled from the city on account of the plague. Now Cosimo had told him that if he was in want of money he could have what he wanted from the Medici bank, the officials having been instructed to pay him whatever money he might need, Messer Palla also authorised his bankers to repay this sum to the Medici when they wanted it.

Now as he had borrowed twenty thousand florins from the Medici, and divers sums from others, it seemed to him that he was spending excessively—not counting money paid for interest—wherefore he resolved to repay all his debts and get rid of the interest. There was in Florence a friend of Palla and Cosimo, by name Piero Bonciani, with whom Palla discussed this project, but Bonciani doubted whether there was the wherewithal to pay, considering the condition of Palla's affairs. Palla told Piero to ask Cosimo to meet him at the hospital of Lemmo on the morrow and that he would have ready all his accounts, so that he might be able to pay all his debts. One afternoon later on Bonciani met Cosimo and, in all good faith, told him that he would lose a good part of what he had lent. But Cosimo, who knew well the state of Palla's affairs, laughed and said, " I shall get every soldo that is due to me, and if he wants more I will let him have it." On the following day he went to the appointed place, and, having investigated Palla's estate, found he would be well off after all his debts should have been discharged. After the investigation Palla said to Cosimo: "I owe you twenty thousand florins, and now request you to pay no more money to my bank, for I will pay you this debt. There are my estates at Empoli and at Prato. You can repay yourself out of these." This Cosimo did, taking from these estates enough to reimburse himself. Palla did the same with all his other creditors. He owed money to Agnolo di Filippo Pandolfini who, as a kinsman, had helped him. Palla gave him parts of his estate and a house at Empoli, still held by the children of Messer

Carlo. So Palla paid all who had lent him money and was in debt to no one. He also paid a large sum to the Commune for the heavy debt he owed for tax.

Thus Messer Palla spent his life, prosecuting his studies, giving counsel to the republic, going as ambassador or serving with the Ten of the Balia whenever the state had need of his services. Florence had long been at peace, the people lived easy and opulent lives, and they soon began to desire to extend their boundaries and hence arose the attempt against Lucca which led to the gravest political discords. The best and wisest of the leaders were opposed to it, such as Messer Palla, Cosimo de' Medici, Agnolo di Filippo and many estimable citizens who had the interest of the state at heart. Those who desired it were led by Messer Rinaldo degli Albizzi and those of his party. Thus, from this clash of will, the city was divided and, as Messer Lionardo d' Arezzo writes in his *History*, the war with Lucca was the beginning of the civil discords and the cause of all the evils which befell Florence ; and Nicolo da Uzzano spake truly when he declared that the first man who should propose a public assembly would be digging a grave for himself ; therefore, as a wise man of weight, he opposed all changes in the state, foreseeing the evils which would follow.

After these troubles, Nicolo being dead, the Balia of 1433 was formed. Palla vehemently opposed its enactments, being certain they would lead to disaster, but the movement was too strong for him to withstand. It was set going by the great crowd of ignorant and turbulent citizens. This was the first trial of such a parliament in Florence, and these men were its promoters.* Palla recognised whither things were tending and the evil consequences which must follow ; so, being unable to do any good was unwilling to do mischief, he let the madness of the leaders run its course in the powerlessness to stem the calamity, as he surely would have done as a foe of all civil strife. In the end the parliament of 1433 banished Cosimo, and, but for Palla, would have done worse. In no case would he have assented to it, nor would it have been carried out if he had possessed enough influence with those

* Vespasiano forgot the Balia of 1378. *Vide* Macchiavelli, *Flor. Hist.*, p. 165.

who promoted it. Moreover, there was his friendship with Giovanni de' Medici and his son Cosimo, who had helped him in his difficulties as has been told. After Cosimo and the others had been banished the city fell into confusion and uproar ; the leaders of '33 seized power and closed the ballot and set up the Balia, wherefore Cosimo's party set themselves to win a majority at the next election of the priors and thereby to secure his recall. The leaders of '33, by way of giving an air of decency to the recent scrutiny, had not deprived all their adversaries of political rights ; and when '34 had come Cosimo's friends deemed that the time was ripe for his recall, and negotiated with those of the Signoria whom they could trust for the change of the state at the end of the year. When the leaders of '33 heard this they at once took up arms and bade their friends do the same. The Piazza was filled with armed men, and when Palla heard of this gathering he, like a man of peace, remained at home, fearing riot and rapine. He also asked that soldiers might be sent to guard his house. Messer Rinaldo now called upon Palla to join his faction with his armed troop, judging that this support would be greatly to his own interest and feeling sure of victory should Palla consent. But Palla steadily refused, saying that he had no mind to destroy what he had not made—to wit, the state, which Rinaldo's party were leading to certain ruin—and that he wished all men to know how entirely he disagreed with them and the changes on which they were bent.

There were some who made rude remarks about him because he refused to show himself, declaring he was poor spirited and that his abstention at this moment would mean his ruin. Palla held firm to his resolve, but certain of his kinsfolk, men of weight, urged him to refuse and to have no dealings with these madmen. To those who urged him on he replied that he had no fear of suffering hurt through well-doing , that, as they all knew, he had always kept clear of dishonour and had censured all those who might strive to provoke it. By this firm attitude he greatly weakened Rinaldo's position and influence ; indeed, it may be said that it was the cause of his downfall. Rinaldo's foes were heartened and his friends cast down. Not only did Palla injure Rinaldo's reputation, for, as this change was a new departure and all men were full of fear, those who would have joined the party of revolution, had Palla gone out, held aloof because he stayed at home. They saw it rested with him whether this party should conquer or be conquered. But he was ill-rewarded for all the good he accomplished. As things stood Palla's followers took courage and Pope Eugenius intervened to still the discord. He sent for all the leaders who had taken up arms and brought about a truce. A new Balia was formed and Cosimo and all those exiled by the last were recalled.

After Cosimo's return everyone thought that affairs would settle down, but the troubles caused by the first Balia were followed by many others. The majority of the citizens who were well disposed to him praised him highly for what he had done, and put him on the Balia as one who had done good service to the state. His mind was at peace and he suspected nothing, but the envy of his foes was too much for him. Having gained control of the government, they held a ballot and formed a Balia in favour of the Otto della Pratica and the captain of the forces. They also put on it Giovanni da Fermo, a brutal fellow. As soon as they thought the city was calming down, they began to exile certain citizens and to threaten others. All were greatly disturbed when they saw what was happening ; this violent seizure of the executive power and notice of a fresh election. By way of carrying out their policy of change they disfranchised a large number of citizens by a scrutiny, working for their private ends and having no regard for the welfare of the state. At this time there was in Florence a party of overbearing men who held that Cosimo was bound to recognise them as the authors of his recall, wherefore he was obliged to be patient, and wary in his carriage, as there were many others who could not keep a cool head. Messer Palla and many citizens made no move, for this fresh step was not what they anticipated. The city being in a state of confusion, and a large number of citizens having been banished (for they banished anyone they would), all good men fell under the displeasure of the dominant faction. Messer Agnolo di Filippo and Bartolomeo Carducci, kinsfolk of Palla, one day got information that the banishment of Palla was contemplated. As they knew the great service he had done in preventing the malcontents of 1433 from taking up arms by his refusal to join them, they were greatly astonished, and enquired indignantly of certain of those in power to hear whether the report was true. Those they consulted answered " No " by way of deceiving them, but at the same time advised Palla to retire into the country for a season, on account of the jealousy against him, and not to show himself in the city for several months. Agnolo and Bartolomeo believed this to be true and reported it to Palla.

Not long after this certain men made bold to say that no judge of appeal was wanted in Florence, and that it would be well to banish Palla, good citizen as he was. He had helped the city with wise counsel and financial aid—no one else paid so heavy a tax as his—but now this did not avail him. The hostile feeling against him was so strong that many of those in power consented to his exile so as to get rid of him, thinking that, were he out of sight, no one would be left to work to their detriment. Thus Palla and his son Noferi were sent into exile for ten years, innocent as they were. When Palla heard the length of the term he was grieved doubly over his son's fate, feeling that, if he himself were innocent, Noferi was doubly innocent.

He himself was sixty-two, an age when men desire to live at home with their friends and kinsfolk, nevertheless he still hoped that God might give him ten years more of life, and let him return and live in peace amongst his fellows, believing that he might placate the envy of his foes, but forgetting that those who injure never forgive. They exiled him to Padua, where he lived the life of a good citizen. He applied himself to letters, both Latin and Greek, living an upright life as did the philosophers of old. He always spoke well of his country and never complained of exile.

He left his son Lorenzo in Florence to manage his estates, for he hoped he had done nothing which would lead to their confiscation; but his good name did not avail him, for in the fourth year of his exile his foes banished Lorenzo as well. Heavy as was this second stroke of ill-fortune, it did not break his spirit, for he went on in the same course of life. Other injuries followed, perhaps with the object of lessening his love for Florence and his desire to return. I have lived long enough to see those who persecuted him fall into the same case—a fate they never anticipated.

It is thus that civil wars and revolutions are caused—wise men have said that our parliament may bring fifty years of ruin on a state. Palla, in his study at Padua, found a tranquil port after many years of shipwreck. He engaged at a liberal salary Giovanni Argiropolo to read Greek with him, and another Greek scholar as well. With Argiropolo he read Aristotle's *Natural History ;* and the other Greek read certain other works he selected. He wasted no time, but undertook the translation of Chrysostom from Greek into Latin. Noferi also attended these lectures and was a diligent student, rarely leaving the house, but when he went out all men honoured him by raising their caps. Whenever exiles from Florence might call upon him Messer Palla would always dismiss them, for he was determined no one should ever hear him speak disrespectfully of the city. When the Florentine ambassador to Venice passed through Padua he always waited on him and conversed with him. I heard Messer Giannozzo Manetti say that he could not sufficiently praise his good manners. When he went as ambassador to Venice he halted at Padua, where he met Messer Palla, who visited him constantly at his lodgings. He marvelled greatly to find Palla so courageous and cheerful and uncomplaining of his exile, scarcely deeming that he could be a banished man.

Thus Palla passed his ten years of exile, and at the end he hoped he had borne himself well enough to secure his recall, but the ill-will of his foes in Florence was active and they suspected that his presence would be an embarrassment to them. Having struck him once they determined to strike him again, and while he was hoping for a recall he heard that he was sentenced to a further exile of ten years. Still, he bore the blow with patience, but being now seventy-two years of age it must have been a heavy grief, seeing that he greatly desired to return. But his discreet carriage in the past availed him nothing. His patience failed him not, and he found comparative ease in his studies, putting his misfortunes aside. The second ten years of exile passed, and his foes were still unrelenting. When he heard that another ten years had been added he merely answered that he feared he would

STATESMEN

not have time to see them out. In addition to exile many other calamities fell upon him. His son Lorenzo was murdered at Gubbio by a Florentine. Heavy grief fell upon him for the death of his son, and despair that he was being left alone in his old age. Soon after his son Noferi, a youth devoted to learning and best beloved by his father, died also, and to crown his sorrow the death of his wife, who had always been most tender and assiduous in her care of him. Misfortune had not yet finished with him. All his hopes now rested in Carlo, his third son, who had been educated for the priesthood. In his present misfortune Messer Palla had little hope of advancement for any son of his, but a career in the Church, seeing that Carlo was a youth of learning and virtue, seemed to promise that he might restore somewhat the fortunes of the house. Moreover, Thomas of Sarzana, who had formerly lived in the house of Messer Palla, was now Pope Nicolas V, a lover of all men of merit, and Palla hoped that Carlo might succeed by the Pope's aid. Carlo went to Rome and prospered, as his father had anticipated. He won the Pope's favour at once and was made private secretary. He was greatly liked by the College of Cardinals and by all about the court, so much so that it was commonly reported that the Pope would cause him to be elected cardinal at the next vacancy. But it pleased God to call the youth to Himself. One can hardly realise what the grief of the father must have been at the loss of this beloved son on whom all his hopes were based. Reft of this last hope there was nothing before him but death, for there was none left now to restore the fortunes of his house.

After Messer Carlo's death he gave himself entirely to the study of sacred things, thinking no more of his earthly state and letting his mind rest in peace. When his exile had lasted twenty years and he was eighty-two years of age, they added ten years more to his term. After this long exile, after the deaths of his wife and sons, he thought no more of a return to Florence, and cared for nought but his soul's health. Realising the sorrows of this life, and that the final cure thereof was to turn to God, he applied himself to the contemplation of the heavenly life and to do everything a faithful Christian ought to do to make a good end. When he had reached the ripe age of ninety-two, still sound in mind and body, he rendered back

244

MATTEO STROZZI

his soul to God like a faithful Christian. If he had lived in the Roman republic when great men abounded, and if his life had been added to those of other illustrious men, it would have been equal to any. As no record of it has been written it has seemed to me fitting that one should be made—even in my humble way—so that the memory of such a man might be preserved as a model to those who are now living and to those who are to come. This example of the fate of an illustrious citizen of Florence should teach them not to trust too much to Fortune.

MATTEO STROZZI

Matteo di Simone degli Strozzi was of the highest birth. He possessed a wide knowledge of Latin letters, but, not contented with this, he devoted himself to philosophy, and, together with Antonio Barbadoro, Benedetto degli Strozzi, Alessandro Arrighi and other citizens with whom he was intimate, heard the lectures of Messer Giannozzo on the Ethics of Aristotle. In the city he won all the civic honours within his reach, and bore himself in a way which gained for him a good name. He devoted himself entirely to letters, was a man of the soundest judgment and widest views and was also of most generous mind. And as the fateful happenings of '34 were distasteful to him and to others not inflamed by factious spirit, he deemed that, as he had always borne himself temperately and had never supported any revolutionary action in the city, he had deserved well and never dreamt of exile.

It never occurred to him that he had done aught to deserve it. Thus, his conscience being clear, he sought to be made gonfalonier of justice, and knowing that the ballot bags were opened and would soon be closed, he went to the registrar of the district to consult him about being made gonfalonier, and this man promised him it should be done. Next he sought a known friend who lived in Santo Spirito for further advice, and, as they discussed the affair, his friend asked him whether he had talked of it to anyone in the quarter, and he replied that he had, and that he had been informed by the registrar that the affair could be carried through. His friend, like an honest man, replied : " Then he was deceiving you, because he was one of those who in the canvassing brought forward your name in order that you might be banished. This will be your fate before fifteen days have passed, and there is no help for it."

When he heard this Matteo was greatly surprised and declared he knew nothing to account for this step. His friend replied that he was grieved then, but that nothing could be done. Fortune had decided that he should be banished, and here was evidence how much envy could do against him. Envy, and not any offences he had committed towards the state, was the cause of his exile. He was a man of quality, and in his quarter there were few who could be placed before him, since he was born of noble and learned parents, a man of good name and reputation who might well have gone as ambassador and enjoyed any honour the state could confer, but for this exile. Moreover, it was greatly to his hurt that he belonged to the same quarter as those who, fearing lest he should outstrip them, helped to banish him. There were some others of his own house who, if they had followed his counsel, would not have fallen into the pit where they ultimately found themselves. He had a clear outlook in all matters, and in his time the house of Strozzi could count more men of weight than any other in Florence. I say nothing of those who lived in Mantua, or in Ferrara in his time : men of mark and of the highest merit. In Florence Messer Palla di Noferi, Messer Marcello degli Strozzi and Benedetto di Peracone. Also at Mantua Messer Roberto, a man of the highest station ; at Florence the Count Lorenzo, and Messer Tito and Noferi di Messer Palla, and Messer Carlo his son, who was highly learned and came near to be made a cardinal, as is told in the Life of Palla.

AGNOLO PANDOLFINI (1360–1446)

He was born of honourable parents, who by their upright life had become kin to the best in the state. He was learned in Latin and philosophy, both moral and natural, beyond most of his equals, for in his time few citizens had any such learning save friars or seculars. Agnolo was the friend of all the learned men of his time, especially with Lionardo d' Arezzo who thought so highly of his judgment that he would never publish any translation or original work until he should have heard Agnolo's opinion of it. He wielded great authority in the republic from which he received every honour a citizen could have, both at home and abroad, having been sent ambassador to the Pope, the Emperor and the King. His character was upright and severe, his advice well-considered, his speech candid, and he was the foe of all deceit. Any opinion he might adopt must be righteous, otherwise he would have let it alone, and he would adhere to it steadfastly. In all his counsels he looked first to the good of the state, and of this his virtuous dealings at home and abroad give ample proof. He was always in favour of peace and never asserted himself unduly, devoting his health, his honour and his time to his country's welfare ; and as to his private estate, because of the tax then levied, his contribution was the third or the fourth largest sum paid in Florence. In his day he paid an immense sum as the records will show. This wealth had been made by his father in Naples, where he had been a merchant and high in the favour of Queen Joanna and the government. All the money he had in the bank was assigned to him in the current coin of the Commune, as was the custom, and it amounted to eighty thousand florins.

At this time the liberty of Florence was endangered by the invasion of Siena and Arezzo by King Ladislas,* who passed on to Cortona through a country fertile enough to sustain the largest army. The rulers of Cortona were divided, so the people, fearing lest their lands should be devastated, gave Ladislas free entry. Afterwards he passed between Scesi and Perugia, and sent to Florence one of his household, a Florentine named Gabriello Brunelleschi, who announced that, if ambassadors were sent to King Ladislas, peace might be arranged. The reason of this move was the death of Pope Gregory, who had allowed Ladislas to occupy Rome. Some of the Florentine leaders approved of this offer and some

---

* Ladislas, King of Naples (1375–1414) He acquired Cortona in 1409 and sold it to Florence in 1411. *Vide* Sismondi, *Republ. Itali.*, Chap. LXI.

opposed it. Those in favour of it held that any offer of peace should be entertained and that Agnolo, as one known and trusted by the King, should be sent as envoy, and he was appointed with Messer Torelli as colleague. They met the King at Scesi and were received with great honour, and began to discuss the terms to which Agnolo gave his approval. Meantime he was warned by his friends in Florence to be very careful over this business as certain of the leading citizens were opposed to the treaty, but he saw no reason for changing his policy. But most of the Florentines did not believe in it or that he would assume the burden of so great a risk; still, both the majority and the minority were bent on ending the dispute with credit. Agnolo had established excellent relations with Ladislas and plied him with arguments every day, wherefore he attained at last the object he desired.

Agnolo pointed out to the King how greatly peace would profit them both, and urged that the advocates of war were looking to their profit rather than his own. While on his way to an audience the military leaders would often taunt him as to the outcome of a cessation of war, whereupon he would bid them not to trouble their heads over the matter as he, and not they, would have the making of peace. In all these difficulties Agnolo thought only of the honour and profit of his state, as was manifest from the advantageous terms he secured. He concluded the peace against the opinions of the citizens for two reasons, the chief of which was that what he demanded of the King was something which involved his honour ; that is the restitution of the money which had been seized from the Florentine merchants in the King's ports and was an affair of great moment to the city. In this matter Agnolo had a heavy task to perform, and it needed all his adroitness to make peace so as to satisfy the Florentines. Nevertheless, he concluded it on the lines he himself had fixed, as will be told presently. In his terms Agnolo demanded that the sixty thousand florins' worth of goods which had been seized should be returned to the merchants. But as Ladislas had no money Agnolo proposed that, instead of payment, Ladislas should hand over Cortona and its territories.* This was a rich prize

* Muratori, *Ann.*, IX, p. 60.

for Florence and a great vexation to the King, who had only recently acquired the city as has been recorded. The Signoria afterwards satisfied the people.

The treaty also specified that nothing in it should prejudice the league between Florence and Rome and King Louis* who were foes of Ladislas, that Ladislas should quit Rome and the adjacent lands, that Siena should join the league, because, through its refusal to give food and shelter to the forces of Ladislas, his plans had failed. Before he set out from Apulia, Ladislas sought leave to pass through Sienese territory and, this being refused, he was forced to pass by Arezzo and Cortona which he seized, and on this account the Florentines now wished to reward the Sienese for this good service. Thus Agnolo made peace and, when he issued from the King's quarters, a number of the men-at-arms, who had before jeered at him about the negotiations, asked eagerly what had been done, and when he told them that peace had been concluded, and that they might go back to their mattocks, they were enraged and would have assaulted him had not the King come out and bade them be silent.

As soon as it was known what he had accomplished, everyone in Florence was amazed, especially in view of the difficulties which had been cast in his way. All good citizens were delighted, and a feeling arose that things were on the mend after many years of war and the consequent heavy burdens. Agnolo's reputation was greatly increased, especially with the Pope and King Louis. But there were certain men in Florence who disliked the peace, and Agnolo stood in danger from their hostility. Few would have chosen to bear such a burden as lay on him, but, in spite of the dangers around him, he took it valiantly when he realised that his country's interests demanded it. One day, after the peace, the King invited Agnolo and Torelli to dine, Agnolo's two sons, Carlo and Giannozzo, being of the party. "Agnolo," said the King, "they tell me these young Florentines are excellent carvers at table." Whereupon Agnolo called his sons and bade them carve the viands for the King, who gave them high praise. They remained with the King several days, and when they had put

---

* Louis of Anjou. Adopted by Joanna II as her heir to Naples He died in 1436.

STATESMEN

all the writings in order, they returned to Florence, where they were honourably welcomed.

But on the way, about two miles from the city, they met a citizen, full of praise of Agnolo and of all he had done. " The city is delighted," he said, " over the benefits you have brought us, nevertheless, when you get to Florence, have care for yourself, for many of the leaders are opposed to the peace and there is danger that this resentment may bring you to the scaffold." Agnolo began to laugh and said, " I will keep a sharp look out if I, who have given to Florence the peace she needs so sorely, am to lose my head." The fine welcome he received forbade any action from those who opposed him.

Duke Filippo at the beginning of his reign sent six envoys to Florence offering peace with Milan with assurances of his especial desire to stand well with the republic and to abandon the hostile attitude of his predecessors. They wished to proclaim their object in public so as to beguile the people with fair promises, but Agnolo and the wiser heads of the state detected Duke Filippo's duplicity in this proposal and negatived it, maintaining the peace he proposed was only a blind to enable him to seize Genoa, that Florence, after concluding such a peace, would be unable to prevent this seizure and that Genoa was the ally of Florence. Peace is a word of power, forasmuch as whoever desires dominion must seek it by a semblance of peace, and this was Duke Filippo's method. As Agnolo had anticipated, the treaty was no sooner made in 1421 than the Duke attacked Genoa and captured it. Then he sent forces into Romagna, contrary to his agreement with Florence, showing that he was set on domination. Shortly before Pope Martin left Florence, greatly angered that the city had remained neutral in this war, the strong army which the Duke had in Romagna attacked the Florentines and put them in peril. Would that the people had only trusted to their wisest heads and refused to make terms with Filippo ! then he would not have dared to attack Genoa and would have lost much valuable time, all to our advantage. Now the Signoria, seeing they had to deal with a powerful foe, hit upon a plan to send Rinaldo degli Albizzi, Agnolo Pandolfini and Nello to ask Pope Martin to arrange terms of peace with the Duke. At the same time they sent Messer Lorenzo Ridolfo to Venice to treat with Venice for a league of mutual assistance in order that one embassy might help the other. Meantime Rinaldo and Agnolo urged the Pope to expedite the treaty, otherwise Florence would be obliged to come to terms with Venice. The Venetians, who were not at war with the Duke, were reluctant to break with him, wherefore Messer Lorenzo informed them that, unless they made a league with Florence, Florence would join the Duke. The Signoria favoured especially the league with Venice. At Rome Rinaldo and Agnolo had settled the peace in form of a convention, and the Venetians, on hearing this, immediately came to terms with Messer Ridolfo. The chief cause of their agreement was the arrival of Carmagnola* in Venice after his desertion of Duke Filippo, when he informed them that the Duke's plan was to seize Florence first and then fall upon Venice. The diplomacy of Agnolo and Rinaldo also helped to bring Venice into the league, and this peace with Duke Filippo was more important than the league with Venice, as it was the source of their greatness.

When the question of Lucca† arose there was a division amongst the citizens, for and against this enterprise, which proved a ruinous affair. Agnolo and many citizens of weight strongly opposed it, while Rinaldo degli Albizzi and his following favoured it, maintaining falsely that Lucca would submit at once. Agnolo pointed out the inevitable dangers, but the people, satiated with wealth, lost their heads and refused to listen. In this turmoil the Signoria called a general council, being in favour of the enterprise, and after one man had spoken for it, Agnolo stood up, but the tumult made by his opponents in stamping of feet and shouting was so great that he was inaudible. The Signoria were alarmed at this behaviour and ordered silence. When at last Agnolo could be heard he brushed aside all the arguments of Rinaldo and his followers, showing by valid reasoning that this question was causing great dissension in the city, and that disaster must follow. He ended by saying, " I have spoken for the welfare of the city, but I see that this attempt is bound to be made, how-

---

* Francesco Carmagnola, the great free captain. He withdrew his force from Milan in 1425 and entered Venetian service.
† 1428.

ever, those who promote it will be the first to repent of it."
After the discussion Rinaldo and his party took courage from
the support they had received from the common herd, who,
like cattle, follow their leaders without thinking of the consequences. The blind populace were numerous while Agnolo's
following was small. The attempt against Lucca was the
cause of the parliament of 1433 which banished Cosimo de'
Medici and other leaders who opposed it. Rinaldo degli Albizzi
was the leader in this, a man whom Agnolo disliked on account
of his overbearing carriage and the mischief he wrought. At
this time* the Emperor Sigismund was passing through Italy to
be crowned at Rome, and Duke Filippo, being his friend,
favoured his passage. He desired to traverse Florentine
territory, but leave was refused on account of the laws, and of
the treaty with Duke Filippo, whereupon the Emperor went by
way of Siena. This roused great fear in Florence, as Sigismund
was a powerful prince, and was now greatly incensed against
the city from their refusal to give him leave to pass. Duke
Filippo was also now their enemy, and the public and private
support he gave to Lucca brought disaster in the attack on it
by the Florentines. For this reason they were much disturbed
by Sigismund's visit to Siena, suspecting that the Sienese,
being friends of Duke Filippo, would seek to prejudice the
Emperor against Florence. In this situation, being in great
anxiety, the Signoria came to a prompt decision to send an
ambassador with full powers to the Emperor. They sent
Messer Agnolo, remembering his ability and uprightness in
other similar missions. At Siena Agnolo was graciously
received by the Emperor and by all his following, and during
discussion he appeased the Emperor's mind of the anger he
had felt against the city, and warded off divers mischances
which might well have ensued. Fourteen thousand florins in
gold were sent to him with instructions that, on a favourable
opportunity, they should be placed in the silver bowl which
accompanied them, and offered by Agnolo in the name of the
people of Florence. Agnolo went one morning, after the
Emperor had dined, into the room, and, after expressing in
appropriate words the good disposition of the people of Florence towards His Majesty, presented the bowl and the florins,

* 1432.

which were accepted with pleasure. Then Sigismund spread the coins on the table and gave them by handfuls to his courtiers till not one remained. He then turned to Agnolo and, laughing, said in Latin that he did not care for the money for himself but for his friends. Agnolo stayed some time in Siena and carried out completely the mission which had been given to him. When he returned to Florence he was graciously received by all, in that he had completely removed the ill-will of the Emperor. Agnolo was consistently opposed to the innovations of 1433, which followed the attack on Lucca, and would concern himself only with the general good of the city. Other matters he put aside as being foreign to the activity of a private citizen. He saw that Rinaldo and his followers contemplated a revolution in the state, and the summoning of a parliament, and the seizure of Cosimo de' Medici with the object of putting him to death, and he desired to deliver a citizen of such eminence from such a fate. He did all he could to let Rinaldo see the danger of the course he was following, and how it must lead to the ruin of the state and of themselves, but these violent and inconsiderate men refused to regard his warning. It would have been wiser to go slowly and to learn from those who had lived before ; men like Niccolo da Uzzano, who always condemned change, and said that the advocates of it dug the graves in which they themselves would be buried : indeed, Rinaldo buried himself, the cause of all the mischief, and his followers and the city as well. Agnolo, seeing how he stood, in all these changes worked as much good as he could, kept clear of offences, would never be one of the Eight nor occupy a post in which he might be obliged to banish any citizen. Nor had he any desire for further honours in the state. For these reasons he won the favour of the whole community, who felt that the course he had taken was for the general good.

After the revolution of 1433 and the banishment of Cosimo, Agnolo, perceiving how great was the disorder and how weak were the authors of it, held aloof from all that might arouse hostility, fearing that trouble might fall upon him and his sons as well. The city had not lived a full year under its changed government, the Signori had not laid down office when, in September, 1434, the public mind inclined to another change of the constitution and the recall of Cosimo. When Rinaldo knew of this he and his followers took up arms, but he feared to approach Agnolo, knowing his disposition. Agnolo did his best to prevent further evil, and when Rinaldo called upon Palla Strozzi to bring out the five hundred armed men he had as a guard,* Agnolo and Bartolomeo Carducci, kinsfolk of Palla, who held him in high esteem, advised him to keep clear of Rinaldo's mad attempt, and exhorted him for the peace of the city that he should hold a middle course and let the others go their way. Palla accordingly held aloof, greatly to the detriment of Rinaldo's enterprise, because Palla's support and the five hundred troops would have been of the greatest service. The advice of Agnolo and Bartolomeo only confirmed Palla in his opinion. As it was now apparent that the government of 1433 was doomed to fall through its weakness, public opinion demanded the recall of Cosimo so that peace in the city might be restored. And when it became evident—except to the few who had brought about the changes in 1433—that Cosimo's return would be a great benefit, those in power determined to avoid the error committed in 1433 by the chief actors who did not think of the mischief which afterwards ensued, such as banishment and ruin. A scrutiny was opened and the government was given to those who were elected. After the scrutiny the ballot was closed and the Balia set up.

But to return to Agnolo. Cosimo had the greatest respect for him and often visited his house, knowing how strong his influence was through his high character, and that he would only use his power for the welfare of the state. After Cosimo's return many changes were made and many citizens exiled by his order, an action which displeased Agnolo, especially as it affected Palla Strozzi his kinsman and friend. One day an official of the state informed Agnolo and Bartolomeo Carducci that, unless some one intervened, Palla would be exiled. They afterwards asked one of the chiefs of the government whether this report was true. He replied that it was not true, but that it would be well for Palla to withdraw into the country for a month or two, by way of disarming his envious detractors. Agnolo and Bartolomeo were men of good faith

* *Vide Life of Palla*, p. 240.

and believed this story and took no action, especially when they remembered how great was the service Palla had done to the state when he refused to support Rinaldo and his party, and to give the services of his five hundred men. But a few days later Palla and his son Noferi were banished.

Agnolo and Bartolomeo were highly indignant at this undeserved sentence on one who had not his equal in the state. Agnolo, seeing how the city had changed, began to consider, as he could not longer aid the state as heretofore, how he might alter his scheme of life. He determined to withdraw from politics and devote himself to letters, but, as he had to take part in the government of 1434, he could not retire as soon as he wished. He discharged his duty on this occasion as efficiently as ever, and then retired from public affairs. He did this without hesitation because his sons, Carlo and Giannozzo, were worthy men, and Agnolo told them that, having come to his present age, he was no longer able to give efficient service. He exhorted them to take their part in state affairs, and to arrange with the authorities that, in future, he himself should be free from them. Henceforth he desired to live a retired life, after having spent his energy in his country's service. He had made the peace of Cortona and added that rich country to Florence. In his time the city held its own against King Ladislas and the Visconti, maintaining themselves by their wisdom and their resources. Florence then was at the highest point of her prosperity; indeed, the great wealth of certain citizens was the cause of the troubles which ensued. Agnolo was at Zagonara* when it was lost. Also he met with a great piece of luck when he and certain other citizens gained a hundred thousand florins in a few hours. He would be a fortunate man who could pay a larger sum than this.

Having done so much good service Agnolo made up his mind to retire into private life and spend his time in reading,† in discourse with learned men and in religious duties. He spent

---

* This was in 1424 when Carlo Malatesta, in Florentine service, was defeated and captured by the Milanese.

† Agnolo has been given the authorship of the *Governo della Famiglia*, a work akin to Leo Battista's celebrated *Trattata*. Later criticism gives it also to Alberti. Symonds deals fully with the matter in *Italian Literature*, Vol. I, Chap. 3.

the summer at his villa in as happy a state as any man of his time and lived the moderate life of a good citizen. He entertained hospitably all the men of mark of his time at Signa. The villa was furnished with all due appurtenances fit for a gentleman's dwelling; horses, dogs, hawks and nets for fowling and fishing. All guests were welcomed. He was most hospitable, and there was no house near Florence kept in such munificent fashion. Thither came Pope Eugenius, King Rinieri, Duke Francesco, Maestro Nicolo and divers other great personages. When his sons came from Florence without some guest he would be greatly disappointed and reprove them. This house was a true resting-place of men of mark. Agnolo was another Lucullus, and the villa was provided with everything his guests might need. If it happened that there were no guests in the house he would send his servants into the road to bid any passers-by to enter and dine with him and after washing their hands they would join him at table. When they had dined, he would thank them and let them go their way. All the exercises of gentlemen were practised, when they went fowling with hawks and dogs there would be fifteen to twenty horsemen besides attendants. They also hunted goats and hares and sometimes fished. These were the amusements of his sons. When they came from the city he cared little to hear about the government, but should he enquire thereanent he rarely heard anything to his taste. Sometimes he would remark, " Government conducted in this fashion is certain to lead to disaster." For some twelve years he lived this untroubled life.

He took a wife of the Strozzi family, a lady of great worth, and the first night, in place of the trifling which is then customary, he told her all she would have to do in governing the house, adding, "Remember these directions, for I shall not repeat them." By her he had three sons, Messer Carlo, a knight and a man of importance in the republic, who after served as ambassador and received the honours due, Messer Giannozzo, also a knight, a worthy and industrious citizen who conducted negotiations between the Venetians and Duke Francesco, with King Alfonso, and another son, Pandolfo, who died young. His wife died after bearing three sons, and though he was still young he did not marry again, but remained a widower for

PANDOLFO PANDOLFINI

fifty years. His daughters-in-law were of the houses of Giugni and of Taldo Valori. These ladies cared for Agnolo as if he had been their father. When he had passed his eighty-fifth year his intellect was equal to that of a man of forty, and he suffered no bodily ailment. In his last illness his mind was so clear that when Messer Alessandro degli Alessandri and certain others came to see him, he turned to them at last and in most fitting words committed the city to their care and exhorted them to bear themselves towards it in such manner as would allow them to hand it over to their sons as worthy as it was when they themselves received it. In conclusion he added briefly, "But I know that what I desire will not be done." This he said knowing their situation, and that what he asked was beyond their power on account of the existing condition of affairs.

PANDOLFO PANDOLFINI

Pandolfo di Messer Giannozzo Pandolfini was born of noble parents, a well-read man and nephew of Agnolo Pandolfini. He was an ornament of letters and, beyond this, he was endowed with great natural gifts, with modesty and temperance. He was grave in childhood and onward through life, and no act or speech of his was unworthy of him. When he grew up he won the general esteem of the citizens, both great and small, by ways of uprightness which he never laid aside. He was eloquent in speech and a patient listener to all who spoke, always ready to do a kindness, wherefore he made many friends. He was polite to everyone and intimate with all the distinguished men of the time ; with Lionardo d' Arezzo, Carlo d' Arezzo, Giannozzo Manetti and all the worthies and men of letters of the day. The charm of his discourse was so great that he won the affection of all, and was held in general esteem. Whenever he spoke in cultured society he was heard with deference as a youth of consideration and promise.

He gave early proof of his merits. When he was eighteen his father was sent as governor of Leghorn at the time when Niccolo Piccinino was with the army of Duke Filippo in the country of Pisa. Messer Giannozzo, who was then at Leghorn, fell ill with fever and was advised by the physicians to withdraw to Pisa. Giannozzo, knowing Pandolfo's ability, determined to leave him in this office at Leghorn, and this he did. Through diligence and probity Pandolfo discharged his duties with extraordinary efficiency. It happened at this time two rascals came along the road from Pisa to Leghorn, apparently about to hold up the highway. On account of the danger of war Neri di Gino had been made commissary. When Pandolfo heard of this he ordered their arrest as highwaymen, and when this was made he received letters both from Neri di Gino and from the captain of Pisa ordering their execution. Nevertheless, Pandolfo was of a discreet disposition and prone to move slowly, so he reprieved them to the morrow. All night long he recalled continuously a verse of Juvenal, that long inquisition is necessary where a man's life is concerned, and on the morrow he gave them the strappado with close examination. He decided that what these fellows had done had been done through mischievous levity and not fault, so he kept them some days in prison and then let them go. Neri di Gino and the rest commended him highly for the course he had taken in establishing their innocence, and affirmed that this decision was that of a grown-up man rather than a youth of eighteen years.

By this exhibition of his ability Pandolfo gave proof of his worth, and he gained more experience every day by his early association with men of weight, and by studying and discussing matters with the chiefs of the state. He desired also to increase the knowledge he had already gained ; so he, together with many other young men of good position, went to hear Carlo d' Arezzo, who read Aristotle's Politics which deal with state government. He had already heard Messer Battista Fabriano on Aristotle's Ethics, and also a part of the same from Giovanni Argiropolo, so that he had a complete knowledge of the book. He combined literature with practice, and when he spoke he was equal to any orator of his time. As he devoted himself to study and practice alike, he was soon drawn for the assembly. Standing so high in general estimation, he was charged with the delivery of the oration De Justitia, a customary function. This duty having been given him, he set to work and produced a fine and graceful speech which won high praise from all who

PANDOLFO PANDOLFINI

heard it. The morning he read it the Signori, the assembly, all the rectors and officials, the mayors of the various crafts, all the literary world of Florence and the chief citizens came to hear him. He gave this oration, *De Justitia*, with so much grace and in such fine style that his auditors felt that no such a feat of oratory had ever been displayed before. His fame was already considerable, but this speech seemed to raise him to the highest level of learning, and he kept on in the path of rectitude and let this practice be evident in all he undertook. His judgment was so keen that immediately anything was told to him he grasped its meaning. At this time happened the re-election of the Signoria, and the city and those who were in power did their best to get control of the state, and, not trusting one another, they sought in every way to secure their own position, thinking more of their private affairs than of the public weal. In the elections to the Priorate* they took good care to select those citizens who would serve their purpose. The procedure in this case lay with the clerks of the ballot, and the clerk now was Neri di Gino Capponi. The clerks could appoint themselves gonfaloniers of justice, or of the Signori in the lack of other candidates. They had settled the seven for the Signori and two others had to be chosen. Some were in favour of Neri and some against him, and he said, " I should like to be elected myself, or some one whom I can trust, and I wish that Pandolfo should be given one vote and that for the other, which belongs to S. Giovanni, six votes be given to the Signori and one for Pandolfo." They agreed that Messer Agnolo Acciaiuoli should be gonfalonier, and that, with regard to the two candidates, one of them should receive all the votes and Pandolfo only one. But there were two others of the quarter who were designated for all the votes and Pandolfo for one only, so it seemed impossible that he should be elected, but in the end he was elected and his opponent defeated. Pandolfo having been elected, the members of the government, who were bent on many changes during their term, perceived that he was not the man to lend himself to their schemes, especially in the matter of exiling citizens and of the enactment of obnoxious laws. As none of Pandolfo's forbears had ever acted thus, he was not likely to begin. To the Signori

* These election details as here given are incomprehensible.

STATESMEN

Pandolfo's election was a surprise, but Neri was well content with the result having regard to the welfare of the city.

Meanwhile Pandolfo remained at his home, where many citizens waited on him ; some to encourage him to keep a firm front and oppose all change, and others to advise him to agree to the proposals which the heads of the government might bring forward, for the time had come when, by following their will, they would make him one of the leaders in that quarter* of the city. Pandolfo had made up his mind and knew what he would do. To all who addressed him he gave a prudent answer and hid certain of his opinions. He was not amongst those who had secret knowledge of what was about to happen, nor was he bound in any compact. All those who knew what was coming were distrustful, and some told him to be watchful and make no opposition to the proposals which might be made, or he and his house might be brought to ruin. Pandolfo answered that he would never depart from just and honest dealing, he had always loved the city, and was not one to withdraw the dutiful service he had given. But he was now suspicious, and as he perceived that things were going amiss he determined to bring off a good stroke, and to beat back the misfortune which he saw was imminent. One evening a very dear friend hailed Pandolfo and took him into his room. This man was one of those who had been told what he was expected to do, and he now cried out to Pandolfo in tears : " Must I, indeed, ruin the city and destroy my own house ? " Pandolfo answered : " Not if you will act as I propose to act. Then you will not be ruined as you fear." These words convinced his friend, so that he agreed to do as Pandolfo suggested. Having come to a secret agreement they enlisted two others, making four in all. Since the Signori were very suspicious if two or three were seen conferring together, Pandolfo arranged that they should betake themselves early one morning to an appointed place and, when they were met, Pandolfo, who had spoken separately to each of the others, said : " We can now do a great service to God and to the world and save the city and ourselves. There is no reason for your fears, if we only stand

---

* Florence was then divided into four quarters: S. Spirito, comprising all beyond the Arno, S. Croce, S. Maria Novella and S. Giovanni.

firm, and keep to our purpose, and give our four votes together, then, as I have said, we shall do a good work indeed." They were all ready to act as Pandolfo directed, and swore an oath together that their votes should all be given for the same names. When he had accomplished his object Pandolfo believed that he had bound the hands of the conspirators who were bent on injuring the state.

A few days afterwards the gonfalonier gave order to the Signori who were assembled that no one of them should go away, and forthwith made them withdraw to the smaller hall, the door of which was then locked so that no one could enter. When the news of this was spread everyone was suspicious, and feared some revolutionary scheme. Pandolfo was president, and the gonfalonier had not let him know what he proposed to do. The Signori were in the smaller hall, and the assembly in the audience chamber, and they could send no message to anyone outside. As soon as the Signori were seated the gonfalonier read his demand, which was as follows : that no decision should be valid unless the gonfalonier—both now and in the future—should be present ; thus all power would remain with him, and the Signori would be impotent in this form as it was put forward by the gonfalonier. When Pandolfo realised the purport of this demand he was greatly disturbed. After the gonfalonier had read it he added it was necessary that this demand should be granted since it was the will of the leaders and that no opposition should be offered to it. When it came to the vote there were five black beans and four white which were cast by Pandolfo and his associates. The vote was taken several times, always with the same result. The more debate there was, the firmer Pandolfo and his associates stood. At last, after a number of votings, one of Pandolfo's party, who had bad eyesight, was so affected that without seeing what he did he cast in a black bean, so that when they were counted they came out six to three.

The one who had made this mistake was dismayed. The Signori at once called upon the assembly saying that this decision gave to the state the powers they wanted, and that all those who had not given their black bean in favour of it were the enemies of the state. The result was put before the assembly, who, out of fear, confirmed it, whereupon all were commanded to remain and the bell was rung to summon a meeting. Everyone hastened to it, as all were anxious to know the decision.

The gonfalonier and the Signori came out. Pandolfo was apprehensive and with an angry countenance, from which all could see that he regarded this demand as unjust and dishonest. As soon as the session began the petition was read, and when the vote was taken there were scarcely any black beans. The gonfalonier was very angry at this, and declared that a fresh vote should be taken ; after this was counted the result was worse than before, and a third voting showed no change. But the gonfalonier urged that the proposal should be again brought forward, whereupon Pandolfo objected, saying that it had been voted on three times and ought not to be further considered. The Council, after further deliberation, determined not to give way. When the gonfalonier saw that the Signori were not all of one mind, he tried hard to get a recommital, but in vain. Then he turned to Pandolfo and said, " If I had my will I would lock them all up in this hall and keep them there till they should agree to a recommital " Pandolfo answered, " That would be the right thing for you to do, but not for me, who have never come to ask favours of these men which we have not full right to ask on account of our grievances. Therefore I will do nothing." Then the bell rang, and as the Council was thereby dissolved, the petition was not granted on account of the many evils which would have followed. The gonfalonier, seeing Pandolfo's strong resolution to act the part of a good citizen, conferred with others of the Signoria and decided to send word to his father, Messer Giannozzo, who was governor of Pistoia, and request him to bring Pandolfo into compliance with their project, wondering the while at such stiff resolution in so young a man. Messer Giannozzo, like a good citizen and a lover of his country, went to Florence and not only discouraged any change in Pandolfo's attitude, but encouraged him to stand firm. Those who fetched him over from Pistoia thought they would win their point, but they lost it, for Pandolfo was quite ready to stand stiffly on his ground, and his father, an experienced and manly citizen, backed him on every point. For, several days after, there came to light various deeds of questionable honesty ; Pandolfo and his three companions held out in everything on account of what was told them concerning the leaders of the state, and thereby worked incalculable benefit in the future. The framers of the aforesaid demand did not lay it aside, and all in the city were full of apprehension lest these men should procure the exile of certain of the citizens, seeing it was understood that this was their intention. Amongst the chiefs there was so great apprehension that no one dare mount the staircase to the chamber, and those who feared exile sent their friends to Pandolfo to beg his good offices ; indeed, I, who write this, went to him several times on behalf of some of the first in the city, and he always replied that, as long as he was at his post, they need not fear. The city was so greatly panic-stricken that not only did men tremble, but also the walls around them.

The chiefs of the government gave out that they would settle the business, wherefore no one need trouble further. Having determined to open the Pratica and to banish certain citizens—not of the lower order—they appointed a day. And because no one went to the Pratica except the gonfalonier, the Signori let it be known that they themselves wished to be summoned, and wrote a request to the gonfalonier. Each one only voted for some one of his own way of thinking, and after they had delivered their requests to the officer, the gonfalonier let them know how many each might vote for to form the Pratica. Pandolfo wrote out his paper and handed it to the officer, his associates did the like. Then the gonfalonier wished to inspect it, and when he found on it the name of one he wished to banish he erased it and substituted another. When the Pratica assembled Pandolfo went to see whether the one he had nominated was present and found he was not, wherefore he sent for the officer of the quarter and made him produce the paper on which the name had been cancelled and another put in. He asked the officer who had done this, and was told it was the gonfalonier, whereupon Pandolfo bade him go to the Piazza to find the citizen he had named and order him in the name of the Signoria to appear before the Pratica. When he entered all those present were amazed, for a resolution had already been passed that he should be banished and others warned ; now when the promoters found their project had been discovered, they revoked their resolution, for none of them wished to be burdened with such a responsibility. Hereupon the gonfalonier rang the bell and dissolved the meeting. This happy result was Pandolfo's work, for he had the gift of foresight as well as decision. He saved this citizen and all his house and many others as well. He earned their gratitude, for they knew that no other could have done so much. By this and many other deeds of the same nature he won a good name everywhere ; indeed, he saved not only these citizens, but the city itself. Many of this family still survive and some of them have been exiled, for, although Pandolfo saved them once, later on, when Pandolfo was no more, they fell into evil case. His career proves what great service a citizen like him can render to the state. Certain of those who had supported the changes which Pandolfo opposed approached him in the palace, letting him see in cautious speech that they disapproved of his attitude, and persuaded him to conform to the gonfalonier's request. They spoke with warmth against any action which would indicate that he was acting against the welfare of the state, and pointed out to him how he would fare if he still persisted, but neither their inducements nor threats availed to move him, and all through his office as prior he continued to work for the public good. He won the highest esteem by the upright and generous course he followed and by the constancy of his unconquerable spirit. While working for justice he let himself be daunted by nothing. After the Signori and the gonfalonier had left office, the last named, being convinced of the courage and good faith of Pandolfo, now felt a warm regard for him, and became his closest friend and said to him, " With reference to those changes in the state which I tried to make, I admit that it was through you that they were thwarted, and that your judgment was sounder than mine." Their friendship became so close that any favour Pandolfo might have demanded would have been granted to him. He was always keen on well-doing, therefore he had no need to fear anyone, and he was popular both with rulers and ruled. He was wary of giving offence, and on this account favour would always be granted him, whether requested for himself or for some other. On the death of Giovanni di Cosimo, one of the officials of the Monte, Pandolfo, though very young for the post, was chosen by the Council to succeed him with general approbation. Many went to the election, and on account of his popularity Pandolfo received nothing but black beans, the same result as when he was elected prior.

In this office, as in others, he achieved complete success, and at the end of it his associates wanted to hand over to him the surplus of taxation, levied by error in computing the super-tax. He refused it, saying it was enough for the citizens to pay their dues, without an extra fine. " I may be poor in estate," he said, " but I am not poor in courage. I will have none of this taxation money. Let it go to the commune." This was done, but his associates did not follow his example in this respect. Pandolfo showed that he cared more for honour than for goods. Cosimo de' Medici and the leaders in the city had the highest opinion of him, both in his public and private life. After his father's death his brothers showed him just the same reverence as to their father. When it was decided to send an ambassador to King René in France, Pandolfo, though a young man, was chosen. He was well received, won golden opinions of all, and succeeded well with his mission. He was helped by his natural parts, and equally by his training in letters, his nurture, and his association with men of fine ideals. He had never had truck with base or corrupt minds, but had always been confronted with lofty ideals, and had been kept free from chaffering and petty merchandise which tends to bring down character to a lower level. He had for a father a most distinguished man, and for many years after Pandolfo's birth no other child was born to him ; thus, having a good competence, he had no need to save. He kept his fine house generously and would have felt shamed to buy common wares ; he left all household details to his staff so as to escape the trouble and deterioration such cares may bring. He hated gambling, which he rated as time wasted.

After the defeat of Duke Giovanni by King Ferdinand at Troja,* the death of the Prince of Taranto and the reconquest

* 1462.

of the greater part of the kingdom, it seemed good to the government to send ambassadors to congratulate the King on his success, and Luigi Guiccardini and Pandolfo were chosen. Great honour was paid to them on their arrival, a crowd of nobles and the King's sons went to meet them and they were lodged in a fine palace, richly furnished. The King showed great favour to Pandolfo, and later, when Luigi was recalled, the King desired Pandolfo to remain. Ferdinand rewarded him generously, and was afterwards a benefactor to his family. Whenever the King walked out in Naples Pandolfo was his companion, and he would talk freely about his private affairs. He became a favourite also with the nobles about the court. His manner of speech was tactful and sympathetic, his words were well chosen and sober, and he knew exactly how to accommodate his discourse to his company.

At this time Count Jacopo* came to Naples and a close friendship arose between him and Pandolfo. They would meet almost every day, for Pandolfo had the gift of attracting men to him as soon as they met. The King was obliged to go to Ischia, which, together with the Castello dell' Uovo, was then held by a certain Catalan. The King desired Count Jacopo and Pandolfo to accompany him in his ship, and no one else went except the secretary. They approached Ischia with the object of finding out the best method of attack, and Count Jacopo, as one well-versed in warfare, gave much advice. Having finished their talk they returned to Naples. Count Jacopo had full trust in Pandolfo's judgment and took him into full confidence. He was still apprehensive as to his own position, not knowing what fate might be before him. Seeing that he himself was maintaining large forces and occupying much of the King's territories,† it seemed that he still held the King in his power. But he could not see his way how to settle the present difficulty. He had often asked the King's leave to return to Lombardy, or whithersoever it might best please His Majesty, not wishing to stay longer where he was, but the King would never give consent. He

---

* Jacopo Piccinino, 1465.
† He held Sulmona, Cività di Perna, Francavilla, Cività di Santo Angelo, il Contado di Campobasso and other lands. Muratori, *Annals of Italy*, IX, p. 292.

often consulted Pandolfo, who, like a wise man, told him he ought not to withdraw without the King's leave.

Whilst these matters were being discussed the King one day after vespers sent for Jacopo. On his way he called at Pandolfo's house and told him how the King had sent for him, that he was now going to take leave, and that to-morrow, with God's help, he would be on his way. Pandolfo had long suspected that Jacopo's liberty was in danger, and had often warned him. Now, being still haunted by these doubts, he was unwilling to let Jacopo go, and told him so, but Jacopo left him and went to the King, who received him at the Castel Nuovo in a private room where there was no one else but the secretary; the Count Brocardo and Jacopo's son and several others remained outside and were at once arrested, as had been planned. The King and Count Jacopo had been conversing some time when a messenger arrived saying that letters had come from France and that His Majesty must go and read them at once. The King left the chamber, and soon after the secretary also withdrew; whereupon some others came in and seized Count Jacopo as the King's prisoner. Count Jacopo complained at this treatment, but he was put in a prison with Galeazzo Pandoni, while the King straightway sent his secretary to inform Pandolfo that, for valid reasons, he had incarcerated Count Jacopo, his son and Count Brocardo. When Pandolfo heard of this he was greatly angered on account of the regard he had for Count Jacopo, and, after several days of chagrin, despatched a messenger to Florence to announce what had happened. Next he went to the King, who vainly endeavoured to justify his violence. After three days' imprisonment Count Jacopo died from some unknown cause.[*] Count Brocardo had induced Count Jacopo to come to Naples. Men are often blind in what they do and are led unawares to their punishment for the purging of their offences. Count Jacopo had received vast rewards in money and land

---

[*] On the 24th of June (1465), under the pretext of showing him the treasure-house, the King took Count Jacopo into the Castello and at once caused him to be put in prison, where he was guarded by two soldiers. Next the King seized his son Francesco and took possession of all his lands. Shortly after Jacopo was strangled in prison by the King's order, and a report was spread that Jacopo, in trying to get sight of the fleet, had climbed up to a high window and had fallen and broken his neck. Muratori, *Annals of Italy*, IX, p. 293.

for his services, but what the King gave to Count Brocardo was measured by his own decision. If these two had duly weighed these matters they would have kept clear of Naples. Jacopo had been told that if he went to Naples he could never leave it alive ; men, however, are not free agents and are led to disaster when they least expect it. Pandolfo was deeply grieved at the loss of his friend.

Pandolfo stayed on at Naples, still in favour with the King, but, as common in men of strenuous intellect, he was frail in physical temper. He fell ill with fever and dysentery, and during his sickness the King often visited him and sent his sons and those of his court to enquire, also his private doctors. Indeed, he was so well cared for in his sickness that, had he been a prince, he could not have been better tended. As Pandolfo wished to return to Florence he asked the King to send him in one of his own vessels to Livorno. The King consented and ordered the ship to be prepared, but Pandolfo's weakness was so great that the voyage was abandoned, and a few days later he grew worse and died in Naples. The King and the court were deeply grieved at his death. Pandolfo won great fame before he died, not only with the King and his nobles, but with all classes in Florence, as may be seen by the banner which was given him by a vote of all black beans The King gave him a funeral at his own charges, as noble a one as would have been given to the chief man of the state.

A short time before this the King had assisted at the baptism of a son who had been born to Pandolfo, and had given him the name of Ferdinand. Now he desired that Messer Tomaso Vasallo, his ambassador in Florence, should also baptise the boy, and he sent, as godfather, a basin and a jug of silver worth a hundred ducats. After Pandolfo's death Messer Garzia Betes, a Spaniard, who was passing through Florence, was commissioned by the King to wait upon Madonna Gostanza, widow of Pandolfo, and to offer her, on the part of the King, all possible services, to exhort her to patience and to assure her that the loss of a friend like Pandolfo was, to the King, no less than was her own. He also directed Messer Marino Tomasello to visit her constantly to see that neither she nor the child should want anything, that the boy should be brought up with all possible diligence and put under

PIERO DI NERI ACCIAIUOLI

teachers who would train him in virtuous ways. For these matters the King sent money through Marino Tomasello, and afterwards made a charge upon the customs of two hundred ducats *per annum* which Pandolfo's descendants collected for themselves. The youth first named was granted his allowance up to the end of his fourteenth year, and he showed by his praiseworthy character that he was a worthy son of Pandolfo. By his munificence to Pandolfo's family the King showed himself a benefactor after death as well as in life, and that the love and respect he had for Pandolfo was real and not simulated. I have here written concerning the life and doings of Pandolfo by way of record, leaving the rest to anyone who will present his Life as a memorial. I have set down certain matters seen and heard by those of good faith, reducing them rather than amplifying them and keeping close to truth so that all may see how great is the force of well-doing in those who persevere therein to the end like Pandolfo. He was set to give a good example to all the city and to its rulers, and to leave to his children and to all his house a possession which could never be taken from them.

Piero di Neri Acciaiuoli

He was born of one of the noblest families in the city, which was held in high esteem by reason of the many distinguished men it had given both to Church and state. To allude briefly to his parentage it may be said that his father, Messer Donato, was brother to Cardinal Acciaiuoli, who was vice-chancellor and held in high esteem at the Papal court. It was commonly believed that Messer Donato was the adopted son of the great Seneschal* who virtually ruled the kingdom of Naples during the lives of several of the kings and of the elder Queen Joanna.

* Niccolo Acciaiuoli was an able ruler who brought prosperity to Naples in spite of the corruption of the court. In 1345 Queen Joanna's husband Andrew, the brother of the King of Hungary, was murdered by Louis of Tarentum, the Queen's lover. The King of Hungary prepared to invade the kingdom, the nobles revolted and Joanna and Louis were induced by Acciaiuoli to fly to Avignon in 1348. By his influence and by the retreat of the King of Hungary, they returned at the end of the year, and Joanna held the kingdom till her death in 1380. She was supposed to have been murdered. Acciaiuoli had returned to Florence, where he died in 1366.

STATESMEN

He was an able ruler, and popular on account of his good government. His sphere was a large one, for he administered both the state and the army. The island of Morea in Greece, an important and rich country, was acquired by him by force of arms, and these lands were afterwards assigned to him by the King and came under his sway. The Grand Seneschal held Thebes, Suschamino, Sesmilia and many other places in Greece, and the revenue of these states amounted to thirty thousand ducats. His father held Prato for King Robert and fortified the palace of the Podesta, having negotiated with King Robert that it should pass to the Florentines. It seems highly probable that Messer Donato was the Grand Seneschal's adopted son, because he was sent to govern the conquered lands in Greece, an office he would scarcely have received had there not been some tie of affinity. Afterwards he returned to his city, where he had ample means of living, and on his return from Greece he brought with him more than thirty thousand florins in current money, though in Greece he had always kept a fine establishment. He had a good name through his pleasant manner, and was of a liberal and candid disposition. As he had been used to state government and important matters he had attained a wide and liberal outlook.

When he returned to Florence the people recognised his merits and high lineage, and that certain of his kinsfolk had filled the highest posts in the government, and for this reason Messer Donato became one of the leaders in the state. His methods were straightforward. Although free speech was allowed, it was well to keep a guard over the tongue. Messer Donato could not escape the shafts of envy, for when the noble family of Uberti were exiled, he tried to get the ban removed in the general interest of the state, but the foes of the Uberti, fearing for their interests on account of their share in this affair, intrigued against Donato and procured his exile for what he had done. He was banished to Barletta in the kingdom, a region held by his own people. His brother was then a cardinal living in Rome, and Donato determined to join him and disregard the limits of his banishment, and on this account he was declared a rebel. The cardinal, however, had sufficient power to rescue from seizure all Donato's houses in Florence by placing on them his own armorial device. On Donato's

PIERO DI NERI ACCIAIUOLI

arrival in Rome, by the cardinal's interest, he was appointed governor of the *patrimonio*, but just as he was leaving Rome the plague broke out and he died. He left two sons and several daughters, Neri, the father of Piero and Donato, and Jacopo, father of Messer Agnolo, born of the two wives he married.

Neri married the daughter of Palla Strozzi, the chief man of his time, and to them were born Piero and Donato and two daughters. After a time Neri went to Greece to visit the lands which had belonged to Donato his father ; they had remained in the Acciaiuoli family until they were seized by the Turks. Most families would have gone begging in such a case as this, but things prospered with the Acciaiuoli, who contracted alliances with all the great houses of the kingdom. Many of their daughters were married to great lords—the Prince of Taranto and others—as may be seen in the Life of the Grand Seneschal. There was Madonna Andrea Acciaiuoli, Countess of Altavilla, a most remarkable lady, to whom Messer Giovanni Boccaccio dedicated his book of Illustrious Women as a woman of the loftiest position. Matteo of Capua, a great captain and the lord of wide lands, was descended from her. Bishops and prelates, men of high rank, were descended from this family : much land of the kingdom is theirs and they built many churches and chapels, and behold ! there is the Certosa near Florence* which was built by the Grand Seneschal in his lifetime, and endowed by him, as no other church had ever been endowed by a single citizen before.

Messer Agnolo Acciaiuoli, Bishop of Florence—for then there was no archbishop—when he saw the city under the sway of the Duke of Athens,† could scarcely endure that the Franks should be in occupation of it by reason of its internal discords and devised a plan for liberating her from this servitude. Seeing that he could not accomplish this end by ordinary means, he took another course and, having come to an understanding with certain citizens that, on a certain day, he would repair with full ecclesiastic state and accompanied by a good

---

* Founded 1341.

† A descendant of the Norman adventurers in Greece. He had been in the service of the Duke of Calabria, and happened to be in Florence when the city was convulsed by the failure of the war of Lucca in 1341. In a fit of frenzy the democracy put him at the head of the state. He was expelled in 1343.

body of the people to the Piazza and then and there request the Duke to leave the city as free as he had found her, and to do everything in his power to bring about this end. When the time came the bishop and his following appeared in the Piazza, but by God's will it happened that, on this same day, several plots against the Duke had been discovered ; wherefore it was decided, now that the bishop and all the people were assembled in the Piazza, that the Duke must resign his power, and an agreement was drawn up between the Duke and the bishop, as chief personage in the city, that the Duke should withdraw to Poppi, which lay outside the lands of Florence, and should despatch therefrom an authentic renunciation of the lordship of Florence—present and future. The bishop attended all these conferences. As the Duke made difficulties about renunciations, the bishop, having received a confirmation of the agreement, made by the whole of the people, told the Duke that, if he refused to agree, he would be transferred back into the hands of the people from whom he had been rescued. As things now stood the Duke saw that he must concede whatever the bishop and the citizens demanded in the name of the state, so he agreed to all the terms of the solemn instrument which was put before him. As the bishop was the chief of the movement which rescued Florence from slavery and restored her liberty, it is certain that the gratitude, not only of his own house but of the whole state, is due to the bishop for the part he played in it.

Having treated of the origins of this house and of its great deeds, I will now say something of Messer Donato, the father of Piero and Donato. He was a tall, fair well-proportioned man of benign and striking presence, so that one who might know nought of him would say, on seeing him, that he was born to command. He wore over his vest a long gown interwoven with gold which reached the ground and was furnished with buttons of silver gilt, worked to look like thread ; these buttons reached from the top to the bottom. Over this gown he wore a cloak of crimson damask brocaded with gold and lined with silk and open on the right side. On his head he wore a grey beaver hat with hood under. He kept a fine establishment of horses and servants. There was a certain citizen who resigned the rectorship of an hospital to take another office elsewhere and, by the influence he possessed, he passed on his former post to one of his kinsfolk with a scanty show of justice. Messer Donato met this man on the Piazza after he had come back to Florence and, being displeased with what he had done, called to him by name and asked him whether he had brought back another hospital in his pocket. As an upright citizen Messer Donato was able to speak frankly. As I am not now writing Messer Donato's Life, I have said enough about him.

To return to Piero. In his youth he was a mirror of good manners and rectitude. He and his brother Donato were always seen together and were well looked upon by all for their gracious bearing and personal beauty. When they grew up the promise of their youth was amply fulfilled. Piero was one of the most highly gifted of his time, and when he came to maturity he put aside all unworthy trifling and devoted himself to Latin letters, and for this reason he sought the best teachers. At this time Messer Jacopo da Lucca, the Cardinal of Pavia, was tutor to the sons of Messer Agnolo Acciaiuoli, and he agreed to teach Piero and Donato, who in a very short time gave proof of their aptitude for letters. Piero, for his part, spent all his time over study and cared not for amusement, looking meantime to the future. Later on the cardinal went to reside with Piero and Donato, who equalled any of the youths of their age in grammar and rhetoric. Piero acquired early an excellent style of composition in letter-writing. He practised oratory, but, not content with this, he studied logic as an introduction to philosophy, and he and Donato would often go to S. Marco to hear the lectures of Fra Agnolo da Lecco, a great logician and philosopher.

At this same time he began to study Greek under Francesco da Castiglione, who had been a pupil of Vittorino da Feltre, and he made great progress in both these subjects. Giovanni Argiropolo had just come into Italy after the fall of Constantinople and was lecturing in Florence at the University on philosophy. Having heard of the particular doctrines of this teacher, Piero and Donato, together with other young Florentines, joined his classes, and in addition studied at home the *Logic* of Aristotle, i.e. the *Categories*, the *Perhiermenia*, the *Priora* and the *Posteriora*. Piero and Donato had gathered the rudiments of Greek from Messer Francesco, and these they followed up with Argiropolo. After a lecture from him they would discuss the same at the University whether in Ethics or Logic. Piero was subtle in intellect and eloquent in speech ; indeed, Argiropolo spent more pains over them than over any others, because, when he had arrived from Constantinople, where he had been robbed of everything by the Turks, the two brothers had relieved all his wants.

At this time the plague came twice to Florence. At the first outbreak the brothers took a house for Argiropolo at Valdipesa and supplied him and his family with all necessaries. Twice daily they went thither for instruction. At home they lived a sober, virtuous life, both in word and deed : more like that of an Observantist monastery than anything else. The city of Florence might well be proud of two such citizens as Piero and Donato. When the plague came a second time they were still at Valdipesa, and it seemed well to go farther away from Florence, so they engaged the apartment of the general of Vallombrosa at Piziano. They also provided lodging near for Messer Giovanni that they might have him as a teacher. Their vacations they spent, together with Pier Filippo Pandolfini, at the Certosa.

On account of Piero's industry in the study of philosophy, there were few in Florence who could match him in learning and eloquence, as may be seen from his letters and other writings. Had not physical weakness hindered him he would have become a man matched by few of his time. He was equally ready in understanding in writing and in speaking. Through frequent use of Latin in writing and in disputation it came to him easily, and with Italian it was the same. This blending of the natural tongue with the accidental produced a brilliant and eloquent success on the history which he wrote of the deeds of arms of the Duke of Urbino at Rimini when he overthrew the army of the Church.* To all the learned of the time it seemed that, had he been less pressed for time, he would have produced a work inferior to none of the period. He received every honour the city had to confer. He was one of the leaders of his party when Messer Piero de' Pazzi came back from his embassy to Paris, where he had been made a

* Battle of Rimini, 1469.

PIERO DI NERI ACCIAIUOLI

knight by the King of France, and, now, as the Order of the Guelfs was to be given him, the delivery of the customary oration was committed to Messer Piero. When this was known in the city a vast concourse gathered to hear him, and the oration was greatly praised by all who heard it.

At this time there came to Florence Messer Giovanni de' Margheriti, the Bishop of Elva (subsequently he became Bishop of Girona,* and was made cardinal by Pope Calixtus), as ambassador from King Giovanni† to urge the Florentines to act up to the treaty which they had made with King Alfonso and Pope Nicolas for the defence of the States. The obligation still held, though the lands had not been regained owing to the war. As Duke Giovanni‡ had entered the kingdom against King Ferdinand, the bishop now asked the Florentines to hold to their bond, and made an effective public speech which was so subtle that it wanted a clever speaker to answer it. Now the chiefs of the government were anxious to evade their obligation, and they asked the gonfalonier if he was minded to answer the ambassador. He replied in the negative, adding that this charge should be given to Piero Acciaiuoli as the most able citizen and an honour to the state. Piero accepted the task and composed his speech. Certain citizens, who were jealous that he should be thus honoured and preferred, went to the gonfalonier and said it was a disgrace that he, in his high position, should be supplanted by one of the Signori, that the honour they thought to do him had miscarried. The gonfalonier then told Piero that he would deliver the speech after all, and Piero agreed. The next morning the ambassador attended to receive the reply, which was to be given in the presence of the Assembly, the Signoria and many citizens. The gonfalonier, who was no orator, as soon as he began lost himself and could not say a word. Hereupon Piero, fearing that such an incident might bring disaster, offered to make the reply, but this offer was refused. The happenings of this morning were a great disgrace and show how a great man may bring honour to his state and how an incapable may injure it. By this action Piero's fame rose greatly, for the speech

* *Vide Life*, p. 151. Gregorovius, *Rome in the Middle Ages*, VII, p. 186.
† John, King of Aragon.
‡ Jean d'Anjou, Duke of Calabria.

which he had prepared and written out gave clear proof of his ability.

As a magistrate he showed his discernment and sense of justice. He was made Governor of Pistoia when he was very young, and left a good name as an efficient officer. He was patient in listening to complaints and was greatly beloved on account of his rectitude and kindness. The two brothers, Piero and Donato, were esteemed by all and were severally nominated gonfalonier of justice, but Donato died directly after his appointment. On account of his high qualities, Piero was chosen, in spite of his youth, to go as ambassador to Pope Pius, one of the most illustrious of men. He was received with much honour by the Pope and cardinals, not only on account of his own reputation, but from the great name of his house. At this time the Cardinal of Pavia, who had been his tutor, was one of the College. Piero succeeded in his mission, for all his requests were graciously granted by the Pope, and he gained great credit on his return to Florence. Had his life been prolonged he would have been employed in many an ambassy, but through the weakness and frailty of his body he died young.

All brothers should note the great affection which subsisted between Piero and Donato. They were always together up to the age of twenty-two, and even when Piero married, some years before Donato, they did not separate. After Donato's marriage they went on as before for a time, and then separated without disagreement. On their marriage at an early age some difficulties arose from the fact that they were marrying two sisters, but in a short time things were brought into harmony and they lived after the manner of worthy gentlefolk. Piero died young by reason of his weak constitution ; had he lived longer he would have been an ornament to the state, and of Donato the same may be said.

Donato Acciaiuoli (1428–1478)

Donato was the son of Neri, son of Donato Acciaiuoli of a noble family. As soon as he had come to the age of discretion he began to read Latin under the tutorship of Jacopo da

DONATO ACCIAIUOLI

Lucca, afterwards Cardinal of Pavia. From his early youth he was a well-mannered and docile boy, and he was a model to all, whether old or young ; he was of rare intelligence, very diligent, and one who never lost a minute of time. His Latin studies soon bore good fruit, and Messer Jacopo made him write exercises in composition so that he acquired an excellent style, and gave good promise for the future. Added to all these qualities, he had a wonderful presence, so that when he passed along the streets all would look at him in admiration. He was a charming talker and won many friends. He hated all foul speech, wrangling and blasphemy. He spoke eloquently and gracefully, and used few and apposite words, avoiding all dissimulation and misstatement. Added to these characteristics, he loved and feared God above all else, and held the Christian religion in highest reverence. Piero and he were left fatherless at an early age with little to live upon, but they managed their income so carefully that they were able to live like gentlefolk. Donato was very liberal and helped out of his own purse those whom he knew to be in want. He was kind and merciful, and he hated all pride and ostentation. When he went back to his studies he worked so assiduously that his teacher found it necessary for him to discontinue them for a time, on account of his weak health, and that he might not suffer therefrom. Nature had given him that seriousness which caused him to disregard the pleasures which youth naturally seeks. His daily course of life was an example to all ; he went to confession every month, communicated three or four times every year, and fasted on all the vigils and throughout Lent. In youth, in order to avoid bad company, Piero and Donato and their teacher entered a company of young men who lived by a very strict rule of life, and made the habit of virtue their chief end. Afterwards he joined the society of San Girolamo which met by night, and he went thither every Saturday when he was in Florence and passed the night there sleeping on a sack. He was several times president, and in the course of their discipline he spoke with wonderful ability, and worked marvellously for good. I know there are many who deem this discipline of which I speak is superfluous, but these people are of a carnal spirit, and have no inclination for spiritual things, they are immersed in the delights and vain pleasures of life, they think of nothing else, and cannot realise what may be the mind and the soul of one who is altogether freed from the hard and tenacious bonds of this wretched and unhappy world, and has turned towards his Saviour in the desire to serve Him, so that, when his soul is separated from this wretched body, it may enter Eternal Life, and never perish when it has clothed itself with the garments of Immortality. Now Donato was one of those who set themselves to adopt this higher life, which will never be realised except by those who have Donato's knowledge of it. Many may think I have digressed too far from the study of letters; I have written thus simply on account of his religious observances, which are to be placed before all the science of the world.

After he had studied grammar and oratory under Messer Jacopo da Lucca, he developed much facility in the writing of themes which demonstrated his great ability, and gave him a high reputation. The first example he gave of his knowledge was at the University of Florence, where there was teaching in every faculty. At this time the court of Rome was in Florence, with its great company of distinguished men, though Florence by herself could show plenty of her own. She had the University as to-day, and the ruling officials, and the Rector who has complete control over the scholars, for the city magistrates have no jurisdiction in any offences committed by these scholars. It was the custom, when a Podestà or Captain was appointed for the Rector, the teachers and all the scholars to present themselves and produce all the laws and regulations, which he would swear to keep. Then a speech would be made, and on one occasion this duty was assigned to Donato when he was only fifteen years old. He made an excellent speech before the Podestà, the whole of the University and a large number of citizens who had come to hear him. He spoke in a way which astonished everyone, considering his youth. This was his first proof as a man of letters.

Having gained a good knowledge of Latin he turned to Greek, and together with Piero he studied under Francesco da Castiglione who was well versed in both languages. After

DONATO ACCIAIUOLI

the fall of Constantinople, there came to Italy Messer Giovanni Argiropolo, a man of the highest learning, and the greatest of philosophers. Donato studied under him for twelve years without intermission, studying both logic and philosophy from the beginnings. He, together with Piero and other youths, heard lectures on the whole of Aristotle's Logic, but it was not enough for him to listen to Argiropolo alone, so he studied also at San Marco, under Fra Agnolo da Lecco who was teaching the logic of Maestro Paolo ; and, every day, either at home or at San Marco, he would debate with other students. He then went to the University to study Aristotle's Ethics, and took down Argiropolo's lectures. He wrote the current hand well and very rapidly. Next he took a course in the Politics and Economics, and all that he had not read in moral philosophy. Every day the students made notes of certain doubtful passages in the lectures, then they would go to Argiropolo and discuss them. In the end he studied moral and natural philosophy ; *De Anima, Metaphysica* and *De cælo et mundo*. At this time the plague again came to Florence and he and Piero took a room close by, so as to lose no time and to have a convenient place for study both in the country and in Florence ; they worked assiduously, losing no time and caring for no other pleasure than the pursuit of letters. Donato had vast learning with which was combined eloquence, a rare occurrence in those who read closely in logic and philosophy.

Messer Poggio praises his eloquence, and as to his writing, having seen two Lives, one translated by Donato and the other by Messer Lionardo, he was in doubt which was the better of the two.

In addition to learning and writing Donato was anxious to know something of practical affairs, and when Messer Diotisalvi went into Lombardy on the outbreak of war between the Duke and the Venetians, Donato accompanied him and gained much experience. He often found himself discussing one science or another with the learned men of Milan, and he won great reputation through his learning. And in addition to his knowledge and worth was added his handsome presence and good manners ; those who knew him only by report would say on seeing him, " This must be Donato." The first office which he held was as one of the Signori in which his carriage showed his bent towards honest dealing. In short, he was admired and beloved by great and small throughout the city. Cosimo de' Medici was greatly impressed by the abilities of Donato, and, being a man of deeds rather than of words, determined to help him to some honour. At this time the gonfalonier of justice had to be chosen for S. Croce and a list was made of qualified citizens, and in Donato's house only Piero was eligible. When he learned this he thought no more of the matter and said nothing to Cosimo or to Agnolo or Diotisalvi, who were the clerks of the returns. Now one of these, who was a friend of Cosimo, called on him and asked whether he wanted anything to be done, whereupon Cosimo said that he especially wanted Donato Acciaiuoli to be made gonfalonier. On the day of election the citizen who had called on Cosimo rose and said : " Cosimo wishes Donato to be gonfalonier," and by means of the schedule which Cosimo presented the thing was done.

Having attained this position it appeared that he was fitted, not only for home government, but for employment as ambassador, and when he was sent to Cesena and to Rimini it seemed as if diplomacy had always been his occupation, so great was the satisfaction he gave. Soon after he was sent on a mission to Pope Paul, who, together with all the cardinals, was much impressed by his ability. It was a great advantage to him that, having to negotiate with such an assembly, he had been born of a noble house, many of whose members had been cardinals and men of mark. In addition there was his own merit, his noble disposition and his profound learning. He rose so high in the Pope's favour that one day in consistory, when he had spoken of certain requests he had made on the part of the Signoria, the Pope said in praise of him that, ever since he had been pope, he had never conferred with an ambassador who had fulfilled his duties so well as Donato. The Pope was an excellent judge in such a matter, seeing that he had lived so long at the court of Rome, and the praise of a man like Pope Paul was worth more than that of one unversed in affairs. Donato was able to hold his own on all points from his education and training amongst those who were used to deal in important matters. In his arguments he was never frivolous or vain like most men ; he fulfilled the commission and returned to Florence with much credit.

On the death of Pope Paul, Pope Sixtus succeeded, whereupon Donato, together with other leaders, were chosen to bear to the Pope the obedience of the state, according to ancient custom. The oration on doing homage was delivered by Donato in public consistory. At this ceremony the Pope, the College of Cardinals, all the ambassadors and the court of Rome were present. He spoke the oration in the best manner. After his return to Florence he was sent ambassador to Duke Galeazzo in Milan,* where he had to discuss certain matters with His Excellency ; matters very unpleasant and perplexing, but through his dexterity these were honourably adjusted. Besides the high position which Donato enjoyed through his merit and distinction, he was courageous ; he never feared to tell the truth, or to speak vigorously upon any business which affected the honour of his city. This should always be the attitude of all those who are called to deal with delicate matters of state, but not everyone has this gift. He was by nature unassuming, and intolerant of arrogance. At this time there were also in Milan ambassadors from Venice, and to these the Duke showed himself more gracious than to any others. The Duke happened to be residing at Pavia, and as he proposed to change his residence he bade Donato join company with the Venetian ambassadors, but Donato, who was ill-pleased with the attitude of the Venetians, told the Duke that he must find some one else to accompany them, as he himself was obliged to go to Milan on certain business. The Duke immediately understood that Donato did not desire their society, because of their scornful manner with others. Donato thanked Duke Galeazzo for the unusual honour done him—which had been extraordinary—an honour which the Duke had been moved to show him for many reasons, the chief of which was to affront King Ferdinand whom he hated, knowing at the same time that the Florentines also disliked Ferdinand as much as he did himself.

The Duke fully appreciated the strength and sobriety of Donato's character. Donato had now been some time in

* 1472. Duke Galeazzo died in 1476.

Milan, living the life of a temperate and religious man, and to Galeazzo and his court it seemed almost impossible that a man should live in such fashion, so he tried by various means to break down his virtue which, to the Milanese, seemed inordinate ; wherefore, on a certain evening he determined to put his continence to the proof. There was at this time in Milan a most beautiful young woman, and the Duke gave orders that she should be taken by night into Donato's chamber and left there. As soon as Donato saw what had happened he called the chamberlain and bade him take her away, refusing to touch her or even to look at her, whereupon they took the woman out of the room. When the Duke and all the court heard what had happened they were one and all struck with amazement at such continence. I will tell of something else which will seem strange and unwonted. When Donato took a wife he had never known a woman before her ; this I know for certain, having heard it from a most worthy monk of the Observantists of San Domenico to whom he had made confession before his marriage, he then being over thirty-two years of age. This is a sufficient answer to those who say that a man of the world cannot refrain from this vice. In Donato were all the qualities which are shared by men who are prone to lust ; handsome in person above all those of his age, nobly born and rich. He had conquered the flesh by abstinence and by habits of virtue. Here we may quote from St. Jerome : that to live in the flesh and to ignore it is angelic rather than human ; this may be said of Donato.

While he was at Milan a ship was captured by corsairs within the limits of the King of France, and in this ship were Florentine goods valued at thirty thousand florins. The Signoria determined to send an ambassador to the King of France* to seek redress, a man of authority and reputation, and they could find no one more fitting than Donato for many reasons ; first on account of his noble lineage, then for the good name he bore everywhere, and last because the King of France had full knowledge of his good qualities ; for, at the time of his coronation, Donato had gone as ambassador with Messer Piero de Pazzi, and had taken as an offering to the King *The Life of Charlemagne* which he had written. The

* Louis XI.

King paid him the greatest honour and gave him certain articles of silver. At Florence they at once decided to write to Donato bidding him go as ambassador to France, with a commission to procure, if possible, the restitution of the lost goods. He took the road forthwith, and when he had arrived in Paris they sent, contrary to habit, certain lords and gentlemen to meet him ; these had secured rooms for him, as the court being then in residence, lodging was scarce. When he saw the King he was informed that he had been lodged in a small house, so that he might escape the annoyance of a crowd. The King received him with more than usual cordiality, and when he spoke he always took him by the hand, as a sign of his great esteem. After he had delivered his credentials the King answered graciously that he would take time to consider the despatch. When Donato came back for his answer he was ushered into a small room adjoining the King's own. The King, as soon as he saw him, said : " Messer Donato, have patience, I want first to send off certain men-at-arms, and then I will see to you." Donato left the room for a quarter of an hour, then the King came back into the room where Donato was and said : " Messer Donato, have patience, I will see to you at once." Then he left and came back a second time into the room and took Donato by the hand, saying : " I wish you to be my secretary and to read certain letters I have received from Spain." They then returned to the apartment of the King, who made Donato read the letters. All this was done to show how much the King esteemed him. As soon as the letters had been read the King told him to wait a little and he would soon despatch the business and let him depart, whereupon Donato went out and after a little was called in again. He then once more repeated his request for the restitution of the thirty thousand florins. The King replied that he would grant it, with an assignment for the payment of the money in Languedoc, as the King had received none of it. After this debate he called the chancellor and ordered him to prepare an assignment, and to hand it over to Donato on his departure. The King asked Donato whether he wanted anything else, whereupon Donato thanked His Majesty for the favour shown him, and for the speedy settlement of the business, and took leave. In this affair it may be seen how strong is the influence of an upright man, even when dealing with a prince, and how great is the benefit and honour which such a man can bring to his state. Donato got all he wanted in this mission, what though few people believed that the King would have made himself responsible for money he had never received.

He took leave and went back to Milan. He had gone through much fatigue and anxiety and had spent double the time any other would have spent, besides laying out money of his own; moreover, he got no gratitude from the merchants for the recovery of their goods. But from this affair he reaped certain benefit, for as he was a gentleman living on a meagre income, the Signoria sent him to Milan, where the Duke gave all ambassadors a hundred scudi a month to keep up their state. But in order to compel him to pay his own charges in France, the Duke curtailed many of his gifts, and stopped his salary, and all the other ambassadors fared the same. So by going to France he lost his allowance and got nothing from the merchants; a double loss. After he returned to Milan he had to settle several matters with the Duke, who was very headstrong, but Donato always upheld his country's dignity and never failed to speak his mind plainly.

Referring to the arrival of the Venetian ambassadors which has already been noticed, when the Duke paid them so much honour that he gave offence to others, certain complaints arose. The " honour " was as follows : on their arrival he gave them the keys of the castle, having dismounted when he met them, but this was not enough ; he must even resign his own private apartments to them ; he sent his eldest son and bade him embrace them, saying at the same time that his son had no other father than the Signory of Venice in whom were all his hopes. What happened will show that the Duke did not mean what he said, for Milan has had no more persistent enemy than Venice. Donato was quite unable to endure these methods of the Duke, and told him tactfully what he thought of him. One day they were at the castle which looks out upon Brescia and Bergamo, and Donato turned to the Duke and said : " Surely it would serve your Lordship better to regain possession of Brescia and Bergamo, which belonged to your predecessors and are so near that you cannot look out of the windows without seeing them. In time your Lordship will know what sort of people the Venetians are, with this instance before you of the treachery with which they treated your father, Duke Francesco of happy memory ; also, it was through them he very nearly lost Milan." At the end of his embassy Donato returned to Florence with the good wishes of the Duke and all the court, and his own city was well satisfied with the result of his legation.

At this time he was made gonfalonier of justice, which office he filled admirably. He was one of those born for high duties, and he had so much firmness and tact that he was always able to bring his associates to his own way of thinking. The King of Norway [Christian I] came to Florence, and the Signori went to meet him. This prince showed him the greatest favour and gave him many honours of the kind which kings can bestow. In those two months he only entered his own house twice, thereby showing others how men in his position ought to demean themselves. Another change which he made was to abolish a strange custom which has obtained amongst the Signori and gonfalonieri in times past, that is never to uncover to those who took off their caps to them, and whenever an ambassador of a king or prince might come for an audience to await him in their apartment and not go forth to meet him. Donato being a man of common sense, ordered the captain that, when the ambassador of the King or of the Duke of Milan called upon him, to come into his room and tell him, then he would go to the entrance of the ante-room and take him by the hand and, having un-covered, lead him into his own apartment. When the dis-cussion was ended he would accompany him back to the same place and remove his cap and take leave of him.

He went a second time to Pope Sixtus to arrange a matter of state which proved to be difficult, inasmuch as it was entirely contrary to the Pope's wishes. He was so alert and painstaking that, although the Pope showed himself hostile to his demands, he achieved a personal triumph, for he was not the promoter of these propositions, but was under obedi-ence to the orders of his own state. After his return to Florence he was soon sent on another mission to deal with a similar question, from which sprang other troubles, for which he was

STATESMEN

in no way responsible ; troubles caused by action which he strongly condemned. One must always look to the end and realise that he who is attacked will defend himself, especially in affairs of state. I cannot treat this question openly, for I should offend those to whom my comments would be distasteful, so I will pass it over,* but I am sure that those who read on will know what I mean. At this time the city of Florence was more prosperous than it had been for many years, and no injury seemed possible or likely, but when princes, or republics, or private men are at the height of their prosperity let them fear that reverse which hardly ever fails to come. At this time the same fate fell on Florence as on those before the Flood and on Sodom, for being sunk in the pleasures and the affluence of this world the people refused to believe that any calamity could befall them. The Flood came upon the world and all those outside the Ark perished, fire and brimstone fell on Sodom from Heaven, and all were burnt save Lot and his family. A scourge fell upon Florence, totally unlooked for, which was the ruin of the state.

At this time the Cardinal of S. Giorgio, the nephew of Pope Sixtus, was living at Florence, and he stayed some time at Monte Ughi, the estate of Messer Jacopo de' Pazzi ; and besides him were present the Archbishop of Pisa, one of the Salviati, Francesco de Pazzi and others. Now Lorenzo de' Medici had invited the cardinal, the archbishop and the ambassadors of the King and of the Duke to join their company, and he had arranged this feast for the morning of Sunday, the twenty-sixth of April, 1478. By way of religious ceremony, a mass had been sung in S. Liberata,† and at the elevation of the Host, Giuliano was assaulted and killed, and Lorenzo slightly wounded. It was contrary to the will of God that such an execrable and wicked crime should happen in His temple. Afterwards more than five hundred were either killed or executed. It is not for me to tell of this barbarous crime. To return, in this tumult the Cardinal of San Giorgio, the nephew of Pope Sixtus, was seized, the Signoria and the members of the government took action to save his life, on

* This refers to the Pazzi conspiracy and the murder of Giuliano de' Medici in which the Pope was implicated.
† All authorities give the cathedral as the scene of the murder. The ancient name of the cathedral was S. Reparata.

account of what might follow. The cardinal was taken to the Palazzo, where he received honourable treatment, and everything was done to save him from the hands of the people who would have made an end of him.

When it was known in Rome that the cardinal had been seized, and the Archbishop of Pisa hanged, there was great commotion and Count Girolamo, having heard the news, stirred up the anger of the Pope and cardinals to make a hostile demonstration against our ambassador at Rome. The Count went to Donato's house, accompanied by more than thirty men-at-arms, each with his halberd on shoulder. Before the arrival of the Count, Donato was much disturbed on account of the events which had happened, since he foresaw their inevitable consequence. While he was considering the matter, the Count entered the house with all his soldiers, and, approaching Donato, bade him come away. This seemed a strange action to Donato and a great insult to his own state, since it was against all custom that ambassadors should be treated in such fashion. He said he was surprised that His Excellency should act in a way contrary to all usage with ambassadors, who were free wherever they might be ; that he could not believe such a deed was done by the order of the Pope and the cardinals, that he would follow the course which he deemed right, and that the Count had better realise that this grave insult would not apply to him, as envoy, but to the state he represented. The Count, a true hothead, endeavoured to answer him, thereupon Donato began to fear for his life, and before he left the house he told the chancellor to take all the cyphers and letters of importance, and set out for Florence with information as to what had happened. When he left the house he was surrounded by the ruffianly soldiers as if he had been a thief or a traitor. Let anyone imagine Donato's feelings when he found his city and himself treated with such contumely, for if ever there was a man in the world who held high his own honour and that of his state it was Donato. When he reached the Pope's palace he demanded to speak with His Holiness, so that he might ask him whether it was his will that an ambassador should be so foully maltreated. He addressed the Pope and complained bitterly of the insult that had been done to his state and himself, and turning to Count

STATESMEN

Girolamo, said, " Sir Count, I am indeed astonished at your rash presumption, that you have ventured to come to my house with an armed band, I being the ambassador of Florence, to carry me off as if I had been a traitor. I will remind you that this injury you have done me is one which my government will not forget, until they have let you see your mistake." Then he turned to the Pope with regrets that he should have sanctioned such an unseemly act, and that His Holiness had not acted justly, knowing, as he must, that ambassadors are always regarded as privileged. Whereupon the Pope swore upon his heart that he knew nothing of this happening and showed by his speech that he was highly displeased, affirming also that this deed had not been done by his will. Having spoken, he gave Donato leave to go back to his house.

Considering the contempt which was heaped upon him as a public man, the disgrace and scorn with which his city and still more he himself had been treated ; his consciousness that this scandal would give rise to future evil on account of his arrest and consequent offence in Rome (which was indeed the cause of future wars) and the love he bore to his state, there is no wonder that a generous-hearted man like Donato felt his position well-nigh intolerable. He wrote word to the heads of the government describing what had happened, and urged them to carry out the promises he had made to the Pope ; to set free the cardinal, since he had written to the Pope that he had been rescued from the hands of the people and was held at his disposition, and that, at any time His Holiness might ask, he would be delivered over. Donato urged this course strongly in order to avoid any future difficulty. And for this reason the Pope sent the Bishop of Perugia to Florence, so that the cardinal might be delivered over to him. Donato exhorted them to liberate him straightway, urging them to do this for the good of the city and knowing that any other course would be dangerous, and lead to no good, especially as they had promised by their letters that the cardinal would be set free whenever his release was demanded. Likewise His Majesty the King urged them in the same terms, and promised that no hurt should ensue in consequence of their compliance. But nothing that Donato said could induce those in office in Florence to consent : the Bishop of Perugia waited on, but the cardinal was not released, and more attention was given to the opinions of obscure men than to Donato's.

In view of this crisis he was seized with great uneasiness on account of the misfortunes which he foresaw must fall upon his country, and, added to this, he was galled by the shame which had been put on Florence and on himself in the matter of his seizure, by the subsequent affront to the city, by the death of so many men, and by the seeds of war which had been sown and future danger to Florence. On account of the recent misadventures, neither he nor Florence were held in respect at the court of Rome, and in these unsatisfactory conditions he could be of no service as ambassador, wherefore he besought the Signoria to recall him. This was done, and before he arrived in Florence he was appointed ambassador to the King of France.* Grief and vexation had brought him so low that he lost all spirit and was sunk in deepest melancholy. Naturally of a delicate sensitive complexion, he lost both sleep and appetite through mental distress. After his recall from Rome he halted at Florence, where his mental perturbation was so great that, however he might strive, he could not conceal it. Now the journey to France lay before him ; the way was long and the heat intense, and he himself in most precarious health. Nevertheless, he would gladly have laid down his life for his country, so great was his love for it. He was urged to go, and he consented, though he knew he would incur great danger, and he had forebodings he would never return, as was shown in the farewell he took of his wife and children and friends. Before leaving, as is the manner with ambassadors going abroad, he confessed and communicated and left full directions by testament. He journeyed from Florence to Milan, where he was received with honour by the heads of the state. It was usual for the resident Florentine envoy to go to meet any special ambassador and to accompany him on his departure, but the present envoy did not attend at Donato's arrival. Donato went to this man's house on a visit of ceremony. When he went to his lodgings he showed himself much perturbed at the slight this man had put upon him, and the fresh irritation added greatly to his other sufferings.

* This embassy was to ask for aid against Sixtus IV and Ferdinand.

STATESMEN

A few days later by the will of God he fell ill, and the distemper from which he had been suffering declared itself ; everything possible was done for him, seeing that he was suffering from melancholia. Physicians were at once called in ; they recognised his disease as dangerous although it had not yet fully revealed itself, and to add to his other misfortunes the chief people in his house, and those who were nursing him, also fell ill and could not give him the care he needed. The unfortunate Donato found himself far from home and separated from his friends and kinsfolk, and all may realise how great his sufferings were. Oh, empty hopes of men, without God everything is wretched and unhappy ! One day when he was lying alone the ambassador of Ferrara came to visit him and found him lamenting and repeating the words, " Oh, my children, where am I leaving you ? " He was so full of anguish, and misery, and bitterness that no hope was left to him, except the hope he had always nourished—the hope in God. He then sought spiritual remedies and bade them call in Observantist friars in whom he had always trusted, and to them he confessed devoutly. When the confessor asked him whether he had anything on his mind, he replied that he had ; that there was in a chest in Florence, written by his own hand, a document telling his last wishes, and he desired that his heirs should see that these were carried out. First, that a farm which he possessed in Valdepisa, which produced a rent of thirty florins a year, should be given to the friars of the Certosa for their enjoyment for thirty years and then should revert to his heirs. He did not make this restitution for himself, but because he felt that some of his forbears ought to have done it. His conscience was so sensitive that he did not deceive himself as is the way of many. Second, that those hundred florins of bank stock which belonged to him should be cancelled for the benefit of the commune. Another matter was, that in all the missions upon which he had been employed, he had taken fewer attendants than he ought to have taken, therefore he desired to make restitution of the sum which their wages and expenses would have involved. Again, as he was a partner in a silk factory, he directed that all the charges which had been put upon the poor weavers, with regard to the third part which they received, should be restored to them, and that this money should be supplied by the sale of his own wares. In everything Donato showed the purity of his conscience. He often revised his accounts and never erred like many others. Having settled all his worldly and spiritual affairs there remained nothing more for him to do ; men of God were continually at his side, and he showed at his end that he had not fallen from the high purpose of his life.

When his death was known in Florence there was universal grief and regard for the loss of so worthy a citizen as Donato. O vain hope of men in this wretched and unstable life ! When men expect some reward for their labours, death comes and all hope is at an end. When it was known that he had died for his country's good, and that he had lived on his own revenues, now much reduced, it was decreed that the state should give him a funeral at its own cost ; with a banner with the arms of the commune, and a train of tapestry ; all these honours were sanctioned unanimously. These honours are shown only to citizens beloved by the state ; others who wish for the honour of the banner must needs pay for it. They excused his children from all taxation, and only asked them for one florin a year for a very long time. As to his two daughters, one of them had no dowry, and the other was only partly dowried ; to the first they gave the whole dowry and to the other they gave what was lacking. They also gave them the money which he had in hand at his death. No one objected to this proposition and everything was easily settled. After this his funeral took place ; it was attended by all the officials and the citizens, indeed there was not absent a single prominent Florentine. Messer Cristofano Landini delivered an oration, over which he showed great emotion ; this emotion I myself witnessed, also that there was no one in the crowd who could refrain from tears and sighs, which evidently came from their heartfelt grief. The illustrious Duke of Urbino, while grief stricken at his death, said that the death of Donato was a loss not only to his city but to the whole of Italy and that he had left no peer. The Duke of Calabria,* who had the greatest regret and reverence for Donato, was deeply grieved by the news of his death and spoke in full agreement with the Duke

* Jean d'Anjou.

of Urbino, saying that all Italy must mourn for the loss of this illustrious man. All grieved for him whether they knew him or not.

I must here speak of his great continence, for before he married his wife no one ever saw him take her by the hand or bear himself otherwise than in seemly manner, and no one ever saw him embrace his sons or put his arm round their neck nor kiss them, and this was solely to maintain the reverence of his sons towards him. Indeed, he freed himself from all fleshly lusts. All his time was taken up with writing and study, except what might be devoted to the duties of his family or of the state, and to both of these he gave diligent care. His first office outside the city was that of Vicar of Poppi, where he won the regard of all the people. He was Vicar of San Miniato and at the same time Podestà of Montepulciano, and in his absence another took his place. He was Captain of Volterra, where he won great favour, and he was the last Podestà of Pisa, where he succeeded as well as elsewhere. In the elections he was returned in most of the contests with all the black beans, on account of the universal regard in which he was held. The same thing happened with regard to the Monte, and every time that he was sent as ambassador he went with the goodwill of all.

As to his appearance, he was a very handsome man, above the average height, his complexion was pink and white, his manner, though dignified, had an unusual charm, which was quite as real as it seemed to be. He was always well dressed, and neat in all his ways, and the sight of him was natural grace displayed. He was temperate in his food and drink, and he ate daintily. Everyone who spoke to him would necessarily depart his admirer. He was very animated and pleasant, and with his friends he would joke freely. He spent his time profitably, and all his leisure he devoted to writing or reading. At the request of Cosimo de' Medici he wrote a comment on the *Ethics*, on which he spent great care; it is a remarkable work now found in all the universities of Italy. When the Duke of Urbino saw it, he begged him to make a similar one upon the *Politics*, whereupon he produced another work of equal merit. Piero di Cosimo besought him to translate two Lives which were wanting in Plutarch*; those of Demetrius and Alcibiades. He made two very elegant translations of them as may be seen ; that of Demetrius had been left out by Messer Lionardo on account of its difficulty. He began the comment on the *Economica* to complete the Moral Philosophy, but death interrupted him. He wrote the Lives of Hannibal and Scipio, drawing a parallel between them and the Life of Charlemagne, which he gave to King Louis of France, as well as many epistles and speeches, but he died before they were finished.

AGNOLO ACCIAIUOLI

He was son of Jacopo and grandson of Donato Acciaiuoli, of noble birth. He gained a good knowledge of Latin letters and spent his leisure in reading history, both sacred and secular. He was kinsman and friend of Giannozzo Manetti and Messer Agnolo. Messer Giannozzo instructed him and divers other young citizens in Aristotle's *Ethics*. He was greatly honoured in the republic, and was employed in every state office that citizens could fill at home, and sent on every diplomatic mission to foreign parts. When Cosimo was banished Agnolo, then a young man, remained at home, and once, when conversing with one of the chiefs of the government, the two disagreed so strongly that Agnolo was carried before the authorities. As he had dealings with banished citizens, they ordered the officials of the Balia to put a seal upon his goods. But his brother-in-law Giacomino, who saw him taken, at once went on horseback to Agnolo's house at Monte Paldi, and, having entered his cabinet, he burned all the writings he found there, which included letters from Cosimo and other exiles, and dealings with them. But for this good fortune these documents might have brought him ruin. As soon as Giacomino had burnt them, the beadle arrived to seize them, but when he realised the position he returned

---

* Donato has been charged with plagiary by later critics. Vossius holds that he did not translate his " Lives " from Plutarch at all, but wrote them himself in Latin ; Naudé accuses him of having taken his treatise on the Ethics bodily from notes by Argiropolo. He translated into Latin Lionardo d' Arezzo's *History of Florence.*

and told the Signoria there were no papers. As there was nothing to justify a process against him they banished Agnolo to Cephalonia. Thus his life was saved by the prompt and prudent Giacomino. He was sent to Cephalonia because this, and Athens and Thebes, belonged to his house, together with other lands of which Messer Donato had been governor.

After he arrived in Greece he was riding one day on the Turkish borders when he was seized and, because he refused to tell who he was and what he was doing, he was imprisoned. Here he found another Florentine, and the two escaped together and went through great perils. He told me that this escape was little less than a miracle. Messer Agnolo's way of life was so admirable that Almighty God naturally delivered him from danger. He was compassionate to the poor, and liberal in almsgiving, for when he went abroad he gave to all the poor he met. When he and Messer Donato went together to Milan they gave, for the love of God, forty ducats in the course of the journey. He was also devoted to religious observances, and during every night he would rise to pray and say the office, spending two hours over his devotions. Every morning he heard mass and was wont to say that the state was saved from many evils by this practice. He was banished in '33, and when Cosimo returned in '34, he was recalled to Florence, where he was welcomed in great state as a member of a noble house and as one high in Cosimo's favour. He was one of the leaders in '34 and, as he could do as he wished in everything, he was sent ambassador on the most important missions in foreign parts.

To refer to his firm belief in the efficacy of religious practices ; when he was travelling in the spring on a mission to the French king it happened that the weather, as it is usual at this season, was variable. In passing through Savoy the road traversed a forest and, just before they reached this place, the day was bright with sunshine, but at the hour of vespers it changed suddenly and snow began to fall so that they lost their way. At dusk they reached a wood in bitter cold and heavy snow to await nightfall, and it seemed to all that in such a place they were bound to die of cold before morning. Not knowing what to do they dismounted, and each one tied his horse to a tree ; the horses, indeed, suffered quite as much as the men. Messer Agnolo and all the rest commended themselves to God, having lost all hope. They were frozen into silence and no one spoke. But God never forsakes those who trust in Him. One of the footmen, unknown to the rest, stole out to search for a village or some human habitation. After going some four miles he came to some peasants' huts, and, as it was winter, all the peasants were at home. At the fourth hour of night he roused the peasants and, having promised them any reward they might ask, he induced six or eight to accompany him with lighted torches. When they were near the wood the servant shouted, "We are saved!" whereupon all the company rejoiced greatly. For those who had remained in the wood the cold was almost unendurable. The peasants took charge of the horses and conducted Messer Agnolo and his troop back to the village, where, though half dead with cold, they soon revived. Agnolo was wont to attribute this miracle to his practice of almsgiving and prayer, and assuredly it was a miracle worked by the grace of God.

Messer Agnolo also tells how once, as he was passing a swollen river in France, he was stranded between two of its branches and could move neither forwards nor backwards. How it happened he did not know, but by God's help he and all his company, who were in danger of drowning, reached the farther bank. He always regarded this as another miracle. At the beginning of Holy Week he went to the Certosa and took part in all the religious observances, and on Saturday returned to Florence to join in the popular Easter ceremonies. During his embassy to the French king * he concluded a treaty greatly to the advantage of the State of Florence, which at this time was hard pressed by King Alfonso. During his stay King Charles gave him a silver table of great value with a sumptuous equipment, but when he received this Agnolo would only accept two silver flasks and returned the rest. These two flasks he presented later on to Duke Francesco of Milan for whom he had great regard, as they had been brought up together.

At the time when the Florentines helped Duke Francesco to become Duke of Milan by going to war with the Venetians,

* Charles VII.

when they refused to observe the provisions of their agreement, thus giving them something to think about, it chanced that certain Venetian soldiers in the pay of the Marquis of Montferrato, whose lands marched with those of Milan, made a strong resistance to the operations against them, harrying the country around Milan and causing great loss and disgrace. When counsel had been taken how they might best abate the insolence of the Venetians and make them keep within their own bounds it seemed best to the Duke and to the Signoria of Florence to send Messer Agnolo on a mission to King René in Provence, urging him to enter Lombardy with as strong a force as he could muster to support Duke Francesco, and pointing out to him that, were this done, his interests in Naples might be considered. When he reached Provence, in company with Giovanni Coscia as a supporter, he laid before King René the advantages he might reap by joining in the assistance to Duke Francesco, but he found the King reluctant to adventure into Italy. Agnolo, however, by his prudence and persuasion succeeded in exhibiting to him so attractive a picture of the gain he would make that René set on foot a force strong enough to bring to reason the Marquis of Montferrato, who had to chose between consent and the loss of his state. By this agreement Duke Francesco was relieved of a serious embarrassment, as the Venetians began to fear the security of their position. When King René's men had joined those of Duke Francesco they came upon the foe at Ponte Vico, and at once scaled the walls and entered the town with great spirit ; indeed, these Frenchmen feared no danger.*
The Venetians were forced to withdraw to a position between the two armies, and they would have been in some peril had not Duke Francesco been short of money on account of the

---

* This happened in 1453. Vespasiano suppresses the horrors of René's campaign. His army was largely composed of French and Burgundian ruffians let loose by the cessation of the English war. After the capture of Ponte Vico they massacred every man, woman and child they met, and attacked those of Sforza's army who tried to restrain their fury. War in Italy at this period was largely an affair of tactics with a minimum of bloodshed, and the savage fury of René's hirelings struck terror into the Venetians who fled in haste, leaving the field clear for Sforza's army. René's men had more taste for massacre than fight, and as winter came on they clamoured to be sent back and Italy was freed of their presence. *Vide* Macchiavelli, *Hist. Flor.*, p. 315 ; Sismondi, *Repub. Italiennes*, IX, p. 423.

failure of payments from Florence. This advance of King René and the consequent relief of Duke Francesco was due to the good offices of Messer Agnolo.

Before this episode of King René, Duke Filippo,* who never could keep the peace, had sent Nicolo Piccinino to attack the Florentines who had no other forces than those of Gian Pagolo. Nicolo advanced with a large army close up to the city walls. Messer Agnolo had gone to Ferrara to enlist the help of Duke Borso, and on his return he found that the way through Lombardy was barred, so he went into Romagna and secured the help of Messer Guidaco of Faenza and other Signori of Romagna with a good force of horse and foot. With this force, and with the influence he commanded, he saved the liberties of Florence which were then in peril. At this period the Florentines and Venetians were in league, and were daily attacked by Duke Filippo, so they resolved to send ambassadors to Milan, and Agnolo was sent as one well-known to the Duke. When they arrived in Milan the Duke fixed a day to receive them and to learn the object of their mission. He received Agnolo very graciously as one he knew and esteemed, but the Venetian had a very cool reception, no respect being shown either to his person or to the dignity of his state. Whenever the two envoys waited on the Duke together, they were refused admission, but when Agnolo went alone he was admitted at once. The Duke disliked the ceremonious ways of the Venetians and preferred Agnolo's ease of manner, acquired by his early association with well-bred people. The Venetian lost all patience on account of these continual affronts, while Agnolo was constantly with the Duke. There was a natural hatred between Duke Filippo and the Venetians on account of the large portion of his lands they held, and he knew not how to hide his resentment. The Venetian waited many days without holding any conversation on the subject of his mission with the Duke, who sent all communications through one of his officials. The ambassador returned to Venice, where he told of the slight which had been put upon him by Duke Filippo, a slight both to the Signory

---

* Filippo Maria died in 1447. Vespasiano has here gone back some ten years, as Piccinino died in 1444. The reference may be to the advance of Piccinino on Florence in 1440 and his defeat at Anghiari.

and to his own person. But at Florence Agnolo was able to report what great honour had been shown to him by the Duke, and he fared just as well in all the missions he undertook.

On the morning of the departure of Pope Eugenius from Florence* there arose a hot dispute as to whether or not he should be suffered to leave. The Venetians desired to hinder his return to Rome, but the majority of the government were for letting him go ; amongst them were Messer Agnolo, who knew the Pope well, and also Messer Francesco di Padua, who was with the Pope. The whole of the night before had been spent in discussing this question. When it had been decided unanimously to allow the Pope to leave whenever he would, Messer Agnolo was sent early in the morning to inform the Pope, who was waiting to hear ; and in S. Maria Novella he met Messer Francesco, who asked if they were prisoners. Agnolo replied that they were not ; if they had been he would not have been sent, but another citizen who wanted them to be detained. The Pope knew everything and had already made Agnolo a knight with the accustomed oath. The Pope thanked Agnolo and the Signoria and rode away with his court to Siena. He left with no friendly feeling towards the city, having made a league with Alfonso and Duke Filippo, wherefore it seemed to the Florentines that they were in a perilous strait, so they sent Agnolo to Siena to appease Eugenius. He spent much time with Pope and cardinals, especially with the Cardinal of Santa Croce, who belonged to the Carthusian order, and also with Messer Thomas of Sarzana. His mediation was successful, and he appeased the Pope largely on account of the support of the Cardinal of Santa Croce who was in the Pope's confidence.

When this mission was finished he returned to Florence and the Pope went on to Rome and died soon afterwards.† Pope Nicolas, whom Agnolo knew well, succeeded him. Agnolo Acciaiuoli, Giannozzo Pitti, Alessandro degli Alessandri, Giannozzo Manetti, Neri di Gino Capponi and Piero di Cosimo de' Medici were chosen as ambassadors to carry homage to the new Pope. They went to Rome with a train of a hundred and twenty horses and were honourably received by all the court. The Pope placed so great trust in Messer Agnolo

* March 7th, 1443. † 1447.

that he charged him with a mission to the King of France, with respect to certain matters concerning the Holy See, which he discharged to the Pope's satisfaction. Agnolo had now enjoyed all the honours the state could give, as well as diplomatic missions to all the principal sovereigns abroad, and several times he was commissary in the field.

Duke Francesco, having got possession of Milan,* and agreed with Pope Pius to aid King Ferdinand against Duke Giovanni, Messer Agnolo, who had often been as envoy to Milan, was again sent thither. Duke Francesco was set on prosecuting this costly enterprise in the kingdom, but many of his advisers condemned it ; even Madonna Bianca who had great influence with him. One day the Duke summoned a Council, at which Madonna Bianca was present, and asked for advice whether or not he should send an expedition into the kingdom, whereupon a unanimous decision was given against it, Madonna Bianca being more emphatic than any. Agnolo, seeing the council was unanimous, said nothing, and, when all had spoken, the Duke turned to him and said, " You and I are the only ones who have been silent. What is your opinion ? " Agnolo said, " In the face of the united opinion of so many worthy gentlemen I did not venture to say a word, but I will speak for myself, and afterwards Your Highness can please yourself. I shall show that, for many reasons, what Duke Francesco has done has been done for the welfare of his state ; also that, for the welfare of all Italy, this expedition ought not to be abandoned ; that it will prove as advantageous to Milan as it is to King Ferdinand. The Venetians are near the borders, and you know what strong foes they are. I urge that, for the defence of this state and the welfare of your son, you should try to secure King Ferdinand from the attacks of Duke John, and restore peace to the kingdom ; that the King, the Florentines and Your Excellency should form a league, for there is no other way to secure the safety of the allied states, and, seeing there is already a tie of relationship,† that each one should work for the common good." Agnolo made this spirited defence

* Filippo Maria died in 1447, but Francesco Sforza, his son-in-law, did not secure the duchy till 1450. Vespasiano here goes on to 1459–64.
† Ferdinand's son, Alfonso, had married Ippolita Maria, Francesco Sforza's daughter, in 1465.

because he knew he was expressing the Duke's will, also because it would be for the advantage of the King and of Florence. Though it was clear that the Duke was disposed to follow the course Agnolo advocated, there were many who dissented and were ill-pleased that he agreed with Agnolo so readily ; and those who favoured Duke Giovanni resented his stay in Milan. But Agnolo by remaining there was the greatest help to the King by supporting Duke Francesco's resolve to aid him, in spite of the opposition of certain factions in Milan and Florence. King Ferdinand was under great obligations to Agnolo, and he was not ungrateful, for he gave him an estate called Quaranto which had formerly belonged to the Acciaiuoli, and Agnolo sent thither his son Jacopo two years before the disturbances of '66.*

Agnolo remained in Milan till the King had regained the greater part of his dominions. Then he was urged by his family to return to Florence in view of the state of King Ferdinand's affairs. He allowed himself to be advised and found he had erred in going back. Just at this time the bishopric of Arezzo became vacant. He had a son named Lorenzo, a well-mannered young man, who had been destined from childhood to become a priest. Now that this bishopric was vacant he made an attempt to obtain it for Lorenzo, because he himself was well known to Pope Pius, and because there was at this time in the Pope's household Messer Jacopo di Lucca, a cardinal, whose word was powerful with the Pope ; moreover, Messer Jacopo had lived in Agnolo's house as tutor to his son Lorenzo. Agnolo, by the favour of the Pope and the Cardinal of Lucca, would have secured the benefice if Cosimo de' Medici had not put forward the name of his kinsman, Filippo de' Medici. At this juncture the Pope was doubtful what to do. Cosimo, a friend and kinsman of Agnolo, was firmly set that Filippo should be nominated, but he promised Agnolo that the next bishopric which fell vacant in Florentine territory should be given to Lorenzo, and Agnolo, for the sake of peace, consented. After a short interval the Archbishop of Pisa died, whereupon Agnolo approached Cosimo, who suggested that Lorenzo should get the bishopric

---

* The struggle between Piero de' Medici and Luca Pitti and his adherents. *Vide* Sismondi, *Republiques Italiennes*, X, p. 290.

of Arezzo and Filippo be promoted Archbishop of Pisa. Thereupon arose a bitter quarrel between the two, and, although Agnolo was obliged to take the bishopric for his son, much anger was generated, Agnolo lost all patience, and, by his demeanour, aroused more opposition than support. He laid his grievances before every one he met, and certain statements he made in the heat of passion were carried to Cosimo in a distorted shape, and these perverted statements proved to be his ruin. Those who embroil themselves in ecclesiastical affairs, except they follow the right path, will meet with serious trouble, as will appear from what now occurred. Agnolo, in the indignant humour which possessed him, refused to be satisfied. Just then (1464) came the death of Cosimo, and at once the city was divided into the factions of Lucca Pitti and of Piero di Cosimo de' Medici. Everyone worked for his party and the names of all were written down. This was the ruin of the city, as in both factions were men of high standing. Agnolo was still hot with resentment, and his friends and kinsfolk urged him to join Messer Luca.* Now Agnolo had been absent from Florence a long time ; he did not realise the treachery of the democracy of the city so, being strongly importuned, he cast in his lot with Messer Luca, whereby he joined that party which had long ago exiled him to Cephalonia. He was turned by the persuasions of a certain kinsman and intimate friend who proved to him that the control of the state must be theirs (but in this he erred), that six hundred citizens had rallied to the support of Messer Luca, and showed him their written signatures. By these advisers and by his own passionate resentment he was driven to his ruin.

In 1466 each faction took up arms, but after a little it appeared that Piero was the stronger of the two, wherefore Luca's adherents began to withdraw, and when they heard that Piero's faction was about to treat with the Signoria, they were greatly dismayed. One evening Piero summoned Agnolo to a conference and asked him to mediate for the settlement of their discords. Messer Agnolo, who deemed matters were now in a fair way to agreement, said that he would do all that was possible, but that should a further crisis

* Luca Pitti.

happen he must keep aloof. Agnolo, indeed, was working in the dark. He wanted to keep a straight path and to avoid all discord. A conference had been arranged ; the party of Luca had disarmed and were at the discretion of their opponents. Ruin fell by God's will without warning. I deem that the confusion of holy things with neglect of duty may have been the reason why events happened as they did. The leaders on each side took the holy body of Christ together before the case came on. The priest broke the sacred wafer into small pieces so that each one took a portion as a pledge that they would act together and forgo all trickery in future. How this pact was broken I know not, but the traitor will assuredly be punished. When the Signoria had met and the Eight of the Balia had been chosen the followers of Messer Luca saw they were ruined. Agnolo worked in good faith up to the end, and failed to see how things were going until the composition of the parliament had been settled. Much might be written on this affair, but I deem it wise to break off, seeing that those who tell the truth often get the blame. I only wish to insist on Messer Agnolo's innocence, seeing that he knew not what he was doing.

One morning I found him at table, greatly disturbed ; he would fain have eaten but he could not, being so much distressed at the trend of events. He cursed those who had persuaded him to quit Milan, where he was living in peace and happiness. He also declared that he had been deceived by Messer Luca's partisans, who declared they had six hundred and more supporters, while he himself had never met anybody who had ever seen a single one of them.

From this saying his innocence is apparent. While affairs were in this state he left Florence and went to stay the night with Ser Nicodemo, a friend, who at once began to hearten him with assurances that no one would deem him in fault. He bade Agnolo wait there while he went to plead his innocence with Piero, who, when he should know that Agnolo had never plotted against him, would surely save him from ill ; also to remain quiet until he should know what was Piero's will. And afterwards Piero often declared that, if Agnolo had followed Nicodemo's counsel, he would never have been exiled. Agnolo, however, was apprehensive of evil, and that same night he left Nicodemo's house for the Certosa over by-paths which he knew well. From the evidence of many trust-worthy persons I know that, if Agnolo had awaited the return of Nicodemo from his visit to Piero, he would never have been exiled, for, only twenty days before his death, Piero discussed with the chiefs of the government the ques-tion of Agnolo's innocence. Messer Marino, the envoy of King Ferdinand, had also intervened, and there was a general desire for the recall of Agnolo. While this matter was pending Piero fell sick and died,* and, as there was no one to look after Agnolo's interests, nothing more was done. All this goes to prove Agnolo innocent.

Agnolo had gone to Barletta,† where he received letters from other Florentine exiles urging him to return. He naturally wished to go back, and left Barletta for Naples. King Ferdinand received him and advised him for the present to keep outside the frontier.‡ In response to certain letters and personal invitations, he went to Rome to Pope Paul. Those who had given unwise counsel in the first instance were now the cause of his second great error, by persuading him by specious arguments that his visit to Rome was the right way to procure his restoration. He let himself be led on by their empty words ; while, had he remained quiet, he would have soon have been recalled, the charge of rebellion would have been withdrawn, and he would have saved his posses-sions. After this second mistake the course of events was exactly contrary to what his advisers had foretold. Happy had he been if he had followed the King's advice not to cross the frontier. He was afterwards convinced of the mistake he made in following the advice of one who had counselled him so disastrously in the first instance. After he had left Rome he encountered the army of Bartolomeo of Bergamo, and, being well versed in military discipline, he saw yet more

---

* 1469. Macchiavelli writes, *Flor. Hist.*, p. 356 : " Insomuch as Piero sent secretly for Agnolo Acciaiuoli and they reasoned at length touching the estate of the Cittie. And surely, had he not been by death prevented, he would have called home all the banished men to bridle the insolence and oppression of those that lived in the citie."

† He and his family were banished to Barletta for twenty years.

‡ He must have been in Naples before Piero died, as Macchiavelli gives an interesting exchange of letters between the two. *Flor. Hist.*, pp. 349–50.

plainly that he had been deceived. After he reached Venice these evil counsellors came to see him and asked him how he fared, whereto he replied : " I should have fared well enough had you let me stay in Naples." Further misfortune soon fell upon him ; he was declared a rebel and all his property in Florence confiscated. At the same time King Ferdinand informed him that, as he had transgressed the bounds of his exile, the estate of Quaranto, which had been granted to him in the kingdom, would he reassumed. This step, the King explained, was necessary on account of the agreement between him and Florence, wherefore this unhappy gentleman found himself stripped of all his possessions both in Florence and in Naples. He wandered about for a long time and finally determined to find a way out of his troubles; therefore, putting his trust in God and in King Ferdinand, whom he had served diligently in the past, he decided to go to Naples and beg the King not to forsake him in his evil case.

When he reached Naples the King was mindful of his past services. He gave Agnolo an income of two hundred ducats a month, which allowed him to live honourably and to maintain his custom of prayer and almsgiving. He cared no more for state affairs, and every morning and evening attended the service at the Certosa. He spent all his time in religious exercises and, by the grace of God, found the right path. I believe that his prayers and fastings and religious exercises were the cause why God gave him such grace at last. Having shaken off all worldly cares he recognised his vocation. He fell ill of fever and at once betook himself to all the practices meet for those who are truly penitent. He took all the sacraments of the Church and showed his repentance before God with sighs and tears, and grasping the Crucifix he gave up his soul. What I have written of Messer Agnolo comes partly from my own knowledge and partly from the report of trustworthy men, and I have set it down in order that all who read it, in marking the changes in his fortunes, may learn to fly low and be content with little.

AGNOLO MANETTI

Agnolo was the son of Giannozzo Manetti, under whose discipline he was brought up. He had a good knowledge of Greek and Latin, for it was his father's wish that he should acquire these in his youth; also that he should be able to write in Latin, Greek and Hebrew. He became so proficient that he composed in Latin better than most youths of his age, and Hebrew he wrote as well as a certain Jew whom his father had persuaded to be baptised under the name of Giovan Francesco, the finest writer in Hebrew of the time. Agnolo would often write verses in Hebrew, and the Jew would write as many, and no one could say one set was better than the other. No one could write Greek better than he, and at the age of twelve he had mastered all these languages. His father never let him waste his time and, as he was studious by nature and possessed of a very active intelligence, he would often write for two hours at a stretch.

Having made him a fine scholar Messer Giannozzo desired that he should now acquire a knowledge of affairs, and when Agnolo was thirteen his father began to take him on all the various missions he discharged, so that in his early years he had gained a wider experience in this field than any other youth of this time. He was by nature very unassuming, sparing of his words, all of which he well weighed. He was an eloquent speaker with quick judgment and sage counsel, of extensive general knowledge and able to discuss every subject. He visited the courts of several of the Popes, Kings and Emperors, Venice and all other regions of Italy, and was well received wherever he went. When he was fourteen, his father, then Captain of Pistoia, was selected to go to Rome after the election of Pope Nicolas. Meantime he left Agnolo to discharge his office at Pistoia. Here he remained for two months until his father's return, and it was a wonder to everyone that a mere youth like Agnolo should have shown so much judgment and reticence. His writings were graceful and eloquent, but the misfortunes which befell his father robbed him of the opportunity of extended study; for wherever Giannozzo went his son always accompanied him. He soon felt the strokes of adverse fate. Giannozzo, after suffering many and varied calamities, died all too soon ; wherefore, as all the charges of the family were laid on Agnolo, he found little time for the cultivation of letters, nevertheless all his leisure he gave to reading.

After his father's death he was forced to go to Naples, as part of the family estate was there. He had several interviews with the King, and complained that justice was not being done to him, and asked for his advice. He also made a strong statement of his case before the Council. After the matter had come before the King and the Council several times, the Council decided in his favour and his conduct won general approval. But after he had dealt with the Grand Seneschal the King refused to allow his petition to be granted forthwith, and bade him have patience. One day the King left Naples to hunt in the country, and Agnolo, seeing how the affair stood, followed him and then, in the presence of certain gentlemen, set forth the wrongs which had been done to him. The King was much disturbed and knew not what to answer, saying that as soon as he returned to Naples he would satisfy him. Like his father, Agnolo was of a high spirit, and was little disposed to submit beyond reason to others for the sake of any gain he might look for.

He was by far the youngest of the city magistrates, and all were surprised to find him so little a novice at his duties. In his decisions he showed an ability which few others possessed : he would listen patiently to both sides of a question, and then would unhesitatingly decide one way or the other. He was often called on to settle mercantile disputes and appeals. His judgments were admirable, as he had a good knowledge of trade and was a skilled arithmetician. I once met a citizen who had consulted Agnolo about a renewal, and about an appeal against some of his kinsfolk which had lasted fourteen years and had never been settled, though they had several times laid it before arbitrators. Agnolo was amongst those chosen to settle the appeal. This citizen waited on Agnolo, who did not despatch the matter in general terms as many would have done, but said, " Come into my office." He then brought out pen, ink and paper, and bade the citizen say all he had to say, and this he wrote down. They then went before the arbitrators, to whom he explained all the arguments of the citizen and of his opponents. Then the disputants were called in to state their several cases. Finally, as Agnolo had taken so much trouble over the affair, it was agreed to leave the settlement to him. Moreover, all the others were glad to shift the trouble off their own shoulders. Agnolo had managed the case so well that his decision satisfied both parties, and no more was heard of it. Many thousand florins were involved in this case, and it would never have been arranged but for Agnolo's care and assiduity. The citizen in question, a cousin of Agnolo Acciaiuoli, let all the city know what Messer Agnolo had done for him.

He was an intimate friend of Agnolo Acciaiuoli, who set great store upon his judgment. If only Acciaiuoli had listened to the wise council Manetti gave him, he would never have been exiled. Manetti indeed foresaw that the course Agnolo was taking would prove his ruin, but men are sometimes driven to destruction against their will. Agnolo Manetti never bore any office outside the city except at Campiglia, where he did excellent service. This was in war times, and he settled many quarrels satisfactorily. Campiglia and Piombino adjoined, and there were continual feuds between one and the other, all of which were settled by Agnolo's ministrations, so that he left the district in excellent order. He had many meetings with the Lord of Piombino with reference to these disputes, and the Lord often said that, if he had a man like Agnolo by his side, he would have no anxiety for his own state. While the officers were always at odds with the Lord and his men, Agnolo was always on good terms with them, also with the underlings of the commune and of the Lord, and with the Lord himself.

When the heads of the government perceived that Agnolo's admirable bearing and character would qualify him for high policy, they determined to send him with Donato Acciaiuoli on an embassy to King Louis of France to procure the restitution of certain Florentine goods which had been seized in one of His Majesty's ports.* The King was so much pleased with Donato that he gave him a cash assignment on Langue-

---

* In Donato Acciaiuoli's Life they are said to have been seized by a corsair.

doc, until the whole of the goods should be restored, to the amount of thirty thousand florins. Now after this assignment had been in force several years—as it often happens with great princes who change their minds—it was withdrawn. This seemed strange to those who held it, and they applied to the Signoria to send a mission of enquiry, whereupon they asked Donato Acciaiuoli for advice as to whom they should send. He replied that, if Agnolo Manetti would consent to go, he would be the most fitting man. There were many reasons for Donato's recommendation. Agnolo was of noble family, with a most distinguished father : he spoke Latin as well as his own language, and had a special faculty for all branches of public affairs ; he was ready in apprehension and clear in statement. He travelled in good state with horses and servants and the King, who was wont to be haughty with most strangers, received him most graciously, and Agnolo bore himself so well in his mission that he won as much favour from the King as Donato. In the end the assignments were renewed and were to be collected as long as the King lived to satisfy the claim of the merchants. The recovery of this assignment was to everyone an unexpected success.

When the government learned what he had done, and the high place he held in the favour of King Louis, it was decreed, in the name of the people of Florence, that he should be re-elected for two months to give advice day by day as to the situation of affairs. Letters were at once written to him from the Signoria giving him full instructions, and his answers to those written to the Signoria were deemed of great value on account of their sound judgment. Now Agnolo knew the King's temper exactly ; how eccentric he was and how suspicious lest others should know what he did, that it was necessary to walk warily and be well prepared lest some untoward accidents should happen—as indeed they did happen on most days, according to the mood which might be upon the King. Shortly before Agnolo's arrival, the Pope's ambassador had come and had been kept more than a fortnight for an audience, because the King had a suspicion that he was friendly to the Duke of Burgundy.* One day the King gave him audience in the presence of many courtiers, whereupon the

* Charles the Bold.

envoy announced that he had been sent by the Pope and that he had met with many hindrances through snow and ice on his journey over the mountains. The King gave him a whimsical answer, " I am well pleased that you have suffered discomfort on the road, since I am well assured that you are a good servant of the Duke of Burgundy." The King then turned his back on him and left him without another word, whereupon it seemed to the ambassador that he had been unjustly censured by the King's suspicious attitude. As to King Louis, no persuasions could move him from the opinion he had formed.

When Agnolo was told by the other ambassadors that the King was subject to these moods, he became anxious for the honour and interests of Florence, so he wrote to the Signoria that it was not meet for him to tarry longer in France, seeing that he had discharged his business, and that they might with advantage recall him. On his return he would make it clear to them that the course he now proposed was the wisest. Thereupon they recalled him forthwith. But there was a certain Florentine who had no wish that he should return with credit and dignity. On his return Agnolo gave the reasons why he had asked for recall ; the varying moods of the King and his suspicion over the smallest trifles. The majority highly approved his action and found no cause for blame, seeing that he had walked in the steps of his father and had gone straight to his object. It was very difficult to deflect him from any course he might have chosen, and he deserves a place amongst our most worthy citizens, for he showed more and more his noble and generous nature.

After his return he once more took up letters, but the city was at this time in a state of turmoil and fear of war with the Pope and King Ferdinand. The Florentines had already lost several fortified towns and were daily losing more from the attacks of these two potent princes and were in danger of losing Campiglia, which was a remote place and peopled by Corsicans and lawless folk. Agnolo had already acted as magistrate there and retained much influence, so the Ten of the Balia sent him there again with plenary powers and letters, announcing that his word was to be obeyed as if he were the Signoria itself. When he reached Campiglia he saw at once what had to be done. He put everything in due order and

brought the people to such obedience as had never been known
in Florence, all by his goodwill and sagacity. Thus Agnolo
saved this place, but by a cruel stroke of fate plague broke
out and many of his household died. Agnolo felt that he
would imperil the town by his withdrawal, so he determined
to stay on, but soon the disease fell on him and he died in the
cause of his country. When he was taken, Florence had left
few citizens whom she could send to protect her interests
abroad and deal with affairs at home with equal skill and
integrity.

Piero de' Pazzi

Messer Piero, son of Andrea, of the noble Florentine family
of Pazzi, was well versed in Latin letters, but he knew little
of Greek. The reason why he was not a zealous scholar was,
that being a very handsome youth and greatly given to the
pleasures and delights of the world, he took little thought of
study. His father was a merchant, and, like those who know
little of learning, thought it to be of little value, and had no
desire that his son should spend time over it. He had already
determined that Piero should take up commerce. One day
it happened that Nicolao Nicoli, who was as Socrates combined with Cato in temperance and virtue, met Messer Piero
to whom he had never spoken, and in passing him close to
the palace of the Podestà, he spoke to him, seeing that he was
a very attractive youth. Nicolao was a very distinguished
man and Piero at once came to him, whereupon Nicolao
asked whose son he was. The youth answered that he was
the son of Messer Andrea de' Pazzi, and when Nicolao asked
him his occupation, he answered after the fashion of young
men, "I am giving myself a good time." Nicolao said to him,
"As you are the son of such a father, and of such good
presence, it is a shame that you should not take to the study
of Latin, which would make a polished man of you. If you
neglect learning, you will win little esteem, and when the
flower of your youth has passed you will find yourself a good-
for-nothing." Messer Piero, when he heard these words, at once
understood their meaning, and knew that Nicolao spoke the
truth, so he answered that he would set to work as soon as he

had found a teacher, if Nicolao would advise him in the
matter. Nicolao told him that he might leave it to him, and
that he would see to the teacher and the books and everything else. Piero realised his good fortune. Nicolao sent to
him a very learned man named Pontano,* a fine Greek and
Latin scholar, who went to live in Piero's house. He held
there an honourable position, being provided with a servant
and a salary of a hundred florins a year. Piero forswore his
wanton dissipations and pleasures which had hitherto occupied him, and gave himself up entirely to letters, and studied
day and night. In a short time Piero, who was a youth of
quick intellect, soon acquired a good knowledge of Latin
letters. Through his association with Pontano he became
acquainted with the chiefs of the city, especially with Piero,
son of Cosimo de' Medici, who had the greatest affection for
him. The Pazzi family had sunk from their high station, and
were heavily taxed, because they were reported wealthy, as
indeed they once were, but they had a hard fight with Fortune.
Now this friendship between Piero de' Pazzi and Piero de'
Medici led to a matrimonial alliance, by the marriage of
Guglielmo de' Pazzi with Bianca, daughter of Piero de'
Medici. Had it not been for this friendship between the two
Pieros, this kinship would never have come to pass ; now,
by means of it, the Pazzi recovered their position, and were
able to meet their taxation, as they would never have done,
but for this marriage. It may be truly said that this alliance
restored their house to prosperity, and if only Messer Piero,
who was the most prudent member of the family, had lived,
the calamity which followed and brought ruin upon them
would never have happened.

Messer Piero was a man of noble and generous spirit,
always at the service of his friends, and the master of a splendid house, where he would often entertain eight or ten guests
at dinner or supper, all of them of the lettered and cultured
youth of the city. The republic showed him much consideration in the honours it bestowed upon him, both at home and
abroad. The first office which he held which brought out

* The famous humanist and friend of Alfonso II and founder of the
Academy of Naples. He was sculptured by Mazzoni as Nicodemus
on a tomb in Monte Oliveto in Naples. He died in 1503.

his merit was that of member of the Assembly, in which he delivered a fine oration, *De Justitia*, in the hearing of all the lettered men and chiefs of the city. He soon showed that he had not studied Latin in vain when he was gonfalonier of justice, which office he discharged with much distinction and won universal praise from all in the city. When Louis* became King of France and the whole of Italy sent embassies of congratulation, the Florentines sent Messer Filippo de' Medici, the Archbishop of Pisa, Bonaccorso Pitti and Messer Piero de' Pazzi. I can affirm that in my time no ambassador ever left Florence in such stately guise as Messer Piero, nor with such fine clothes and jewels for himself and for his train of attendants, nor with such magnificent horses ; assuredly he did all that was possible, and the Signoria desired him to ride through the city so that the people might see such stately pomp as they had never seen before. Donato Acciaiuoli begged leave to accompany him, and he took with him the *Life of Charlemagne*, which he had written, as a present to the King of France. Piero was highly honoured by His Majesty and by all the court, for his noble birth, his fine presence and his learning and eloquence. He travelled in such state that every day he would change his sumptuous attire once or twice, and all his attendants would do the same. Donato Acciaiuoli was also greatly honoured for his illustrious house ; he was well known to the King and all the court for his worth and high reputation. His Majesty the King on a day of solemn ceremony, when all the lords of the court and ambassadors were present, made Messer Piero a knight, thus showing distinguished honour to him and to his country. After the accolade a great band of nobles, gentlemen and ambassadors accompanied him back to his house. Piero bore himself so gallantly that when he left he carried away universal regard and fame, and having fulfilled his duties as ambassador to the King of France, he returned to Florence. When he entered the city all the notables went out to meet him, the city was full of joy at the return of one beloved by all on account of his generous nature. In the city itself the streets and the windows were full of spectators who awaited his coming. He and his following were all clad in handsome

* Louis XI in 1461.

new garments, with silken cloaks, with sleeves embroidered with pearls of great value. No cavalier ever before entered Florence with such pomp as this, which conferred great honour upon his house. He dismounted according to custom at the door of the palace, and then went up into the hall of the Signoria to receive the banner of those who come back as knights. On leaving the palace he remounted and went to the Guelph quarter to take up the standard of the party, and there he found Piero Acciaiuoli, who made a graceful speech in Italian to the great crowd which was waiting to hear him. When the speech was finished and the standards of the party and of the palace unfurled, he went, accompanied by the crowd, to his house where a sumptuous feast was held, and for several days they kept open house and no citizen ever bore his dignities more worthily than Piero. No one could ever accuse him of being avaricious, as so many are—on the other hand, he was rather a spendthrift ; often he deserved blame rather than praise for his lavish outlay. No one asked of him in vain. When, after the death of his father, the brothers divided the estate—Salviati and other kinsfolk also took their share—it was found that Piero had spent twelve thousand florins, and had nothing to show for it. It was decided that he who had spent this money should be reimbursed this cost, because he had spent it in splendour and liberality. It was agreed that, up to the time of Messer Andrea's death, Piero had maintained himself and all his establishment at his own cost. The overflowing wealth of the family had tempted him to extravagance, as is the case with many who are inclined to prodigality. It is a fact that all, or a greater part, of the money he had spent was laid out in honourable fashion according to the way of the world.

Messer Piero was singularly endowed by nature ; he had a powerful intellect and a most retentive memory, a proof of which was that he learnt the whole of Virgil's Æneid by heart and many orations of Livy during his solitary walks in a place called Trebbio, one of the estates which had been assigned to him for his share, which brought in a rent of five hundred florins. He had many other possessions in these parts which were securely held for him, he being a spendthrift.

STATESMEN

He often walked with the tutor of his children, and would return to Florence, also he would go to Fiesole and Santo Chimenti, and on the way he would learn by heart the triumphs of Petrarch. He declaimed verse and prose marvellously well, for he knew how to manage his voice and his chest, which was finely developed, and if he, like so many others, had not wasted so much time on useless things instead of studying Latin few would have excelled him. He caused many beautiful books to be copied, and always kept scribes in his service, so he spent much money in books, and manuscripts, and in miniatures. All these were executed in the best manner, so that at his death he left a fine library.

Messer Piero was an intimate friend of Duke Giovanni, and when King René and all his family came to Florence they lived in Piero's house, and the King was godfather to Piero's son Renato. Afterwards, when Duke Giovanni came to Florence and King René crossed over into Lombardy, a great friendship sprang up between the Duke and Piero, who was an accomplished courtier. Indeed, while the Duke remained in Florence Piero was his constant companion. When he returned to Naples their friendship was still so close that, had the Duke retained the kingdom, Piero would have been one of his chief ministers. He often wrote to Piero, and induced him to send him a large sum of money, and on Piero's security, Giovanni, son of Cosimo de' Medici, lent him two thousand florins. When things were prospering for the Duke, Piero helped him greatly, both by word and deed.

It happened one day that Messer Piero met an intimate friend and said to him, "In a fortnight Duke Giovanni will be King of Naples without any opposition." Before this fortnight had passed the Prince of Rossano, Jacopo da Gaviano and Deifebo, enemies of the King and friends of the Duke, sent word to the King that if His Majesty would pardon them, they would come to sue for forgiveness and be his followers hereafter. The King, who saw that he would be a gainer, answered that he was content with their proposition, and that they would discuss the hour and the meeting. When these were settled the King went to the appointed place, taking with him a certain Count Ventimiglia, a wise and cautious Sicilian, who advised His Majesty to have a care what he was doing, for these men were not to be trusted. The King determined to go on and took with him four squadrons of cavalry under Count Giovanni, all well armed, and when they had come to the meeting-place, he left Count Giovanni and his men half a bow-shot aside, with orders that if they should hear nothing, they should quickly ride up to the rescue. When the King had gone on, he came up with the three who, on his approach, knelt down on the ground as a sign of respect, and a request for forgiveness. The King held out his hand, whereupon one of them sprang forward, holding a knife, to seize the reins of the horse, and stab the King, but he, who was a good horseman, as soon as he saw this move spurred on his horse, which went at a great speed, and leapt, so that he evaded the grasp of the assassin, and the knife fell upon the man who had attempted to kill the King. When Count Giovanni saw this, he quickly came up with all the horsemen to the King's rescue, while the traitors fled leaving the knife behind them. The King bade them pick it up, and, to test it, thrust it into the back of a dog which at once fell dead, a proof that these traitors were minded to kill the King by poison. Now as this treachery happened within the fifteen days of which Piero had spoken to his friend, as the time for the acquisition of the kingdom by Duke Giovanni, the friend aforesaid went to him and said, " Sire, it is not the act of a prince to win a kingdom by such a deed as this ; these are not the ways of the royal house of France ; if the kingdom could be won by feat of arms, it would be a deed worthy to be praised, but if by such treachery as this, No ! And this, Signor Piero, you cannot deny, that the reason why these men chose this course was because it fell in with the saying about Duke Giovanni winning the kingdom without opposition within fifteen days. But this attempt failed, since Almighty God will not allow such deeds to succeed."

After this event it happened that Giovanni Coscia, a Neapolitan gentleman who had been, and still was, in the service of Duke Giovanni, was asked one day after the defeat of Troia who he thought would win the kingdom, made a witty answer to this effect, that as long as their sins weighed more than those of their adversaries, the kingdom would remain theirs. From this time onward many misfortunes befell Duke

STATESMEN

Giovanni, so that he was obliged to quit the kingdom, and abandon all that he had won. Apparently by the will of God, after this act of treachery, everything went badly with him. It now happened that, after the attempt on his life, the King, who seemed to be brought to a pass for which there was no remedy, with the greater part of his nobles in rebellion, with no money and no army, rapidly repaired his fortunes, so that in a short time he regained his kingdom as history shows. To return to Piero, many things could be said of him ; about his employment in another place, and of his administration of the city, but this is enough for a brief record.

LORENZO RIDOLFI

Lorenzo Ridolfi was a worthy Florentine citizen born of a good stock. He was upright and conscientious, and, though he had great influence in state affairs and might have done whatever he willed, he was like an ancient Roman in integrity —a poor man who lived on his own income. Although he was learned in Civil and Canon Law he would not practise in them through qualms of conscience. His opinions were sound and were much sought, both in the city and without ; also he was employed as envoy on many occasions and always discharged his duty with credit. He concluded the treaty with Venice in 1425* on the outbreak of war between Duke Filippo and the Florentines in Romagna in spite of the league between them. When Messer Lorenzo and the heads of the state met the Duke, in compliance with his request to make peace, they deemed it would be better to refuse, for it was plain that he only asked for peace in order to be able to occupy Genoa. His policy was to show favour to the Genoese until he should be able to seize the city and then, having acquired it, he would at once attack the Florentines though he was now preaching peace with them. This was the wise counsel given by Messer Lorenzo and the other citizens who foresaw what happened later, for, as soon as peace was made with Florence, the Duke seized Genoa and attacked the Florentines

* Muratori, *Annals*, IX, p. 125. Poggio writes that the treaty was made by Palla Strozzi and Giovanni de' Medici.

in Romagna, where they were defeated three times in one year and reduced to great straits.*

From these events sprang the mission of Lorenzo to Venice, where a peace was made on terms which the Florentines needs must accept, as the Duke was a potent and ambitious prince. The Signoria decided to send Lorenzo alone as the most capable citizen, and at the same time they despatched a mission to Pope Martin begging him to intervene in favour of peace between the Duke and Florence. The Venetians had been at peace with the Duke for a long time, and they were now loth to go to war. Lorenzo, however, put forward strong arguments to show the bad faith of this tyrant who was not likely to keep any of his pledges. From Rome Pope Martin put in a plea for peace, and each mission supported the other, but the Venetians could not be moved. While Lorenzo was thus striving for peace it happened that Francesco Carmagnola† withdrew from the Duke's service and entered the territory of the Venetians, to whom he disclosed the secret projects of Filippo Maria, which were that as soon as he should have mastered Florence would seize Venice also. When they heard this from Carmagnola they were greatly shaken, but not enough to induce them to change their policy straightway. At Rome the envoys were working in conjunction with Pope Martin to arrange a peace with Duke Filippo, and the negotiations were on the way to completion, and the report of them to Venice caused the Venetians to hold out some hope to the League. In the end Duke Filippo favoured the conclusion of peace, deeming that it might bring the project of a league to nothing. When he heard how things were going, Lorenzo cut matters short and let the Signory know his mind plainly. He proved that by making peace at Rome with the Duke, Florence would be at his mercy, and that they must now understand he would no longer be satisfied with mere words ; if they had said their final word he would at once avail himself of their permission to depart. He then showed to them clearly what end Duke Filippo's conditions must inevitably lead to, and by his firm attitude

* Niccolo Piccinino had left the service of the Florentines for that of Milan. They were beaten at Anghiari on October 9, 1425, and again on the 17th at Faggiuola ; their sixth defeat since the war had begun. Sismondi, *Republiques Ital.*, Ch. LXIV. † 1424.

he obtained the support of Venice for the League.* His success won the highest approval in Florence, because he had induced the Venetians to break peace with the Duke. The Venetians required certain conditions to safeguard their interests, to which the Florentines agreed, in view of the state in which they found themselves. Also they knew that, if they made a peace with the Duke, he would probably break it, as was his wont, so of two evils they chose the lesser.†

Wherever Lorenzo went he added to his country's honour. He never considered his own interest, always setting the service of God and the claims of the world at large before his personal advantage. The integrity of his character may be judged by his book *De usuris*, which deals with legal contracts and restitution, a book which has had great weight everywhere and has never been censured. Archbishop Antonino often quotes it in his *Summa* on contracts with full agreement; indeed, he gives it an authority almost equal to that of the Gospels. Lorenzo spent immense trouble and labour over this book, as all things are given consonant with reason and authority. He consults all the writers on cases of conscience, on exchanges, on unjust contracts, all these he upsets and condemns exchanges of all sorts. No one writes more forcibly or more reasonably concerning the Monte at Florence. He took an austere view of life, and in state affairs never swerved from the ways of justice and honesty. He was religious and assiduous in Divine worship; his works show how rightly he felt on holy things. Besides his devotional exercises he greatly admired S. Jerome and made a collection of his Epistles larger than any other in Italy or elsewhere. It contains some on the interpretation of the Psalter, and differences of translation, and many Greek and Hebrew texts. This shows him to be a jurist and a canonist, also a profound scholar in sacred learning. The book of the Epistle of S. Jerome in one volume he gave to the Church of S. Spirito for the library, for the use of

* His speech was a triumph of oratory, ending thus : " My lords, your sluggishness has already made Filippo Visconti Duke of Milan and Master of Genoa, now by sacrificing us you propose to make him King of Italy, but if we submit our turn may come, and then we will make him Emperor." Poggio, *Hist. Flor.*, L, 5, p. 336.

† The League was signed in January, 1426, between Venice, Florence, King Alfonso ; the Marquis of Mantua, the Duke of Ferrara and the Duke of Savoy.

all who might wish to consult it. Messer Lorenzo was inferior to no citizen of an age when Florence was rich in distinguished men.

To the praise which I have given to Messer Lorenzo I wish to add a particular instance, which is that, in all the changes which happened in the republic, he always fled from dishonour and followed the path of justice and honesty as the universal friend of every good citizen, and one who desired that the public life of the city should spring from good deeds. He had no mind to rise through the exile of his fellow-citizens, or through fomenting state revolution of which he was the determined foe. He knew well how to use his power and position and thus became everybody's friend; but no one would ever venture to ask him to put his hand to any deed which was not just and honest. Let this stand as a memorial of this righteous man as an example for all to follow.

SER FILIPPO DI SER UGOLINO (d. 1454)

Although Ser Filippo called himself the son of Ser Ugolino he had no right to this style. He studied Greek and Latin, and became a learned scholar as will afterwards be noted. His father was a very poor man of Vertine di Chianti. Neither the eloquence of Tully nor of Demosthenes would suffice to tell of the excellencies of this youth, who was so pious in life and habit that he excelled all other youths past and present. He was master of all the seven liberal arts, well versed in Greek, a distinguished theologian, much given to the studies of astrology, geometry and astronomy, upon which he wrote many treatises which may be seen in the many volumes written by him and in S. Marco, also in the large theological library which he left to the monastery of Settimo. He was a man of few words, but what he spoke was always well judged. Messer Ugolino wished to make him a notary, and when he was very young the notice of his appointment was sent to him as the ablest youth of his time. This post is granted to merit and not to the man, as will appear in this case of Ser Filippo, who assuredly did not obtain it by any claim of kinship. This office he discharged with authority; and it is one which sways the good or evil fortune of the state by the laws which there originate. The notary allows no laws to pass which do not make for the benefit of the republic, and when there comes before him a law devised by the government which appears to him unjust he speaks plainly about it and will not allow any obscurities to be inserted. If at any time he cannot prevent the enactment of a law, he finds some means of making it ineffective. Ser Filippo never betrayed his trust and therefore enjoyed the full confidence of the people. When he had fully considered and approved any law, it would always be passed ; if he condemned it he would let his opinion of it be widely known, and it would always be rejected unanimously on account of his knowledge and integrity. If any of the leaders brought before him a bill on any subject which he found to be incorrectly drawn, Ser Filippo would turn to him and begin to laugh—a favourite trick of his ; he would go over the rough draft and point out its mistakes. He had also a way of telling anyone who seemed inclined to play dishonest tricks to go mind his own business. He held this office for a long time and was an admirable public servant, as will appear from the laws passed in his time.

He was small in stature with a handsome sagacious face. He wore a long purple mantle with armholes on each side. He was of a lively humour and cheerful, and it was considered a marvel that he should remain insensible to the charms of the ladies. He never married. He led a religious and God-fearing life, simple and temperate in his diet, with one old woman as housekeeper and one manservant. He did much secret almsgiving and built the two cloisters in the Badia at Florence ; also the two new dormitories in the field adjoining the garden. Over good works he never laid down his arms. He gave dowries to many young girls, and devoted to God's service more than half his income, as may be seen in the records of the Monte from which he received his salary. He would never accept a gift. One day a Pisan, who had suffered much ill-treatment, left at his house a gift of sea fish, and when Filippo returned he sent the fish back by his servant. When the Pisan came again Filippo was very angry and told the man he must never approach him again, as he was not one to be influenced by presents.

SER FILIPPO DI SER UGOLINO

He was of a generous nature, not like one born of common folk ; he might well have come of the highest nobility. In questions of honour and justice he would make way for no one. He had great scorn of unlettered folk, especially if they should be in the service of the state. About this he told me a story. The Emperor sent as ambassador one who was of the Gherardini, and the gonfalonier then was one of the Veccheti who, together with all his associates, was completely illiterate. After the ambassador, who was also an archbishop, had delivered his message in Latin, the chancellor was chosen to answer it, and a day was fixed when this reply should be given. The archbishop duly attended and waited in the hall ; but as the chancellor was absent not one of the others could say a word in answer, and the gonfalonier was at his wits' end. Ser Filippo, in his vexation that such disgrace should have fallen on the Signoria, said that he would have paid heavily to be able to teach the gonfalonier enough Latin to make an answer ; after having done this he might have forgotten it as soon as he would. Here it is shown how much honour and profit letters may bring, looking at the disgrace the Signoria suffered on this occasion. Ser Filippo was, as has been already told, temperate in his eating and drinking, taking only what was needful. He spent all the leisure he had outside the palace in studying sacred books, and he kept in his service scribes who were constantly employed in writing out the Lives of S. Jerome, S. Augustine and the other doctors. In the morning he would hear mass, and then to the palace, where he would be amongst the earliest to begin his service to the state, over which he was most diligent. After his dinner he would visit Friar Ambrogio, and then to the Badia to converse with the abbot and the monks. He would go round the stationers' shops to see whether they might have for sale any book he wanted to buy. He was often with Giannozzo Manetti, Messer Lionardo and Carlo d' Arezzo and, at the time of the court, with Thomas of Sarzana, who was afterwards Pope Nicolas. Thomas had great confidence in him by reason of his many merits. Later in the day he would return to the palace to finish his duties and give audience to many visitors, all of whom, rich and poor, he would dismiss satisfied.

STATESMEN

Some time after the changes in the state, Ser Filippo found that affairs were not working according to his wishes, which were all on the side of justice, and did his best to amend matters. When these failed, he realised that he could not go on with his public duties without offending God and, as he desired to avoid bringing ruin upon himself, he determined to give up his office and live a life of privacy. While he was still in office the Assembly decided to renew a certain law, and this decision was passed, and the conservators were elected from the leading men of the city ; but, on a sudden, the heads of the government, in opposition to those who had favoured this law, proposed to annul it. This they could not do while Filippo was in office and exercised such strong influence, and while it lay in the power of the conservators to keep him in office or not. Should Ser Filippo be in office they, with his support, could establish the law. In this case the heads of the government determined to pass a vote for Ser Filippo's dismissal, and this was carried by six beans one day while the gonfalonier, who was a friend of his, was away asleep. As soon as the vote was taken they sent a beadle to inform Ser Filippo who, as soon as he heard of his dismissal, took up his cloak and walked away without showing the least sign. After Ser Filippo's dismissal they imprisoned and banished a great number, some of the conservators amongst them. The aforesaid change of leaders took place between the parliament of '34 and the present time. These are the benefits which Ser Filippo brought back to the state : in having established the regular working of justice while he was in office and all the blessings which resulted therefrom. All this calamity happened to him because the leaders were impatient of legal restraint, and that state is in a bad way when its citizens are more powerful than the laws.

After he had been dismissed Ser Filippo returned home, but the one who had begun the attack on him did not rest but was fain to injure him yet more, and all those who were moving in this matter of the law brought forward all sorts of strange arguments. Filippo, realising the nature of these, left his house quickly and withdrew secretly to the house of one Goro, who was governor of S. Maria Nuova outside S. Friano, and there abode, unknown to anyone. The house was guarded to see who might come to visit him, and his foes were greatly chagrined. He now found himself with nothing but a hundred *grossi* in silver, for he always kept his accounts even, giving a portion to God and spending the rest on necessary things. He remained with Goro some days till the panic had subsided. Then came the reaction of '34, and a first banishment and imprisonment of citizens, and when the city settled down they made him retire to a house of his own near Chianti called Vertine. He caused many of his books to be sent to him there, and spent his time peacefully in reading and study. He used to say that, after he had come through all these troubles, this was the happiest time of his life. So far from blaming his foes he blessed them for thus delivering him from trouble and danger. Not long after this Pope Nicolas, who esteemed Ser Filippo very highly, requested the Florentine ambassadors, who had come to convey the obedience of the state on his election, to procure the recall of Filippo from exile as a personal favour. He made earnest solicitation, and even wrote a letter, but neither was of any avail on account of the resentment of the one who had originally attacked him. Had he gone to Rome he might have lived there under pleasant conditions, but he preferred his peaceful course of life free from further entanglements and aloof from the world.

After he had lived several years at Vertine, those in power at Florence revised what had been done at the time of his exile, and considered what had ensued therefrom ; but, so as not to give offence, I will pass on. They relaxed the limits of his banishment and allowed him to live wherever he would up to the gates of the city. At this time there were at Settimo twelve monks from the Badia at Florence who had come to reform the monastery there, and Ser Filippo was on friendly terms with these. The monastery was now admirably governed, both in spiritual and temporal matters, wherefore Ser Filippo determined to reside there. He took with him all his books, and gave to the monastery more than enough to support himself and certain companions. He set himself, in spite of his age, to live the life of a friar, to eat with them in their refectory, to attend church night and day and to keep all their fasts. His leisure he spent in study or in teaching Latin to the younger monks, and he varied his teaching according to the knowledge of his pupils, but he always lectured on sacred subjects. Many eminent men came to visit him and to listen to his discourse, which was marvellously interesting on account of his knowledge on all subjects. He was happier and more light-hearted now than he had ever been before, and he would jest with everyone, never mentioning his exile or what he had suffered.

I, who write this, went often to visit him at Settimo and took with me divers youths in order that they might be led into virtuous ways by intercourse with such a man ; amongst these were the sons of Messer Giannozzo Pandolfini, Pier Filippo, the present Bishop of Pistoia, and Messer Niccolo, and their brother the prior. It was wonderful to hear him ; what with his memory, his universal knowledge and experience of state government, which indeed seemed the least of all, his holiness of life and his perfect integrity. In attire, in speech and in all his moods he was like an ancient philosopher. Those who only knew him from his outer aspect would say he was a marvel. To fit any proposition he would bring out a text of Scripture, as he had it all by heart. He had this great gift that the more he spoke the more you would wish to hear.

When he spoke of our city he gave us this parable : That he was like a man on a level plain who must needs mount a hill and then return to the plain, and that he had to descend as much as he had ascended. I took his meaning to be that any man who might rule Florence without doing his full duty, and had climbed to a height he did not merit, must sink to the level from which he had started. When he quitted the palace, Florence enjoyed a prosperity greater than she had known for many years : afterwards there came a vast change as everyone saw. He spoke another parable dealing with those who are lacking in judgment and intellect. He said that there were not enough cornices in Florence to shelter those who go begging their bread for the love of God ; these should rather seek protection under a roof so as not to be drenched. Those who take shelter from the rain are the prudent, for they cover themselves with the cloak of good sense ; those who are soaked by rain are the rash and foolish, for they seem to think they can never err whatever they do. Unsheltered they find themselves wet to the skin alone. This is the garnered wisdom

SER FILIPPO DI SER UGOLINO

of a sage, which will never corrupt in its storehouse ; common-sense which may be to every man's advantage. He once said that two things were necessary for the preservation of the city ; one, that the Monte should be made level with the plain : the other that the taxation should not be controlled by certain officials, but imposed by law. He was one of the most clearminded citizens, and he had no other thought than the welfare of Florence.

Ser Filippo continued his life in the monastery, but occasionally he would go on foot, staff in hand, from Settimo as far as Ingesuati, where he would recreate himself and regulate certain private affairs. He would tarry there several days, and many men of religion would come to hear his wise counsel. He censured many of those who visited him and neglected their religious duties ; for instance, a certain citizen was seeking an office, and went constantly to learn whether he had been chosen. At last he was appointed and he began to weep for joy, and he went to Ser Filippo when he knew and told him that this office had just come in time, for he could not have maintained himself much longer as things stood. Ser Filippo spoke to him openly, " Does it not seem to you an infamy that you should trade upon this office and make profit thereby instead of gaining sustenance elsewhere, instead of living on the labour of poor men ? These offices were never devised to furnish plunder for you and your fellows, who think of nothing but pillage and let your public duties go unfulfilled. Indeed, they would fare better under a band of mercenaries than under you. The distress around Florence is largely caused by the ill-administration of your class, a distress which grows worse every day. You should discharge the duties for which you were appointed, but you neglect them altogether."

The misfortunes which befell Ser Filippo came by Divine permission in order that by their agency he might be purged from the sins he had committed. For many years he lived under the rule of S. Bernard, keeping all the observances of the Order and communicating and confessing like the friars. He spent all the time he had to spend in the most worthy fashion ; he gave the best example to all and taught the younger monks, many of whom became learned scholars. His love of God gave him a humble spirit, and for this reason

STATESMEN

Almighty God permitted him to make the finest end that a gentleman of his quality in Florence had ever made. To the end of his long life he kept his body free from infirmity by his wonderful temperance. By his will he left all his sacred books to the Abbey of Settimo, and a certain number of secular works, some dealing with history, to the same abbey. He gave many things in his lifetime to the abbey rather than wait for his death. He settled all his affairs in the fear of God, and kept himself prepared to render up his soul to God whenever He might call for it. He made a holy end with the friars, with whom he had lived in the Badia at Florence and at Settimo.

BERNARDO GIUGNI

Messer Bernardo Giugni was of good Florentine family. He was a Latin scholar and a worthy servant of the state, having filled with credit all the chief offices in the government. He was temperate, modest, averse from brawling, just and single-minded in his dealings ; and no one could turn him from the paths of honesty. Florence would have been happy had all her citizens been like him. Revolutions and new methods were distasteful to him, and no citizen ever suffered exile or imprisonment because of him. There was no need for him to use these methods to secure promotion : this came to him from his natural merits. He had a sympathetic disposition, and was a patient listener to all who approached him. He was unassuming and chose the middle way of life, and hated arrogance and display in apparel. On account of his prudence and integrity, whenever an embassy had to be sent to any place of importance he would be one of the first to be chosen. When King Alfonso entered Naples for the second time* Messer Bernardo and Messer Giuliano Davanzati were sent to greet him. The King, knowing how much Bernardo was beloved in Florence, received him with great honour, and when he conversed with him saw that his merits were real. Messer Bernardo

* In 1442. His first entrance was after the death of Joanna II in 1435, but he was almost immediately defeated and captured by the Genoese fleet and sent a prisoner to Milan. Filippo Maria Visconti released him at once, but he did not recover the city of Naples till 1442.

BERNARDO GIUGNI

often was obliged to restrain his companion, who was somewhat of a hothead and carried away by passion. One day when the two were talking with the King, Davanzati spake words which were both unseemly and inappropriate. Bernardo, so as not to shame him in the King's presence, kept silence, but when they returned to their lodgings he told Davanzati that he must be more careful in his speech, especially with a prince of Alfonso's temper. Messer Bernardo returned to Florence in high favour with Alfonso, having discharged his mission admirably and strengthened the King as a peacemaker in Italy.

Bernardo's fame now stood so high and the government valued his services so greatly that no one would dare approach him with any discreditable suggestion. Pope Nicolas* was now zealous for peace throughout Italy, wherefore he called on all the powers to send representatives. Florence sent two ; Bernardo, who was known to desire peace, and Messer Giannozzo Pitti. These two, when they reached Rome, talked only of peace to the Pope, and they found him to be of one mind with them. Some there were who had no desire for peace, and opposed it as strongly as the Florentines worked for it. But the Florentines, having the Pope to back them, held to their view.

One of those who opposed peace insisted that King Alfonso opposed it also, and asserted that he would never give up Castiglione della Pescaia to the Florentines,† but this was false, and the speech was only made to hamper the King, who, when he heard of it, at once sent for all the Florentine merchants who were at Naples, and told them how he had been accused of opposing the peace and of refusing to surrender Castiglione to Florence. He complained bitterly of this accusation and asked them to send messengers to the ambassadors in Rome to inform them that he was not an opponent of peace, but

---

* His action led to the Congress of Lodi, 1453.
† He ultimately kept it on condition of surrendering all other Florentine lands he held. At this congress Alfonso was irritated by the action of Milan and Venice who, with the assent of Florence, had signed the Treaty of Lodi in April, 1454, which professed to bind all the other Italian powers without their consent. After some delay he signed it, but only on condition that the Genoese, Malatesta of Rimini and Astorre Manfredi of Faenza, should be excepted from its protection in order that he might attack them.

desired it as strongly as anyone in Italy and was ready to surrender Castiglione at once without conditions. These messengers were sent to Rome and the King fulfilled his promise. The ambassadors, as soon as they heard of this, went to the Pope to tell him the news from Naples and of King Alfonso's goodwill. As soon as this was known they, together with the Pope, drew up conditions of peace according to their instructions. When this was settled, together with the restitution of Castiglione, the Pope decided the treaty should take the form of a papal bull, with as many clauses as were necessary to make it binding. When the general peace was concluded, and only the seal was wanting, Messer Bernardo and Messer Giannozzo deemed that they had wrought a good work in bringing honour to their city, and liberating her from her troubles. Having notified to Florence what they had done in discharge of their commission, they awaited its publication. Letters came to them from Florence bidding them delay for good reasons until the arrival of another envoy. On hearing this Bernardo and his associate were displeased, because certain reports which had come from friends in Florence made them suspect that all the good they had hitherto done would be nullified. When the new ambassador arrived Bernardo and Giannozzo had leave to return to Florence. They started at once and left the treaty concluded, and the bull complete except the sealing. The reasons for this I will not give,* but I will give praise for these two for their good work towards settling the peace. I need not write more on this affair, as it will be fully explained by what follows. The ambassadors received a joyful welcome in Florence, for the city was much distressed by the long warfare. All were uncertain, wild rumours went about and most men blamed the government for trying to hinder the pacification. When the heads of the government realised the situation they were alarmed to find the whole of the blame laid upon themselves: in fact, the city talked of nothing else. After the return of the ambassadors

---

* This is one of Vespasiano's many reticences, imposed no doubt by the fear of offending some powerful person in Florence. He does not name the new ambassador, but Sismondi writes of Diotisalvi Neroni as being present at the conference and pleading for peace at any price, since he had no money for warfare. *Republiq. Italiennes*, IX, p. 430.

the govérnment was asked to explain why they had not concluded the peace, a matter which was in their own hands, and
they made the best excuse they could. Meantime they would
not excuse others so much as to allow themselves to be
accused, and they assured their friends that they had not failed
through their own fault. When they found they were in bad
repute throughout the city, they called together a council of
requests to free themselves from blame. This was made up of
the Signori and the Assembly, beside all the important citizens.
They called upon the two ambassadors who had been in Rome
to attend, and desired one of them to explain why the peace
had not been definitely concluded, also they affirmed that any
delay in this affair was not the fault of the government. As
they knew Bernardo's disposition they were unwilling that he
should enter the rostrum and speak, so they gave this duty to
Messer Giannozzo, believing that he would excuse them, but in
this they were mistaken as the truth prevailed. He mounted
the rostrum and narrated what had happened since he went to
Rome to arrange a peace with Pope Nicolas in compliance with
his instructions ; how certain difficulties had arisen on account
of the demands of King Alfonso which had been afterwards
satisfied, and how they and Pope Nicolas, who was more set
on peace than any, had brought things to a satisfactory conclusion. Although there were certain ambiguities in Giannozzo's
speech, it was clear enough to let most of his hearers understand that their objęct had been peace. He went on to say that
the Pope, in order to make the treaty more binding, had
caused it to be drawn up in the form of an apostolic bull, which
had been written out and completed, except for the sealing,
when orders came for them to return and make room for other
ambassadors from home. At this point of the speech many of
those present observed that Bernardo Giugni, who was seated
in the middle of the hall, began to weep, and this demonstration dissipated the doubts of those who hesitated, and turned
the feeling of the audience against those who maintained that
no peace had been made. Those who had not heard the true
state of affairs were now convinced by Giannozzo's speech and
Bernardo's emotion, and those who had attacked the ambassadors suffered greatly in public opinion. Pope Nicolas was
greatly annoyed when he heard of this episode, because he

believed that peace had already been made by himself.* The peace ultimately took a form differing from that settled by the Pope and the Florentine ambassadors, and whoever writes the history of this time must study it : it is enough to record that Messer Bernardo in will and deed always strove for the honour and benefit of his city.

On the death of Duke Francesco Sforza† it was resolved to send ambassadors at once on behalf of the state, and Messer Bernardo was chosen as a fitting person for this office. When he arrived in Milan he was honourably received by the rulers, who took no action without first consulting him. He remained there several months until affairs were settled, when he begged leave to return to Florence. He found some difficulty in gaining consent from the Milanese, who would fain have kept him there premanently, seeing that, with him as counsellor, nothing would go wrong. He returned to Florence with his reputation greatly increased. In the offices he filled he won honour, and in his legation to the Emperor when he came to receive the crown at Rome. Messer Bernardo, in company with Giannozzo Manetti and Carlo Pandolfini, met the Emperor at Ferrara and accompanied him to Rome, where he remained till the Emperor's departure, when he also went to Venice and to other cities, where he was graciously welcomed. Whoever may write his Life will find therein many things worthy of praise, which entitle him to a place amongst the most worthy citizens Florence ever produced.

COUNT CAMARLINGO (d. 1481)

Count Camarlingo, whose name was Messer Inigo Davalos, born of the royal Spanish house of Ignarra, left his country when King Alfonso went to take possession of the kingdom,

---

* There is something ambiguous in the Pope's attitude over the peace. Censure is hardly to be expected from such an ardent church-man and bibliophile as Vespasiano, but Giannozzo Manetti in his "Life" is more outspoken. "Prudence had taught him that war between the rulers of Italy safeguarded the peace and interests of the Church, while perfect agreement would threaten its welfare." Manetti also hints that the undue prolongation of the negotiations was the Pope's work. Muratori, *Rerum Italic. Script.*, T. II, part. 2, p. 666.
† 1466.

with his fleet, when he was captured by the Genoese and sent to Milan. Duke Filippo asked the Count whether he would enter his service, and being in prison and not knowing how they would ultimately fare in the hands of the Duke, so as to escape imprisonment he accepted the Duke's offer by leave of the King. He was a good Latin scholar and was greatly given to all courteous usages, a good musician and skilful with all instruments. After spending some time with Duke Filippo he returned to the kingdom at King Alfonso's request, having been treated with much honour in Duke Filippo's house.* In Naples there was four brothers all high in the King's favour, and greatly honoured by His Majesty on account of their noble birth and manners. They had been brought up in the King's household from boyhood, and they held all the principal offices in the realm, which offices are now held by their descendants. After King Alfonso's death Count Camarlingo enjoyed the favour of King Ferdinand, and served him faithfully; the King employed him in many embassies to the popes, which he discharged honourably with the reputation of being a man equal to deal with all matters.

Count Camarlingo was the most refined of courtiers, and his house was the haunt of all the distinguished men of the kingdom. He was most liberal, and whatever he had he shared with his friends. He kept a fine establishment and there were always foreigners amongst his guests. Being a bibliophile he had a beautiful library of books, all written by the finest scribes of Italy and adorned with miniatures. Everything he had was superlatively good, and he never considered the price if the books were worth it. He took an interest in everything ; he was an excellent talker, because he had seen many things and had always lived with men of distinction. He was very handsome and was gracious to everybody ; he had one habit which becomes a gentleman, that is at the end of the year he would have spent all his income and sometimes would have trenched upon that of the next year. He loved the society of learned men wherever he might find them, and showed much favour to those who frequented the courts of King Alfonso and of King Ferdinand.

---

* He was a great favourite of King Alfonso. Masuccio dedicates to him the twelfth story in the *Novellino*.

STATESMEN

It is impossible to praise him too much, especially for his inviolable fidelity which never failed him. After the death of King Alfonso the greater part of the kingdom broke their oath, but Count Camarlingo kept his unchanged like a man of good faith. He was well trained in military discipline, and always took the field on the King's side in the wars with Duke Giovanni, thus on every occasion he took service, and finally went to the Turkish war with the men put under his command, and fought strenuously throughout. Wise in counsel he brought up his sons under the best discipline, giving them good instruction in Latin letters, and in all other things befitting the sons of a gentleman such as he was.

MICHELE FERIERO

Messer Michele Feriero was a well-born Catalan gentleman who lived in the time of Pope Calixtus. He was in the service of the Pope, who trusted him completely. He sent out all the bulls, which were written by him and signed at the foot. While he was in office an important case arose in which his handwriting was forged, that of Count d' Armagnac, an infamous person who had been living in incest with his sister. When the King of France heard of this he took away his rank, whereupon Armagnac repaired to Rome, where he met an ultramontane prelate whom he knew. This prelate had high rank at the court, and Armagnac, who was rich, promised him a large bribe if he would obtain for him a papal dispensation. They approached one of the papal scribes, who was a fellow-countryman, and by his instrumentality a document was prepared, the register was signed and all completed in such fashion that it seemed to be genuine. Amongst other signatures they forged that of Michele Feriero. On the death of Calixtus, Pius succeeded, and Michele returned to Catalonia. Armagnac went back to France with these documents, and the whole country was in uproar that he should have been able to obtain them in such scandalous fashion, whereupon messengers were despatched to Rome. When Pope Pius heard of this he was greatly distressed and caused the registry of petitions and of apostolic bulls to be

332

searched, but nothing applicable to this affair was found, wherefore he summoned Michele to return at once. Michele set out and when he saw the documents he perceived that the signatures were forged, but so well imitated that they were scarcely to be distinguished from his own. Then the prelate, who never expected to be detected, was seized and, having been put to the strappado, confessed his offence and was reft of all his rank and sentenced to spend the rest of his life in seclusion as a Benedictine monk ; the papal scribe fled and his office was forfeited, while Michele returned to Barcelona after having vindicated his honour. Pope Calixtus had full confidence in him and was satisfied that he was incapable of fraud and simony, seeing that he was honest in all his dealings, and open and downright in speech. He bore himself throughout as a gentleman should, because those in his station are not wont to fall away from their traditions.

MATTEO MALFERITO

He was born in Majorca of noble parentage of knightly rank. He was well read in Civil and Canon Law, in the Humanities, and accomplished in other ways. He was a valued servant of King Alfonso, who several times employed him as ambassador, for he was a pious, conscientious man, liberal and free from all double-dealing. He told me he had suffered much misfortune, having been three times shipwrecked, but always rescued in the end. Once when he was returning to Majorca, after taking his doctor's degree, and bearing with him all his books, clothes, silver ware and other chattels, he was shipwrecked and lost all his possessions. He had always trusted that God would not forsake him, and indeed he always contrived to gather together other goods after each misfortune. He was of the most kindly nature and was always ready to help those in distress. He used to say that it was a man's duty to make the world pleasant for his fellows, and never to disparage them by speech ; for instance, one day when King Alfonso was in camp near Piombino, Messer **Matteo** saw a poor man led out to execution with a halter round his neck. Matteo besought the guard to halt while he went to the King and begged pardon, which was freely granted. Then Matteo took the halter from the neck of the man, who at once made off. Matteo never thought to see him again ; he only acted out of compassion.

Soon after this Matteo was sent on a mission to Catalonia, the King being at war with Genoa, and on the voyage the ship met some Genoese galleys, by which Matteo's ship was captured. He was stripped of all his belongings and put into the well of the ship. As there was enmity between the King and the Genoese, it did not seem likely he would ever be set free. But in the well he was accosted by the youth he had saved at Piombino, and, when no one was by, he said to Matteo, " Signor, I owe my life to God and yourself, and I will never rest till I have set you free as a return for what you did for me at Piombino." Matteo recognised the youth and, finding himself quite helpless, trusted to this deliverer. When the galley entered a port to take in water the youth carried Messer Matteo on his back ashore and thus delivered him As this port was in King Alfonso's dominions, Messer Matteo was freed. Let everyone therefore be kind and courteous to others, for no one knows what the future has in store.

Matteo was in the King's service for twenty-two years and then desired to take a wife and return to Majorca, but the King was unwilling to part with him. At last he determined to marry in order that the King might more readily consent. The King ultimately gave way and, after the marriage, he again asked leave to retire as he needed rest. Many times he complained to me of the irksomeness of royal service, comparing it to a gilded bird-cage which those inside wish to leave, while those outside wish to enter. At last the King allowed him to go back to Majorca, and he left at once. He was well read in the liberal arts, a man of universal culture and constant in his religious duties. He was a worthy gentleman, therefore I have added his name to this collection.

FRANCESCO DEL BENNINO

Francesco Bennino was of good birth, he was learned in Latin and he held in the city every office that a citizen can fill. He bore himself so well that he acquired the best of reputations, was much given to religious observances and of distinguished manners, a good example to all. He disliked all worldly display, was most temperate in everything, a most worthy citizen and a great friend to everybody, lay and cleric alike. He delighted greatly in the Holy Scriptures and would read them whenever he had leisure ; sometimes indeed he would cause them to be read to him, as his sight was short. He discharged his official duties outside the city with the utmost justice and mercy, and would hear every case which was brought before him, and was most temperate in his decision. He was the foe of all ribald persons and blasphemers ; these he punished in a way which they would never forget, and more often he punished them by corporal chastisement than by fine. Instead of passing his time uselessly as others would over gambling and vanities, Francesco would always, during his daily work, and at dinner, and at supper, cause to be read to him either Giovanni Cassiano, or the sermons of S. Efrem, or some other devotional work. He ordered his house by an upright rule of life and decent manners, as all those who fear and love God are bound to do. He was a citizen most worthy to be included in the number of those remarkable men in this collection. Happy the republic which has men like him to rule it !

DUCA DI WORCESTRI (JOHN TIPTOFT, EARL OF WORCESTER)
(1427–1470)

John, Duke of Worcester, an Englishman of the noblest birth, quitted England with a large following for Venice at that season when the land was torn with disputes in which he, like a wise man, had resolved to take no part. Later, the pilgrims' galley being ready to leave Venice for the Holy Land, he embarked thereon and went to visit the holy places of Jerusalem. Having made this voyage, he returned to Venice and thence journeyed to Padua, where is the University, to study Latin, though he was already well versed in the same, and after he had been there some time the troubles in England came to an end. As soon as they were settled many noblemen, and the King as well, wrote to him asking him to

return. He went from Padua to Florence with the purpose
of going on to Rome, taking with him great store of books,
and in Florence he bought others which he happened upon,
and collected a vast number. While certain books which his
lordship desired were being transcribed, he tarried in Florence
several days, and was minded to visit the whole city, alone
and unattended. He would turn to the left hand, then to the
right, and next to the left again and in this fashion he went
into every part of it.

Now, having heard the fame of Messer Giovanni Argiropolo,
he went one morning to the University to hear one of his
lectures. His presence was unknown to anyone, and the
teaching of Messer Giovanni gave him much satisfaction.
When he had seen all there was to see in Florence, he quitted
it and went to Rome, where he saw the whole city and visited
the Pope and cardinals and many prelates who were there.
Afterwards he passed through Florence on his way to England,
where, on his arrival, he was much honoured, and, on account
of his learning and his great wisdom and prudence, was
counted one of the chief men of the government.*

Nevertheless, there are many men of high estate who know
not how to rule themselves within, and this nobleman was
amongst them. He held in his own hands the whole of the
King's treasure, and of the affairs of state there were few
which he did not control. While things stood thus, new
broils broke out in King Edward's kingdom, and he fled to
avoid capture by his foes, who were by far the stronger party
on account of foreign support. The Duke, wishing to keep
faith with his sovereign, left London in search of him, taking
with him a large sum of money. Thinking how he might best
escape his enemies, he hid himself in a wood where there
were some shepherds with their cattle, and this thing happened. Having disguised himself, he took up his quarters
with them, and gave money to one of the shepherds to lay out
for bread. The shepherd went to a farm hard by, and, seeing
that he had been wont to buy bread for himself alone, and
now bought more than was usual, the people of the farm

* Lionardo Bruno dedicated to him his translation of Aristotle's
Politics ; but, dissatisfied apparently at Tiptoft's reception of the
gift, he dedicated it afresh to Eugenius IV.

became suspicious, because a close search was then being made for the Duke. And when the shepherd went away they sent for certain men-at-arms to search the wood, and see if he might be hidden therein. They soon discovered him and sent him to London. Then the people, according to their disposition, all clamoured for his death, the chief plea for his condemnation being that he had procured the revival of certain laws which the people did not favour, and for this reason he was condemned to death. They wished that he should die as the kings had died, and therefore they caused a great scaffold to be built and covered with tapestries and carpets and other ornaments. And when it came to the taking of his life the populace, minded like most of those who support the winning side, made great rejoicing and cried out that he must die because he had brought into England certain laws of Padua, the city in Italy where he had studied, which were hateful to the people. However, men ought always to do right, and never trust the favours of the crowd, which are like fair days of winter which quickly come and quickly go.

On the day of his death he went forth accompanied by many priests, some English and some Italian. There was one Italian of the Dominican Order, a man of fine presence and eloquent in speech,* who went to him and said : " My Lord, you are brought here to-day by reason of your unheard-of cruelties, especially when, desiring to put an end to certain leaders, enemies of the state, you killed also two innocent yearling children, urged on by the lust of power." When the Duke said that this was done for the good of the state, the friar answered that it is right to do those things which are just and honest in the service of the state, but not evil deeds ; moreover, it was a maxim of S. Jerome that no righteous man ever came to a bad end, and that the opposite happened to the impious and the cruel. These ultramontanes showed the greatest devotion, especially in religious affairs. The Duke, when the time for his decapitation had come, turned to the executioner and besought him to take off his head in three strokes in honour of the Holy Trinity, though it might have

---

* Vespasiano probably gathered from this friar the details which follow, as well as the story of his betrayal by the shepherds, which do not appear elsewhere.

been done in one ; a sign of his great faith and of his magnanimity. The headsman promised this, and struck off his head in three strokes. He met his death fully penitent for his sins, and with the hope that God would have mercy upon him, seeing that he died in the fear of God, and that death was the punishment of his offences. Many of the greatest men are blinded by ambition, and know not God, therefore they come to an evil end.

ALVARO DI LUNA (*d.* 1453)

Alvaro di Luna was a Catalan, sprung from honest parents and a man of great ability. His influence with King Juan* was so great that all the government became centred in his hands. This caused great indignation amongst the leading nobles of the kingdom, for it seemed to them strange that a foreigner of ignoble birth should rule the state, and they bore it unwillingly and worked assiduously with the King to procure Alvaro's dismissal, but for a long time the King would not listen, and was determined that the government should remain in the hands of Alvaro, who was a very able ruler and bore himself so prudently that he governed this kingdom for more than forty years, and by the will of God was the means of breaking the arrogance of these nobles.

Alvaro fared as most great men fare, who are blinded with the pomp of power and with long success. Stung by the annoyances he suffered from the envy of the nobles he became lacking in due restraint ; he assumed more authority than was becoming, for he imagined that he could do what he liked. Once he sent for a certain nobleman who, while he was in Alvaro's house, was wounded almost to death to the disgrace and shame of the King and the constituted authority. When this outrage became known to the barons of the kingdom they deemed the time had come for the punishment of Alvaro, and for revenge for the many insults they had suffered at his hands. They went before the King at once and pointed out to him all Alvaro's misdoings, the wrongs he had done and the power he had usurped without warrant. As they knew

* Juan II, King of Aragon and Navarre, *d.* 1458.

well how to deal with the King's humour, and had duly preferred their charges they aroused the King's anger so strongly that he ordered Alvaro's arrest at once and condemnation to death, without permission to address a word to the King. When he was seized by the ministers of justice, before being sent to execution, he asked permission of the King to speak to him, whereto the King answered that what he had determined to be done should be carried out in this case, and that he had already told him that any man, whom he desired to die, should hold no further speech with him, and this rule should be followed with regard to himself. Princes, and those who advise them, should take note here, and also governors of republics and cruel men, that they will meet with the same treatment which they have unjustly dealt out to others, as Christ says in His holy evangel : " What men sow, that they shall reap."

When Alvaro had received this answer from the King, those who had to carry out the sentence set him upon a mule with his face towards the tail, as is the custom with traitors, and along the way by which he passed there went before him a trumpeter who cried out, " This is Alvaro, traitor to the Crown of Spain." Alvaro answered saying that this was not true, for he was faithful and loyal. Passing along, they came to the place of execution where was gathered a vast crowd awaiting them, as is always the case in spectacles like this. They then cut off his head, but before this he cried out that everyone should take warning by him, and dread the strokes of Fate, for now they could see what end he had come to, and to what misery, after so much good fortune. He begged them to pray God for him. This should be noted well by all rulers, and by those who advise them, and by those who hold office in republics and democratic states and teach them the fickleness of Fortune, even though they may wish to live justly and within the bounds of the Law and not to trust too much to their own strength ; seeing that everything is prone to change, as in the case of Alvaro,* a striking instance of the working of Fortune.

* Alvaro was a wise and beneficent statesman, under whose rule Aragon rose to its highest power and prosperity. He became over-confident and exasperated his enemies by arrogance and by refusing

STATESMEN

Antonio Cincinello

Messer Antonio Cincinello was a Neapolitan gentleman of good family. He served King Ferdinand many years and won a good reputation in the several legations on which he was sent. He was upright, sober and trustworthy; he spoke his meaning openly and with due prudence, and he was the finest of the gentlemen about the court. He never took meat or wine, save when his health demanded. While he was ambassador at Ferrara in the time of the Marquis Borso, an envoy came from Duke Giovanni who tried secretly, by Borso's aid, to win over Count Jacopo* into the Duke's service, and the safety of King Ferdinand depended upon whether he should succeed or not, for Jacopo was then in the King's pay. This business was being conducted so privily that Messer Antonio could learn nothing of it. He thought out many plans for fathoming the secret in order to secure the King's safety, and endeavoured to discover whom this ambassador had in his house and what people might be in the habit of going there. They told him of a barber who used to shave the ambassador, so he let this same barber cut his own beard. He used to pay the barber above his charges, and give him presents beside, questioning him now and then if he knew where the ambassador's papers were kept, and if he had the courage to get hold of them he would reward him so liberally that he would be happy for the rest of his life. The barber agreed, whereupon Messer Antonio gave him some more ducats. Afterwards the barber went into the ambassador's room and having found the writings, carried them to Messer Antonio who, when he had read them, found out what negotiations were going on with Duke Giovanni, who it appeared had arranged for the invasion of the kingdom by Count Jacopo. Immediately Messer Antonio sent off post-riders to warn the King who, thus forewarned, was able to safeguard divers state interests, for he knew of this business fifteen days before anyone else.

to allow the nobles to plunder the state for their own benefit. The King was weak, and the Queen, his bitter enemy, is said to have intercepted a reprieve on the morning of his execution. The state declined rapidly after his death in 1453.

* Jacopo Piccinino.

ANTONIO CINCINELLO

While Antonio was ambassador at Rome, and Duke Giovanni was maintaining himself in the kingdom by the favour of the revolted barons, and had sent an envoy of his own to the Pope to treat on certain important affairs, Antonio tried to discover, by all possible means, the nature of the negotiations between the Pope and the Duke. He often passed the envoy's house to see whether anyone he knew might frequent it, and one day he came upon a man he had formerly known, whereupon he sent to this man a messenger, who made a sign to him that he wanted to speak to him on a private matter. Afterwards the man went secretly to Antonio, who received him most graciously and, when he dismissed the man, he let drop that he might be able to entrust to him a matter of business which, if properly discharged, would lead to his profit. The man thereupon agreed to do anything Antonio might ask. He came secretly a second time to Antonio, who told him that, if he would bring him the correspondence between the ambassador and Duke Giovanni, he would pay him any price he might ask. The man agreed to this, and went several times into the ambassador's private room in search of any documents which might serve his purpose, and one day he found copies of the letters to Duke Giovanni and the cyphers. These he took to Antonio straightway, and Antonio gave his agent a good sum of money for the letters, which revealed many important matters referring to Duke Giovanni, and sent all information to the King, who thus was able to safeguard himself against many dangers, and was also informed of the secret dealings between the Pope and Duke Giovanni. All this shows how a prudent man can safeguard the state.

When Antonio was in Rome a foe of the King was constantly going backwards and forwards between Rome and the kingdom, wherefore Antonio resolved to have him seized and brought before King Ferdinand. He contrived to have this man lured out of Rome, and at the same time engaged a band of well-mounted young men to seize him in the Campagna and hurry him away over the Papal frontier. He was brought before the King, who, being a clement man, had no mind to use violence but reproved him for his persistent hostility, saying that his conduct was not that of an upright

341

man, and that he hardly knew what to do in this case. At
last he agreed to pardon the man for this once, and warned
him not to repeat his offence. He then freed the offender,
who humbly assured the King that he could never trespass
again, and if he did he would be willing to undergo any punishment the King might inflict. He never erred again, and,
when free, deemed that he had done well in escaping the
King's anger, seeing that he had often been guilty of
unpardonable actions. There are many who deem that
Antonio ought not to have employed the methods he followed
in this case, and in that of the ambassador of Duke Giovanni
at Ferrara, in safeguarding the King and the state by dis-
covering the schemes of his opponents, but Antonio believed
that any means were lawful in the preservation of his master.
I will not judge this matter one way or the other. I know
Antonio to have been an honest man, and I will leave the
decision to those better informed than I am. When Antonio
was appointed ambassador to Pope Paul to deal with certain
differences between him and the King, he found it necessary,
as these affairs were very important, to present a protest,
attested by a notary and two witnesses. As a protest like
this had never been made before, the Pope was very angry.
Messer Antonio answered in becoming terms saying that the
Pope had no reason to take this action amiss as two courses
were permissible to everyone—to protest or to beseech.
Antonio used these words to the Pope in their natural sense
and managed to appease him.

Antonio was for a long time in King Ferdinand's service
and gained a complete knowledge of his character. On two
points he praised the King ; one was that, unlike most men,
he knew how to endure ill, as well as good fortune. When he
heard how the barons of the kingdom had revolted he
observed that it was so much the worse for himself. This
revolt almost led to the entire loss of the kingdom, but he
never lost his head or gave way to despair. When he was
brought to his lowest extremity, with little hope of saving
his kingdom—with no army, an empty treasury and the
barons in revolt—he turned to Antonio and some others who
were by and said : " When I have exhausted every remedy
and lost all hope of winning back my kingdom, I will put

myself at the head of the few men I can find and go in search of my foes, for I would rather die sword in hand like a man than live in disgrace." He was in such straits at this time that he wanted the bare necessaries of life. No one need ever despair after seeing how low the King had been brought, and how fair fortune may follow upon foul.

When his affairs mended the King had many examples of this. When he had a success he never changed, but went on in the same mood. After he brought off his feat of arms at Troja, where he was opposed by Duke Giovanni, Count Jacopo and the Prince of Taranto and other leaders and a force far stronger than his own, he was supported by Signor Alessandro* and other captains such as Count Orso and others in the Papal interest. After the battle opened they drove the foe from a certain hill and forced him into the open plain, whereupon Signor Alessandro wanted to cease fighting, saying to the King, " We have done enough for to-day, let us now stop the fight." But Ferdinand, who was lacking in money and arms and men and in danger of losing his kingdom, turned to Signor Alessandro and said, " I am determined that the end of this day shall see me either a King or nothing, so the battle must go on." Then the fight was resumed through the King's courage and resolution. The enemy was broken and the battle ended with a glorious victory for the King. The enemy was broken and put to flight. Before the fight began Count Jacopo was uneasy as to the enterprise, suspecting that it might end in failure. When the battle ended with great profit and honour to the King, I met Messer Antonio and Messer Marino, and from them I heard that when the army went back into quarters everyone was joyful except the King, who seemed as if he had taken no part in it.

When they prepared to take food the King washed his hands and said nothing, so everyone was amazed that he should have given no sign of joy. On leaving the table he called his secretary and some of the captains and said : " By the grace of God we have won a victory and all seem to think I have done enough, but if I fail to follow up this victory at once I shall be in a bad case, for the Prince of Taranto after this victory will offer money to my men-at-arms. All of you

* Alessandro Sforza.

know my condition. I have no money and everyone knows it, and my soldiers, if they are determined to be paid, may go to the Prince of Taranto. I am penniless, therefore this victory we have just won may prove to be a disaster. I can only think of one remedy ; that you, Marino, should go to the Baths of Petriuolo, where you will find Pope Pius, and you must tell him of the battle we have just won and ask him to lend me twenty thousand florins. I shall then be able to put heart into my soldiers by the help of Pope Pius and thus may save my kingdom." Everything turned out as the King had planned and showed the King's prudence in providing for the future, for the Prince of Taranto, when he saw how severe the defeat had been, began to distribute large sums of money amongst the men-at-arms, and he would have won them over if the King had not provided for their pay. Strength is no service to a ruler unless it be seconded by intelligence.

I will tell here something worthy to be remembered, especially by all who are in the service of great men, most of whom know how gross is the ingratitude which these, as a rule, deal out to those who serve them. The grandfather of Messer Antonio was named Giovanni Cincinello, one of the wisest men in the kingdom, of great weight and judgment, and one possessed of more than a hundred and fifty thousand ducats. He was a faithful subject of the house of Aragon, the father of a son, Messer Bufardo, whose son was Messer Antonio. When King René was in the kingdom, a report was spread that Messer Giovanni was an adherent to the Aragonese party, as it often happens in court where one man is jealous of another. Thus it came to King René's hearing that Messer Giovanni was inscribed on King Alfonso's books, and against King René. For this reason, without making further enquiry, he and his son Messer Bufardo were seized and Messer Giovanni was put to the strappado to make him confess a crime which he had not committed or even thought of. One day when father and son were in prison one of the King's men came and said that Messer Bufardo would be beheaded at once if sixteen thousand ducats were not handed over. Messer Giovanni said this was the last thing he wanted and he would pay the money, and this he did. After a long imprisonment they were set free and Messer Giovanni, having spent all his substance and being very old, fell ill and died in a hospital, the Nunziata, at Naples. After his father's death Bufardo remained in Naples, and when Alfonso regained the kingdom Bufardo acquired a post which allowed him to live, but he never was duly repaid for the fidelity his father and he had given, in fact he was ill to do.

Messer Antonio has served the King from his youth till the present day in all important affairs of state to which he has devoted the whole of his life. Antonio is a trustworthy and upright man, who has occupied many responsible offices with a very small salary. His own income was a very small one and he would never have asked the King for higher reward ; if any increase came to him, it was through the King's liberality, moreover, he had many envious rivals who strove to keep him away from the court. When he was ambassador in Florence and when his mission was well-nigh completed, a letter came ordering him to go to Milan, with letters of authorisation, the commission and a special letter from the King directing him to set out at once. Messer Antonio was assured that, by obeying this command, he would risk his life, because he had been involved, albeit unwittingly, in the capture and death of Count Jacopo. Though he was known to be truthful, nevertheless the people are brutal and it is dangerous to put oneself into their power. When he read in the King's letter that he was ordered to go to Milan he quickly decided to refuse to go and to write to the King that he might do what he would with him, but that he would not go to Milan on account of the wrongful reports concerning himself which were current amongst the people there. The King fathomed his meaning and wrote in reply that he might go or not as he pleased.

Many events of this nature happened to him, but to avoid prolixity I will not tell of them all. A Diet met in Germany, at which were assembled many lords and prelates, and a request was sent to the King to despatch thither two distinguished men to meet a gathering of the leading personages of Germany. There was at the court of Naples a certain Catalan who had been in King Alfonso's service, a man learned in all the seven liberal arts and of high reputation. Now all those who were jealous of Messer Antonio did all they could to procure his selection for this post, so as to rid the court of his presence. As he was superabundantly fitted for it he was obliged to go. He won the highest esteem of the Emperor and of all the nobles present and saw that nothing was done against the King's honour. As soon as he had discharged one commission as ambassador, he would always be asked to undertake the next which might arise, and he remained many years in this service. The Duke of Calabria, the King's heir, had a son, the Prince of Capua, who would ultimately become King, and it seemed good to King Ferdinand, who was convinced of the worth and wisdom of Messer Antonio, that he should become the Governor of the young prince and be relieved of all other duties. He saw the importance of this charge which he accepted, and brought up the prince in a suitable manner.

The King met with great troubles in governing Aquila; the people were factious and disobedient, and especially the party of the Count of Montoro who was very powerful. The people's allegiance was due to the King, but they only gave it to him as far as it suited the Count, who was ultimately seized, with his wife and family, and sent to Naples. Messer Antonio had now become weary of court life and wished to retire, alleging that he was going to visit S. Jacopo and S. Antonio in the spring. He purposed to travel slowly, and to rest in his lodging whenever gout might trouble him. But in this life man proposes and God disposes. The King was keeping the Count of Montoro in Naples and looked about for some man of experience to govern Aquila, wherefore he sent Messer Antonio to regulate affairs. He laboured hard to settle the region, but this was difficult, for the Aquilani are a coarse and brutal race, especially those who live in the mountains and herd with their cattle. This charge was an unfortunate one for this poor gentleman. The Aquilani hated the King and the Duke of Calabria and sought by every means to get the better of them, and they turned to the Pope, as their lord, for they deemed that the King was a vassal of the Church. The King kept a guard of soldiers in Aquila, and the chief of these and some of his men were killed in a brawl with the citizens. On hearing this Antonio mounted his horse and rode into the Piazza, where certain friendly citizens warned him to return to his house and avoid the brutal mob. He returned home and left the door unsecured and unguarded, never deeming that the people would attack him. A tumultuous crowd followed him, and when he saw them approaching went on to the roof so as to escape into the house of a friend, but this friend, through fear of the people, would not admit him, so the unfortunate man was forced to return to his own house, which was soon forced by the crowd. They asked where his possessions were kept, and, after they had seized everything, one of these miscreants gave him a blow on the chest ; others fell on him and murdered him and finally his body was hacked to pieces and thrown out into the street.* Alas, this was the end and the reward of Messer Antonio who, together with his family, had given so long and faithful service. Almighty God, marvellous are Thy judicial decisions, and inscrutable Thy ways !

Messer Antonio was one of the most religious, merciful and beneficent of men. I will here give an instance of his piety. When he was on a mission from King Ferdinand to Rome, a youth named Rinaldo Gianfigliazzi—whose father and grandfather had been rebels and exiles—begged to be taken into his service and to become a soldier. Messer Antonio dissuaded him strongly against such a course, saying, " You are a gentleman and should sit upon the bench : the calling of a soldier is not for you," and added many other reasons, but the youth induced several others to press his suit on Messer Antonio, who finally consented. Soon after Messer Antonio went into camp and, when he found Rinaldo to be honest and worthy, he handed his establishment over to him and let him keep the keys. On the first evening he bade the youth see to the forage of the horses, whereupon he gave it to them and also their bedding, which he spread in the stable. It appeared as if he had been at this work all his life. Every day he served Messer Antonio as gentlemen should be served, and no one could have done better. From the camp he accompanied Messer Antonio to Naples, and every day he became more efficient. Often when the King took Messer

* Macchiavelli, *Flor. Hist.*, p. 414.

STATESMEN

Antonio out hunting with him the youth would lead a dog like a practised hunter. So he became well known to the King and all the court.

When this young man had managed Messer Antonio's house some three years, his mother, who lived in the Marches, desired his return and sent two friars to Naples to fetch him —one, Don Tulbia, son of Rinaldo degli Albizzi, and the other her own brother. Arrived at Naples they sought Messer Antonio and begged him to allow the youth Rinaldo to return to his mother, now a widow, her husband having been exiled as a rebel in the civil broils. Moved by the insistence of the friars and by the unhappy case of the mother Messer Antonio urged Rinaldo to return, but he, who loved Messer Antonio and deemed that he had met his chance in life, demurred at this, but Messer Antonio ordered him to go back with the friars. After spending some time with his mother he determined to become a soldier, and as he was ashamed to apply to Antonio he joined a free company; but he was ill-content here, and shortly afterwards he again applied to Antonio, who, seeing him in such an evil plight, gave him three horses and seventy ducats. Soon afterwards the luckless Rinaldo died and, when Antonio learned this, he tried to recover what he had lately given him, not for himself, but for the unfortunate mother who was now a widow and homeless. He got back forty ducats which he sent to the mother at Ancona, and soon after recovered the rest. The mother went to Florence, and when Antonio was in the city he found her and asked her to meet him one morning at the Church of S. Teresa, but as she was sick with fever he sent to her the thirty ducats which he had last received. When she received this and remembered Antonio's great kindness to herself and her son, she cried, weeping, " It is now thirty-five years since my husband was expelled from Florence in 1434, and I have been wandering about the country ever since without finding anyone to help me. Messer Antonio alone has been kind and charitable to me and my son. I pray God that He may reward him, in that now when I am sick and wretched he has again come to my aid."

Before I end this notice of Messer Antonio—who as we see was a most generous man—I will say that this youth Rinaldo

348

ANTONIO CINCINELLO

was the grandson of Messer Rinaldo degli Albizzi,* his father being one of the Gianfigliazzi. When he went to his mother at Ancona he arrived barefoot and clad only in an under-vest. When his mother saw his plight she cried, " What does this mean, my son ? " Whereto he replied, " I have been robbed and left with naught but my shirt, and this waistcoat I took from the body of a man who had been hanged." We can imagine the mother's grief at this sight of her poor and homeless son. Although this last episode in Rinaldo's career may be of no great weight, it may be warning to those who read this Life to guard against the strokes of adverse fortune.

Regarding the death of Messer Antonio at the hands of an execrable mob like that of Aquila, many reflections will ensue. Nevertheless, the judgments of God, as it is written, are as a vast gulf which no one can explore, although S. Paul declared, " O the height of the riches, O the knowledge and wisdom of God. How inscrutable are Thy judgments ! " And S. Jerome says, " If thou wouldst not err, give no opinions."

NOTE.—Having come to the end of the spiritual and temporal leaders, I will write of those who have left their written compositions to be the light of their own age and of those ages which are to come.

* Cosimo's chief opponent. He was exiled in 1434.

VI : *WRITERS*

POGGIO FIORENTINO (1380–1454)

MESSER POGGIO was born at Terranuova, a Florentine village. His father sent him to the University, where he remained as a teacher, being very learned in the Latin tongue and well conversant with Greek. He was an excellent scribe in ancient characters, and in his youth he was wont to write for a living, providing himself thus with money for the purchase of books and for his other needs. It is well known that the court of Rome is a place where distinguished men may find a position and reward for their activity, and thither he accordingly went, and when his quickness of wit had become known, he was appointed apostolic secretary. Afterwards he opened a scrivener's office, and in these two vocations was known as a man of integrity and good repute. He had no mind to enter the priesthood, or to accept ecclesiastical preferment, but he took as wife a lady of the noblest blood of Florence, one of the Buondelmonti, and by her had four sons and one daughter. He was sent by Pope Martin with letters into England,* and he found much to censure in the way of life of that country, how the people were fain to spend all their time in eating and drinking ; indeed, by way of joke, he would tell how, when he had been invited by some bishop or nobleman to dine or sup, he had been forced, after sitting four hours at table, to rise and bathe his eyes with cold water to prevent him from falling asleep. He had many marvellous tales to tell about the wealth of the land, especially concerning the old cardinal† who had

* 1429.
† Cardinal Beaufort. Poggio had met him at the Council of Constance, and had been attracted to England by promises of preferment which Beaufort neglected to perform. Some of his comments on his English experiences are interesting. He writes : " The nobles of England deem it disgraceful to reside in cities and prefer to live in country retirement. They reckon a man's nobility by the size of his landed estate. They spend their time over agriculture and traffic in

directed the government of the kingdom for so many years. It was said that his gold and silver plate was of enormous value, and that all the kitchen utensils were of silver, as were also the andirons and all the smaller articles. Another fellow-citizen of ours, Antonio dei Pazzi, went thither also, and one morning, on a solemn feast, the cardinal assembled a great company for which two rooms were prepared, hung with the richest cloth and arranged all round to hold silver ornaments, one of them being full of cups of silver, and the other with cups gilded or golden. Afterwards Pazzi was taken into a very sumptuous chamber, and seven strong boxes full of English articles of price were exhibited to him. I set this down in confirmation of what Poggio has stated.

When the Council of Constance was assembled, Poggio went thither, and was besought by Nicolao and other learned men not to spare himself trouble in searching through the religious houses in these parts for some of the many Latin books which had been lost.* He found six Orations of Cicero, and, as I understood him to say, found them in a heap of waste paper amongst the rubbish. He found the complete works of Quintillian, which had hitherto been only known in fragments, and as he could not obtain the volume he spent thirty-two days in copying it with his own hand : this I saw in the fairest manuscript. Every day he filled a copybook with the text. He found Tully's *De Oratore*, which had been long lost and was known only in parts, Silius Italicus, *De secundo bello punico*, in heroic verse, Marcus Manilius on Astronomy, written in verse, and the poem of Lucretius, *De rerum Natura*, all works of the highest importance. Also the *Argonauticon* of Valerius Flaccus in verse, the comments of Asconius-Pedianus on certain of Cicero's Orations, Columella on Agriculture, Cornelius Celsus on Medicine, the *Noctium Atticarum* of Agellius, some additional works of Tertullian, the *Silvæ* of Statius in verse, and Eusebius, *De Temporibus*, with manuscript

wool and sheep, not deeming it derogatory to trade in the produce of their land. I have known a rich merchant, who had retired from business, invested his money in land and retired into the country to become the founder of a noble race, and I have seen him admitted into the society of the most illustrious families." Shepherd's *Life of Poggio*, p. 127.

* *Vide* his "letter to a friend." Muratori, *Rerum Italic. Script.*, XX, p. 160. This friend was Guerino da Verona.

additions by Girolamo and Prospero. Next at Constance
he found Tully's letters to Atticus, but of these I have no
information, and Messer Lionardo and Messer Poggio together discovered the last twelve comedies of Plautus, which
Gregorio Corero, Poggio and certain others amended and set
in the order which they still follow. The Verrine orations of
Cicero also came from Constance and were brought to Italy
by Lionardo and Poggio.* Thus it may be seen how many
noble works we possess through the efforts of these scholars,
and how much we are indebted to them ; and how greatly the
students of our own time have been enlightened by their
discoveries. There was no copy of Pliny in Italy ; but, news
having been brought to Nicolao that there was a fine and perfect one at Lubeck in Germany, he worked so effectively
through Cosimo de' Medici that he, by the agency of a kinsman
of his living there, bargained with the friars who owned it,
giving them a hundred Rhenish ducats in exchange for the
book. But great trouble followed, both to the friars and to the
purchasers.†

After his return from Constance Poggio commenced author,
and to show his quality as a speaker. He had a great gift of
words, as the study of his writings and translations will show.
His letters are most delightful from their easy style, written
without effort. He was given to strong invective, and all
stood in dread of him. He was a very cultured and pleasant
man, sincere and liberal, and the foe of all deceit and pretence.
He had many witty stories to tell of adventures he had
encountered in England and Germany when he went thither.
As he was very free of speech he incurred the ill-will of some
of their learned men, and was prompt to take up his pen in
vituperation of certain men of letters. He wrote a very abusive
letter to Pope Felix, the Duke of Savoy, and took up the
cudgels in defence of Nicolao Nicoli, on the score of his many
virtues, against a learned man who is now dead. Nicolao

---

* He also found Cicero's *Oratio pro Cæcina* in a Cluniac monastery
at Langres. Also Lactantius, *De via Dei ;* Vegetius, *De re Militari ;*
Ammianus Marcellinus, *vide* the preface of the Abbé Mehus to the
Vita Ambrosii Traversarii.

† He employed a certain Nicolas of Treves as a teacher, who found
in Germany a volume containing twelve comedies of Plautus hitherto
missing—only eight being extant. A copy by Nicolao Nicoli is in the
Marcian Library at Florence.

was devoted to Carlo d' Arezzo on account of his learning and of his excellent character, and procured advancement for him in many ways. By his influence Carlo was appointed to teach in the University in competition with the learned man before named, against whom Poggio, from his love of Nicolao Nicoli, had written his invective. The gathering at Messer Carlo's lectures was marvellous; thither came all the court of Rome, which was then at Florence, and all the learned Florentines, and from this cause arose the differences between Nicolao Nicoli and Filelfo, through the great reputation which Messer Carlo had thereby gained. Poggio defended Nicolao Nicoli against an attack made by Filelfo, and on this account ill-feeling arose between Nicolao and Filelfo. As much abuse passed from one to the other, and as Cosimo de' Medici was well disposed to Nicolao and Messer Carlo, Filelfo began to trouble the state, and for his misdemeanour was banished as a rebel; so high did feeling run. To return to Messer Poggio. His fame increased all over the world wherever his works were known, and he spent in original writing or in translating all the time he had to spare after attending to his secretarial and his scrivener's office. One of the first books he translated was the *Agropedia*, a famous work amongst the Greeks, and this he sent to King Alfonso. This translation was highly thought of by the learned of the time, and after it had been sent to Alfonso, the King, quite contrary to his practice, omitted to send to the translator a remuneration for his trouble, where-upon Poggio wrote to Panormita, lamenting this neglect, and when Panormita reminded the King of it he at once sent four hundred Alfonsini, equal to six hundred ducats. Poggio henceforth remembered gratefully the King's action and praised it, whereas up to this time he had felt something of a grudge. While he tarried at Rome, enjoying the highest favour of the Pope, Messer Carlo d' Arezzo, the Chancellor of the Signoria, died at Florence and Poggio was elected to the office forthwith on account of his fame, and his appointment met with general approval. When this news was brought to him, although from his high position at the court of Rome, and the profit he made, he could not hope to better his con-dition, he felt a desire to return to his country, so he accepted the office and made Florence his fatherland, as it was just to do.

POGGIO FIORENTINO

Coming from the court of Rome, and being of a disposition open and frank, and without any leaning towards falsity or dissimulation, Poggio by his character was unacceptable to many of those who ruled their conduct by opposite maxims, saying one thing and meaning another. It happened that an election was held and that he was put forward as a candidate, wherefore he sent word through one of his friends to the electors, who gave him favourable promises as to what they would do. Messer Poggio, who knew little of the Florentine character, took all this for truth, having yet much to learn ; and after he had come to an understanding with his friend, and after the ballot boxes had been emptied, he found that he had received nothing but white beans.* Deceit was foreign to Poggio, and up to this time he had believed that what so many citizens had said must have been near the truth ; but when he saw that he had been tricked, he lost patience at the duplicity of the Florentines, and broke the peace with them, saying that he could never have believed that men would have trangressed into such evil ways, and lamenting that he had come to live in Florence. He believed that this false trick had been played on himself, and not on his friend.

After he had lived some time in Florence he was chosen into the Signoria in order to honour him with civic dignity. When he ceased to attend the Signoria—still retaining the chancellorship and discharging his duties—he went to the Roman court, having won approval from the papal authorities by his letters from all parts of the world. Then it was that certain Florentines, of the sort which is always ready to find fault with everything, began to censure him, scheming how, by the agency of Cosimo de' Medici, who was well disposed toward him, they might drive him out of the chancellorship and put another in his place. Let everyone mark what great danger a man incurs who, with many competitors, submits to the popular vote. Messer Poggio, who was growing old, perceived he could not satisfy this demand because it was mixed up with various parties and policies, decided to retire, in order to have more rest and leisure for study, and let them put another in his office. Life in the city was uncongenial to his

---

* In Florentine elections white beans were negative and black affirmative.

habits and pursuits. Cosimo was much attached to him, and would never have wished to see anyone else in the chancellorship, but when he saw that Messer Poggio cared naught in the matter, he let things take their course, otherwise he would not have allowed the change. Messer Poggio was at this time very rich through long residence at the court of Rome. He had much ready money, property, many houses in Florence, fine household goods and a noble library: wherefore there was no reason why he should save. Having done with the Palazzo, and with time on his hands, he began upon the history of Florence, taking up the work where Messer Lionardo had left it, and bringing it down to his own day. In Florence it was considered a work of great merit. It had been agreed that he should pay to the state a certain annual sum so that neither he nor his children in the future should be subject to the public burdens of Florence. It came to pass that this privilege was abrogated by an additional tax which laid upon him the insupportable levy of two hundred florins. Hearing the same, Messer Poggio lost patience that the exemption granted to him should be broken in his own lifetime, and if it had not been that Cosimo, who had great influence with him, was able to moderate his anger, he might have taken some imprudent action, for he could not see that a return like this was the meet reward for all his labour. The city itself, and all those who had the Latin tongue, were under great obligations to him, to Messer Lionardo, and Fra Ambrogio, the first exponents of Latin, which had lain obscure and neglected for so many centuries. Thus Florence found itself, in this golden age, full of learned men.

Amongst the other exceptional debts which the city of Florence owed to Messer Lionardo and to Messer Poggio may be reckoned the following: From the times of the Roman republic onward there was not to be found any republic or popular state in Italy so famous as was the city of Florence, which had its history written by two authors so illustrious as were Messer Lionardo and Messer Poggio; indeed, before they wrote all knowledge of the same lay in the deepest obscurity. If the chronicles of the Venetian republic, with its numerous men of learning, which has wrought such great deeds both by land and sea, had been written down and not left unrecorded,

WORKS WRITTEN BY MESSER POGGIO

the renown of Venice would stand higher than it stands to-day. Likewise the affairs of Galeazzo Maria and Filippo Maria and all the other Visconti would be better known than they are. Every republic ought to set high value upon its writers who may record what is done therein ; as we may see from what has been done in Florence, in a narrative from the very beginning of the state, to the times of Messer Lionardo and Messer Poggio ; every deed done by the Florentines being set down in Latin in a narrative appropriate to the same. Poggio let his history follow that of Lionardo, writing also in Latin, and Giovanni Villani wrote a general history in the vulgar tongue, telling of what happened in every place mixing with it the history of Florence, and following him Filippo Villani did the same. These two are the only historians who exhibit these times to us in their writings.

Anyone who may have to write the Life of Messer Poggio will find many things to tell, but having had to make something by way of a commentary, this, which is written here of him, is enough for the present. At the end is added a list of all the works which he wrote or translated, in order that it may be seen how greatly the Latin tongue was enriched by his learning. Before he died, having left to his children a good income as it has been already noticed, he made plans for a marble tomb in S. Croce and stated his wishes as to the erection of the same, writing the epitaph with his own hand, but afterwards, while the affair was in progress, the money was put to bad use and the tomb was never built.

WORKS WRITTEN BY MESSER POGGIO

(1) Epistolarum libri decem (immo XVIII). (2) In avaritiam liber unus. (3) De infelicitate principum lib. unus. (4) An seni sit uxor ducenda lib. unus. (5) Contra hypocritas lib. unus. (6) Dialogus trium disputationum lib. unus. (7) De miseria conditione humanæ lib. duo. (8) De varietate fortunæ lib. quattuor. (9) De præstantia Cæsaris et Scipionis lib unus. (10) Oratio in laudem Cardinalis Florentini.* (11) Oratio in laudem Nicolai de Nicolis. (12) Oratio in laudem Laur-

* Cardinal Zabarella, who died during the Council of Constance in 1417.

entii de Medicis. (13) Oratio in Laudem Leonardi Aretini.
(14) Oratio in Laudem Cardinalis Sancti Angeli. (15) Oratio
ad Nicolaum quintum. (16) Oratio in laudem matrimonii.
(17) Oratio in coronatione Federici imperatoris. (18) In-
vectiva in Thomam Reatinum. (19) Invectivæ quinque in
Philelphum. (20) Invectivæ quattuor in Nicolaum Perrottum.
(21) In Jacobum Zenum episcopum feltrensem. (22) In
Franciscum Vallatinum. (23) In Felicem antipapam. (24)
Contra delatores. (25) Facetiarum lib. unus. (26) Historia
populi florentini.

WORKS TRANSLATED

(27) *Cyropædea*, Xenophon. (28) Diodorus Siculus libri VI.
(29) *Asinus*, Lucianus lib. unus.

LIONARDO D' AREZZO (*d.* 1443)

Messer Lionardo was of humble birth and left Arezzo to
study in Florence, where he became a teacher. Messer
Coluccio was at that time the leading man of letters, and he
showed to Lionardo, on account of his merits, especial favour
in teaching him the Latin tongue. Having mastered this, he
worked hard at Greek letters under the tuition of Manuel
Grisolora, a learned scholar, and gained a greater proficiency
in Greek and Latin than any other student of our time. He
then began to write on his own account, and in his first works
showed himself most eloquent and learned, attaining a
position such as no one had reached for a thousand years.
His fame began to spread through all Italy, wherefore he
determined to seek his fortune in the court of Rome under
the advice of Messer Coluccio, who gave him a commendatory
letter to Pope Innocent.* After his arrival in Rome and
reception by the Pope, there came to the city Jacopo di
Agnolo della Iscarparia, a man learned in Greek and Latin.
It happened that at this time it was necessary to appoint a
secretary to replace one who had died ; so it was settled that
these two should write a letter to Pope Innocent to decide
which of the two should succeed. Each had to write the same

---

* Innocent VII, 1404–6. *Vide* Milman, *Lat. Christianity* VIII, p. 97.

form of letter, so that whichever showed himself the better scribe should be appointed secretary. When the letters were written they were laid before the Pope. Messer Lionardo's was pronounced to be the better and he was appointed. He was well liked by all the popes he served, especially by Pope Baldassare Cossa* of Naples. At this time Messer Lionardo was very poor and the Pope, having great regard for him, put him in the way of making money. While Pope John was at Bologna Lionardo was in Mendara, and once when he went to Florence on his own business one of the servants he took with him stole from him goods and money worth two hundred florins. On his return the Pope heard of this, and asked whether it was true. On hearing that it was, the Pope told him the loss should be made good, and on the following morning he sent off a bull to the chancery, saying that he wished it to go through the camera and be taxed for a sum of six hundred florins. This sum he handed over to Lionardo as a recompense for that which the servant had stolen.

Pope John had been asked to attend the Council. While he tarried in Florence, at S. Antonio del Vescovo, he was undecided whether to go or not, chiefly because he had promised to go, wherefore he sent ambassadors to the Emperor with instructions to say that there were certain places, which he specified, to which he would not go, while to certain others he would. After he had given directions to the ambassadors to go to the Emperor with the names of the places written in a document, he became almost mad with fear and regret that he had not written otherwise. Then, as it was willed by Almighty God in his divine justice, he got back the document from them and tore it in pieces, telling the ambassadors that he would go to any place that the Emperor might select. When the ambassadors had told the Emperor their commission he at once named Constance, which indeed was one of the places to which Pope John was loth to go. God Almighty had prepared his punishment. Having chosen the place, and knowing all about it, Pope John at once prepared to go to the Council against the advice of all his friends, who knew that his journey would end in his deprivation. Messer Lionardo accompanied him and lodged with him, and as soon as

* John XXIII, deposed by the Council of Constance.

they came to Constance a combination against the Pope was at once set on foot to deprive him of the pontificate, and the chiefs of the Council gave written support to it. A friend of Pope John who had notice of what was going on, warned him in a letter, and one evening after supper, while Messer Lionardo and others were in the house, this friend went to the Pope to let him know what was being done against him. Messer Lionardo was present and heard all that was said. The friend, who was an Italian prelate, took the Pope aside and told him of the plot against him, showing the list of the conspirators, and imagining that he might thereby win some favour from the Pope. He added that the conspirators had sworn to seize him and put him in prison. As soon as the Pope heard this he seized the letter and tore it to shreds and then, being furiously angry, took hold of the prelate and made as if to throw him out of the window. Certain others who were present and Messer Lionardo came forward, astonished at what had happened, not knowing the reason, and the prelate, who thought to win some favour, found he had not done much for himself when he saw that the Pope had escaped. The next day the Pope was told he must either fly the city or go to prison ; so after he had put on a friar's hood he and Messer Lionardo and those about him went out of Constance on foot. They halted at an abbey, where they determined to stay three days, and ate nothing but mildewed pears, since there was naught else, so that they might not be discovered and taken prisoners. After his flight the Pope's deprivation was declared at once and he returned a simple priest. Thus divine justice was done to Pope John, because everyone had declared to him that if he went to Constance he would surely be deprived ; nevertheless, he told himself that he must go, whether he would or no, so it was not in his power to stay away.

After Pope John's deposition Pope Martin was elected and at once went to Florence. Messer Baldassare Cossa, formerly Pope John and now merely a priest, also went thither. Pope Martin, on the petition of Bartolomeo Valori, a citizen of importance and of others in power, made him a cardinal, in which state he lived a few years at Florence where he died. Messer Lionardo relates how the Emperor Sigismund, the Council being assembled and the constitution ordained, rose and said, " Omnes nationes consentiunt, et vos Italici, quare non vultis consentire." Then rose a priest of Prato and said, " Nos sumus hic sub tyranno." Whereupon the Emperor in a rage turned to him and said, " If I were a tyrant you would not have dared to utter those words : for this reason the constitutions are revoked." At the end of the Council Pope Martin repaired to Florence to set about the reform of the Church of God, then in great disorder on account of the existing schism. The city of Florence was rich and very populous, but in the midst of plenty the majority of the city knew not how to govern themselves and the higher classes were as bad as the lower. If due precaution had been taken this humour might not have prevailed, but it became universal and the well-to-do citizens began to sing all about the town a song, " Papa Martino non vale un lupino," and the children went about singing it in all parts, in S. Maria Novella and elsewhere. Blindness seemed to have come over all, and when the children sang the grown-up people laughed to hear them : which was a great mistake on the part of the men and women rather than the children. When he was conscious of this insolence the Pope lost all patience, seeing that the offence came from the adults and not from the children. As soon as Lionardo heard of the Pope's anger he went to him forthwith, knowing what his temper was, hoping to appease it. He found the Pope walking up and down an open gallery which opened upon his chamber, muttering as he went, " Martinus, inquit, quadrantem non valet," * adding, " and it seems to me that each day will be as a thousand till I get to Rome."

Messer Lionardo, knowing well his disposition, did all he could to placate him and said : " Most blessed Father, these are but the utterances of children and not worthy of your notice." The Pope's reply was : " If the men had not agreed with it, the children would not have spoken it. It is in God's hands, and if I go to Rome I will show them whether it is the adults or the children who say these things." Messer Lionardo could not appease his anger, and he left for Rome forthwith. A short time after this war broke out with Duke

---

* " Papa Martino, papa Martino," the popular street cry in Rome, " non vale un quattrino."

WRITERS

Filippo in the Bolognese, and afterwards in Romagna with Madonna Caterina degli Ordelaffi, who was supported by the Florentines, in which war Florence suffered three defeats and was driven into a dangerous position. Moreover, everyone knows how great may be the effect of a false move over some small matter in a state affair if it be not corrected ; to have one like Pope Martin as a friend of the state of Florence and then, by the merest trifle, to change him, who would have been friendly, into a foe.

Messer Lionardo condemned the citizens of these times in the strongest terms for having suffered such an untoward event to occur and for having missed the chance of a remedy when one was possible. Here lay the cause of the greatest misfortune for, when the Florentines found themselves over-thrown by a very powerful army and routed—as it happened thrice in a single year—they were forced to make the best terms they could arrange with the Venetians, whence arose the greatness of the republic and the acquisition of the larger part of their territory on terra firma, and the numerous troubles which ensued therefrom.* All this Messer Lionardo clearly recognised and did all that was possible by word and deed to remedy it, but unsuccessfully, and the saying, " Papa Martino non vale un lupino " well-nigh robbed the city of Florence of its liberties and of several millions of florins.

To return to Messer Lionardo, he came to Florence in the time of Pope Eugenius, for he resigned the secretariat and writership he held to be appointed to the chancellorship. His prudence and his universal knowledge of affairs, through his experience gained in his long sojourn at the court of Rome, were well known, and they gave him a status which made him one of the Signori and often of the Ten.† He proved to be a man of great capability, and was called upon to deal with business of all kinds ; he showed himself a man of wise and temperate opinions and one averse from rash or sudden action in affairs. He was one of the Ten when Niccolo Piccinino was defeated at Anghiari.‡ Concerning Messer Lionardo many things commendatory might be said, and of

* War between Florence and Milan. *Vide Life of Lorenzo Ridolfi,* who gained the support of Venice, 1425.
† The body charged with military affairs. *Vide* Appendix.
‡ 1440. The Florentines were defeated here in 1425.

LIONARDO D' AREZZO

these Messer Giannozzo, in his funeral oration, and Messer Carlo have said enough. Here I will tell only one special matter which I both saw and heard, a counsel of great wisdom given by him to Pope Eugenius when he quitted Florence in order that his leaving might not turn out like that of Pope Martin. When the Pope was about to leave Florence for Rome there arose discord between him and the Venetians, on account of which Pope Eugenius allied himself with King Alfonso and Duke Filippo, wherefore there was grave fear lest war might break out in divers places after the Pope should have departed. The Venetians, who were in alliance with the Florentines, gave instructions to their ambassador at Florence to induce the Florentines on no account to permit the departure of Eugenius in view of the difficulties which might ensue therefrom, and in this matter they went far beyond words and many laid wagers whether he would be suffered to go or not.

Then, as was the custom in the city at this time, a Council of Requests was assembled where all the leading citizens, including Messer Lionardo, were gathered together. When the gonfalonier entered the Council he proposed, according to precedent, they should decide whether they forbid the Pope to depart or no; and added that the Venetians were in favour of retaining him in the city. Messer Lionardo, being chancellor and minister of the Signoria, was the last to speak. All who had hitherto spoken had spoken for retaining the Pope, and now Messer Lionardo ascended the rostrum and spake as follows: " Most Potent Signors and worshipful citizens, I am not sure whether any one of you has duly considered the matter concerning which you have spoken. Whether you know it or no, you have spoken about the Vicar of Christ on earth, who ought to be honoured and venerated as the head of our religion, and, if the Venetians back you up in forbidding him to leave the city, for the reasons which they have assigned, I hold an opposite opinion, because they are urging you on to a policy which they themselves would at once refuse to adopt, were such a request made to them. They are doing everything to lay the burden of this weighty decision upon you, one so important in its nature that, if you are determined to engage in it, you must be prepared

363

to justify your action to all Christian nations, otherwise every Florentine, when he goes outside the state, will be treated as worse than a Jew. Your ruin and undoing will follow and you will never purge yourselves of this infamy." After Messer Lionardo had spoken at length to this effect, and midnight had struck, he could go on no longer—being eighty years of age—and took his leave. As soon as he had gone the greater part of the citizens, who had advised the opposite course, acted like wise men on account of Messer Lionardo's speech and set about altering the decision and confirming all that he had advised. There was but one exception, a man who that evening had spoken strongly against the Pope, going so far as to offer to lay hands on him, if necessary ; and, after Messer Lionardo had gone, this citizen censured what he had said. Nevertheless, the speech of Messer Lionardo had such strong influence that, being confirmed by all the rest, the debate ended by letting the Pope depart, and this counsel of Messer Lionardo came to be more highly appreciated hereafter.

Messer Lionardo had a generous mind, and, when he learned that this citizen had spoken ill of him, on the following morning, when the Signori and the Collegi were assembled according to procedure for debate, he went up into the hall to say what he had to say to the Signoria when the citizen aforesaid should be present. They straightway called him in and then Lionardo warned him, saying that against all procedure he had mounted the rostrum to speak against him (Messer Lionardo) and what he had said in support of the honour and welfare of the state, which he valued above his own life, and not passionately or without consideration. In giving such advice it must be realised that he had acted for the common weal, and not for private passion, he was fully aware of his own status and circumstances, concerning which words of disparagement had been uttered ; though he was born in Arezzo he had made his fatherland that Florence from which city he had received all the honours which could be given to a citizen of the state which was truly his country, and that in all the advice which he had been called upon to give for so many years past, he had acted with the good faith and love as was the duty of every loyal man. Not only had he counselled and acted like a good citizen, he had attempted, to the best of his feeble strength, to honour and exalt the city by writing its history to be included in the roll of literature and thus rendered eternal. One can see how Rome has become celebrated through the illustrious writers—especially Livy—whom she produced, and will be famous through all ages. And though the deeds of the Florentines may not be compared with those of the Romans, he had endeavoured, to the best of his powers, to celebrate their fame without departing from the truth ; it was very difficult to discover the events of past times for want of written records, but he had written from the beginnings to the wars of Galeazzo Visconti, Duke of Milan. If it seemed that he had been somewhat fugitive in his narrative the illustrious Signors must pardon him, seeing that he had been touched in his honour, the preservation of which had been his constant labour to the present day. But now he would turn, with the leave of the illustrious Signors, and deal with this man who had slandered him and who was now here before them. " What advice was it that he gave to the state ? What profit has it brought ? Whither has he gone as envoy ? He knew well that I was an upright man and that, if he had given the matter a thought, he would not have censured what deserved praise and commendation, but would have realised that I gave to my state, without hatred or passion, good advice as a loyal citizen is bound to do." Thus Messer Lionardo reduced him to such a plight that he did not dare reply or speak in his presence, because the respect all men paid to his integrity was so great, because all these false statements had been made in his own presence, and because the government had a good opinion of his honesty, wherefore this citizen found he had not gained much profit when Messer Lionardo had done with him.

Now about Messer Lionardo many things might be said, but these are the affair of whosoever shall write his Life. I have only set down certain incidents I have heard of him which appeared to me worthy of some memorial. Messer Lionardo was, as I have already said, much esteemed by the Signoria, and was often made one of the Ten of the Balia ; the last time was during one of the most arduous and difficult crises of the republic. Niccolo Piccinino appeared before the gates without anyone in Florence being aware of his approach. The Ten made large preparations and engaged the principal leaders of Italy. After Piccinino with his strong force had passed by the city he, persuaded by the Count of Poppi,* led it into Casentirco. Then, after a riot in Florence on account of the preparations made by the Ten, Niccolo Piccinino was routed and overcome between Borgo and Anghiari.† After having induced Niccolo Piccinino to make this move the Count of Poppi, seeking to gain Bibbiena and Castello Santo Nicolo, lost his dominion ; because, after the rout of Niccolo Piccinino, the Florentines took the field at Poppi with two of the Ten as commissaries. After a few days the Count, not being able to defend it, lost Poppi and all his territories and many villages which had belonged to the Counts of Poppi more than six hundred years. During these events the Ten of the Balia—Messer Lionardo amongst them—were in a position of great danger, but in the end—through their great prudence—they were held in high honour and esteem for their good government of the city during their time of office.

At this time the fame of Messer Lionardo was great in Italy and in other lands. In Florence a large band of scribes were always copying his works, some for the city and some to export, so that, wherever he might go, he would find some transcripts of his writings which, through his great name, were in demand throughout the world. I will speak of what I have seen, how many learned men came from Spain and from France led by his fame. Many of these had come for no other reason than to see Messer Lionardo. Every day he received letters from this or that side of the Alps, written by those who were hoping to see him, especially while the court of Rome and Pope Eugenius were in the city. I once went with an envoy, sent by the Spanish King to greet him on his account, who, on entering his house, knelt to him and was loth to rise. The Spaniard said that he had been commissioned by the King to pay this visit, and Messer Lionardo received him with gracious speech, begging that he might be commended to His Majesty. King Alfonso was greatly devoted to him, and begged him to go and reside at

---

* Piccinino's father-in-law.
† 1440. Macchiavelli, *Flor. Hist.*, pp. 269–73.

LIONARDO D' AREZZO

his court on such terms as might seem fitting. He enjoyed the highest consideration in England, especially with the Duke of Worcester, to whom he dedicated his translation of Aristotle's Politics and sent a copy to England. The Duke sent a reply which, in Messer Lionardo's opinion, did not show due appreciation of such a fine work, so he withdrew the dedicatory proem and added another to Pope Eugenius who was then at Bologna. He bore the book in person to His Holiness, who received him with distinguished consideration.

Messer Lionardo was grave in seeming, small in person and of middle height. He wore a cloak of red camlet which came almost to the ground with lined sleeves turned back, and over the cloak he wore a red mantle open on one side and reaching the ground. On his head was a red hood arranged after the fashion. His manners were gentle and pleasing and he had many good stories to tell about Germany, whither he went to attend the Council. He was sparing in words and he looked with especial favour upon those whose worth he knew. He was of choleric nature ; at times he would become angry and then quickly let his anger cool. As an instance of this sudden anger and sudden cooling it may be told, to his credit, how one evening he was with Messer Giannozzo Manetti and other learned men on the Piazza arguing on various matters. Messer Giannozzo was keen upon the subjects in debate, and had an answer ready for everyone, disentangling every problem which was discussed, whereupon Messer Lionardo gave him a reproof somewhat sharper than was his wont. Messer Giannozzo, who had the greatest reverence for him, then excused himself, and Messer Lionardo with his generous nature, deeming that he had given offence, was privately vexed so that all that same evening and night he fell ill at ease. Early in the morning he left his house and went to call on Messer Giannozzo, contrary to his habit, and bade his servant knock at the door. A servant opened it and Messer Lionardo bade him go and tell Messer Giannozzo that one of his friends would fain speak with him. As soon as he heard this, Messer Giannozzo went to the entry and, as soon as he saw Messer Lionardo, he grieved greatly that he should have come there, for, had he heard a single word trom Messer Lionardo, he would have waited on him at once. Messer Lionardo replied that he should not be troubled, but put on his cloak and come with him and listen to what he, Messer Lionardo, had to say. They went out together and, as they passed along the Arno, Messer Lionardo began : " Giannozzo, I know well that last evening I was guilty of bad manners in the Piazza, and I am heartily sorry on this account. After I returned home I was so displeased with myself for what I had done, that all night I had neither peace nor slumber and could not rest till I should have seen you and begged your pardon." Messer Giannozzo replied that he was as his son, and that Messer Lionardo had said nothing he could not put up with. But even if he had spoken any words of this nature there would have been no necessity for him to make any apology. Seeing how great was the respect he had always borne to Messer Lionardo he remained his constant friend. A short time afterwards it was resolved to send an ambassador to Genoa, according to the custom of the time. Every assembly, when naming one, might appoint whomsoever it would, and Messer Giannozzo, who had never yet acted as ambassador, was nominated. Messer Lionardo was present and said, " Send him instead of me, for he is a distinguished man and will do the state much honour." On account of this honourable mention he was sent ambassador to Genoa, to Messer Tomaso da Campo Fregoso, together with the Venetian ambassador. All this was brought about through Messer Lionardo's influence. Messer Giannozzo, as a member of the Assembly, delivered a just and worthy funeral oration at his death in praise of his virtues.

Messer Lionardo left the following works :—

The History of Florence.
The First Punic War. (The second decade of Livy.)
The History of the Goths.*
Oration to Madonna Battista Malatesta.
De temporibus suis.
Oration on the Death of Messer Giovanni Strozzi : Contra hypocritas : Pro seipso ad præsides : Contra nebulonem

---

* It was asserted by Christopher Persona that Aretino's work is only a translation from Procopius. Bayle also remarks that there are forty MS. letters in the Library of Oxford University. *Vide Dict. Hist.* Art. *Aretin. Leo.*

CARLO D' AREZZO

maledicam : De origine urbis romanæ : De recta interpreta-
tione : Dialogi ad Petrum Historium : Isagogicon moralis
disciplinæ : Vita Aristotelis liber unus : Vita Ciceronis :
Epistolarum suarum.
Translations from Aristotle. Ethicorum X* : Politicorum
VIII : Œconomicorum II.
Translations from Plato. Phædo, De immortalitate
animarum : Phædrus : Gorgias : Crito : Apologia Socratis :
Epistolæ Platonis.
Translations from Plutarch. Lives. Marcus Aurelius :
Cato : Pyrrhus : Demosthenes : Sertorius : Paulus Æmilius :
Xenophon.†

CARLO D' AREZZO (MARSUPPINI) (*d.* 1455)

He came of a good family. His father, Messer Gregorio, was
a doctor and well-to-do, and at one time lived with Bucicaldo.
Carlo went early to Florence to study letters, and became
proficient both in Latin and in Greek. Then he studied
philosophy, which he cultivated more on the positive than on
the speculative side. He won the regard of all men of learning,
especially of Nicolao Nicoli, who brought him forward and
thus greatly enhanced his reputation. He had a remarkable
memory. He was introduced to Cosimo de' Medici, who,
together with Lorenzo his brother, showed him much kindness,
and when they fled to Verona on account of the plague
they took with them Nicolao Nicoli and Carlo. When they
returned to Florence, Carlo resumed his studies and Nicolao,
having realised his fine scholarship and his knowledge of Latin,
urged him to lecture in public when Pope Eugenius was in
Florence. Carlo assented, and thereupon was appointed by
the University authorities as lecturer at a liberal stipend.
His lectures attracted a very large audience, not only of
Florentines but of others drawn from the surrounding country.
The nephews of the Pope and cardinals attended likewise.

* Lauro Quirino, a young Venetian, who was at Florence with
Eugenius, wrote an invective against Aretino's work, maintaining
that he had mistaken " Summum bonum " for " Bonum per se."
Vide Life, p. 175
† Corniani, *Secoli della Litteratura Ital.*, names Lives by Aretino of
Dante and Petrarch, which he condemns for their style and matter.

WRITERS

He was recognised as the best read man in Florence. At his first lecture, before a great concourse of learned men, he gave proof of his wonderful memory, for he quoted every known writer in Greek and Latin. Before this Filelfo had been lecturing and now, through jealousy of Carlo, he behaved in a fashion which brought about his banishment. The influence of Lorenzo, who was all-powerful with Pope Eugenius, and the good name Carlo had made procured him the office of papal secretary; moreover, he had shown that he was as efficient in affairs as in the classics. He was sober and modest by nature, and a man of few words; handsome in person, giving an impression of a somewhat sad and meditative temper. His speech and manners were polite, and indecency of any kind was offensive to him. Having given proof of his high capabilities he succeeded to the chancellorship on the death of Messer Lionardo d' Arezzo, which office he filled most efficiently. He was inclined to the making verses and epigrams and showed much facility, he translated the Batracomio-machia of Homer which was much commended, also two books of the Iliad, and spoke a funeral oration on the death of the mother of Cosimo de' Medici. If he had given himself entirely to letters and spent less time over other works his labour might have produced a rich harvest. In many respects he was worthy of praise. He was given a stately funeral, and a poet's crown was laid on his bier by Matteo Palmieri who delivered the funeral oration.

BENEDETTO D' AREZZO (1415-1466)

Messer Benedetto d' Arezzo was of worthy parentage. His father was a doctor of laws who was anxious for his sons to study law under him in Florence, where he taught at the University. These youths were afterwards two of the most famous lawyers of Italy. In intellect and memory Benedetto excelled all others of his time. He was a skilful dialectician both in Civil and Canon Law, and lectured to large audiences in Florence where he had a wide reputation, because in his audience were students from all parts of Italy. His rapid intelligence enabled him to grasp a question as soon as it was put before him, and he was a profound scholar in the Humanities, both prose and verse. He had a wide knowledge of sacred history and literature, and likewise a pleasant trick of repeating popular songs and verses. With his wonderful memory he could converse on every subject, for he never forgot anything he read, so that when he was with well-read men this memory of his did him good service.

Benedetto, with his genial and sympathetic manner, was popular with all learned and unlearned alike, wherefore when the chancellorship became vacant it was given to him. This election and his subsequent administration of his office gave universal satisfaction. When suits came before the Signoria for decision at home, or disputes had to be settled with other states, Benedetto would be called in, and any misunderstanding would be cleared up at once. He was indeed a great ornament in the palace, for when ultramontane envoys came to Florence it would be his duty to answer them. Once an ambassador from the King of Hungary laid before the Signoria in Latin the object of his mission. Benedetto, who heard him, committed the speech to memory and wrote it down word for word in Latin and translated it into Italian for the Signoria. He was then instructed as to what points he should notice in his reply. He made his answer in Latin so excellent that the envoy, who was a learned scholar, was astonished. On his departure Benedetto bade him farewell and, when the ambassador again complimented him on his oration, he again recited the whole speech in Latin. The envoy again expressed his astonishment that he should have repeated it without missing a word and praised his talent and his memory.

By reason of his geniality he was known to all the learned and worthy citizens of Florence in questions of the law and its interpretation ; in those which called for lively treatment, all others would be silent if he chanced to be present. He was glad to get clear of the law, and used to declare that it was concerned with nothing but wrangling. I heard from some of those about the Signoria that no man had borne himself better there than Messer Benedetto. While he was at the palace he began to study history with the intention of writing a continuous narration down to the present time, and he completed it as far as the expedition of Godfrey de Bouillon to the Holy Land. This was a notable achievement, for hitherto this campaign had never been described except in French. He knew this language and made a Latin translation in excellent style. The book was as big as Cæsar's Commentaries, and from his retentive memory he was able to reproduce the style of whatever historians he might have read, but when he left these entirely aside his prose was less distinguished. He deserves great praise, for though he was of the class of lawyers where writings rarely show elegance, he acquired this by diligence. If death had not come to him, and if he had persevered in his studies, he would have done wonders, for there were few Latin books which he had not read.

GIANNOZZO MANETTI (1396–1459)

Messer Giannozzo Manetti was of good birth and, judging from the commentary on his Life,* it seems that he has a claim to be added to the list of distinguished men who have adorned our century. He wrote a number of books and was an ornament to the city, not only from his writings but from everything he did. He was a fine scholar in Greek, Latin and Hebrew, eminent in moral and natural philosophy, and a theologian equal to any of his time. He learned Hebrew solely for the better understanding of the sacred writings, and would say that he knew three books by heart, the epistles of S. Paul, *De Civitate Dei* by Augustine, and from the pagans the Ethics of Aristotle. With his knowledge of Hebrew he was able to write a treatise in ten books for the confusion of the Jews, which he afterwards amended. He was an ardent controversialist ; always ready to argue with the Jews, with whom no one can dispute who is not versed in their tongue. In these contests he would always say to his opponent, " Put yourself on guard, with your arms ready, for I will only attack you with your own weapons," and no Jew, however learned, ever met him without defeat. Because the Jews declared that the edition of the Psalter, made by the seventy-two interpreters, had been augmented and altered, he published a translation of it from *De Hebraica veritate*, whereupon certain

* By Naldo Naldio. Muratori, *Rerum Italic Script.*, XX.

men, who were ignorant of the language, endeavoured to censure it from envy, so Manetti published five apologetic treatises in defence of the Psalter. In these he showed everything that had been added unaltered, without leaving unconsidered a single iota, thus proving his own knowledge of the Holy Scriptures. He demonstrated that he had read and studied the whole of the Bible, in Hebrew as well as in Greek. He read twice all the Hebrew commentators with the view of denouncing their perfidy. He studied Hebrew under two learned teachers, and his intimate knowledge of Greek is shown in his translations of the New Testament, the Ethics of Aristotle, as well as the *Magni Morali*, the *De Memoria* and *De Reminiscentia*. He was taught Greek by the learned Friar Ambrogio degli Agnoli, and acquired learning very quickly, simply because he knew how to divide his time rightly. He gave no more than five hours to sleep, and devoted the rest to study. He began to study Latin in his twenty-fifth year, not having been able hitherto to follow his own wishes on account of his father. For nine years he never crossed the river. He used to go to S. Spirito, to which he had opened a way from his garden, and at S. Spirito at this time there were divers learned men, Messer Vangelista of Pisa and Messer Girolamo of Naples. The first taught logic and philosophy, and Giannozzo attended all his lectures, and every day would argue at the clubs over one doctrine or another and soon acquired a good knowledge of logic and philosophy.

After this study of the liberal arts he began the study of theology, under Messer Girolamo of Naples, by reading *De Civitate Dei* by S. Augustine, of which he made a special habit. Added to his other virtues was a spirit of religion of which he always spoke with reverence, saying in praise of it that our religious faith was not faith but certainty, because whatever things concerning religion were written and spoken by the Church are as true as it is true that a triangle is a triangle, which is a demonstrative figure. So great was his integrity that he would never exhibit one thing for another or dissimulate. I do not believe that he ever spoke falsely. With him it was " yea yea, and no no," and in his decisions he was void of passion. He would say, in confirmation of faith and truth, that he had never known an ill-doer to escape vengeance.

WRITERS

At one time Giannozzo had to arrange a dispute between a friend of his and another who, knowing his integrity, had made him arbitrator. It was necessary for him to investigate divers accounts and writings between the two, a task for which he was as well fitted as any in Florence. The question itself was easy to solve—a glance was enough. When he looked through the accounts of the man with whom his friend had to do, he found them full of errors as to interest and usury. He called this man before him to point these out, wishing to settle the dispute, and to cast no blame on anyone. But the other proved obstinate, whereupon Messer Giannozzo, in the presence of several persons who knew the case, said to him, " Come here, I have taken account of you, and also of your sons, as to your lives and way of living, and I wish to prophesy what will happen to you. I have read much of the Holy Scriptures in my time : you may be certain that you and your family as well will be punished by nature so as to give an example to the city before long. Beware of God's judgment." This man, as to his family and his estate, was then at the height of his fortunes, and believed not that either Heaven or earth could hurt him. But in a short time punishment fell upon him in his person, his household, his family and his estate, which punishment should be an example to all the world. Messer Giannozzo spoke of this case as if he had it all before his eyes, and affirmed that, of all the punishments God could send on man, the greatest was the loss of his children.

At this period, when ambassadors were appointed by the Signori and the Collegi, Giannozzo was sent several times on missions, and always received all the black beans on account of his popularity. His first mission was to Genoa when Tomaso da Campo Fregoso was Doge, Pasquale Malipieri, a distinguished Venetian, being his colleague. It was a great honour to Messer Giannozzo that he, an untried man, should have been chosen out of the many men of eminence who had been nominated. Messer Lionardo d' Arezzo, who was present, said that he would prefer Messer Giannozzo as Genoese ambassador to all others—even to himself. When the ballot was taken not a single vote was given against him, and in this mission he served the state with the greatest honour.

GIANNOZZO MANETTI

He had a wonderful memory, forgetting nothing. He valued time so highly that he never wasted an hour, notwithstanding his many public and private duties. He used to say that of the time which is given to us in this life we must give an account for every moment, basing his argument on a text in the Gospel which declares that Almighty God is like the master of a business who gives money to his treasurer and requires him to render an account as to how it may have been spent. So God wills that when a man quits this life he shall account for how he has spent his time, even to the glance of an eye. He condemned the sluggards and the worthless. Gamblers and gaming he hated as pestiferous abominations, and deemed that of these few would escape destruction.

He showed himself to be a man of great weight in his missions to Pope Eugenius and Pope Nicolas, to King Alfonso and to the Venetians. To Pope Eugenius he was sent to settle an affair over which the Pope had taken great offence, but he knew his task so well that he won full success and high favour from the Pope and cardinals. Indeed, though Pope Nicolas already knew him well, he knew him still better through this transaction with Pope Eugenius. In company with the Emperor he went on a mission to Pope Nicolas,* and was so acceptable to all the court that the Pope made him secretary and offered him an order of knighthood. Twice he went to King Alfonso at Naples, then to the marriage of Don Ferdinando, the heir to the crown, when he was met on his arrival by a host of cavaliers, ambassadors and all the gentry of the kingdom. The court was then full of distinguished men, and from these he met with a fine reception when he made a public oration, at which King Alfonso and all the court were present and the foreign ambassadors also.

Giannozzo's great gifts were well known to the King, and as many distinguished men were now about the court, he determined to make trial of Giannozzo's knowledge before these. One morning, when the King gave audience, Giannozzo was summoned to join it, whereupon now one and now another would put before him some doubtful question, but he answered

---

* This mission was to the Pope on the occasion of the coronation of Frederic III, and was in no sense connected with the Emperor. It happened in 1452.

and explained them all, whether in moral philosophy, or theology, or in any one of the seven liberal arts. Having replied with wonderful skill, the King and all the disputants were astonished, and Giannozzo's fame was greatly increased. While he was at Naples the feast of Corpus Christi took place, to which he and his kinsman Noferi, together with all the ambassadors, were invited. At this feast the King would bear the first of the staves of the baldachino which was over the body of Christ, and the others would be carried by Signori according to their rank. Giannozzo went to see whether the position given to him was worthy of his city ; and when he found that the Genoese had been put before him, his patience gave way and, turning to the rest of the Florentines who were present, he went back to his lodgings. Thereupon the King showed much chagrin and sent the Count of Fondi and others to appease him and beg him to return, but he would not give way, saying that he would not take a place inferior to that given to the Genoese ; and that, whomsoever the Genoese might wrangle with on this point, it would not be with the Florentines, seeing that they paid duties to the King, as the tax accounts would show. The question was ultimately referred to arbitrators, who decided that he should attend the ceremony in his due position. Giannozzo won universal approval for the course he had taken.

He stayed in Naples until the wedding festivities were finished and then went to Rome to wait on Pope Eugenius, with whom he had a disagreeable matter to settle ; moreover, the Pope at this time harboured a grudge against Florence. But he arranged the affair to the satisfaction of the Pope and cardinals. He was well known to the Pope through something which had happened during his sojourn there. Eugenius took Baldaccio d' Anghiari into his service at a salary, but the next day the Signoria sent for Baldaccio and had him thrown out of the window. The Pope was much enraged at this, wherefore Giannozzo was sent to appease him, and he succeeded perfectly by the skilful use of his tongue, for when the Pope recounted certain great benefits which he himself had conferred on the city, Giannozzo fully acknowledged these, and judiciously reminded His Holiness of certain others he had failed to mention and so peace was made.

GIANNOZZO MANETTI

He went as Vicar to Pescia* at the time when Niccolo Piccinino was harassing Florence. A bushel of wheat was then worth three lire and six soldi both at Pescia and at Florence. It was an ancient custom at Pescia that straw and wood should be offered to the Vicar on his arrival, but now, when large loads of straw and wood were brought to him, he ordered their removal, saying that he had enough money to pay for what he wanted. He also remitted the duties, and paid more for the goods duty free than any other Vicar had paid with the duty. This made him popular. He abolished the custom of giving presents, but if at any time he was obliged to accept one, he would always return it to the giver or pay for it. There was then a great shortage of grain in Pescia and, after he had noted the amount of it, he advised that enough should be purchased in Lombardy to make up the deficiency. The town had not funds available for this, so he offered to lend them about three hundred florins, and directed that every day a portion of the grain should be offered for sale in the Piazza. In a few days the price of grain was twenty-five soldi a bushel less than in Florence. In every office he held he closely supervised his subordinates, but on a certain day he found that one of them had done something for his own private gain. On learning this Giannozzo sent for him and told him that were it not for the respect he had for the man through whom he had engaged him he would have let him know it was no light matter to disobey a chief. He then let him depart. He thus taught everybody that honesty pays best. He settled many disputes, and the memory of his pacific deeds remains to this day. He held that the duty of a deputy was to keep everything in good order, and, in the midst of his many duties, he found time to write Lives of Socrates and Seneca.

When he returned from Pescia he was sent to King Alfonso, who was then in the Marches fighting for the Church against Duke Francesco.† Many gentlemen were with the King, who every day caused Panormita to read aloud the third decade of Livy, and Giannozzo was always amongst them. There was also present Messer Zaccaria the Trevisan, representing the Signory of Venice, and when the embassy to the King was finished Giannozzo and Zaccaria went to Duke Francesco,

* 1431.   † Francesco Sforza, 1433.

where they found Messer Agnolo Acciaiuoli. At this time Niccolo Piccinino had been sent by Duke Filippo to support the Church against Duke Francesco, but every day he lost ground and with difficulty escaped capture. While Giannozzo was passing by Piccinino's camp five of his horses were taken— he not having a safe conduct—and when he arrived at Duke Francesco's quarters, he told what had happened to Agnolo, who assured him that they would be recovered, as he had influence with Roberto del Monte Alboddi. He suggested that Giannozzo should write to this Roberto. The letter was written with no result. Then Giannozzo said, " I will try the effect of a letter to Piccinino himself, and I have good hope of getting everything back." Whereupon he wrote a very serious epistle, full of praise of His Excellency and showing that this thing had been done as an exhibition of prowess and not for the sake of gain. This he sent by one of his company with directions that it should be given to Niccolo himself. But Niccolo was away when the messenger arrived, so he awaited him. When he appeared he dismounted and, leaning on a javelin which he carried, took the letter and gave it to his chancellor to read. When this was done he directed that the bearer should be duly lodged and that on the morrow an answer would be given. Then everything was given back and a courteous letter was written to Giannozzo. Both the Duke and Agnolo were surprised at Giannozzo's policy in this affair, whereupon he said with a laugh to Agnolo, " Which method succeeded best ? Your trust in Roberto's friendship or my letter to Niccolo ? "

On his return to Florence he was drawn for the Assembly, and about this time Messer Lionardo of Arezzo died (1443). The Signoria decided that his memory should be honoured in every possible way. It was decreed that the custom of delivering a funeral oration should be revived and Giannozzo was charged with this duty, and that he should be crowned with laurel after the ancient custom. To these obsequies all the illustrious men of the city came to his coronation. Many prelates attended, as the court of Rome was then in Florence, and Giannozzo delivered an oration worthy of the subject, and they crowned him with a laurel crown, a custom which had not lately been observed.

GIANNOZZO MANETTI

At this time Giannozzo, being a member of the Assembly, it was resolved to enact a retrospective law to compel those who in the late troublesome times had not returned the full amount of their dues, to pay the arrears within a certain time or come under the penalties of the taxing laws. This law, directed against the rich, having been duly enacted, the legal authorities put it in action against all who disregarded it. This matter being settled, the gonfalonier and Filippo d' Ugolino were doubtful about Giannozzo's attitude. At last, fearing that Giannozzo would oppose them, the gonfalonier determined to call him into his private room and read the enactment to him in Ser Filippo's presence. After it had been read, Giannozzo turned to the gonfalonier and told him this law affected him more than anyone else, seeing that he paid more super-tax than the Signoria and the Collegio put together, and that if they could lighten the weight of his responsibility in any way his liability would be so much less. Nevertheless, on account of a possible mischief he would have nothing to do with the matter. Then turning to Ser Filippo he said, "And you, Ser Filippo, will be driven out of the city." They advised him to go to his place, but he refused, to show his friends that the matter did not concern him. The Collegio met, and the Signoria also, and all their propositions were carried : in the assemblies there was not a single vote in opposition, because the democracy always hanker after new ways and never look to the end. Ser Filippo was exiled, and many other citizens interned, which things caused the ruin of the city.

Giannozzo was governor of Pistoia and, as at Pescia, would accept neither gift nor tribute. He kept more servants and horses than the law allowed. The place was given over to gaming; indeed, the people thought of little else. Hating this vice as he did, he resolved to put an end to it as long as he was there, and to effect this he issued a proclamation that whoever should play any forbidden game should be taken and treated with four strokes with a rope. Moreover, he fixed a fine which every offender would have to pay, wherefore during his time of office gaming ceased. He worked for peace and soon established order throughout the country. It is commonly known that in these days Pistoia was divided into two factions, but he bore himself in such fashion that no one knew whether he favoured this faction or that, therefore he won the favour of all. The people would have given him rich reward, but he would accept nothing. He wrote the history of Pistoia in four books, and when he went away he was presented with the standard of the city worked with its coat of arms, and a helmet, enriched with silver, of marvellous beauty.

While he was governor of Pistoia in 1447 Pope Eugenius died and Pope Nicolas was elected. It was necessary to send an embassy to convey the obedience of Pistoia to the new Pope, and a law had to be passed to enable Giannozzo to go with this, seeing that he would have to be absent some two months. He went in company with Agnolo Acciaiuoli, Allesandro degli Alessandri, Nero di Gino Capponi, Piero di Cosimo de' Medici and Giannozzo Pitti, and travelled in great state with a hundred and thirty horses. Pope Nicolas showed much favour to our state and bestowed great honour on our embassy, giving audience in public consistory, a form observed with the emperors and kings. In this public reception Giannozzo revived the custom of a public oration; hitherto the Florentines had been received in private and only a few words spoken. Giannozzo spoke his oration with much dignity before the most illustrious men of Italy, some of whom had travelled a hundred and fifty miles or more to hear him. This I heard from Cardinal Niceno. At the end of the speech all the Florentines shook hands with one another just as if they had acquired Pisa and all its lands. In the court men talked of nothing but this oration, and the Venetian cardinals at once wrote home to suggest that an orator might be added to the embassy which had already been chosen.

His third embassy was to King Alfonso on Duke Filippo's death, but, after he was appointed, the government sent him instead as envoy to Signor Gismondo* to induce him to revoke a compact he had made with King Alfonso to the hurt of Florence. At Rimini he found King Alfonso's ambassador, Frate Puccio, who had come to set Gismondo's forces in motion

---

* " In this year, 1448, the Florentines were much troubled by King Alfonso's forces and sought to enlist other troops in their service. Amongst these they engaged Sigismondo Malatesta, Lord of Rimini, a man of great courage and of greater profligacy. He had already agreed with Alfonso, but the Florentine offer was higher, so he left the King in the lurch." Muratori, *Annals*, IX, p. 129. Filippo Maria Visconti had died in 1447.

and had given him twenty thousand florins. Gismondo had promised to march in a few days' time. When he met Gismondo Giannozzo put forward powerful arguments to persuade him to enter the service of Florence, showing him that service under King Alfonso would not be to his interest. Gismondo began to waver and ultimately told Giannozzo that, if he would settle certain differences between himself and the Duke of Urbino, he would join the Florentines, whereupon Giannozzo assured him that if the matter were left to him it might be settled at once, so great was the confidence he had in the Duke. He mounted his horse forthwith and rode to Urbino, where he received a gracious welcome and, as soon as he had explained the reason of his coming, the Duke answered that all the disputes between himself and Gismondo should be arranged forthwith on the full trust he had in Messer Giannozzo. With this understanding he returned to Gismondo, who was satisfied to leave the matter entirely in his hands, so the parties compromised their dispute through his agency. He went back to Urbino and finally settled the affair with the Duke. All praised him highly for this exploit, over which he had laboured so strenuously ; and few believed he would be able to bring it about. The Duke of Urbino commended him specially by publishing the treaty and depositing a copy in his library *ad perpetuam rei memoriam.* Giannozzo next enlisted Gismondo in the Florentine service by treaty which, by securing his support instead of his opposition, was a great advantage to the state, and Bartolomeo Fazio, who wrote the Life of King Alfonso, says that this detachment of Gismondo from the King ruined his plans, which were to despatch Gismondo into Pisan territory and thus open a double campaign. This the Florentines could not have sustained and would have fallen into perilous case. The action of Gismondo led to his own ruin and the salvation of the Florentines, for the King, seeing that he had been duped, determined to have vengeance on Gismondo in the peace which was made afterwards at Rome in 1454 between the King, the Venetians and Florence,* through

---

* This was the outcome of the Congress of Lodi which had met in April, 1454, when Venice and Milan had made peace and invited all the other powers to ratify. The fall of Constantinople was the reason of this meeting, but little was done to resist the Turk, as was shown by the jealousy and quarrelling at the subsequent congresses. Alfonso

the intervention of Pope Nicolas, the Venetians agreed to evacuate all Alfonso's territories, but he, being incensed against them, refused to join, and only consented when he was granted a free hand to attack Gismondo and the Genoese. Soon afterwards Jacopo Piccinino was sent by him to seize a portion of Gismondo's state.*

In the same year Manetti was sent on a mission to Venice to seek support against King Alfonso by bringing King René with an army into Italy. He was honourably received at Venice by the Doge Foscari and granted a public reception in the Council : his fame attracted more than five hundred gentlemen and as many others as could get entry. Giannozzo spoke for more than an hour without interruption, and at the end all were amazed by the power and vigour of his rhetoric, and, as they quitted the palace, all declared that if Venice possessed such a citizen as this the finest estate in the republic would not be too much to offer him. He gained the greatest reputation a citizen could gain. To help King René he asked Venice to furnish four thousand horsemen and two thousand foot, but the Venetians only offered two thousand horse and wanted to bind the Florentines not to make peace without their express consent. As to the renewal of the alliance Giannozzo had authority to act, but not to decide finally on certain points.

When Giannozzo dealt with the League itself he affirmed to the Doge and the Signory that it was made for the common defence of their states, whereupon the Doge interposed and declared it was made with reference to Milan against Duke Filippo, his heirs and successors. Messer Giannozzo here denied that a league of this kind could have anything to do with civil matters. The Doge answered that with regard to Milan, the question now before them, Venice was unwilling that we should support Duke Francesco—Filippo's son-in-law—to gain the

was indignant that the treaty should have been made without consulting him. He never fully ratified the treaty, and signed it only with the provision that he should be free to attack Genoa, Sigismondo Malatesta and Astorre di Faenza.

* Vespasiano has little to say of this notorious personage. He has been held up as the blackest monster of the age, but he may have been judged by the report of his enemies only. Pius II attacked him furiously, but later writers have pointed out that he was a man of culture and an enlightened art patron as well as a murderer.

inheritance of Madonna Bianca—that is Milan, and that if such support were given the league between Venice and Florence would become void, because it specified that Florence was bound to oppose Francesco as Duke of Milan. The Venetians then began to demur as to their contribution of four thousand horse, affirming that they had already fifteen thousand in their pay and ten thousand foot. While this question was in debate came the defeat at Caravaggio* which plunged the state in terror and despair. When he heard of it Giannozzo went to the palace to condole with the Signory, and found there the deepest dejection. All were in black, and the first words of the Doge were, " Messer Giannozzo, the state is wrecked beyond repair. See here the result of a decision made without due consideration, a decision which has handed over the realm of Duke Filippo to Duke Francesco." When Giannozzo heard these lamentations he reproved them strongly for their panic-stricken attitude, asking what had become of their courage : this was the time to repair their loss and not to grieve over it : at the same time he offered the help of his government, and of himself personally in every possible way. The Doge thanked him generally and assured him they would rouse themselves to active effort. Giannozzo wrote to Florence concerning the disaster of Caravaggio, but of his own commission he said nothing, deeming that they had already enough on their hands. He heard from Florence that the Signoria was negotiating for peace with King Alfonso, and this news he reported to the Doge, who agreed to it, but asked to be further informed before the pact should be finally concluded. Later on the Doge informed him that they were negotiating with Duke Francesco† and ultimately let him know the terms of agreement, which were that after fifteen

---

* The shifting of dates here is very confusing. The battle of Caravaggio was in 1448, and the negotiations to bring René into Italy happened in 1452. *Vide Life of Agnolo Acciaiuoli*, and Sismondi, *Republiques Ital.*, Chap. LXXIV.

† Filippo Maria died in 1447, but Francesca Sforza did not become Duke till 1450. The leading citizens of Milan, the Trivulzi, the Bossi, the Lampugrani and others had no desire for another Duke, and set up a republican government on the Florentine model. The Doge Foscari was just as much opposed to Sforza's succession, but at the same time he attacked the republic. Also he managed to affront Sforza, who turned upon the Venetian force at Caravaggio and completely crushed it.

days they were to pay him forty thousand ducats and beyond this fourteen thousand a month till he should win Milan. When the Signoria heard this they cancelled the instructions given to Giannozzo, doubting whether the Venetians would honour their agreement with Duke Francesco, and sent a fresh proposal for a league between Venice, Florence and the Duke for the defence of their states, the object of which was to compel the Venetians to keep their word with the Duke. When Giannozzo received these fresh terms he laid them before the Venetian government and put forward many good reasons for their adoption, but the cautious Venetians at once divined the object of them and took time before answering them. When he received the answer he found it was given in very obscure terms, which affirmed there was no reason for making any change at all, for in the agreement they had made with the Duke they had spoken of the Florentines as their colleagues, an expression he had received with gracious words and had pledged himself never to make war on them again. The Duke also affirmed that if the Florentines would favour him—according to the pledge given by the Venetians—he also would observe all pledges made. Thus there was no need for any fresh compact. Giannozzo at once perceived that the Venetians objected to the fresh proposals in order to get rid of their former promise to Duke Francesco to aid him in gaining the Duchy of Milan, especially as they believed they would master him. This was their firm conviction, but they were grievously mistaken, as Francesco seized Milan and stirred up war against Venice. When Giannozzo found they were obstinately set on doing nothing, he took his leave and returned to Florence.

On his return to Florence he was made one of the Eight,* and as there were misgivings as to the preservation of peace, a term of ten years was granted to them, and in this affair he conducted himself as well as heretofore. At this time the plague broke out, but Giannozzo, for the welfare and credit of the city, refused to depart. As so few citizens were left there were no resources to pay the men-at-arms, and these— especially those of the Duke of Urbino and of Napoleone which

* The *Otto della pratica.* *Vide* Appendix.

384

were in Florentine service—when they got no pay after many
demands for it, began to plunder in S. Miniato. This being
made known to the Signoria, ambassadors were at once sent
to the Duke and to Napoleone to promise pay, and for this
office Giannozzo and Agnolo Acciaiuoli were chosen. When
they met the Duke they urged him to have patience and in a
short time his demands would be satisfied. The Duke, who was
not one to be satisfied with words without deeds, gave an
eloquent and dignified reply, saying how he realised that
what they had done was caused by stress of fortune, but that
they must understand that so large a body of soldiers could
not be held together by promises alone. In a later discussion,
after their return, Messer Agnolo and Messer Giannozzo
maintained they had never met a more eloquent man than
the Duke of Urbino. In the subsequent parley over the pay
for the troops, they went back to their lodgings without
further mischief, though they had not been paid. The
Signoria was gratified that the Duke had been contented with
promises, and the Duke was highly complaisant to Giannozzo
for the services he had rendered in the negotiations with
Gismondo.

Giannozzo next went for the fourth time as envoy to King
Alfonso by way of confirming the pact between him and
Florence. The great success he now accomplished will be
found written in his Life.* The King had made a treaty
with Venice for the expulsion of all Florentines from their
several dominions, but this treaty he had kept secret. In
his interview with the King, Giannozzo, who had got wind of
this affair, asked Alfonso several times what was his object,
and what had prompted him to it. Certain Venetians in
Naples had been urging the King to act at once, wherefore
Panormita and Frate Puccio were despatched to Florence on
this business. They then went to Venice and concluded the
treaty for the expulsion of all Florentines from Venice and
the kingdom. When he heard of this Giannozzo went to
Torre del Greco, where the King was, and spoke to him fully
—as is told in the commentary of his Life—and having
described to the King the policy and anger of the Venetians,
he ended by saying that in four months' time they would

* By Naldo Naldio. Muratori, *Rerum Italic. Script.*, Vol. XX.

have broken all their promises. Before twenty days had passed the King sent for Giannozzo and said : " Giannozzo Manetti, you should be called Giannozzo the prophet, for not twenty days have passed since the treaty with the Venetians and they have already broken all their promises." By this Giannozzo gained so completely the confidence of the King that he might have had anything he demanded. The Florentines were granted a safe conduct and an extension of several months before quitting the kingdom.

The Signoria sent him as ambassador to Pope Nicolas, who made him secretary and granted him many gratuitous privileges, and gave him handsome presents with gracious words. Shortly after his return to Florence he was again despatched as one of the ambassadors to receive the Emperor, who had come to Italy for coronation. Amongst this dignified company Giannozzo was selected to act as spokesman for the Signoria. The embassy went by way of the Mugello, and on reaching Veglia encountered the Emperor accompanied by Carlo Pandolfini and Otto Niccolini. The Emperor and all his company dismounted—amongst them Messer Æneas,* afterwards cardinal and Pope through the Emperor's patronage ; Giannozzo and the other ambassadors also dismounted, whereupon Messer Æneas made a suitable speech in the Emperor's behalf, and this done they all took their way to Florence, where they were received with much honour. Besides the fifteen ambassadors all the citizens of condition rode on horseback in the train of the Emperor, who after his arrival was lodged in S. Maria Novella. The Signoria waited on him, as they were bound to do by their office. They called upon all the citizens who were about the palace and bade them attend, dressed in their best, the reception of the Emperor, and all the leading citizens assembled and made a grand spectacle. However, jealousy often takes a part on such occasions as these. An address had to be delivered on the Emperor's visit, and it would have been more seemly if this had been made by one of the Signoria than by some one who was only attached to it as chancellor. Messer Giannozzo, who was a member of the College, ought to have spoken it, rather than Messer Carlo d' Arezzo, who was chancellor.

* Æneas Silvius Piccolomini, made cardinal in 1456.

However, some of those who were unwilling that Giannozzo should have this honour settled that it should be given to Messer Carlo and told him of it several days before. On the appointed day some two hundred citizens attended, and according to the arrangement Messer Carlo addressed the Emperor. When he had finished the Emperor requested Messer Æneas to reply, proposing in addition divers other matters which required an immediate answer, whereupon the Signoria called upon Messer Carlo to reply to them. He, however, affirmed he could not do this without due preparation. The Signoria called on him several times, but he always refused on the same plea. And now those who had plotted to deprive Giannozzo of his due honour turned to him begging him to answer so that they might not be shamed, as they would be, before the Emperor, the King of Hungary, and all the nobility. Giannozzo, seeing that disgrace was imminent, turned on those who had worked against him, accepted, as the Emperor was awaiting a reply at once. His speech had not the air of an impromptu, but of one which had been more carefully prepared than that delivered by Messer Carlo. When he had finished all men of intelligence who understood Latin decided that Giannozzo's unprepared speech was far better than Carlo's prepared one. That day his fame increased greatly, and those who had thwarted him found they had made a mistake. The Emperor and his nobles regarded him as a most remarkable man, as indeed he was, one who need not go begging for words to express his ideas, because he had already good store of them.

After the return to the palace the Signoria, seeing what he had done, chose Giannozzo to accompany the Emperor to Rome, along with Messer Bernardo Guigni and Messer Carlo Pandolfini. At Rome he was honourably received by the Pope, the cardinals and all the court. He made a fine speech at the coronation in precedence of the two other ambassadors who were waiting on the Emperor.

One day the vice-chancellor, a nephew of Pope Eugenius, invited him to dinner without informing him there would be other guests. On arriving he found there Messer Pasquale Malipieri, the envoy of Venice and a man of weight in that state. After dinner the cardinal retired to his cabinet with these two after dismissing the others. Malipieri then asked Giannozzo whether he considered the offences of Venice against Florence to be unpardonable, admitting that the expulsion of the Florentines from Venice was the greatest mistake ever made by the republic, and denying his own complicity therein. He added that he had authority from the Signory to offer such a settlement of the dispute as they might wish—even as far as giving them *carte blanche*. On this Giannozzo said he had no power to negotiate, and that Florence was unwilling to discuss matters. However, by the persistency of the cardinal and Malipieri, he was induced to write to the Signoria concerning the requests of the cardinal and Malipieri, but in his letter he laid full stress on the faults which had led to this disagreement. The Signoria replied that they were not minded to discuss this affair, that he was to confine himself to his special mission and that, with regard to the subject of his letter, he was to do nothing. This answer he handed to the cardinal and Malipieri. When the Emperor returned to Rome from his visit to King Alfonso at Naples, the whole court of Rome and the ambassadors rode out to meet him, and when Malipieri was riding past Giannozzo's house he halted and begged him to ride in his company to meet the Emperor. Giannozzo, recognising the courtesy of this request and feeling that his honour would be in no way impugned, consented to go with him. This was at once reported in Florence, and gave offence to some who were incensed against Venice.

He returned in the Emperor's train to Rome and was at once despatched to Siena, where two other ambassadors were already on the spot urging the Sienese to refuse supplies to King Alfonso who was now in camp at Piombino.* Two of the leading citizens were on King Alfonso's side, Antonio di Cecco Rossi and Gino Bellanti, and these kept the Sienese to their decision to send him the supplies. Giannozzo, seeing that he was being put off by excuses, that no conclusion could be attained, and that the populace were against the stoppage of the King's supplies, asked for a public hearing, saying to the Signoria and to the leaders, " If it is indeed the Sienese people

* 1448. Alfonso had invaded Tuscany from the south and was besieging Piombino, a small seaport.

388

who wish these supplies to be sent to the King, let me be heard in public, so that we may come to a clear understanding, and then we may be able to hold them responsible, and not the Signoria."

He spoke so forcibly that they could not refuse, and a day for the public hearing was fixed at once. Giannozzo, who knew the minds of Antonio and of Gino Bellanti, foresaw what might be the result. He wrote to Galeotto da Ricasoli and directed him to have ready five hundred soldiers on the morning of the audience and to post them at the gate leading to Brolio and to Cacchiano, along the frontier. They were to act as Giannozzo directed. At the audience he spoke and proved by many arguments that these supplies ought not to be sent to the King, for, were they sent, they would be wasted and a loss to those who sent them.

When he had ended the people clamoured unanimously against the despatch of supplies, demanding that everything should be done as Messer Giannozzo had so wisely advised on behalf of the Florentines. Antonio and Gino, men full of craft, turned to Giannozzo and, by way of upsetting this proposition, said that, as the will of the people had now been manifested, they were ready to support him in the future ; but Giannozzo, divining their astuteness and perversity, saw the danger ahead, and, so as not to involve Florence in any calamity, left the palace and went privately to the spot where the soldiers and the horses were in waiting and rode away towards Brolio, thus following the proper course. In due time the King came to understand the real wish of the Sienese, and how Giannozzo had shown them their error. Antonio and Gino profited little by their action in the matter.

On his return from Siena he went as envoy to Pope Nicolas, who made him *cavaliere* with order of knighthood and, while conferring these, commended him in weighty words in that he had so worthily carried out the wishes of His Holiness and his friends ; adding that, if he would come to live in Rome, a pension sufficient for his position should be given to him. This promise the Pope carried out later on. On his return from Rome he was made Vicar of the Scarperia, and this was the last office he held in Florence. Here he found everything in confusion and full of deadly quarrels. He decided that, for his own good and the honour of God, he could not have undertaken a more profitable work than this. He required them all to note down their causes of dispute and with inexhaustible patience he listened to both sides, in each instance suffering each to say all he had to say. Then according to his habit he recited each one, and reasoned it out. He left unsettled no dispute, however complicated, and he would wait personally upon those who did not come to him. He settled more than a hundred disputes and brought peace and unity into this office, receiving a thousand blessings daily for what he had done. In spite of his beneficent work there were many who envied his good repute and the high place he had gained by his merits. He lost no time for, while he held the Vicariate, he wrote his book *De dignitate et excellentia hominis*, which he sent to King Alfonso. Having finished his work at the Scarperia, all the reward he got from the state was a demand to pay an insupportable super-tax by way of ridding the city of such an example of merit as he exhibited. The sum of this tax was one hundred and sixty-six thousand gold florins, of which he had to pay three every month, and at this rate he would have been stripped of everything in a short time. He who planned this was all-powerful in the state, and his object was to force Manetti to follow his orders in everything. One of his kinsfolk who, together with one of the chief citizens,* went to sympathize with him over this exaction, said to him, " Giannozzo, this hurt is not deadly," whereto he replied, " *Erit ad mortem corporis, sed non animæ*," adding, " They will not get from me what they expect, and what I have not given willingly to the city they shall not have ; moreover, my sons shall never be reproached that I was the cause of these doings, but that I would have left things as I found them." And as he was not minded to act against his conscience, and feared personal danger should he tarry in Florence—having been warned by a friend—he determined to withdraw to Rome. After his arrival there Pope Nicolas received him with honour and allotted him a

---

* According to Naldo's " Life " (Muratori, *Rerum Italic. Script.*, XX, p. 583), this was Franco Sacchetti, probably a kinsman of the novelist.

pension of six hundred ducats a year in addition to his salary as secretary.

When he left Florence he left it penniless ; he left all his possessions, his houses, his money at the bank and all else. Now that he was in Rome he imagined, that as he had stripped himself of everything, his person would be free. Still, knowing the Florentine disposition, he said to those about him, " My masters and he who rules Florence will not be satisfied with what they have done to me, but will work me further ill if they can." One evening while he was discoursing in this vein a sudden knock was heard at the door. He said at once to his companions, " This is a rider from Florence." The door was opened and a messenger from the Signoria delivered to him a letter bidding him present himself at Florence within ten days under penalty of banishment for himself and his sons to Piacenza for ten years. In case of a month's delay, they would all be banished for rebellion. When he had read the letter he went at once to Pope Nicolas, who was greatly vexed about it and the persecution of Giannozzo, but he quickly found a way out of the trouble and bade Giannozzo obey the command of the Signoria and repair to Florence. He called Piero di Noceto and bade him prepare at once a letter of credit and a commission for Messer Giannozzo to act as his ambassador at Florence, and a similar letter to the Signoria. Then he bade Giannozzo go to Florence and, should any offence be offered to him, to present his letter of credit as ambassador, but not to present it if no need arose. The Pope's proposition pleased Giannozzo, who at once prepared for the journey and started for Florence with this commission. Those citizens who had not looked for his return were anticipating the ruin of his affairs, but when it was known that he was returning they arranged for his arrest at Borzo and at Castel San Giovanni, and that he should be sent a prisoner to Florence. The Vicar and the Captain of Borzo were ashamed to commit such an outrage. This is fully told in the commentary of his Life.

He reached Florence on Holy Thursday and reported himself at once to the Signoria, who granted him an audience. He knelt before them, although they would have hindered him, and spoke thus : " Excellencies, if I had served God who created me, with as much love and fidelity as I have given to the Signoria of Florence I should think I was kneeling at the feet of S. John the Baptist, and your Excellencies will know if I have gained any merit thereby." Hearing these words many of them were moved to tears, and suggested he should take rest and that they would hear him later.

He left and went to the captain in charge to announce his arrival. The officer, when he met him, uncovered and took him by the hand saying that it shamed him that so distinguished a man should be forced to report himself thus. Later he went back to the Signoria to show what his present position was ; how up to this date he had paid a hundred and thirty-five thousand florins and was willing to pay as much more as he could ; how he had left in Florence his children, his money and all his possessions ; and how under these conditions he deemed he ought to be free to go whithersoever he pleased and earn a living creditably. Wherefore he begged the Signoria to dismiss him and allow him to serve Pope Nicolas with whom he had made an agreement. He had paid all that was due to the state, and had served it truly both in person and in pence ; indeed, only a few days ago he had paid two thousand florins current, to raise which he had sold one property at ten per cent and another at four per cent ; these having originally cost a hundred. He had never bought any property, and everything he possessed was money which had been paid to him. Having done what was required of him the licence to leave was granted.

After he had obtained this grace, while he was preparing for departure, there was an election of councillors to make up the Ten of the Balia, and each member of the Signoria and of the colleges had a vote. Amongst the first to be nominated was Messer Giannozzo, who was elected unanimously on account of the high respect felt for him. This was a staggering blow for those who had looked to be chosen amongst the first. The more he was persecuted the more his reputation increased. At this time there were many territories which had been lost to Florence during the war with King Alfonso, and when the Ten had been constituted they at once set about the recovery of these, but they found themselves opposed by a certain one who, through envy, wished to discredit them by putting every possible obstacle in their path and having no care for the welfare of the state. Giannozzo was made field commissary and went to Vada, where he handed the baton to Gismondo Malatesta. He there made a most important speech in public and finally regained Vada and all the other lost territory. While on this service Giannozzo's manner suggested that he might have lived in a camp all his life. The Ten led out a force of twenty thousand men and recovered all they had lost. Moreover, the opposing leaders offered to the Ten to deliver up within fifteen days the whole of the country of Siena, but this offer was not found acceptable at Florence because of the envy which was felt over the great honour which the acceptance of it would have brought to the Ten. Moreover, it was thought that enough had been gained, so this was the end of the business. Nevertheless, the mission of the Ten was marvellously successful and they won the greatest honour.

At the end of his service Giannozzo revised his position and called together his sons and addressed them : " I have now ascertained what your position will be ; all that I have are the few things I have about me and the houses we inhabit, and knowing this I have arranged that this property may produce enough to support you and your children, but time will show this better than I can. With the leave of the Signoria I will go to Rome so as to earn enough to keep me honourably for the rest of my life." He set about to get the necessary licence, and after receiving it on his way home he met a kinsman who was of high standing in the city ; a man who never deemed that adversity could ever strike him. When Giannozzo spoke of his project the reply he got was not what he looked for. When they parted I, the writer, was present. Giannozzo turned to me and said : " See this kinsman of mine and his grand position in the city ! He cannot believe that anything like my ill-fortune could ever befall him. But bear this in mind, you will see that he will be driven out of Florence like me, and that this blow will come from an unexpected quarter." Not long afterwards the event Giannozzo had predicted came to pass.

After he had taken leave of the Signoria and the leaders he bade his friends and kinsfolk to dine with him, not knowing whether he would ever see them again. He addressed them in gracious words, especially his wife and children, exhorting them to be patient and to pray God for him. There were many tears and sighs at this farewell dinner owing to the cruelty of parting. In this last gathering he wished to give an example to his sons, urging them to act as he had acted so that they never need to repent of anything they had done. As to his eating and drinking no one ever found out whether he liked one thing better than another, for it was, he said, a poor business to waste thought over such poor trivialities, and that we were born for higher aims than these. After he had thus spoken he mounted his horse quickly, having taken no one by the hand lest he might be induced to alter his purpose. Then he turned to them and said, " I commend you all to God," and took the road to Rome. Considering what the carriage of Messer Giannozzo had always been towards the state I cannot refrain from censuring my country for its ingratitude towards him ; for at the time of life when men desire to enjoy repose in their own land with wife and children and friends he was driven forth to find a new country and home.

On his arrival at Rome he was honourably received by the Pope and the whole court and confirmed in his office. There was then a movement by certain Conventuals to deprive the Observantists of the Vicariate and hand it over to the General, which would have been the ruin of the Order. They had worked so strongly on the Pope by misrepresentation that he had given way and the treaty was ready for sealing. Concerning this business, letters were written to Messer Giannozzo from Florence, begging him to prevent it, and as soon as he heard of the project he demonstrated to Pope Nicolas the importance of it and that, if he desired the overthrow of the Order, this was the way to accomplish it. The Pope happened to have by him the bull in question, and now in Giannozzo's presence he destroyed it. Thus he always worked for good whenever it was possible. Shortly after this Pope Nicolas died,* and Giannozzo could not have sustained a greater misfortune. Pope Calixtus now succeeded, and at once confirmed Giannozzo's appointment as secretary by a deed

* 1455.

which was handed over to him. Giannozzo now went to Naples * where he employed his time in letters, being greatly sought by the leaders and learned men of the city. His conversation was most polite and pleasing ; humane and tolerant with a delicate wit.

While he abode in Naples, through the assistance given to him by the King, he translated the Psalter, *De Hebraica veritate*, and five books of apologetics in defence of it on account of the envious attacks on his honour made by some of his assailants. He translated the New Testament from Greek into Latin, the Nicomachean Ethic of Aristotle and another ethic hitherto untranslated—*Ad Eudemum*—and the *Magna Moralia*, and corrected as much as he had done of *Contra Judæos et Gentes*. He added to this other books, making ten in all, which ought to be remembered for the high character of the subject. In all these he showed his virtuous mind and his devotion to the religion in which he had been born ; he loved and rated it so highly that he spoke of it not as faith but certainty. No modern scholars have written against the Jews save a certain Genoese, Porchetto, and Piero d' Alfonso, a Spaniard, but neither wrote with the elegance and style of Giannozzo. For these and for all his other works he deserves high praise, in that in spite of all his worldly cares and persecutions he found time to leave behind him such a literary monument. In the midst of his busy and useful life, when at last he seemed to have found a refuge against ill-fate, the heaviest blow of all fell upon him in the death of King Alfonso. As was his wont, he bore it patiently. King Ferdinand, on his accession, confirmed the privileges given by Alfonso. Not long afterwards he passed from this life and rendered up his soul like a Catholic and a good Christian. I have given his Life as briefly as possible, referring to the commentary on his Life in which it is more fully told.

NICOLAO NICOLI (*d.* 1437)

Nicolao was well born, one of the four sons of a rich merchant, all of whom became merchants. In his youth Nicolao,

---

* The account of Giannozzo's reception in Naples by King Alfonso is given on p. 385.

by his father's wish, entered trade, wherefore he could not give his time to letters as he desired. After his father's death he left his brothers so as to carry out his aims. He was the master of a good fortune and took up Latin letters, in which he soon became proficient. He studied under Grisolora, a learned Greek who had recently come to Florence, and although he worked hard in Greek and Latin he was not content with his progress, so he went to study with Luigi Marsigli, a learned philosopher and theologian, and in the course of some years' reading gained a good knowledge of the subjects he studied. He here acted like a good and faithful Christian, for, putting all else aside, he studied theology alone. Nicolao may justly be called the father and the benefactor of all students of letters, for he gave them protection and encouragement to work, and pointed out to them the rewards which would follow. If he knew of any Greek or Latin book which was not in Florence he spared neither trouble nor cost until he should procure it; indeed, there are numberless Latin books which the city possesses through his care. He gained such high reputation amongst men of letters that Messer Lionardo sent him his *Life of Cicero* and pronounced him to be the censor of the Latin tongue.

He was a man of upright life who favoured virtue and censured vice. He collected a fine library, not regarding the cost, and was always searching for rare books. He bought all these with the wealth which his father had left, putting aside only what was necessary for his maintenance. He sold several of his farms and spent the proceeds on his library. He was a devoted Christian, who specially favoured monks and friars, and was the foe of evildoers. He held his books rather for the use of others than of himself, and all lettered students of Greek or Latin would come to him to borrow books, which he would always lend. He was guileless and sincere and liberal to everyone. It was through his good offices that Fra Ambrogio and Carlo d' Arezzo achieved success, on account of his gifts, the loan of his books and the fees he paid to their teachers. If he heard of students going to Greece or to France or elsewhere he would give them the names of books which they lacked in Florence, and procure for them the help of Cosimo de' Medici who would do anything for him. When it happened that he could only get the copy of a book he would copy it himself, either in current or shaped characters, all in the finest script, as may be seen in San Marco, where there are many books from his hand in one lettering or the other. He procured at his own expense the works of Tertullian and other writers which were not in Italy. He also found an imperfect copy of Ammianus Marcellinus and wrote it out with his own hand. The *De Oratore* and the *Brutus* were sent to Nicolao from Lombardy, having been brought by the envoys of Duke Filippo when they went to ask for peace in the time of Pope Martin. The book was found in a chest in a very old church; this chest had not been opened for a long time, and they found the book, a very ancient example, while searching for evidence concerning certain ancient rights. *De Oratore* was found broken up, and it is through the care of Nicolao that we find it perfect to-day. He also rediscovered many sacred works and several of Tully's orations.

Through Nicolao Florence acquired many fine works of sculpture, of which he had great knowledge as well as of painting. A complete copy of Pliny did not exist in Florence, but when Nicolao heard that there was one in Lübeck, in Germany, he secured it by Cosimo's aid, and thus Pliny came to Florence. All the young men he knew in Florence used to come to him for instruction in letters, and he cared for the needs of all those who wanted books or teachers. He did not seek any office in Florence, he was made an official in the University, many times he was selected for some governorship, but he refused them all, saying that they were food for the vultures, and he would let these feed on them. He called vultures those who went into the alehouses and devoured the poor. Master Paolo and Ser Filippo were his intimate friends, and there were few days when they would not be found at the monastery of the Agnoli, together with Fra Ambrogio and sometimes Cosimo and Lorenzo de' Medici, who, on account of Nicolao's great merits, treated him most liberally, because he had spent in books almost all that he had. His means only allowed him to live very sparingly considering his position. The Medici, as they knew this, gave orders at the bank that whenever Nicolao might ask for money, it should be given to him, and charged to their account. They afterwards told Nicolao not to let himself want for anything, but to send to the bank for whatever he needed. So Nicolao, being in sore straits, heartened himself to do what he would not otherwise have done. They supported him in this way till the end of his life, and they showed the greatest courtesy in aiding him in necessity. In 1420 Cosimo fled from the plague to Verona, taking with him Nicolao and Carlo d' Arezzo and paying all their charges. Afterwards, when Cosimo was banished to Venice, Nicolao was deeply grieved on account of the love he had for him, and one day he wrote a letter to Cosimo at Venice, and when he gave it to the horseman who would deliver it, he said in my presence : " Give this letter to Cosimo, and tell him, Nicolao says that so many ill-deeds are committed by the state every day, that a ream of paper would not suffice him to write them down." And he spoke these words in so loud a voice that all those present could hear them. If he had uttered them to-day he also would have been exiled.

His was a frank and liberal nature. One day when he was in company with a friar who was learned rather than pious, he addressed him, saying : " There will be few of your kind in Paradise." Another friar, Francesco da Pietropane by name, lived with a few others in the mountains near Lucca, in pious community, and was a man well versed in Greek and Latin. Nicolao showed them much favour and let them have all the books they wanted. At his death he had lent here and there more than two hundred volumes, amongst which were some of the Greek books which had been lent to Fra Francesco. This friar, amongst many other gifts, had that of predicting the future, and before Cosimo was banished he informed Nicolao that the year 1433 would bring great danger to Cosimo ; he would either lose his life or be exiled, whereupon Nicolao sent word to Cosimo to be on his guard, for in this same year he would be in peril either of death or exile. Cosimo was loth to believe this, but these words proved true. Nicolao had a pure mind, and his conversation was that of a good and faithful Christian, for he would say that there were many unbelievers and rebels against the Christian religion who argued against the immortality of

NICOLAO NICOLI

the soul, as if this were a matter of doubt. That it was a great misfortune to many that they were only able to care for their bodies, thinking of their souls, which are no way concerned with their unbridled lusts, as something which could sit in a chair, as something substantial enough to be seen with the eye. All those who were not good Christians and doubted concerning that religion to which he was so firmly attached, incurred his strongest hatred; indeed, it seemed to him stark madness to have any doubt of anything so noble which had won the support of so many wonderful men in every age.

Beyond his other remarkable qualities he had a wide judgment, not only in letters, but also in painting and in sculpture, and he had in his house a number of medals, in bronze, silver and gold ; also many antique figures in copper, and heads in marble. One day, when Nicolao was leaving his house, he saw a boy who had around his neck a chalcedony engraved with a figure by the hand of Polycleitus, a beautiful work. He enquired of the boy his father's name, and having learnt this, sent to ask him if he would sell the stone ; the father readily consented, like one who neither knew what it was nor valued it. Nicolao sent him five florins in exchange, and the good man to whom it had belonged deemed that he had paid him more than double its value. Nicolao afterwards exhibited it as a remarkable object, as indeed it was. There was in Florence in the time of Pope Eugenius a certain Maestro Luigi, the Patriarch, who took great interest in such things as these, and he sent word to Nicolao, asking if he might see the chalcedony. Nicolao sent it to him, and it pleased him so greatly that he kept it, and sent to Nicolao two hundred golden ducats and he urged him so much that Nicolao, not being a rich man, let him have it. After the death of this Patriarch it passed to Pope Paul, and then to Lorenzo de' Medici.

Nicolao had a great knowledge of all parts of the world, so that if anyone who had been in any particular region, and asked him about it, Nicolao would know it better than the man who had been there, and he gave many instances of this. Nicolao always had his house full of distinguished men, and the leading youths of the city. As to the strangers who visited Florence at that time, they all deemed that if they had not visited Nicolao they had not been to Florence at all. Many prelates and learned youths and courtiers frequented his house, and amongst those who often went to see him was Messer Gregorio Correro, nephew of the Cardinal of Bologna, who himself was the nephew of Pope Gregory. This Messer Gregorio was a mirror of conduct, well read in prose and in verse and much devoted to Nicolao. As soon as Gregorio, or any other of these youths should come to him, he put a book into his hand, and bade him read it. There would often be, at the same time, ten or twelve noble young gentlemen with books in their hands reading ; after a time he would bid them put down the books and tell him what they had been studying. Then there would be a discussion on some matter of interest so that no time might be lost. Indeed, with Nicolao the custom was absolutely different from that of other houses, where men would sit down to play or gamble at once. It chanced one day that a scholar brought some of his writings to show to him, but neither the subject nor the style of them was to Nicolao's liking. After he had read separate portions of the work, the writer begged for his opinion, but Nicolao demurred, being unwilling to vex him, and answered, " I have already to deal with several hundred volumes of authors of repute before I shall be able to consider yours " (for every writer of that time would ask him to read his work and give an opinion), and handed the manuscript back to the writer, who was much astonished, and failed to understand what his verdict was. He was very apt at composition, but his taste was so delicate that he could rarely satisfy himself. I have spoken formerly with some who have seen his Latin epistles and other elegant writings, but these were not shown to me for reasons which I fully understood.

Nicolao always encouraged promising students to follow a literary life, and he nobly aided all those who showed merit in providing them with teachers and books, for in his time teachers and books were not so numerous as they are to-day. It may be said that he was the reviver of Greek and Latin letters in Florence ; they had for a long time lain buried, and although Petrarch, Dante and Boccaccio had done something to rehabilitate them, they had not reached that height which they attained through Nicolao's cultivation of them for divers reasons. First, because he urged many in his time to take to letters, and, through his persuasion, many scholars came to Florence for study and teaching; for instance, he and Palla Strozzi induced Manuello Grisolora to come by providing money for his journey. He did the same for Aurispa and other learned men, and when the question arose of spending money he would say to certain of those he knew, "I wish you would help bring over Manuello, or someone else," and then he would say what each one might give.

Nicolao patronised painters, sculptors and architects as well as men of letters, and he had a thorough knowledge of their crafts; he especially favoured Pippo di Ser Brunellesco, Donatello, Luca della Robbia, Lorenzo di Bartolaccio and was on intimate terms with them. He was a true connoisseur of all fine things. Friar Ambrogio, Messer Poggio and Carlo d' Arezzo were his friends, and it was through him that these men of genius became public teachers in Florence in the time of Pope Eugenius. He was on terms of friendship with all the learned men of Italy, and he corresponded with them both at home and abroad.

After having done so many good deeds, and gathered together a vast number of books on all the liberal arts in Greek and Latin, he desired that these should be made accessible to everyone. He directed that, after his death, they should continue to be at the service of all, so in his will be designated forty citizens to see that the books in question should be made a public library in order that all might use them. There were eight hundred volumes of Greek and Latin. He gave directions to these forty citizens that these books should be given to Cosimo de' Medici for the library of San Marco, in fulfilment of the wishes of the testator, that they should remain in a public place for the use of those who might want to consult them. Also that it should be written in the cover of every book how it had once belonged to Nicolao Nicoli, and thus they remain to the present day. The value of them was six thousand florins. At the end of his book, *De longævis*, Messer Giannozzo mentions Nicolao and his way of life and the high praise he earned. Amongst other things he praises most highly the gift of this library, and says that he did more than Plato, Aristotle or Theophrastus had done, for in the last testaments of Plato and Aristotle are named certain goods which they left to their children, and to others, but they made no mention of their books. Theophrastus left all his possessions privately to a friend ; Nicolao alone dedicated his to the public use, therefore much gratitude is due to him. Nor was this all, for Giovanni Boccaccio at his death had left all his books to Santo Spirito, where they were kept in chests, but Nicolao decided that they ought rather to be in a library available for all, so at his own expense he built one for their reception and preservation, and for the honour of Messer Giovanni. As they were for public use he made shelves for them, and they may be seen there to the present time.

To describe Nicolao, he was of handsome presence, lively, with a smile usually on his face, and pleasant manner in conversation. His clothes were always of fine red cloth down to the ground ; he never took a wife so as not to be hindered in his studies. He had a housekeeper to provide for his wants, and was one of the most particular of men in his diet as in all else, and was accustomed to have his meals served to him in beautiful old dishes, his table would be covered with vases of porcelain, and he drank from a cup of crystal or of some other fine stone. It was a pleasure to see him at table, old as he was. All the linen that he used was of the whitest. Some may be astonished to hear that he possessed a vast number of vessels, and to these may be answered that, in his day, things of this sort were not so highly prized as now ; but Nicolao, being known all over the world, those who wished to please him would send him either marble statues, or antique vases, or sculpture, or marble inscriptions, or pictures by distinguished masters, or tables in mosaic. He had a fine map of the world on which all places were given, and also illustrations of Italy and Spain. There was no house in Florence better decorated than his or better furnished with beautiful things. Nicolao was now over sixty-five years of age ; his life had been occupied with good deeds, and when sickness came he was fain to show how his death might be worthy of his life. He was aware that he was near his end, so he sent for Friar Ambrogio and several other holy men and begged them to stay by him till the end. He was a great friend of Maestro Paolo, who, besides being a physician, was a man of holy life, and he begged him to remain also. As he could not rise from his bed he bade them prepare an altar in his room, and all things necessary for the mass; he also made full confession, and then begged Friar Ambrogio to say mass there every morning. After the mass an epistle of Saint Paul, for whom he had the greatest reverence, would be read, and during the reading, when the friar came to any fine passage, he would beg him to stop and would reflect over what had been read, and according to Friar Ambrogio he rarely heard one of these fine passages without tears. He also told me that his fervour and his devotion were wonderful, the result of a well-spent life. He knew that his conscience was clear; that he had never deprived anyone of wealth or fame, and that he had never desired any office in which he might have to pass sentence on others. His room was always filled with those who were the servants of God; unbelievers kept away, knowing that he did not care for them.

At the end he did his religious duties with great devotion. First mass was said, then he had himself placed on the ground on a carpet, with a large number of persons kneeling around him. When the Host was presented he showed the greatest devotion, and he turned to his Redeemer and accused himself as a sinner, and as one unworthy of this holy sacrament. Those around him could scarcely restrain their tears. This wonderful grace came from his habit of always reading holy books. Having taken the sacred body of Christ from the hands of Friar Ambrogio he seemed greatly consoled, and would only speak of his own salvation or read some book of devotion or discourse with the holy men about him. These were the exercises of his last illness, and when his end came he died in the arms of Friar Ambrogio, like a holy man who from his childhood had lived a godly life.

FRANCO SACCHETTI

Franco Sacchetti came of ancient and well-born Florentine stock. He was a good Greek and Latin scholar and a friend of all the learned men of his time and inclined to well-doing. Nicolao Nicoli left him the executor of his will, together with certain other learned men and chiefs of the city. He enjoyed all the dignities which Florence could give to its citizens, he was graciously received by those of every class through the politeness he showed to all, and it was no easy matter to please everyone in a democratic state. He was sent on all the chief diplomatic missions ; several times to Venice, and to King Alfonso in company with Giannozzo Pandolfini to settle the peace between the King and Florence, on which occasion they were greatly honoured by the King. He also went again to Naples and afterwards to Pope Pius, to the Diet of Mantua, whither came all the Christian ambassadors, and to divers other places, having been honourably received everywhere.

Franco lived entirely on his income, which was a meagre one. He followed no calling, but devoted himself exclusively to letters. He lived an upright life without ostentation : satisfied with little and always living within his means. Some may have deemed him over-sparing, but this tendency arose from the paucity of his means. He preferred to live on his own income—narrow as it was—rather than trench upon that of other men, as is the fashion of those who are not troubled with an over-delicate conscience. He hated vice and gave a good example to all. His garb was simple and worthy of his station. He kept servants and a saddle-horse, and maintained his house on an appropriate scale, and would often bid his friends and kinsfolk to his well-appointed villa near the city. His custom was to invite ten or twelve men of letters twice a year to his villa, where he would entertain them handsomely for two or three days. He led a refined life, and those who frequented him were literary men of good position and conduct. No games of any kind were played in his home, as is now the present custom : the chief entertainment was the discussion of literature or affairs of state. He received all his guests with easy familiarity, and his house became the resort of the best people. He was always anxious to welcome Giovanni Argiropolo and most of his scholars. No unseemly word was ever spoken in his house. Men like him, meritorious and liberal with their store, ought not to be called avaricious.

Amongst those invited to his villa every year were Giovanni Argiropolo, Pandolfo di Giannozzo Pandolfini, Alamanno Rinuccini, Marco Parenti, Domenico Pandolfini, Piero di

FRANCO SACCHETTI

Neri Acciaiuoli, Donato di Neri, Carlo di Silvestro, Piero Filippo di Giannozzo Pandolfini, Banco da Casa Vecchia, all Greek and Latin scholars and learned in all branches of philosophy, and I, a mere scribe, was included in this illustrious company.

Argiropolo was a stranger in this country, having lost his own ; Franco gave him aid, and every year at harvest sent him corn and wine. He often went to Argiropolo's house to hear if he might be in need and to help him. This is true liberality, to help deserving people who are in want, unlike those who are prodigal and waste there substance over a crew of profligates. Indeed, Franco may be well called a good and liberal man, for there are not many who stand so firmly for virtue against vice as he did. Would to God that Florence held more men of his sort ! How strong is the power of virtue in everything ! There was woven, between him and those named above, a bond of love from which there seemed to spring a unity of several souls in one body. These are the fruits of true friendship; the sympathy between these men was so quick that a day rarely passed without a meeting. Their high character was so well-known in the city that they could obtain almost anything they might require. It seems to me that the best people and most worthy of praise are those who live on what is their own, without preying upon others. And assuredly Franco Sacchetti was one of them.

He did honour to his state and elsewhere. He held no office, but was the friend of the leaders and the men of letters. He was much beloved by Cosimo and Lorenzo de' Medici, Fra Ambrogio degli Agnoli, Lionardo and Carlo d' Arezzo, Nicolao Nicoli, Giannozzo Manetti and all the men of mark of that time. His death proved that those who deemed him rich were wrong. These are the citizens whom a republic should honour, who only leave the store they inherited from their ancestors, and not great wealth gathered by all ways indiscriminately without regard to the welfare of the state or the individual. This brief record of Sacchetti has been written without trouble, for he was one of those who do nothing about which mistakes can be made.

WRITERS

Giorgio di Trabisonda (1396–1468)

He was of Greek nationality, a learned scholar both of
Greek and Latin, as is shown by his writings and translations,
and, like most Greeks, was well versed in the seven liberal
arts and amongst the most elegant writers of his time. He
lectured ably in many parts of Italy at high fees, and wherever
he discoursed many of his pupils afterwards became good
scholars. When the Pope was at Florence the city was crowded,
and at this time he lectured in public and in private : at his
house and in the schools, in Greek, Latin, Logic and Philosophy.
He held a discussion for the instruction of his scholars and
treated rhetoric in a fashion which won high praise ; he also
made them write exercises. In his time he was the most
valuable teacher in Florence and in addition the most
eloquent. He became famous both in Florence and in the
court of Rome.

At this time the Council of the Greeks was sitting at Florence,
and he took part in all the disputations between the Greeks
and Latins before the Pope (for he was well known to Cardinal
Niceno and others) as to the tenets of the two Churches. He
was asked to translate S. Basil, *De deitate Filii et processione
Spiritus Sancti*, and after it was finished he dedicated it to
Pope Eugenius. It was greatly praised by all contemporary
scholars, both for the language and the exactitude of the
rendering. Pope Eugenius appointed him secretary and his
son a writer. He accompanied the Pope from Florence to
Rome, and Pope Nicolas who succeeded esteemed him greatly,
and soon after his accession asked Trabisonda to translate
other sacred works from the Greek, amongst which were the
residue of S. John Chrysostom on S. Matthew, from the twenty-
five homilies translated by Orontius many years ago. This
being a valuable book the Pope directed Giorgio to finish it.
This work of S. John Chrysostom had always been highly
esteemed, for, when S. Thomas Aquinas was in Paris, it was
shown to him, whereupon he said he would rather possess
these twenty-five homilies than the whole of Paris. This
shows how highly he valued the portion now translated by
Trabisonda. At the Pope's request he did many other

GIORGIO DI TRABISONDA

translations—notably Aristotle's great work, *De Animalibus*. On the invitation of King Alfonso he withdrew from Rome on account of certain dissention and went to Naples, where he translated the *Tesori* of Cyril, a book of great value. He translated many books from Greek into Latin, showing greater facility than any other writer of the time on account of his accurate knowledge he had of each tongue. Also he translated works in all the faculties, philosophy and astrology, and that wonderful book by Eusebius Pamphilius, *De preparatione evangelica*, which has proved so valuable to Christianity. The rewards which Pope Nicolas and King Alfonso gave to Trabizonda and other learned men, brought about the revival of Latin; and, by the hope of gain, induced many others to obtain honour and emolument which would not otherwise have been theirs. I give all the works written and translated by Messer Giorgio to be noted by all who read his Life.

WORKS WRITTEN

Compendium grammaticæ. Dialectica ad intelligendos quamplures libros Ciceronis. Rhetorica, magnum volumen. Defensio problematum. Aristotelis contra Theodorum. Commentum super almagestum Ptolomei. Commentum super centiloquium Ptolomei. Commentum super orationes Ciceronis de suo genere dicendi. Responsio ad Guarinum veronensem.

TRANSLATIONS

Sancti Basilii contra Eunomium. Vita sancti Basilii. Vita sancti Athanesi. Almagestum Ptolomei. Centiloquium Ptolomei. Liber Chrysostomi super Mattheum. Sancti Cyrilli super Johannem Evangelistam. Sancti Cyrilli thesaurus. Eusebii Pamphili de preparatione evangelica. Sancti Gregorii Nysseni de vita Moysis. Rhetorica Aristotelis magna. De cælo et mundo. De generatione et corruptione. Meteorologica. Physica. De Anima. De animalibus. Problemata. Oratio Demosthenis contra Ctesiphontem.

407

WRITERS

Francesco Filelfo (1398–1481)

Messer Francesco Filelfo was of Tolentino in the Marches. He began to study in Latin, and later went to Greece to learn the language, in which he soon became as proficient as he was in Latin. Even as a youth he was well known as a scholar, and when a lecturer in oratory was wanted in Florence he, by the influence of Nicolao Nicoli, was chosen. The sons of all the chief citizens attended his classes, and often he would lecture to two hundred students, of whom many afterwards became learned scholars. Besides lecturing at the University he gave private tuition at his own house, and, to satisfy literary sentiment, he consented to read Dante in S. Liberata on days of *festa*. For the sake of practice, and to make them known to the public, he made his pupils write papers in Italian and deliver them from the pulpit in S. Liberata. He used the same method at the University, and proved the most successful teacher in the city.

His fame would have waxed greater had he not marred it by interference in the public affairs of a state of which he was not a citizen, and by giving active support to a particular party. For this reason Nicolao Nicoli and Cosimo de' Medici and all the friends of Messer Carlo determined to bring him forward as a competitor with Filelfo. When Carlo began to lecture the whole of the youth of Florence went to listen, wherefore Filelfo lost many pupils and much reputation. When Filelfo saw that Cosimo and his friends were favouring Carlo (with justice, seeing his worth and learning) he joined the faction of Rinaldo degli Albizzi and the '33,* and traduced Cosimo and those of '34. When Cosimo returned and changed the constitution, Filelfo was banished as a rebel, and this caused his ruin.

He wandered about Italy without finding any place where he could live with the comfort and consideration he had enjoyed in Florence. At last he went to Milan in the time of Duke Francesco, who gave him an honourable office and a liberal stipend. Nevertheless, he, restless by nature, tried unceasingly to return to Florence. He stayed several years

* Cosimo was banished in 1433 and recalled in 1434.

in Milan, where, at the request of King Alfonso, he wrote a book, the *Intercennati*, and afterwards left for Naples. In passing through Rome in the time of Nicolas V, he determined to visit His Holiness on his return. When the Pope heard he was in Rome he sent for him, whereupon Francesco went to His Holiness, who at once addressed him, " Messer Francesco, we are astonished that you have not yet visited us." Francesco answered that he had planned first to see King Alfonso, and then to wait on His Holiness on his return. Pope Nicolas, who was a generous patron of men of letters, wished to do a kindness to Francesco and brought out a bag of five hundred ducats and said, " Messer Francesco, I give you this so that you can pay your charges on the road." Francesco thanked the Pope for his generosity and left Rome for Naples, taking his book, *Intercennati*, which he had written at King Alfonso's command. The King gave him an honourable reception and rewarded him liberally. On his return from Naples to Milan he asked permission to pass through Florence—being a banished man—and this was granted to him.

On his return to Milan Duke Francesco granted him a salary, as he was writing an account in verse of his doings and those of his house, called the *Sforziade*. Amongst his other gifts Filelfo had great facility of writing verse and prose, both in Latin and in the vulgar tongue. His wit was nimble, but he knew not how to keep it in order. He wrote and translated many books and showed a pretty fancy, especially in his later time. He had not much knowledge of philosophy, having read it but little. He brought out a version of Aristotle's Ethics, but does not treat of the disputed doctrine of virtue. He produces proofs from the authority of Holy Writ and from other writers, likewise he condemns vice. He wrote a book on Positive Matter, most necessary and useful to every scholar and a guide to Christian living. He translated the Lives of Galba, Otho, Lycurgus and Numa Pompilius with the laws they made ; also the *Cyropedia*, which had already been done by Poggio, because this translator had left out one book which he deemed unnecessary. He wrote many satires with great gusto, a comment on Petrarch's Italian sonnets, a book which he called *De exilio*, in form of a dialogue, a very prolix production, into which he brought many exiled Florentines

WRITERS

talking together, amongst these Messer Palla who grieved sorely over his banishment. And because this book was a libel on a certain citizen, it was condemned, as Filelfo holds, only because its author, now a decrepit old man more than eighty years of age, desired to return to Florence.

Filelfo at last induced Lorenzo de' Medici to remove the ban of exile, so he was suffered to go back to Florence to resume his lectures, but soon after his return he fell sick of fever and died.

VITTORINO DA FELTRE (1399–1447)

Vittorino came from Feltre in Lombardy, a man of good position and of sober life, learned in Greek, in Latin and in all the seven liberal arts. He lived in Mantua in the time of Francesco Gonzaga* and Madonna Pagola dei Malatesti his wife, who had a large family of fair children, both boys and girls. He was known throughout Italy as a virtuous and learned man, and on this account many of the Venetian aristocracy sent their children to be under his tuition in matters of conduct as well as in polite letters. Amongst his disciples were two distinguished Florentines : Francesco de Castiglione, a man of saintly life and habits ; and Sasero, son of Maestro Lorenzo da Prato, a fine Greek and Latin scholar, possessed of a good style as may be seen in his writings, especially in his Life of Vittorino, which was lost at the time of his death from plague after he left Mantua. Vittorino had many pupils whom he supported and taught for the love of God ; and because of his benefactions to these and almsgiving he found, at the end of the year, that, in addition to his salary of three hundred florins from the Signori, he had spent three hundred more. When he revised his accounts and saw the amount of his debt he went to Gonzaga and said, " I have received three hundred florins as salary, and I have spent three hundred more, wherefore I appeal to your Lordship to help me to pay this debt." Gonzaga had great affection for Vittorino : he knew his worth and honesty and liberality, and that he had put by nothing for himself, so he made a grant of money without demur.

* Gian Francesco.

VITTORINO DA FELTRE

So that his studies should not be disturbed, he never married. It was said, moreover, that he had no desire for women. He was a professed Christian and recited the office every day. He fasted on all the prescribed vigils, and directed those of his pupils who were under discipline to do the same. When he went to table he said the benediction like a priest and returned thanks afterwards, and all the rest did the same. During the meal some one read aloud that silence might be kept. He practised confession and wished all his scholars to use this same habit. His house was as a sacrarium of deeds and words. He allowed his pupils to play fitting games, and the sons of the gentry were required to learn riding, throwing the stone and the staff, to play *palla*, jumping and all exercises good for bodily training, permitting them these recreations after they had learnt and repeated their lessons. He lectured in various subjects appropriate to the separate classes, and would give instructions to all in the liberal arts and in Greek at various times of the day. He made an accurate time-table and never allowed an hour to be wasted. Few of the scholars ever left the house and these would always return at the appointed hour, and at evening all were obliged to be back in the house early : thus he brought them into the habits of order and well doing.

From his school came many men distinguished for their worth and literary attainments. Amongst his scholars were cardinals, bishops and archbishops, as well as temporal rulers and cultured gentlemen from Lombardy, Venice, Padua, Vicenza and all the chief places of the province. In the time of Pope Eugenius many sons of Venetian gentlemen entered the Church, and on festal days, when special orations were delivered, they would always be spoken by pupils of Vittorino. Amongst these I knew Messer Gregorio, nephew of the Cardinal of Bologna, and of Pope Gregory, a learned and eloquent youth, who wrote good verses and was high in his praise of Vittorino as a teacher.

Amongst his pupils was a daughter of the Marquis of Mantua, one of the most beautiful maidens of her time, who studied under Vittorino, and in learning and conduct surpassed all other women. In her life of self-denial she abandoned all her own desires to carry out the wishes of her Redeemer, and when her father betrothed her to the Lord of Urbino* against her wishes—for she had always declared she wanted no other spouse than her Redeemer, for whom she wished to preserve her body intact and immaculate. In this mood she persisted, although gently dissuaded by her father and mother and friends; she finally determined to renounce all worldly things and become an heiress of eternity, to fly to religion as a safe nest for her salvation. One day she withdrew from her father's house to a monastery of holy women in Mantua, and on arrival she cut off her hair and put on a black habit until the time of taking the veil. When her father and mother and the citizens of Mantua heard of this act they were deeply grieved, for all loved her for her charm and goodness. When her father and mother went to her they failed to shake her resolution and even had to listen to an exhortation from her, bidding them shake off the pomps and vanities of the world. Vittorino, who knew the strength of her purpose, encouraged the father and mother to bend to God's will and to thank Him for having wrought such a work of grace in inducing her to renounce the world and its enticing pleasures. So strong was the mind and the constancy of the maiden that no persuasion could move her. When her father and mother saw this they realised that they must let her go her own way, and submit to God's will. Messer Gregorio wrote a learned epistle, *De Contemptu mundi*, exhorting to perseverance in religious ways. Her doings in the convent were wonderful. In her profound humility she wished to take the lowest place. Almighty God! how illimitable is the grace granted to those who turn to Thee, like Cecilia, who would fain imitate the saint whose name she bore in all other ways as well as in her virginity.

This was Vittorino's system: to give a good example in his own life ; to exhort and stimulate all about him to live worthily ; to show that all our actions in life should lead us to live in a fashion which would allow us to reap the fruits of our labour in the future. He was not content to give his own alms for the love of God ; he was always urging others to do the same. He taught gratuitously the needy youths who came to him and supplied all their other wants ; he made

---

* Count Oddantonio, *d.* 1444. His tragic career is one of the unexplained historical mysteries.

no profit by them, for every year he spent more than his income and was forced to beg help from others to make good his losses. Great God! how strongly Thy light shone upon Vittorino! Having read Thy sacred Evangel where it is written, ' Give, and it shall be given unto you,' and fearing the day of judgment when it will be asked of all whether they have fulfilled the seven works of mercy, Vittorino not only carried out Thy commands himself, but likewise persuaded others to do the same. All teachers should be fashioned after this model, not merely to teach Latin and Greek, but also good conduct, which is the most important thing in life. I have heard of books he wrote, but I will say nothing of them, as I never saw them. He was in stature small and lean, and animated and cheerful in aspect. He was dignified in carriage and somewhat taciturn, being always clad in sombre-hued garments which reached the ground. He wore a small cap on his head with narrow opening. I saw him in Florence and spoke to him several times when he came there from Rome in the train of Madonna Pagola Malatesti. In his company was also Signor Carlo da Gonzaga who had been his pupil. In their house, to which they were returning, the life was almost that of a monastery. This is a brief record of his life and manners.

GUERINO VERONESE (1370–1460)

Guerino was born at Verona, and after he had spent some time over the study of Latin, of which he acquired a good knowledge, he went to Florence, which at that time was the mother of learning and of the arts. There were many good teachers in Latin letters, and amongst these was Antonio Corbinelli, a man whose practice it was to teach both Greek and Latin, wherefore he took Guerino into his house at a good salary. He had also brought over from Greece Manuello Grisolora, a man of great distinction, and Guarino, Antonio Corbinelli, Lionardo d' Arezzo, Palla di Noferi Strozzi, Nicolao Nicoli, Fra Ambrogio and many other distinguished men, who at that time were studying with Corbinelli, put themselves under Grisolora's teaching. Later on Guerino was invited by the Marquis Nicolò to go to Ferrara to teach

WRITERS

his sons. He therefore left Florence for Ferrara, and amongst his pupils was Messer Lionello, son of the Marquis, who was much more learned than most gentlemen of his rank, and virtuous withal. Afterwards he ruled the state with great ability. In Lombardy Guerino trained many pupils who became learned men; these pupils came not only from Lombardy, but from Hungary, and from other far countries; youths were sent to study at Ferrara, and to learn under Guerino, not only literature, but also good manners and conduct, for he was scrupulously honest and most particular in his view of life. I once saw a Hungarian youth* who had been sent by the Archbishop of Strigonia to study under Guerino. He was a good Greek and Latin scholar, and had a pretty trick of verse and of prose, as is fully told in the account given of his Life. Guerino was the means of leading many into a good way of life, being himself an example of virtue. He lived at Ferrara for some time in easy circumstances with his wife and children, taking no heed of aught else but letters, and for this reason he won general regard. He conducted his profession of tutor as a man should, for he employed all his time in teaching, in translating or in composing. He was the second in merit of Grisolora's pupils as a writer; Lionardo d' Arezzo stands first. In their writings may be seen how widely the style of these two scholars differs; Messer Lionardo reached the highest level of writing, but both he and Guerino deserve the greatest praise in that they were the first to bring into the light the Latin language which for so many centuries had been obscured. If any one of the learned scholars of his training had done his duty he would have written his Life, for assuredly his memory deserved to be handed down in the world of letters, so great was his worth. He translated from Plutarch, *De liberis educandis*, and the lives of Marcellus, Alexander the Great, Cæsar, Pelopidas, Sulla and Lysander.

Pope Nicolas asked him to translate the *De Situ Orbis* of Strabo, divided into the three parts of Asia, Africa and Europe, and paid him five hundred florins for each part. Before the Pope's death he had translated two parts and had received a thousand ducats. After Nicolas died he translated the third part, and he wished to send it to some one who would

* Bishop of Fünfkirchen. (See *Life*, p. 122.)

414

pay him for his work because, with his children and his slender resources, he was obliged to earn money by writing. He offered it to one of the chief men in Florence, and, on refusal, he sent it to a Venetian gentleman who was quite ready to pay him for his labour. When it was finished the Venetian offered it, with a proem attached, to King René. Enough cannot be said of Guerino and his many good qualities.

BIONDO DA FORLI (1388-1463)

Messer Biondo was a fine Latin scholar with a certain knowledge of Greek. He was apostolic secretary ; also a diligent antiquarian who wrote several works which threw considerable light on past times. Rome had held the dominion of the whole world, *Domina Orbis*, but the history of many of her victories and triumphs was imperfectly known to later generations, wherefore Biondo searched so diligently that he unearthed many facts relating to the Macedonian war. He wrote four decades, beginning prior to the Goths, and recording all events worth notice down to his own time. For this work he deserves the greatest praise, for he expended enormous labour in illuminating the events of these obscure centuries. Ancient Rome had been enriched with magnificent structures and gay with gorgeous spectacles, all mundane amenities were to be found within her streets, fine sculpture and stately triumphs. She was the meeting-place of all the illustrious men in the world, and the seat of the noblest republic that had ever existed. The palace of Nero covered an area of four square miles, and was filled with marvellous objects. For many years it consumed the entire revenue of the Empire. Also the palaces of the Cæsars, of Lucullus, of Marcus Crassus and of the numerous remarkable men whom the Roman Empire produced ; all these were blotted out and lost to memory on account of the calamities which fell upon the Empire, first through the civil wars of Marius and Sylla, in which at one blast of the trumpet twenty thousand citizens died, then from the overthrow by the Gauls, the Goths and other barbarous nations. For a long time Italy remained enslaved, and Rome ruined and deserted. Concerning all

WRITERS

these calamities, of which there was no record, Messer Biondo produced a book called *Roma istaurata*, wherein he wrote luminously concerning the splendour of the republic, of its buildings, and of everything else, for the benefit of those who desire to possess some knowledge of the times. For this reason we, and those who may come after us, are under great obligation to him.

After finishing *Roma istaurata*,* he saw how greatly Italy had changed ; a number of cities and towns which were formerly inhabited now lay deserted and ruined, and without any record that they had ever existed. Not only had the cities themselves disappeared, all knowledge of the men of mark who might have inhabited them had also perished. Therefore Biondo determined to revive and illuminate the Italy of the past by writing a book, *Italia illustrata*, describing the country as it once was, not only those places and districts which remain, but every village, however small and humble it might be, and every river, and if any one of these had been the scene of memorable events in the past he names it. This is a work worthy of notice, and one over which he spent great care and close investigations. Biondo also deserves praise for the vast labour he devoted for the benefit of all, and, if others before him had been as diligent recorders as he was, we should see the past more clearly than we now see it, for it is a thousand years and more since anyone wrote as he has written. Therefore the whole world should be grateful to Messer Biondo for what he has given us.

MATTEO PALMIERI (*d.* 1433)

Matteo di Marco Palmieri, a Florentine, was of middle-class birth. He was the founder of his house and ennobled it by his worthy life. He took up the study of Latin and became a good scholar. In the course of his studies he won a high position in the city, and ultimately enjoyed all the honours it could give. Both within and without the city he was engaged in

* First printed in 1471. In 1472 *Roma triumphans* was printed, and *Italia illustrata* compiled for King Alfonso in 1474. Biondo was the first to write comprehensively on antiquities and to collect inscriptions. He denounced the clearances made by Nicolas V. in Rome.

divers offices and missions. All this preferment came to him without any family influence, for, as it has been said, he was the first of his house. He was known in the republic as a grave and prudent man and a wise counsellor, wherefore he was reckoned by those in power to be amongst those who gave the wisest and best matured advice to the republic, advice which was always most temperate. This was not merely the opinion of the home government, for the King's ambassadors, in their dealings with him, invariably commended his judgment. On account of his merits he was sent as ambassador to King Alfonso's court, where, through his learning and wisdom, he was received with honour. There were many literary men in Naples who knew Matteo by his works. In several of these missions he was successful. Besides his other gifts, his handsome presence favoured him, but he became bald when he was very young. He went on his last mission to Pope Paul on important matters when he was old and decrepit, and satisfied both the Pope and the city which had sent him.

He wrote in excellent style, both in Latin and Italian. In Latin he added to the *De Temporibus* of Eusebius the events of more than a thousand years, taking up the work where S. Jerome and Prospero had left it. It is evident that he must have had great trouble in his researches to give an account of what happened in those ages of obscure writers. Both he and his work became famous. He made many copies of it so that it was found in all parts of the world. It comes down to the ruin of the state of the Counts of Poppi.* He wrote in Latin the Life of the great Seneschal of the Acciaiuoli† in an elaborate style, the history of Pisa to the time of its acquisition by the Florentines, a funeral oration on the death of Messer Carlo, which he recited in public and crowned him as poet. He wrote a book in Italian,‡ in which he taught how to rule both the public and the family; it is in the form of a dialogue, dedicated to Messer Alessandro degli Alessandri. Last he wrote some Italian verses in the manner of Dante, called Città di Vita, a work which cost him much

* Macchiavelli, *Floren. Hist.*, p. 265.
† *Vide*, p. 269. He ruled Naples successfully under Joanna I.
‡ Vespasiano probably refers to the *Vita Civile*.

WRITERS

labour, as the subject was a very difficult one ; there are fine passages in it in which he shows his talent. However it may be, he went astray in this book while writing of religion, because he had no knowledge of sacred things, and the chief mistakes are those which he makes in dealing with those matters which are opposed to our religion. This is the lot of those who, as St.'Paul says, would be wise in the things of this life ; they have gone mad with the madness of the world, for of a truth those may be called mad who lose the knowledge of God through straying from His path. Matteo almost certainly fell into this error through ignorance, for at the end of this work he admits to the Church that on no account did he desire to go astray, and lets the Church approve what was right and disapprove of what was wrong. After he had finished his book he did not discuss its subject with anyone ; had he done this he would not have made this mistake. He had it written in antique lettering on kid's skin, and illuminated and bound, and wrapped up in a sealed packet and put under lock and key; he then gave it to the proconsul with the request that this book should not be unsealed until after his death. When he was dead they at once brought out the book, and showed it to certain learned theologians, with the intention that it should not be published if anything contrary to the Faith should be found in it, and after having carefully examined it, they found but one error in the whole of the book, which showed that Matteo had no ill purpose, for, had he known of it, he would have rectified it. This book is now in the keeping of the proconsul of the Guild of Notaries and has never been published.*

MAFFEO VEGIO (1406–1458)

Maffeo Vegio was a native of Lodi in Lombardy. He wrote well in Latin and Greek, both in prose and in verse. He was a man of upright life who began as a secular priest and gained

* The charge of heresy made against him seems to have been his adoption of Origen's theory of the Nature of Christ and of the Soul, vide Muratori, Rerum Italic. Script., XX, p. 541. Possibly Palmieri was one of the victims of the persecution which Paul II set up against the humanists Platina Pomponius and Callimachus in 1468.

his living by his pen and sought no other emolument. He was devoted to the memory of S. Augustine and of his mother S. Monica, whose Life he wrote. After this he built in S. Agostino at Rome a fine chapel with a beautiful tomb, to which he caused to be transferred S. Monica's body and composed an epitaph for it.* He provided the chapel with all needful ornament, and endowed it out of his estate so that now each morning masses are said in honour of the saint. So skilled was he in verse that he added with the greatest ease a thirteenth book to Virgil's Æneid, which was greatly praised by all the learned men of the time. I once saw a vocabulary for the use of jurisconsults which had much merit. He also wrote a version of the Psalms of David in Latin verse, and a Life of S. Bernadino of Siena.

Vegio proved himself a faithful servant of God. It would have been easy for a man of his fame and learning to obtain any post of dignity in the papal court had he desired one, but, knowing the dangers which hang around these places, and wishing to live a life of safety remote from worldly vanities, he resolved to withdraw from the world to the religious life as a haven of safety. Wherefore he made over all his substance to God's service, and became a regular canon of S. Agostino d' Osservanza on account of the devotion he had always felt for that saint and for S. Monica, giving thereby an example of the saintly life. He showed his profound humility not only by his words, but by his deeds likewise. There we see this man of rare excellence submitting himself to the yoke of obedience ! He valued immortal treasures more than the perishing ones of earth, and set his face toward that true end which every Christian should seek. He hid his virtues and made no show of them, sure that they were known to the Redeemer of the world who rewards all those who serve Him willingly. His good deeds were so many that he deserves to be kept in memory by all learned men. I am unwilling that his fame should perish, wherefore I have placed him amongst the men worthy to be remembered.

* By Isaia da Pisa.

WRITERS

Zembino of Pistoia (Sozomen) (1387–1458)

Messer Zembino was a priest of Pistoia, learned in Latin and Greek, also a canon, and the holder of another benefice without profit, for, being a conscientious man, he did not care to hold a paid office without work. He was austere by nature, and had no hankering after pomps and gaieties. He gained a living by instructing the children of the chief citizens in humane letters and good conduct ; Messer Palla Strozzi and other leading citizens sent their sons to him for teaching. He lived a life of severe chastity for fifty-two years, from the day that he was ordained priest until his death. He never left his chamber in the morning to go to teach his scholars without first saying his prayers. He was contented with little and desired no more than he had, being engaged to lecture at the University, where he taught publicly together with other learned men, and was well thought of. He spent his time so profitably that he never had any to spare. Having made up his mind to lead a simple life, he gave up all his superfluities to God, or spent his money in buying books, as may be seen, for amongst the hundred and fifty volumes which he left to Pistoia, some are written by his own hand, and some of the Greek and Latin books were purchased. These books are now in the palace of the Signori for the use of any student who may need them. He cared nothing for honours or fame.

It happened one day, when Pope Eugenius was in Florence, that a certain Cardinal Moriense, an ultramontane, sent for Zembino and asked him to act as tutor to his nephew, but Zembino answered that he was in no need of such a post and declined to wait on the cardinal, who was greatly astonished at this reply and sent one of his household to repeat the message, whereupon Zembino answered again in the same words. He went to the Council of Constance, where he was highly esteemed, and in the elections he gave his vote with the Italians. One day when he was riding from Pistoia he encountered a party of Florentine fowlers, one of whom called out to him : *domine a concilio*. Zembino turned his horse and said, " I have been there and I counted as one ; is there anything else you want? " The citizen excused himself that he had thus jested, and seeing that he had offended, begged pardon. Zembino trained many excellent scholars in Florence—Matteo Palmieri, Pandolfo Pandolfini, Bartolomeo Strozzi, Francesco Vettori and many others of the leading families. He desired to leave some worthy and valuable work behind him, and, having decided that he would never do this at his present employment of teaching, he calculated how he might live on the small income he had, and, like a philosopher, he went to Pistoia at the time of harvest, and sold of his grain and wine enough to pay for his sustenance for a year. After he had made this provision he returned to Florence and put the money he had received into a purse which he hung on the hat-stand in his room ; he then calculated his daily cost of living which came to about two loaves a day, the price of which he took every day from his purse and never exceeded his limit.

He wrote one very valuable book which gives an account of every event worthy of notice which has happened since the beginning of the world, set forth year by year. In those places where Eusebius is meagre Zembino has amplified the narrative from trustworthy sources ; otherwise he has let it stand ; and in the life of Moses or of other great men, he has made succinct additions of new matter. He gives fuller information on many subjects, profane as well as sacred. After the history of the world he passes to that of the Assyrians, the Medes and the Romans, all excellently arranged, with dates given in the margins so that any event can be found with the greatest ease. All the authorities given are authentic, otherwise Zembino could not have used them. The making of these works was a great labour and took a long time, seeing that he amended and set in order all events down to the time of Pope Celestine and filled therewith eighty script books of royal size. But when he had completed it he took no steps to have it copied, but, by my persuasion and encouragement he let it be done and it quickly attracted so great notice that it was sent to all parts of Italy, to Catalonia, Spain, France, England and Rome. Cosimo de' Medici had it copied in Florence as a gift to the Badia of Fiesole. He wrote a third volume covering the period down to his own time,

but he had not leisure to amend and revive it before his death.*
I could not omit his name from a collection of illustrious men
deserving of commemoration, for I knew him as a most
interesting man of admirable life and conduct.

GIOVANNI TORTELLO (1400–1466)

Messer Giovanni was an Aretine, a good Greek and Latin
scholar, an apostolic sub-deacon, and greatly esteemed on
account of his worth by Pope Nicolas, who saw that he was
both learned and diligent and put him in charge of the library
which he had collected. He made a catalogue of all the books,
their number reaching to nine thousand. I have heard from
him much praise of Pope Nicolas, of his great liberality
towards learned men, and of his hatred of the unworthy. He
told me that one evening, when he was in the library with
the Pope, he found him greatly displeased at the habits of a
certain cardinal at the court. He had done all that was possible
to make this man change his habits, but without success.
Pope Nicolas now told Tortello that he meant to try a different
method with him. He gave orders that when the cardinal
should come to the palace in the morning, he should be detained, in order that he might try to effect by force that which
he could not effect by kindness. Having heard this, Messer
Giovanni warned the cardinal not to go to the palace in the
morning, and the cardinal, thus warned, kept away, and
having got some inkling of the Pope's purpose, he spent the
whole day in trying to find a way of appeasing him. Pope
Nicolas was disposed to forgive him, and he did not go any
further in the matter for this was his benevolent humour
which, up to the day of his death, he never changed. It
happened not long after this that the plague broke out in
Rome, and as all the court dispersed, this cardinal besought
Messer Giovanni to go with him to Florence and stay in his
house. Giovanni assented, for he thought after what he had
done for the cardinal, that he might trust him to behave

* This chronicle is a very remarkable work. It professes to deal
with the history of the world from the creation to 1455, divided into
three sections. Sozomen went with Poggio and Lionardo Aretino to
S. Gall when they made their discovery of the lost classics.

decently and occupy himself by study. But after they had spent some time in Florence, he broke all his promises of amendment and bore himself in a fashion which may not, for the sake of decency, be described. Messer Giovanni now saw that he had made a false move in not allowing the Pope to chastise him, and he was wont to say that this was the greatest regret of his life.

Giovanni was very learned, and at the request of the Pope he wrote a book called *Ortografia*, which describes words with wide exposition, and when he meets with a word, the name of a place, he describes its origin, also its position and any event which may have happened there ; thus he may be called an expositor, a cosmographer and an historian. From this book it will appear that Giovanni had a wonderful knowledge of many things, taken both from Greek and Latin sources. Through this book he won great fame all over the world, and those who have to study Latin owe him a great debt. He translated the Life of St. Athanasius from Greek into Latin, and other works of which I know nothing. Giovanni was a man of fine character, humane by nature, and could talk on any subject. He was grave of aspect and highly esteemed by all those who had dealings with him ; he sought honour rather than wealth, and was content with little, working hard at letters, which were his delight.

MASTER PAGOLO (1415–1474)

He was the son of Domenico, a Florentine, of respectable parentage. He was a good Greek and Latin scholar and proficient in the liberal arts, which he began to study in his youth. He was learned in astrology above all others of his time. He never flaunted his scholarship before the world and was slow in giving an opinion, but should a friend ask for information in his science he would receive it. Also he was a very religious man, and most people held him to be a virgin. He slept on a mattress beside his desk, and for a long time he ate no meat and little of anything else. He ate plenty of fruit and vegetables and drank much pure water. He never wore a lined cloak, but one of cloth in winter and in summer a light one. He was one of few words, and of the gentlest natures I ever knew, of decent speech, and, should an unseemly word be spoken before him, his face would change. He loved everything that was good, especially monks and friars and others whom he knew to be lovers of God. He was learned in geometry, and the friend of all lettered men of his time, especially Nicolao Nicoli, Filippo di Ser Ugolino, Lionardo d' Arezzo, Friar Ambrogio and Giannozzo Manetti. He often went to visit Cosimo de' Medici when he could not leave his house and was always welcome. Master Pagolo thought less of riches than of virtue on which all his hopes were set. A day seldom passed when he would not meet Cosimo and the aforesaid men of letters and talk with them and discuss matters worth remarking.

Here I cannot refrain from protest against the swarm of ignorant charlatans and hot-heads who find their highest good in pleasure of the senses, such as eating and drinking, recking of naught else. None of these illustrious men cared for them, and Master Pagolo often studied far into the night. He had collected a great number of books on all the liberal arts both in Greek and in Latin, and when he was not studying he would go abroad and treat the ailments of a friend, although he did not practise medicine largely. The residue of his time he would spend in the company above named. Nicolao had the highest regard for him and desired him to act as executor of his will. In Nicolao's last illness he and Friar Ambrogio were always with him. Pagolo spake ill of no man, and was most careful over his duties. Whenever he visited a sick man he would refuse to enter unless he had confessed, for such was his rule. His life was devout with no burden on his conscience, he never neglected abstinence, and fasting, or sleeping in his clothes, or temperance. He died at eighty, rendering his spirit to God with devotion and repentance of his sins.

Lapo di Castiglionchi

He was a Florentine of reputable descent. At the time when Filelfo and Trabizonda came to the city, and Carlo d' Arezzo was lecturing, Lapo, then about twenty-five years

of age, began to study Greek and Latin and in a short time
became proficient in both. The court of Rome was then at
Florence, and, both in the court and among the *literati* of
the city, he was much praised for his translations of Lucian
and Plutarch. He was taciturn by nature and made no display of his quality, but Lionardo d' Arezzo and Giannozzo
Manetti knew him well and commissioned him to do the
rendering of *De Longævis* by Lucian. Being well known in
Rome and Florence, Pope Eugenius made him secretary and
gave him certain other offices. As he was a favourite with
the cardinals he would probably have risen yet higher had he
lived. Lapo was a poor man, consequently many of his Greek
and Latin books were written by his own hand. He went
with Pope Eugenius to Ferrara and there died of plague.
He wrote many books, amongst which were translations of
Lucian and Plutarch and others. He was an excellent
translator and his fame still lives. He was a small melancholy
man who rarely laughed ; one of seemly life and very poor,
so that all the books he possessed were those he had himself
copied. I myself have seen some of these in Greek and Latin.
This is all I know about Lapo.

LAURO QUIRINO (1424–1466)

He was a Venetian learned in the liberal arts. When Pope
Eugenius was in Florence, Lauro was a young eager student
who had the audacity to contradict Messer Lionardo over
his translation of Aristotle's Ethics, speaking especially against
the passage *Summum Bonum* which he declared was incorrect
and ought to have stood *Bonum per se.* Messer Lionardo
was then a famous scholar and took it ill that a youth like
this should undertake to set him right. Lauro, who at this
time was in the house of Cardinal Niceno, made answer to
Lionardo's invective by a letter in which he said it was
better to follow Francesco Barbaro and Lionardo Giustiniano
than to foregather with dolts and fools. Lauro was a poor
writer in spite of his learning, and when his reply was shown
about at the court of Rome he gained little credit therefrom.
When Cardinal Niceno read it he began to laugh, and sincerely

WRITERS

blamed Lauro in that, youth as he was, he should have dared to speak in such terms to Messer Lionardo, who was then at the height of his fame, and saw that Lauro would lose rather than gain over the business. Later Messer Lauro gained a good name and position in Venice. Of his other works I know nothing.

MALRASO CICILIANO

He came to study law in Florence when the University had a general faculty and many learned men attended. He was a good jurist and canonist and also devoted to the humanities and to poetry, in which few equalled him. Many of his elegies were highly praised, and he reached so high a position that, according to report, he gained the laurel. He wrote verse so readily that few could come near him; it seemed to be an especial gift of Nature.

ENOCHE D' ASCOLI (d. 1450)

Enoche came from Ascoli and, after learning Latin, went to Florence, where he studied in all the faculties and subsequently entered the house of the Bardi as a tutor. He was a marvellous grammarian, having spent much time over this study. Pope Nicolas was anxious to procure certain books which could not be found in Italy, wherefore he sent Enoche into Germany to all religious houses with apostolic briefs to require all the libraries to be opened to his emissary under pain of excommunication. Enoche made search through part of Germany, but he brought back nothing worth noting. He found Porfirio on all the writings of Horace, and Apicius *De Cænis* in ten books. I imagine that he failed because he lacked a complete knowledge of writers of the past.* As he was a learned man I have added his name to the list.

* There is a touch of jealousy here rare in Vespasiano. It reads as if he resented the action of Nicolas in letting another buy books for him. Mai, in his preface to the *Vite*, refers to a Latin poem which he found in the Ambrosian library at Milan, *Orestis fabulam longo hexametro scriptam que ab Henocho asculano reperta dicebatur.* This codex contained also certain poems attributed to Virgil.

LIONARDO DEL BENNINO

Lucio da Spoleto

Messer Lucio was a man of learning and eloquence. He lived with the abbot of Monte Cassino as tutor to his nephew, Messer Marino Tomasello. The castle of Spoleto* was in the possession of the abbot who became embroiled with Eugenius IV concerning the same. The abbot sent Messer Lucio to the Pope to justify himself and his position. Meantime the Pope had placed his claims in the hands of the Cardinal of Capua, a Neapolitan. Messer Lucio, besides defending his claims by a speech, made a written report which he sent to the Pope, the cardinals and the court of Rome. This report was finely written and full of cogent argument, but force was stronger than reason. Messer Giovanni Vitellesco, a foe of the abbot and powerful with the papal court, led his men-at-arms against the Castle of Spoleto which, after some time, he stormed and plundered. The Patriarch was the most cruel warrior of the age, and his end shows what his life had been. As to Lucio, he showed such promise as a scholar and a rhetorician that had he lived he would have equalled any one of his time.

Lionardo del Bennino

He was a Florentine of high birth with a good knowledge of Latin, to which he was devoted from his youth. He remained for a long time at home and gave the best possible example in his life and manners. He had a generous spirit and cared naught for fleshly pleasure. He took a well-born girl for wife, reared a family of sons and daughters as well and diligently as any paterfamilias in the city. In no other house was there better economy or better care of the children, for Lionardo recognised that, by such practice, he would best discharge his duty to God and the state. By way of example he tried to make himself a mirror, in which all the virtues and none of the vices should be exhibited, for the benefit of his

---

* *Vide* Alfonso, King of Naples (p. 60) ; Muratori, *Annali*, IX, p. 160. Vitelleschi was in the Papal service. He fell into disfavour and died a prisoner in the Castle of S. Angelo under Eugenius IV.

family ; and in all the offices he held his good qualities were manifest. He had high courage, and whenever he was required to discharge any duty, which he deemed just and honest, no persuasion otherwise would hold him back. His judgment was unerring on account of his keen insight, and no one would venture to urge him to do any equivocal act. He was open in speech and spoke his mind freely. He was generous and hospitable and given to entertaining the lettered and well-bred young men of the city who were his chief companions. His fine presence well became his way of life and character. Many of the acts of the city authorities displeased him, and, had he wielded greater power, events would have been different. He disliked the practices of exile and confinement and would have nothing to do with their use ; for it seemed to him that the state ought, by itself, to have sufficient regulative power without such methods as these. But in this matter his father was inclined one way and he himself to the other, and if he had not died so young he would have had the chance of showing how strong was his opposition. In spite of his youth he might well have been employed in any mission or office of state.

CIPRIANO RUCELLAI

He was a Florentine of honourable birth who became a good Greek scholar. He kept in his house teachers of one language and of the other, and led a reputable virtuous life ; in order to have the more time for study he never married, and died when young, so had no time to show his powers. Had he lived longer he might have written some work which would have been an honour to the state. It must suffice to know that he made a good beginning, and recognised the rich fruit which might have followed.

NICOLÒ DELLA LUNA

Nicolò della Luna was born of Florentine parents of good standing, and a good Greek and Latin scholar. He was industrious, well mannered and of seemly life, having studied Latin and Greek under Francesco Filelfo and Carlo d' Arezzo.

FRANCESCO DI LAPACINO

He never married, so as to have more leisure for study, and spent most of his energy over Greek, in which he composed several works, and, but for his early death, he would have translated certain Greek vocabularies which do not exist in Latin. I have seen two Greek-Latin vocabularies prepared by him which show the method he used.

VERI SALVIATI

Veri di Giovanni di Messer Forese Salviati was well born and learned in Greek and Latin and a diligent student. His teachers were Carlo d' Arezzo and Filelfo. He worked at Moral Philosophy and heard lectures on Aristotle's Politics from Messer Carlo, and on the Ethics from Battista da Fabriano, working so diligently that he became very learned in the subject. He was a well-conducted man of virtuous life. He wrote a good style, as may be seen from his letters and translations.

FRANCESCO DI LAPACINO

He was a well-born Florentine who received from the state all the honours due from a citizen. He was studious by habit and knew both Greek and Latin. He undertook a work which has been of great service to all learned men ; namely the transcription of the *Cosmographia of Ptolemy** which had been brought into Italy from Constantinople, in its large form with maps, the text and the names of the various provinces being given in Greek. Francesco was amongst the first who undertook to reproduce the maps with his own hand, writing the Greek names in Greek and the Latin in Latin, a change which had not been made since the book had come from Constantinople, although before this the Greek text had been done into Latin by Jacopo della Scarperia, but the maps were left out : now Francesco restored the maps with the Greek names, adding the Latin names as stated. From this revision many copies have been made, some of which have been sent

* First printed in Rome in Latin, 1462. The first Greek text is of Bale, 1533, edited by Erasmus.

429

as far as Turkey. For this work, undertaken in the cause of the Latinists, Francesco deserves the warmest praise. He was akin to Nicolao Nicoli, who held him in the highest esteem for his virtues, and wished to include him in the group of distinguished men he had appointed executors of his will.

Giovanni da Miles

He was a Roman, consistorial advocate and distinguished jurist and canonist. He devoted his life to the law, was most conscientious, cared little for gain and would undertake no case which was not just and honest. He wrote many books on the law, amongst others a work of great value, a Repertorium of Civil and Canon Law. His intellect was ready and active, and his decisions much commended. He was assiduous in his religious duties like the good Christian he was.

Cencio Romano

Cencio was a Roman, learned in Greek and Latin. He was apostolic secretary and wrote several works which, by their apt style and composition, won the praise of all the learned men of the time. He was taciturn and cold in manner, and with such a temper he failed to gain full recognition. I know nothing of his work.

Antonio Cafferelli

He was born in Rome and became a learned jurist and canonist with a subtle intelligence in the law. In his time he held a high place as a consistorial advocate, and had a large practice by which he gained great sums of money, as was evident from the fortune he left to his heirs. No man would have been a greater adept in every legal faculty if only he had spent more time in study and less in gathering riches. He was a man of moody temperament and few words, but when engaged in a case would be most vehement, with an admirable faculty of defence. He spent so much time in making money that he left no legal writing.

NUGNO GUSMANO

Nugno Gusmano

Messer Nugno, of the house of Gusmano and allied to the royal family of Spain, came to Florence at the time of the Council of the Greeks from the Holy Land and Mount Sinai. He was a man of generous and liberal mind, on account of which he had left his father's house in Spain to see the world and learn its spiritual and temporal governance. He travelled through France and remained four months at the court to study the conditions of the kingdom, and then he went on to Florence with five or six servants in attendance. He lived handsomely there, but he was so melancholy by temper, that often, when I have sat with him at table, he would be so deeply sunk in thought, that he would be forgetful of his food and all else. One evening I marked that he never ate anything, but at the time I said nothing ; the morning after I asked him what he had eaten for supper, and why he had been so absent-minded. He answered that it was now eight years since he had left his home to visit all the Christian courts and to study their manners and customs, then he had left these parts and had travelled in the Holy Land, to Mount Sinai, to Cairo and had explored the whole of Syria. He had made all these voyages against the will of his father, having been provided with a good sum of money by his mother, who was a very rich lady. He had now received letters from his mother, his sisters and his father who were all greatly angered with him. I answered him saying that this was a very important matter, and that he would do well to take the advice of a very dis tinguished citizen of Florence thereanent, Messer Giannozzo Manetti. He replied that he would be very glad to do this.

The next day Messer Giannozzo went to his house, and after he had listened to the story, said that Nugno would do well to write a complete account of his wanderings during the last eight years. And this he did. After he had finished it I went to Messer Nugno and arranged that the book should be transcribed, and sent by private messenger to his father in Spain, Messer Lodovico, who was Master of the Order of Calatrava. This book, which he wrote on Messer Giannozzo's advice, he called *Apologia*, that is an excuse for his conduct.

WRITERS

He sent one of his servants named Roderico de Mires to Spain, to present the book to his father, who at once gave it, according to the messenger's account, to one of his attendants, and made him read it straight through to him several times without stopping, and he could not keep back his tears on account of the dignity of the composition, and exclaimed that he would willingly forgive his son and welcome him back. The messenger departed with letters from father, and mother, and the whole family, urging Nugno to return to Spain. It would be hard to describe how touching and vivid was the picture which the messenger brought back to Nugno of the love and kindly feeling of the father towards his errant son, and how completely the *Apologia*, suggested by Messer Giannozzo, had worked upon this gentleman and had changed his mind. He sent to his son through Barcelona fourteen thousand florins, requesting him to make certain benefactions in Rome before his return. A great fraud was, however, practised on Nugno by certain Florentines, who induced him to give money on a bill of exchange, which was dishonoured, and for which he had no legal remedy; and thus fourteen thousand florins were thrown away. And in addition to the loss of this money, he took certain jewels, which he had brought from Cairo, amongst which was a fine table diamond valued at a thousand florins, to show them to a certain prelate. This prelate offered to buy the stones, whereupon Nugno gave them to him. He was betrayed by his easy-going nature and by a certain Spanish affectation. He understood the Tuscan speech marvellously well, and would read in that language better than one Tuscan born, having composed in it a number of books, which he sent to Spain.

In the course of his wanderings he met with many untoward adventures, as is the fate of those who roam the world. He went to Cairo and after he had explored the Holy Land and Mount Sinai, in the journey between Mount Sinai and Jerusalem, through the desert, all the horses and the attendants were seriously injured by the hornets and other strange beasts of the deserts, and on account of the long journey their money grew short. At Cairo they found a Catalan merchant, who traded with Barcelona, named Giovanni Andrea, who, when Nugno told him of his need, gave him credit for two

432

hundred ducats, like a good-hearted man. When later on this kindly act was known to Nugno's kinsfolk they repaid the merchant double, and felt a sincere friendship for him and all his house. They did not reckon anything for exchange or interest, but paid him most liberally according to the usage of the time. When he got back to Cairo his mother knew that from the length of his travels he must be in want of cash, and when she heard that he was going to the Holy Land she reckoned that he would pass through Venice on his homeward way, wherefore she sent his servant, one of those whom the Spaniards call *creati*, that is to say one brought up in the house, with five thousand florins to await the arrival of galleys from the Holy Land. As soon as the servant saw Messer Nugno, he recognised him, and threw himself at his feet, whereupon Messer Nugno was joyful indeed, for he realised that he had now plenty of money for his own needs and joyful also over the good faith of his servant. When Messer Nugno had received the sum which the servant had deposited in a bank in Venice he gave himself a handsome outfit, as he was going to Florence, where the court of Rome was then residing ; he bought himself fine apparel of gold brocade in the fashion of gentlefolk of the time, and travelled to Florence in good state with servants and horses, reaching the city at the time when Pope Eugenius brought about the union with the Greeks in Santa Maria del Fiore.

I will tell an instance of his extraordinary fortitude ; for eight years he travelled all over the world, always suffering from ague ; when it was upon him he rested, and on other days he travelled; he was always content, and when he could go about he enjoyed himself. He spent the most of his time in Florence with Giannozzo Manetti, Lionardo d' Arezzo and other learned men, others he did not care about, for he only took pleasure in conversation with men of letters. He had many other good qualities which I will omit for fear of being too prolix. He left Florence for Spain, where he met a joyful reception from his kinsfolk. He had a wonderful knowledge of most things gained by observation in all parts of the world ; he could converse as to the management of the state and customs of various countries, of all the regions of the earth and of all the places he had visited, which really included the whole of the habitable world. He knew about these matters so intimately that, were it necessary, he could have described them in writing. His liberality was great, and in Florence he made generous gifts to learned men and others. The Spaniards are acute by nature, but Messer Nugno would have been reckoned acute even amongst them. He was so much devoted to Tuscan letters that he often sent scribes to Florence at his own expense to copy various books, and they remained in Florence till the work was finished. He caused to be translated many Latin works into the Tuscan tongue : the *Tuscalane* of Tully, *De Oratore* and *Declamazioni* of Quintilian, *De Saturnalibus* of Macrobius. He collected a fine library of books in this language which, after his death in Seville, came to grief.

VELASCO DI PORTOGALLO

Velasco was born of noble Portuguese parents and went to Italy to study Civil and Canon Law, of which he became a learned exponent. He won a great reputation on account of his learning : also because his father, a wealthy nobleman, was in high favour with the King of Portugal. From some cause, unknown to me, his father incurred the King's displeasure and was fined a sum of twenty thousand ducats, and was forced to leave the kingdom. At this time Velasco was living at Bologna, and there, as his father was still rich and he himself of nimble intellect, he found no need to labour for his living. He spent his nights in merriment, and little time over the revision of his lectures on the sonnets of Petrarch, which, as he told me, were the only ones he delivered at this period ; most of his time he passed in useless frivolity and trusted to his natural ability. After spending some years in this fashion, he heard that his father had lost the favour of the King and a large sum of money, wherefore he determined never to return to Portugal, and began to study diligently Civil and Canon Law, in which, owing to his high talent, he soon became distinguished. In a short time he became one of the most prominent exponents of these faculties, and passed for the doctorate with great brilliancy. Few in Bologna ever equalled him. He, like most other canonists and jurists, used a flowing and pregnant style in writing, through study of the humaner letters, as may be seen in his compositions. He was bold and forcible in speech, as lawyers are bound to be.

He went to the court in the time of Pope Eugenius who, having recognised his great gifts, appointed him advocate to the consistory, a post which brought him into such prominent notice that most of the causes came into his hands, and over a great part of them he was successful. He had a voice like thunder, and with this, and his legal skill, his audacious manner and his natural wit he won almost every case, and made a large fortune. His books were worth many thousand florins, for he would only have the best. His satin robes were all lined with sable and he had the finest horses in Rome, where he lived in state. He spent liberally over everything, and sometimes got into trouble on account of his headstrong temper and impatience, for he could not brook contradiction. One day, when Pope Eugenius was in Florence, a public consistory had been convened at which Messer Velasco appeared before the Pope to conduct a case against a certain abbot, and what with his learning, his insolence, his eloquence and a voice which would have thundered round the world, he reduced the abbot to such a state of desperation that he did not know where he was. He then turned and began to abuse Velasco who, losing all patience, seized the abbot and, after belabouring him soundly, threw him on the floor at the feet of the Pope and cardinals. The Pope was highly indignant and, but for the interference of some of the cardinals, Velasco would have suffered heavily, as the Pope was strongly disposed to have him put in prison, so he narrowly escaped severe punishment. After this he retired to his house and only went forth by night to beg other cardinals and prelates to intercede with the Pope, who refused to listen to them. After much intercession, and having appeased the abbot as well as he could, Velasco began to suspect that he might come off even worse than the abbot, and it was only with difficulty that he contrived to get a pardon from the Pope. Indeed, in one way, the abbot had come off the better, for Velasco did not appear again in this cause.

When he left Florence Pope Eugenius tarried some time in Siena, and Velasco did the same. But when the Pope went on to Rome, Velasco did not propose to accompany him, for the last time he was there he, being handy with his fists, had quarrelled with certain Roman gentlemen and had given them some shrewd blows, so he was apprehensive that they would take their revenge on him. This affair had happened when Pope Martin died, when the Bishop of Tivoli, one of the heads of the government, had been put in charge of the castle of S. Angelo. Velasco gave out that he wanted to see him, and went thither and, because in time past the bishop, when, as is often the case with men of importance, refused to admit Velasco to an interview, Velasco now sought the bishop with a stick in his hand, and, when he found him in S. Angelo, he gave him a sound beating, saying, "Don't you remember that you once refused to be addressed by anyone, and made a mock of everybody, so now I give you a drubbing and a good stock of bruises so you may not forget it." I believe this affair was the reason why he suspected hostility in Rome. He remained at Siena, where he became popular and gained both credit and riches. He decided to stay there for some time.

One day, after he had been some months in Siena, he was arguing a case before the Signoria and broke into violent language, since he deemed he was right. Now it happened that he was opposed by another who was still more intemperate, so things came to such a pass that the Signoria threatened to have him thrown out of the window. He did his best to appease them till he should be out of their reach, and after he had left the court some of his friends warned him to depart in God's name or he would fare ill at the hands of the Signoria, whereupon he fled the city at once, leaving behind all his goods and several thousand florins and never halted till he came to the house of the friars of Scopeto near Florence. When he arrived here, he could not rest till he had put upon paper those opinions of his concerning the Signoria of Siena and their doings, which he had not been able to give them *viva voce*. So he wrote a long and most vituperative invective in elegant terms against them, which he sent to Siena and to all parts of Italy. To the learned this document commended itself highly as a most finished example of abuse. It was held to combine the eloquence of Tully with the vehemence of Demosthenes. He lost the greater part of

436

the possessions he left at Siena and this proved to be his undoing.

He next went to Florence and practised as advocate in the episcopal court with much success, for in this faculty few equalled him. As he lost a good part of his substance at Siena, was now old and in a strange country and separated from his kinsfolk, he began to think of resting and quitting his profession so that he might have a care for the salvation of his soul. A few of his books he had saved and these he sold for six hundred florins, which he handed over to his friend Guglielmo Tanagli, on condition that Tanagli should supply him with food for the rest of his life. He also reserved a few books and his raiment. One evening in Messer Tanagli's house he lamented the offences he had wrought to his Redeemer through never having known Him, or done any good whatever. His contrition was so great that he wept bitterly, and grieved especially about certain unjust gains he had made and now wished to reimburse. Messer Guglielmo, seeing that there was no remedy, gave him the best consolation he could, and asked whether anyone had ever taken money from him, referring to the twenty thousand florins seized by the King of Portugal from his father, and of the goods and money of his own confiscated by the Sienese. Velasco replied that what he had taken unjustly must be restored : as to his own losses he must bear them himself. Almighty God gave him abundant grace in bringing him to repentance : few have been so highly favoured. When he had determined to cut himself free from the world and to retire into a retreat, where he should only have to deal with religious folk, some one told him he had better go into Paradise at once, where he would find only the most religious of men and the holiest of women. He came to terms with some friars to give them a good part of what he had, provided they would maintain him in a house where he could read and pray and see to the salvation of his soul by repentance of his sins ; all this he did and found peace. He prayed and fasted often by day and night, confessed and abjured all intercourse with the world. He found the true grace of God, and became as humble as he had been arrogant. He confirmed all he met in their good works, and while he abode in this house wrote many devotional books I have not seen, and in the end yielded his spirit to God in the care of these holy men after taking the sacraments like a good Christian. God gave him grace by bringing him, worldly man as he was, to repent of his sins and to make a good end. The friars erected to his memory a marble tomb which stands by the door opposite to a crucifix.

VII: *PROEM AND SUPPLEMENTARY LIVES*

WRITTEN BY VESPASIANO TO THE LIFE OF ALESSANDRA DE'
BERNARDO DE' BARDI

To GIOVANNI DE' BARDI

THE strength of virtue is so great that it has always availed to arouse sympathy for those of the present, as well as those whom we have never seen. Now I have long known that you are gifted with all the qualities of a just man, and that you have maintained the generous traditions belonging to your house. I know that you have lived a long time in England, and that, on account of your seemly carriage and trustworthiness, the most serene King of that island, and all the nobles with whom you have had to do have taken your plain word for gospel truth; moreover, in the court of Rome your credit has stood as firm as in that distant isle. You followed the honourable calling of a merchant in transporting the goods of one land to another and selling them at a just profit. As to the management of a house which, according to Aristotle, is a republic in little; I have always remarked in yours the greatest seemliness of deed and speech, as well as a temperate and tranquil scheme of life and an observance of everything concerned with the Christian religion which is duly observed, and no opposition thereto permitted. The discussions held therein had nothing to do with empty frivolity, but with weighty subjects of the present or the past, or of the rule of popes, cardinals, kings or emperors; or the wonderful men of the Roman republic, compared with those of to-day. The same may be said of Florence which has surpassed all the other cities of Italy in distinguished citizens, in the seven liberal arts, in state government and in all beside. Your house has never lacked great men in military and civil service, or in the rule of the republic, for among the first magistrates appointed to rule the city there was one of your house. In spiritual affairs

439

it was the same : bishops and prelates have been chosen from it for other cities besides itself. Even in the days of Aquinas and Albertus Magnus, Roberto de' Bardi flourished at the University of Paris as a great philosopher and theologian ; so profound was his learning that, with the glance of the eye, he could detect faults in the writings of S. Thomas and Albertus Magnus. That this was in the times of these two great men is clearly proven, for some writers have recorded thus, " He impugned certain articles of Thomas Aquinas and of Albert of Cologne." This extract shows that Thomas had not been canonized and that Albert was not called " Magnus " till after his death.

The reputation of Roberto de' Bardi was so great that he was made Chancellor of the University of Paris, an office he held forty years. This is always given to the most distinguished member. With his deep learning and saintly life he, though a layman, was an example of holiness. He died and was buried at Paris, where his fame still lives. Your house has given to Florence many noble citizens who, through the want of recorders, are unknown ; and not merely great men, but great women as well—as great as any in Italy. A few evenings ago, when you, Alessandro de' Bardi, and I were together, and discussing the members of your house who had been examples of temperance and integrity, we praised, amongst others, Alessandra, daughter of Bardo de' Bardi and wife of Lorenzo the son of Palla Strozzi. We praised her as one not inferior to the Roman Sulpicia, nor to Porzia, daughter of Cato and wife of Marcus Brutus the defender of the Roman republic. Boccaccio honours them in his pages and describes them as the most illustrious women. Now though it is strange to me to write in polite fashion—as is due—I have done the best my feeble wit can compass in writing a Life of Alessandra, and the affection I bear you, rather than any aptitude on my part, has led me to undertake the province of an historian and compose this dissertation. Now that I have finished it I deem it right to send it to you as the chief of that house, the one who has brought it back to the dignity and welfare it enjoyed in former years. Accept it therefore from your most faithful friend who, if he had any more worthy offering, would certainly give it to you.

LIFE OF ALESSANDRA DE' BARDI

PROEM

To the Life of Alessandra de' Bardi

WRITTEN BY VESPASIANO

Forasmuch as all men are naturally eager for knowledge, those who are in the darkness of ignorance owe gratitude to learned men, seeing that all knowledge comes through them. See what S. Jerome writes in praise of righteous teaching, saying that the wise and learned are as stars in the midst of the heavenly firmament. Daniel also declares that the just shine like the sun. S. Simplicita affirms that simplicity and ignorance are only good when they are holy, that they are less beneficial to those possessed by them than hurtful to others. Consider what evils may arise from them when they are not holy, as is often the case! Ingnorance indeed is the source of all worldly evil. But writers have brought enlightenment, especially those of past times. The Greeks had writers in every branch of knowledge, noting down the history of other lands as well as of their own. Plutarch, that most exact of writers, gave forty-eight Lives; half of Greeks and half of Latins, always comparing a Greek with a Latin. Up to the present day they only existed in Greek, but are now rendered into Latin by Messer Lionardo and others. He also wrote Lives of illustrious Greek women to save them from oblivion, and this book of illustrious women has been translated by Alamanno Rinuccini, a learned scholar. The Latins also had certain biographers, Suetonius, author of the Lives of the twelve Cæsars, Æmilius Probus wrote short Lives of outlanders, Cornelius Nepos wrote of Atticus and Cato, Pliny wrote succinctly a volume, *De viris illustribus*, Œlius Spartianus and others wrote Lives of the emperors, ineptly enough because, in the civil commotion and warfare during the Empire, power was seized by a nefarious set of adventurers in place of the worthy citizens of the Roman republic, and in this turmoil there was no inducement to men of worth to devote themselves to letters. All these evils arose from civil broils, for there are no worse foes to a state than promoters of abuses and revolution. Cornelius Tacitus wrote a fragmentary history

PROEM AND SUPPLEMENTARY LIVES

containing a Life of Nero and other emperors. This age is obscurely known through the lack of writers for several centuries, as is shown in the case of Messer Lionardo's history of Florence, when he went searching for information. Then after several centuries came Dante, that great philosopher and theologian and Latin scholar. Then Petrarch and Boccaccio, and these three revived the Latin tongue which had been neglected for many centuries. Petrarch made a collection of the Lives of illustrious men and wrote the Lives of several popes and emperors. Boccaccio wrote a book called *De' casi avversi degli nomini illustri*, which came down to Walter Duke of Athens,* Lord of Florence. This treats of the disorders during his rule of ten months and eighteen days. Next the life of Dante by Boccaccio in very elegant Italian and a volume, *Della donne illustri*, in Latin in order that women might not be forgotten, beginning with Eve. Colluccio Salutati, a learned scholar, improved the Latin style by his writing, but left no biography. Messer Lionardo d' Arezzo carried the movement still farther, as may be seen from his writings and translations. From S. Jerome, S. Ambrose, S. Augustine, S. Gregory and Bede there had been no writers until Messer Lionardo. S. Cyprian was a fine writer, but he lived more than a hundred years before S. Jerome. Orontius translated twenty-five homilies by S. Chrysostom on Matthew, and Messer Lionardo was one of the first to translate Greek into Latin. He rendered seven Lives by Plutarch in fine style; also he wrote the Life of Tully, not being satisfied with Plutarch's treatment. He translated the Ethics, the Politics and the Œconomics of Aristotle and seven Orations of Demosthenes and several works of Plato, besides other works all in excellent manner. Then came Friar Ambrogio, a man learned in Greek and Hebrew, as fine a Latin scholar as Messer Lionardo, as will appear from his translations, such as Diogenes Laetius' *Della vita e costumi de' Filosofi*. He was a great light in religion and in learning—the second of the translators. The son of a peasant of Portici in Romagna, he entered the Monastery degli Angioli as a youth and became a great scholar. This monastery was then the centre of all the religion and learning in Florence. Then came Messer Poggio, apostolic

* Walter de Brienne, a Norman adventurer from Greece, 1342.

secretary and learned in Greek and Latin, who wrote and made divers works and translations, amongst which were *Della varietà della fortuna*, a book of the Lives and vicissitudes of great men, and a Life of Cyrus, King of Persia: Messer Giannozzo Manetti, the ornament of his age, who enjoyed all the high offices the republic could give and brought the greatest honour to the state. I never knew a man more respected by high and low on account of his virtues. He was the most learned classical scholar of his century, because he was the first in this material age to approach and to master the difficult study of philosophy. At the request of Agnolo Acciaiuoli and others he lectured on Aristotle's *Ethics;* also on a portion of the *Politics* with Jacopo da Lucca, afterwards Cardinal of Pavia, and read the whole of the Natural and Moral Philosophy to Manuello Ebreo, who in turn read to him the whole of the Bible and the comment thereon in Hebrew, of which he had complete knowledge. Pope Nicolas, then Bishop of Bologna, was in Florence on his way to Savoy to put an end to the schism, in the year when he was made cardinal and Pope, spake to me thus: One evening when Giannozzo had been to visit him at his lodgings and was about to leave, Nicolas insisted in leaving the room with him and descended more than thirty steps of the staircase ; but even this was not enough, for he insisted on going half-way back with him to the astonishment of the gaping crowd who have no regard for good manners. When he came back into the house he turned to me and said, " Vespasiano, you are amazed at the honour I have done to Messer Giannozzo this evening. I have done it on account of his fine qualities of which I have had long experience, and especially on account of a recent mission to Pope Eugenius, about which the Pope and cardinals were greatly displeased. He, however, carried out his mission so well that they completely changed their view, which was a great feat. His fine parts would have fitted a citizen of Rome at her greatest." Giannozzo translated the Psalter from the Hebrew, and from the Greek all the moral works of Aristotle, besides writing the Lives of Socrates, Seneca, Petrarch, Boccaccio and of Pope Nicolas who, when he left Florence for Rome, made him secretary with a salary of a hundred ducats a year. When Pope Nicolas died, King

Alfonso sent for him and gave him nine hundred ducats a year. You Florentine citizens should teach your children arithmetic as soon as they are born : there are many accomplishments you do not esteem because you do not understand them. He also wrote a set of Lives of illustrious men, who had passed sixty, down to the time of Nicolao Nicoli, also a Life of Philip of Macedon and of King Alfonso which he left incompleted. Next came Messer Donato Acciaiuoli of a noble house whom I name for his virtues, well known to the whole of Italy. Donato was one of the lights of his state and safeguarded the fame and fortune of his family. He enriched his country and his house by his learning and his knowledge of Greek, Latin and philosophy, as may be seen by his translations from Greek into Latin. These include the Lives of Homer and Demetrius, which had been omitted by Messer Lionardo, and others, and also the Life of Alcibiades. All were done in the finest style and show his wonderful learning. He wrote commentaries on all Aristotle's works and exhibited the conclusions of the philosopher. They were left incomplete at his death. We may see from these that, besides being a master of the Greek language, he had thoroughly comprehended the doctrines of Aristotle. He wrote Lives of Hannibal and Scipio Africanus, which had never been done before, also one of Charlemagne. These works have given him a lasting renown. By his comments he cleared moral philosophy of much of its obscurity, so that anyone who reads it now will find it much easier than did the student of past ages. I cannot omit a saying of the illustrious Duke of Urbino which I once heard when he was lamenting Donato's death. " His death has been a misfortune not only to his city, but to the whole of Italy, on account of his distinguished virtues." I know of no other modern biographers or historians, since many lettered men are incapable of composition, wherefore we owe gratitude to all these writers, for without their work the lives of many great men would have been unknown. Men who have been brought up in easy conditions are stronger than women, who require more care and advice. I have been unjustly accused of maligning women, but I have never spoken ill of virtuous women who devote themselves to their children and follow the rules given by S. Paul. The first is that they bring up their children in the fear of God, and the second that they keep quiet in church, and I would add that they stop talking in other places as well, for they cause much mischief thereby—and men do the same. Many women encourage their daughters to disregard S. Paul's directions, but they are mistaken in thinking they win approbation, even though they speak well. This sort I blame and always shall, for their daughters, educated in this fashion, bring ruin to any house they enter by marriage. I wish to show that virtuous women please me, so I will write the Lives of certain women of Florence who may be reckoned equal to those of antiquity, and as an example to present times will write the Life of a most noble lady who combined all the virtues, so that she may be a mirror to all the women of to-day. She excelled all others in beauty of mind and body, having been born of one of the noblest houses in the city. and married to a husband aş well born as herself. Her fortune ought to have brought her the highest earthly happiness, but the worst of misfortunes befell her and those she loved with the greatest constancy. Now let all women read her Life and follow her example and win the favour of God.

ALESSANDRA DE' BARDI*

Alessandra de' Bardi was a daughter of Messer Alessandro de' Bardi, as noble a family as any in Florence, especially distinguished for the many illustrious men it has produced, and still produces, and of women no less. Her father was greatly esteemed, and received every honour which the republic can give to its citizens. Her mother was a Rinuccini, also of a noble family and respected for her many virtues, especially for the care she gave to the education of her family, as is shown in the case of Alessandra, for with her and the other children she followed the practice of past times.

Alessandra was generously gifted by nature and beautiful beyond all the other maidens of Florence. She was so tall that she rarely wore street shoes; indeed, she was taller than any other lady of the city. Her mother began her training

* Macchiavelli, *Flor. Hist.*, p. 341, writes of an Alessandra de' Bardi, who was married to Raffaelo, son of Agnolo Acciaiuoli.

as soon as she was born, and when she came to the age of discretion followed the practice of that noble Christian lady, S. Pagola Romana, born of the house of Scipio Africanus, who brought up so fine a family that she became an example to all the world. She trained Alessandra in Christian ways, and in all usages a modest girl ought to observe, teaching her psalms and prayers, and, above all, the love and fear of God, the first consideration of all. Thus she set her in the ways of right living, and having done so much she would never allow her to waste her time, for she knew that for men and women alike there is no worse ill than idleness. Amongst other habits she was not suffered to address any servant except in her mother's presence, and this salutary teaching led her to avoid the servants' outlook and their habits. It would be well if the women of our time would take similar care, for from this practice many unseemly results ensue. She taught her all that a gentlewoman ought to know, the control of a household, and especially needlework of all kinds in silk and in all kinds of stuffs. In this respect she had many examples, such as the Emperor Octavian, who let his daughters learn weaving, and when asked his reason replied, " I am now an Emperor ; to-morrow I may be dead and who knows whether my children will have a coin left, so they must learn an art by which they could live if need comes." Now most children are reared in the belief the world cannot fail them, but how often are they deceived ! Charlemagne also followed Octavian's practice and was not ashamed. Alessandra was not provided with a troop of servants, as is the present custom with young girls, who demand excessive service at home, and when they marry ruin their husbands by the debts they make to pay for their luxuries. Her mother saw that she learned everything necessary for household economy, so that in her own house she might show she had been educated by a wise mother, that she could practise as well as preach, and rule her house herself, instead of leaving it to servants who, as I have noticed, are the last to rise in the morning. Many of our most prominent citizens will rise early and search the house throughout to see whether it is in order or not. I have known many ladies who were most thorough housekeepers, notably Madonna Nanna, daughter of Bartolomeo Valori, a citizen of repute, and wife to Giannozzo Pandolfini. She, indeed, was the highest example of a good housewife ; witness the excellent education she gave to her sons and daughters. Under her wise rule her house, her possessions and her children became a temple dedicated to God, of fasting, and prayer, and almsgiving. After managing her house, all her time was well spent. She visited the sick and poor, and made them tell her their wants ; in short, no one ever came to her house and went away without succour. I note this so as not to omit an example to other women, which may teach them not to talk too much, for her words were few, and to the point. God kept her house from all calamity on account of her worth, and, as long as she lived, it prospered.

I also knew a lady of noble birth, Madonna Francesca, married on account of her virtues to one of the richest men in Florence. Afterwards, through misfortune and through civil strife, of which our city has known too much, he had to leave his country for a foreign land. His wife would never desert him, but determined to share his ill-fortune, as she had shared his prosperity. A still greater grief befell her while she was yet young, for her husband died a rebel and in exile, and only one child remained. She went to live in Rome in the house of her brother-in-law, who was one of the first in the College of Cardinals, and was kindly received by him. She was the most beautiful woman of her time, but her mental gifts were still finer, so that she became a pattern for all the women of her age. She devoted all her youth to the education of her son, and cared for nought else.

Let young widows take note that they may be the prop of the house. After she had been some time in Rome, the cardinal sent her back to Florence, for he had contrived, by his influence, to preserve for her certain property and many houses, although her husband had been a rebel. At this time the cardinal died and the youth inherited great riches, and was known as the wealthiest, the most noble, the most seemly and talented youth in the city. When the time came for him to marry he could choose any maiden he would, so he took the daughter of the foremost citizen, who was also rich and of high birth. By this lady he had four beautiful children, two boys and two girls. But there was laid upon this young man an insupportable tax, which absorbed a great part of his wealth, and he was obliged to seek another country, where he could live appropriately to his condition. His kinsfolk possessed large territories in Greece, therefore he retired thither. He died suddenly and left his young wife with four children. As she wished to marry again, and to reclaim her dowry, which was large, she arranged that her children should be given into the charge of their grandmother, of whom I have already spoken as a lady of wonderful parts, who had been the mainstay of the house while her son was living in Florence and afterwards.

The repayment of the dowry consumed almost all the estate, and left an income of only five hundred florins for the grand-mother, the grandchildren and the nurse. Although she had been accustomed to many servants she willingly reduced her establishment, and even worked with her own hands and made the two girls do their share. She brought them up honourably and supplied all their wants, and kept together the whole of their patrimony. She married the two girls, and educated the youths so well that they ranked with the best in the city. It was only the wisdom and prudence of this lady which saved the house from ruin. The women of our time might well imitate this illustrious lady (whose name for good reasons I suppress), and follow her example as did the mother of Alessandra, who, when she found herself in evil conditions, took as a pattern not only the women of antiquity, but those of her own day. It seems as if God taught her to walk in the steps of this illustrious lady when she also suffered a like mis-fortune. She also followed the steps of Carilla Romana, the wife of Tarquinius Priscus, who thought it no shame to spin wool for clothing ; this was reckoned honourable labour in the days of the Roman republic, before Asiatic luxury had brought it to destruction, as it did in old times and may again. This noble dame became so famous in the republic that she was cited as an example for all Roman women, so much so, that when young girls were about to marry, all claimed her name ; and when they entered the house of their husbands, they always gave the name of Carilla in answer to the enquiry as to how they were called.

Alessandra was eager to learn all those duties which are

distasteful to many girls of our time, who think it disgraceful to do aught except self-adornment and think of nothing else. Her mother searched the past and present for knowledge in order that Alessandra might be completely trained as a modest girl. She taught her reading, then the office of the Madonna, which she was obliged to repeat every day and to return thanks to Almighty God, and to the glorious Virgin Mary seven times in the seven hours. She was seldom seen either at the window or at the door, because she found her pleasures in more useful matters. Her mother took her out nearly every morning to hear early mass, with covered head and face scarcely to be seen.

On feast days, when she was young, she was taken to certain convents of holy women, where she might find an example of virtue in their constant acts of devotion. She did not bear herself like many of the women of our time, who, instead of holding converse with holy women, spend the nights in dancing and in other vanities, and take infinite pains over the choice of their dancing masters, and think more of letting their feet move exactly in time with the music than of aught else. Indeed, they are content to be known for these vanities, and care nothing for a modest and reputable way of life ; I should be ashamed to write of some of their ways and habits. Alessandra's mother would have countenanced none of these doings, for she had determined not to bring up her daughter for passing vanities, but to take care that she occupied her time over gathering the knowledge which was fitting for a modest damsel. When Alessandra was fourteen years old she was known for her good manners and carriage ; she had a beauty both of body and of mind unequalled by any young girl of her age, everyone spoke of her and everyone praised her. In addition to all I have said of her, she was of noble birth on both sides, and she was always held up as a model of excellence to all the citizens. At this time there was living in Florence Messer Palla di Noferi degli Strozzi, a man of noble birth and gifted with all those qualities which become a gentleman, indeed, that most distinguished man, Messer Lionardo,* used to say that the happiest man of his age was Messer Palla, for he had everything that makes for happiness in this life, was highly

* Lionardo d'Arezzo.

449

gifted in mind and body, a fine scholar in Greek and Latin, alert in intellect. His family of sons and daughters was the finest and the most gracious in Florence. The men learned scholars and gentlemen, the women, brought up under the care of Madonna Marietta, the most distinguished woman of his time. He married his daughters to the leading citizens, and the race is still extant ; it has been, and still is, the chief honour of our city. He had riches in other parts, greater than those of any other citizen, he was most popular in the state, and on this account all the honours which can be bestowed upon a citizen, both at home and abroad, were given to him. He went on all the chief missions, and in these he reaped honours both for his country and himself. In my time he engaged Messer Giovanni da Imola, a very learned man, as instructor to his sons. When these youths went about the city there was no need to ask whose sons they were, for everyone knew that by the look of them.

It was through Messer Palla that Greek literature and numerous Greek books were brought into Italy by Manuello Grisolora ; the greater part of the cost being paid by him. Afterwards he procured from Greece many other books ; he purchased at Constantinople the Greek cosmography in manuscript with illustrations. It may also be said that he was the first to reveal the Latin language, for, if Manuello had not come over, neither Lionardo Aretino, nor Friar Ambrogio, nor Guerino, nor any one of the other learned men would ever have arisen. All honour to Messer Palla as the cause of all the good which ensued !

The eldest of Messer Palla's sons was Lorenzo, a goodly youth, and he wished his son to marry, for the time had now come for him to take a wife. He looked about amongst his friends and kinsfolk for the most suitable match in the city, as was the custom. At this time, in 1428, Florence was most flourishing ; a long time had elapsed since any disturbance, and the citizens were ostentatious, ambitious and well-to-do. Alessandra was now of an age meet for holy matrimony, and all the kinsfolk and friends of Messer Palla agreed that Lorenzo should choose her as the best match in all the city. Because it was Messer Palla's part to choose a wife for his son, he approached Messer Bardo, her father, as to the alliance ; the circumstances on both sides were equally satisfactory, whereupon the match was settled with the greatest satisfaction to both families, and all the city was loud in the praise of it. Lorenzo at once went to see the damsel, and the two met in seemly modest fashion, as was the custom at that time. Not like most of the betrothals of to-day, which are not true matrimony, but unions which would be rated lewd and unseemly, even amongst the basest.

At this time the Emperor Sigismund went to Rome for his coronation. Pope Eugenius IV was then in Florence, a city in which the laws denied entrance to Pope, or King, or Emperor without leave ; wherefore the Emperor went on to Siena, and sent to Florence as ambassadors four of the chief noblemen he had about him. He had indeed a noble train, for besides the Imperial court the King of Hungary was there. These gentlemen were also curious to see the city itself, which at this time was full of splendour and riches and famous throughout the world. They were received with the highest honour by the Signoria, and by all the citizens, who showed them all possible courtesy and, in order to entertain them and let them see the most accomplished and seemly ladies and the most goodly youths of the city, they determined to give a ball on the Piazza dei Signori, where was constructed a platform, stretching from the lion of the Piazza as far as the Mercatanzia. Steps led up to this platform, and there were seats from the corner of the Mercatanzia as far as the corner which leads into the Garbo, and espaliers festooned with carpets and the finest tapestries. They arranged that the noblest youths of the city should be placed in order, uniformly dressed in rich green cloth trimmed with fur as far as their stockings. They invited a great crowd of the young women of Florence finely dressed, most beautiful and seemly in body and mind, splendidly decked with pearls and jewels, wonderful to behold. Their dresses were not cut low in the neck as they are to-day, but cut high in a fair and modest fashion. Amongst these ladies, Alessandra, who was reckoned the comeliest of all, was placed beside the chief of the ambassadors. Her companion in this honour was Francesca, daughter of Antonio di Salvestro Serristori, the rest were duly placed amongst the company. In this year Alessandra had been betrothed, and when she and her young companions stood up to dance, the ambassadors were also invited to join, and the grace with which Alessandra danced was a marvel to all beholders; indeed, everything she did was well done. After they had danced for some time a choice feast was served, an unaccustomed feature in entertainments of this kind. On account of her dexterity Alessandra was chosen to take a dish full of sweetmeats and bear it to the ambassadors, with a napkin of fine linen on her shoulder. She offered it to them most gracefully, curtseying to the ground as if she had never done anything else in her life, whereat the ambassadors and all those around were greatly delighted. After the sweetmeats she handed them glasses of wine in like manner, and all this she did as to the manner born, showing how carefully she had been trained by her accomplished mother, who had taught her well even in the smallest things. After feasting and more dancing the ambassadors rose to depart, as the hour was late, and they left, accompanied by a great number of citizens together with the young people of the feast. Alessandra and the most beautiful and noble of the young women walked on either side of the chief ambassador, she holding his right hand and her companion his left. They went with the ambassadors to the inn where they lodged, and then the first ambassador took from his finger a beautiful ring and gave it to Alessandra, and gave a second ring to her companion. The young people having bidden farewell to the ambassadors, the youths accompanied the ladies to their houses. After the great honour that had been done to the ambassadors they longed to return to Siena and tell the Emperor what they had seen; they told him of their doings, praising greatly the city itself and its seemly ladies, especially naming Alessandra, for her charming manners and her great beauty. The Emperor made an effort to visit Florence, but found it impossible, and for this reason he continued his journey greatly angered towards the city, as appeared from his subsequent action.

Alessandra lived in her father's house from 1428 until her marriage in 1432. During that time the plague broke out in Florence. Her heart was firmly set to love her husband only, to cleave to him faithfully, and, if widowed, to refuse second marriage. In this respect she followed the example of Portia,

ALESSANDRA DE' BARDI

the daughter of Cato of Utica and wife of Marcus Brutus, the saviour of the Roman republic. Alessandra was as steadfast in mind as Portia when evil fate befell her. In 1432 she was married with a splendid feast in her father's house, as was the custom. There was also rich feasting in the house of the bridegroom, and the greater part of the city was entertained at a generous public banquet. She had never been allowed to go about the city until she came to her husband's house, and when she went out she was always accompanied by the elder ladies of the house, not as is the custom now, when young girls are suffered to go where they please with only the escort of a servant. Such doings would have been deemed unseemly in those days, as no lady of rank ever went abroad except in the company of one of her kinsfolk.

But soon afterwards a noble youth, handsome in person, but with an ill-directed mind, was attracted by her beauty and, like the giddy wastrel that he was, became enamoured of her and pursued her, knowing nought of the vows of constancy which she had made. This youth told me, after he had undertaken this difficult task, that he could never sway her mind ; she always remained as hard as a diamond, and whenever he happened to be in her presence she never looked at him. Alessandra tried hard to let him see how foolish and flighty he was, like all other youths who are given up to pleasures and lechery ; she did all she could to cure him of this obsession, but the more she tried the more violent his passion became. Her husband, who was told everything, laughed at the matter, for he was secure of the constancy of his high-minded lady. In the course of time Alessandra, according to her usage, went to the monastery of San Giorgio, occupied by religious women of the Order of St. Francis, accompanied by two elderly ladies of her household. From her childhood she had been accustomed to visit these holy women. Now this youth, overcome by his passion, and uninfluenced by all the tokens which Alessandra had shown, watched her return from the monastery ; he waited for her concealed in a turn of the street, and as she passed, went down on his knees and held out a naked knife to her, but she turned from him feigning not to see him, whereupon he cried, " Since you will not look at me, take this knife and kill me." She took no notice of his words, and indignant at his presumption went on her way without a word.

Alessandra in this adventure proved herself superior not only to her whole female sex and the women of her own time, but to those who came after her, for these plume themselves when their beauty is praised, and they find themselves the cynosure of all foolish amorous youths. These have no desire to imitate the constancy of the ancient Romans. This youth, finding that Alessandra was obdurate, soon after abandoned the pursuit.

Alessandra's good fortune lasted but a short time, because in 1433, the year after her marriage, came the revolution in the state. Messer Palla, like a peaceful citizen, refused to take part therein. Before another year had passed came fresh changes, for in 1434 that illustrious citizen, Cosimo de' Medici, who had been banished in 1433 was recalled. These two revolutions were the ruin of the state, for in the last many of the most noble citizens were banished, and amongst these was Bardo, the father of Alessandra. Envy, the enemy of all that is good, must needs strike also Messer Palla, a man of extraordinary merit. At these two blows of ill-fortune Alessandra was confounded; she now imitated the King of Nineveh, in the first place she commended herself to God, she then stripped herself of her wedding garb, and, having clothed herself in black, threw herself at the feet of the Crucified like the Magdalen, with prayers, and sighs, and tears she prayed God to grant patience to her afflicted father, and mother, and husband. After Messer Palla was banished, she went herself and sent others to divers holy places to pray to God, that, in this bitter sorrow, He would grant them patience. The unhappy Alessandra had only just passed her twentieth year when she was thus smitten by adverse fortune. Let us consider the condition of this unfortunate girl; when she went to her father's house, she found him and her mother in the deepest grief; she saw her father driven into exile at the time when he was longing to rest in his beloved country, with his kinsfolk and friends, seeing that he had come to an age when men yearn especially for quiet. Now he had to seek a home in an unknown country, and leave his property in the fatherland from which he was exiled, and being of gentle birth he

ALESSANDRA DE' BARDI

was unaccustomed to earn his living ; neither was he rich as were many others of his class. He was forced to seek another country and to become the laughing-stock of Fortune. Let everyone try to imagine the state of mind of this noble citizen, of his wife and of Alessandra.

Added to all these misfortunes the unhappy sisters of Alessandra, who were unmarried, wept and cried aloud, " What will become of us ? In whose care will you leave us ? " Everywhere was grief, especially when she thought of her noble father with his sixty-six years, forced to abandon the land he loved. And now he had to seek a home in a strange country. Messer Palla remained in exile for twenty-six years, living an upright and quiet life and an example to all the world. He never spoke ill of his country, and would never listen to those who vituperated it. He spent his time in honest fashion with only one or two in the house ; the most distinguished men sought his company, Giovanni Argiropolo and other learned Greeks visited him. He wrote constant themes in Greek, and translated many of the sacred writings, and after his death many were found which had not been revised. Messer Palla would have been no unworthy citizen of the Roman republic when it was at its highest glory. In Padua, where he abode, he was held in such reverence that he could never walk abroad without receiving tokens of the greatest respect. All, small and great, took off their caps to him, contrary to the Florentine usage. He did not become, like Coriolanus, hostile to his country, and there was no need to send ambassadors, or priests, or his mother, or his wife to exhort him to refrain from his attacks on his fatherland, for he always worked for its honour and good fame, and spoke in the same strain. He died in exile, which was several times prolonged, at the age of ninety-two, healthy both in body and mind.

As to Lorenzo, left in Florence under conditions which may be imagined, he was thrown about, now here now there, by the blows of ill-fortune. And he fared as those fare who have no one to care for them, or, if any address them they speak as if they were Jews, or excommunicate, or worse. While this was his fate, his poor young wife, finding herself bereft of all aid, turned to Almighty God, and to the glorious Virgin Mary,

455

with prayer and fasting ; she fasted throughout Lent and on all the appointed days. Her husband seldom returned home without a tale of some fresh insult which had been put upon him, and the two mourned together. She consoled him the best she could, and so as not to sadden him yet more she forced herself to appear as cheerful as she might, declaring that they must be patient, and that, through adversity, they would be brought to know God better than in prosperity, and thus she lessened somewhat the burden of his grief.

Alessandra did not follow the way of the wife of Tully, whose lamentations her husband found more intolerable than exile itself, for she determined that she herself would be his comfort and refuge. Let all those who would take a wife look at her way of life and character, and not merely at her dowry as is the custom with most ; let him seek in his wife the virtues of Alessandra, so that his fate may not be that of Tully, who, when he returned from exile, had to live apart. The law of Lycurgus was a just one, for it forbade the giving of dowries, so that men might regard good wifely qualities and not money. Learn from that philosopher who, when he was questioned by one about to marry what sort of wife he should choose, answered that he should choose a maiden sprung from a chaste mother and a chaste grandmother.

Meantime Lorenzo in Florence did not realise that a more cruel stroke of fate than that of 1438 could befall him, but now his enemies plotted to banish him also so as to rid them of his presence. He had now three children, two boys and one girl, with no expectation of more. After the decree of exile was passed, a messenger was sent one evening to his house and announced the decree to him in the presence of Alessandra. The unhappy woman stood for some time speechless at this third blow of fortune, even more cruel than death ; a blow which pierced her to the heart and dazed her brain. In their bitter grief both were silent. Lorenzo, after a long pause, turned to Alessandra and thus addressed her : " Alessandra, since it is the will of God that I must quit the country where I was born, for no fault of my own, and leave my children and you, my most beloved wife : you who since we have been married have never vexed me in the smallest matter. Now you see that Fate is leading me to some place

ALESSANDRA DE' BARDI

in a strange land ; my unhappy fate thus wills it. Stay here, my beloved wife ; you know how we both of us love our children whom I must now abandon. There are three great griefs in my mind : to be an exile from my country, to be parted from my children, and to be parted from you, which is not the least of these. I must go forth alone and leave my children to you, also the charge of saving for them the small remnant of my estate which remains to us, also I pray that the fatherland which is now denied to me may not be denied to them. Now be content and bow to God's will. As to our separation by exile, our bodies only are divided, our souls will still be united." Here Alessandra might have acted like Carilla Romana by concealing her husband somewhere in the house.

Then she replied, " Your exile is the worst evil I could have foreseen. Death would mean one blow, but now I must die every day, and I have also to mourn the loss of my father and mother, so no one is left to help me. I will spend my days over duty, but I shall be tossed about like a ship in a storm and helpless in my wretched plight." Here she was overcome by her sighs and tears, but she restrained them as well as she could so as not to add to his affliction. Lorenzo answered, " I have no doubt of your constancy, and the greatest comfort I shall find in adversity is to know that you are patient."

When the day came for Lorenzo to quit Alessandra and his children, the house was full of mourning. All constant wives and husbands will know what pangs these luckless ones must have felt at this hour. They could not restrain their grief. Let anyone calmly consider the cruel separation of these two, bound together as they were by the purest love, without knowing if they would ever meet again. Oh, tragedy of life ! How great and how brief had been their happiness ! In 1432 she was married, in 1434 her father was exiled, and shortly afterwards her husband followed him, all the residue of her life must needs be passed in want and affliction.

After the exile of Lorenzo, she devoted herself to the education of her children, and in employment to add to the slender income which remained to her. Another most worthy lady was her companion in misfortune, her husband being also an exile. This was Madonna Caterina, the wife of Piero di Neri, one of the Strozzi family. These two ladies won the highest respect and spent their lives on good works.

It was not long before fresh misfortunes fell upon Alessandra ; the first was the death of her mother, a very noble lady, and then that of her father exiled and separated from his friends and kinsfolk. Let us consider her case in this fresh access of disaster, robbed of all aid and comfort. She was truly a Job in patience, and indeed patience was needed, for now after the death of her father and her mother she could hardly expect any new afflictions.

But Fortune had not yet done with her, but was fain to treat her as fire treats gold by refining her through adversity. She left Florence and went to Gubbio, Lorenzo's place of exile. A noble citizen of Gubbio had appointed Lorenzo as governor of one of his sons, who needed discipline and direction to restrain him from falling into evil ways, as many young men are prone to do. But this vicious youth, not content with ordinary outlay, and inclined to scatter his money with both hands, thwarted Lorenzo whenever he tried by word or by deed to curb him, and took a hostile attitude towards him. At last, instigated by the devil he determined to kill him rather than submit to guidance. Lorenzo thought only of this young man's good, and never suspected that he contemplated such a wicked deed. One day, however, like an infuriated madman he carried out his wicked intent and slew Lorenzo unawares in the streets of Gubbio.

Alessandra never expected such a sudden blow, never thought that his death would come otherwise than by the course of nature ; as soon as she heard what had happened she nearly died herself. Surely it was impossible that further adversity could befall her. She turned to Almighty God in grief which was almost inarticulate, and after many sighs she cried, " O miserable that I am ! after enduring my husband's exile, the exile and death of my father and mother, the exile of Messer Palla who was as a father to me, I never thought to see my beloved husband come to such a death as this, nor to see my unfortunate children deprived first of their country and then of their father by outrage. And what adds sorrow to sorrow is that I and my children are away

458

from home and bereft of all consolation. Death, O God, would be better than life in these conditions."

Her children and her friends did all they could to console her, exhibiting to her other examples of calamity, but their task was an impossible one. Bewailing her fate she cried, " If God wept human tears over the sorrows of the sisters of Lazarus, why should not I in my unhappiness weep also? This grief is mine alone. And if the religion in which I have been educated, and have always observed, did not forbid me to take my life, I should act like Portia, the wife of Brutus, who, when she heard of the death of her husband, took a live coal from the fire and thrust it down her throat. If I may not do this lest I should offend my Creator I must needs weep. As S. Augustine said after the death of S. Monica, his mother, that his grief was so great that the fountain of tears was exhausted, and his eyes had become dry. Or, as S. Jerome writes of S. Pagola Romana, whose husband died a natural death, how she, being a saintly woman, died of grief and tears. Now that my husband Lorenzo has perished by violence, what forbids me to weep? As I can no longer endure this immensurable grief, why should I wish to live, I who have passed my life in tears and sorrow, with all my days darkened by misfortune? Who would have believed that the most prosperous house in Florence should in such brief time suffer so great a change? Let the citizens beware, though good fortune seems to wait upon them now, lest calamity should be near at hand, for this is the drift of all mortal affairs."

She went on, " My one hope is that death will soon release me from all my sorrows, and may God Almighty forgive me my sins."

Her unhappy children did what they could to console her, without success; indeed, they themselves were also in need of consolation. Having composed herself she invoked God and the glorious Virgin Mary, and after her prayers she felt she had reconciled herself with God's will and had found patience. Her mind began to recover and she prayed devoutly:

" Almighty God, who out of nothing hast created everything, the heavens, the angels, the earth, men, the sea, the fishes and everything else which serves men's need ; also the human race, which, on account of disobedience of the first man, had been damned eternally, was so mercifully redeemed by the death of Thy only Son. And after graciously allowing mankind to participate in Thy everlasting bliss. I, thy humble hand-maiden, beg Thee, by the majesty of Thy holy name, to show grace to one of the least of Thy servants, to have mercy on my husband, and forgive his sins and take him into paradise, the sure refuge of the blessed, and give me leave to live as long as Thy mercy shall allow, and to forgive my sins and give me strength to bear my misfortunes without offence to Thee."

This is the service a chaste woman should offer over the death of her husband, according to S. Paul's words; to shun delights and fine clothing; to avoid delicate dishes and spend her time in prayer and fasting, like the prophetess Anna, daughter of Samuel the prophet, who, after her husband's death, fasted and prayed till she died at eighty-four. This was her life for sixty years and it was so acceptable to God that she was rewarded by the sight of God incarnate in the hands of Simeon. She was truly a pattern to widows, and Alessandra took her as a model, as may be seen from her Life. She devoted her life to her children and lived according to S. Paul's directions and as a widow for the most of her life. S. Paul says that those who live in pleasure are dead to God, but without it they will live in Him. S. Paul also divides true widows from false. What shall I say about garments lined with black fur or cloth, or miniver, of which I am ashamed to speak! They know not God, and when He speaks to them they heed Him not. Let them obey His commands, and let them ascertain whether, in the lifetime of her husband, Alessandra ever heeded such base vanities. Her cloak was quite plain, her dress high up to her neck, as becomes a widow, with a veil over her eyes. The widows of our time might well follow this excellent lady who gave so striking an instance of purity. She cared little as to what she ate, and never changed her purpose of denying a second marriage. Her affairs obliged her to visit divers parts of Tuscany. She lived a widow for fourteen years after Lorenzo's death, and before this they were living for some time apart. In her widow's life she made her model Madonna Caterina degli Alberti, a lady who realised S. Paul's idea of a true widow. She was wife of Piero, son of Filippo Corsini, of a noble house. They were married when she was fifteen, and after a year and eleven months her husband died, leaving her a widow with two children. She lived for sixty years in widowhood. She had a good knowledge of letters and studied the lives of the women of the Old Testament especially, also of the prophetess Anna. O wonderful power and wisdom of God ! how great is their force that they should be able to bring this young beautiful high-born woman, rich and talented, to this resolve never to marry again ! She was young and subject to youthful desires, which she would fain subdue, so she always wore a garment of coarse fabric, she never slept in a bed, but on one bare mattress. She never went to bed except when ill or infirm. Further, to subdue the flesh, she fasted on all the appointed vigils and during Lent, also Advent. To avoid idleness, the cause of all evil, she spent her time in repeating the offices and the breviary. She drew great comfort from her Bible, besides homilies on all the Gospels, which she read day after day as appointed, and other expositions by holy writers of old. She spent all her time in good works and gave freely to the poor and to others who were ashamed to beg.

Her house was kept like a well-ordered convent, and during the exile of her brothers she endeavoured to cause the ban against them to be removed and, so great was the influence she exercised through her worth, that she rarely failed in her attempt, and in due time the brothers were recalled. She had no children of her own, but certain nephews whom she nurtured from their infancy. She educated them well under tutors and managed excellently the estates of her brothers and her own, living a frugal life. She rarely left the house except to hear mass. Her clothes were suitable to widowhood and her face was always covered. The women of our time should take as a model this excellent lady, and act as did Alessandra de' Bardi. I put her here as an example because, as she had to bear with the exile of her brothers as Alessandra had to endure that of her kinsfolk, I thought it meet to include her with the others whom Alessandra imitated. Lorenzo died at Gubbio in 1451. Alessandra then lived partly in Florence and partly in Bologna. Afterwards she went to Ferrara, where also were Gian Francesco and his children, and then to the Badia di Pulesone.

PROEM AND SUPPLEMENTARY LIVES

Having been driven about by fate for so many years, she now settled in this spot and devoted herself to her children, especially to her excellent daughter, the wife of a gentleman named Theophilo, a man of property. After her long misfortune it now pleased Almighty God to remove her from this vale of misery. When she was fifty-four she sickened with fever, and she at once sent for her confessor and desired to take the holy sacrament, although she had been wont to confess and communicate on all festivals of the year, and after these exercises she could say with S. Paul, " I wish to shake off this body and be with Christ."

Truly Alessandra might speak thus, for she had been a martyr in this life to the love of God. She spent her time in lamentation over her sins and was always attended by religious persons who ministered to her soul, showing in her end what her life had been. She gave up her soul with these words, " *In manus tuas Domine commendo spiritum meum.*"

Honour is due to her for her virtues, and also for her descent and her marriage with one of the noble house of Strozzi. It is not to be doubted that God would take her after her righteous life into eternal glory. Her life should serve as a model to all the women of our city, especially mothers with daughters to rear, and should forbid them to read such books as the Cento Novelle, the novels of Boccaccio or the sonnets of Petrarch, which, although they are polished, are not wholesome for the pure minds of young women who should consider naught but God and their own husbands. They should be led to read the Lives of the holy fathers, history and other books fitting for the regulation of their lives. They are by nature prone to frivolity, therefore let them realise that a dowry of virtue is infinitely more valuable than one of money, which may be lost, but virtue is a secure possession which may be retained to the end of their lives.

BARTOLOMEO DE' FORTINI

Bartolomeo, son of Ser Benedetto de' Fortini, was of honourable birth. He had a good knowledge of Latin letters and was highly esteemed by all in the city for his worthy character.

BARTOLOMEO DE' FORTINI

He was most religious, frequent at public worship and the friend of all religious persons and servants of God. He was respected in the state and proved an upright public servant in every office he filled.

The Florentines had once more occupied Borgo San Sepolcro, a place much given to armed brawls and changes of government, and, as it seemed well to the Signoria to institute certain reforms, they chose Bartolomeo as a fitting person to go thither on account of his worth and his good repute. He went at once to Borgo, where he was honourably received. On taking office he deliberated how he might cure the sloth and indolence which pervaded the city. He caused to be made a list of all the citizens of Borgo, and, when this list was completed, he sent every day for one or other of them and questioned him as to his occupation. If he came across an idle man he would demand of him what work he would be able to do. He would then reprove him for his idleness and show him the evil consequences of a lazy life, both for himself and his family. Next he would demonstrate by way of contrast how much happier was the lot of the man who followed some useful calling, for soul and body and well-being ; let him, for instance, follow the calling of a wool-comber rather than remain idle. He succeeded so well with his pleasant counselling that in a short time most of the people gave up their idle habits and gambling and civil broils and took up some useful work. And this he did for two reasons, one that they might give up their idle life and show due obedience to the Florentine state, otherwise they would not be able to maintain themselves ; and the other that they might work for the good of the state and give up their continual strife with which they occupied their time through having naught else to do.

He abolished gambling, knowing well the evils thereof, and he gained such great favour through his beneficent action that the people held that God must have sent him there for the general benefit. Having made a good beginning he desired to go on, and determined to become acquainted with all the disputes which troubled the country. He would begin by summoning one of the parties before him to hear his version of the dispute. When he had mastered it he would address the litigant with the most powerful and appropriate words—for no man in the country, priest or layman, spake better than Bartolomeo. Amongst his other talents he possessed the gift of convincing anyone, who might submit a question to him for decision, that the verdict he might give would be just and correct. He would then send for the other litigant and treat him in the same manner. Then he would bring the two together and place all the arguments before them ; indeed, few cases were settled without the shedding of tears, so moving were the words of Bartolomeo, and always backed up by texts from Christ's words which he would have ready for use on every occasion.

He governed the state in such fashion that to-day it bears traces of his hand. He was one of those citizens to whom office should be committed ; men who regard the general good of the places they administer and think nought of their own advantage, as most will do. All who knew Bartolomeo liked him and he made friends of the best. At that time the notary of the Law of Ordinances in Florence was Ser Filippo di Ser Ugollio, a man of the highest character. He knew Bartolomeo well and liked him for his many virtues. His reputation in the city was so great that he attended to many disputes and settled them more readily than anyone else in his quarter. There was nothing he could not accomplish with his unassuming ways, his diligence and his knowledge of the Holy Scripture which he had, as has been said, at his finger-ends. Good men are always envied by the depraved. It chanced that there took place in Florence an election of officers of the Monte Vecchio, an institution of much importance. Bartolomeo, without seeking for it, was nominated thereto. Another citizen, a man of standing in the quarter, was very anxious to be chosen, but he was beaten at the election, Bartolomeo being returned by all the black beans.

Bartolomeo was in the Piazza when the news was published. He went into the shop of a friend where several citizens shook hands with him, but he began to weep and said, " To-day's work means ruin to me and to my family. I know that he who set his heart on this office will not rest quiet now he has lost it. My friends, who thought to serve me by supporting me, have really done me an ill turn." What Bartolomeo

BARTOLOMEO DE' FORTINI

feared occurred too exactly. Not being able to get an office by just means, his opponent chose a most nefarious one. He managed to procure the internment of a number of citizens, amongst whom was Bartolomeo, whose place he took as an official of the Monte Vecchio.

But Almighty God could not suffer this man to go unpunished for this great wickedness, for it often happens, in the vicissitudes of state, that those who have unjustly punished the innocent are stricken with the same evil fortune when they least expect it. Not long afterwards, in a time of civil disorder, this citizen who had ruined Benedetto was interned and his sons with him. Moreover, because they did not keep within their bounds, they came under the ban of rebellion and suffered confiscation of all their goods. Bartolomeo, living under the conditions aforesaid, was greatly chagrined over his fate and that of his sons, being conscious that they were innocent. The greatest sympathy was shown to him by everyone in Florence, for all knew his virtues and innocence and the injustice he had suffered. In this Bartolomeo kept his soul in peace the best he could, hoping the time would come when he would be proved to be blameless.

Thus it happened, when in the course of time those who had brought about Bartolomeo's ruin were also banished, although they were of high rank, it came to light that a great wrong had been done to Bartolomeo, and all his former honours and emoluments were restored to him. At the election Bartolomeo and all his sons were chosen. In future times Bartolomeo's name stood high in the city, and to this day his children deservedly enjoy the fruit of his industry. To the end of his life he kept to honest ways. If a man acquires a good habit it is easy to keep it, and the end of his life was as was the beginning. And, because he was such a worthy citizen and example to all, I have thought it well to write this brief comment to serve as a pattern to present and to future times.

APPENDICES

I

U P to 1282 the government of Florence was conducted by twelve *Anziani*, two elected from each *sestiere* of the city; but in this year they were superseded by eight priors, one chosen by each of the greater trade guilds and a new officer, the Gonfalonier of Justice, whose function was to keep order and restrain the Ghibelline aristocracy who had been excluded from all participation in office by the recently enacted Ordinances of Justice. The eight priors and the Gonfalonier made up the Signoria, who lived at the public charge in the Palazzo during their two months' term of office. It may not have been an unmixed benefit to be ruled by traders, but the condition of Florence rapidly improved, and showed a favourable contrast to the state of cities like Perugia and Bologna, which remained battle-grounds of patrician rivalry. The Florentine executive was, I. The Signoria already described, II. The College of Buonuomini—twelve special advisers and III. The gonfaloniers of the greater guilds, two elected by each. The union of these three orders was known as the Collegio. There was also the Senate, with varying numbers, and the larger Councils of the People and of the Commune. The appointment of magistrates was vested in a body of experts, who were supposed to make a searching examination into the merits of the candidates— the *squittino* or scrutiny. Instituted to achieve perfection it became a most destructive instrument and led to flagrant abuses. All laws were proposed by the Signori, approved by the College and Senate, and finally by the Councils. The gonfaloniers were entrusted with the preservation of public order, and a body of experts, " The Eight of War," established

467

APPENDICES

in 1386 during the war with the Pope, directed the military forces. The higher offices of the magistracy were open only to Guelf citizens, affiliated to one or other of the trade guilds or arts, the names being drawn by lot. But the *squittino*—corresponding to a modern list of voters—and the *borse*—the bags from which the names were drawn—lent themselves as instruments of corruption to the dominant faction. The Guelf leaders were reinforced by the rich traders—*popolani grossi*—and they strove to restrict still more the number of active citizens. In 1378 Salvestro de' Medici, an opponent of the extreme Guelfs, was chosen gonfalonier, and the conflict became inevitable. The papal war which had just come to an end had been a brilliant success to Florentine arms, and the Ghibellines had played a worthy part and, in conjunction with the " Eight of War," had won great popularity in the city. Salvestro determined to destroy the oligarchy which deprived so many citizens of their rights. He enforced the Ordinances of Justice and restored the rights of the *ammoniti*—those who had been warned to keep clear of politics. Owing to the opposition of the Guelfs in the Signoria his laws were rejected, but were subsequently passed by the larger Council of the People. After 1380 the Albizzi faction recovered their position and was the dominant power till 1434, the year Cosimo de' Medici was recalled. On the whole their influence was salutary, and they certainly barred the way to supremacy against Gian Galeazzo and Filippo Maria Visconti and King Ladislas of Naples.

On June 22 a Balia, with dictatorial authority to reform the republic, was formed, in which all the chief officers of state were included. As this is the first instance of this sinister institution a short description of it may be permitted. Henceforth the Balia was the instrument by which changes in the constitution were made. Rumours would be spread about the city that there was danger to the state, that the government was mistrustful of its power to deal with it, and desired to call the people together and seek their counsel. Next the great bell would be rung, and the people would rush to the Piazza which, when filled, would be blockaded by soldiers. Then an impassioned speech would be made from the balcony, and the crowd would be asked to commit the government to a

468

council made up from a list of names which would be read. Paid agents of the promoters would swarm in the gathering below, and the result invariably was the adoption of the list.

Almost immediately after the Balia* was set up riots broke out amongst the workers, who had been stirred up by Salvestro's propositions, and the houses of the leading opponents of the new laws were burnt. Salvestro now saw that the best chance of carrying his proposals lay in an alliance with the populace, " I Ciompi," who, having chosen as their leader Michele Lando, a wool-comber, a man of remarkable character, made him gonfalonier on July 22. They seized the Palazzo, and Lando showed admirable tact and ability in restoring order, but, like many other demagogues, failed when he attempted to compromise. His followers fought amongst themselves and riot and bloodshed took place. In September Lando's term ceased, and the next voting placed Salvestro de' Medici, Benedetto Alberti and Giorgio Scali at the head of affairs. Their position was strengthened by the discovery that the Albizzi faction was intriguing with Charles of Naples to bring his army, which was on the frontier, into Florence to coerce the republic, but discord soon broke out over a quarrel between Alberti and Scali, which led to Scali's execution. Meantime public opinion turned to support the Guelf leaders, and in January, 1382, a Balia was called which replaced them in power. Lando, Alberti and many others of the popular party were banished.

The term " Pratica," which often occurs, was in later times applied to the " Eight of War " when this body was authorised to act together with the Podestà as a military commission. Afterwards its functions passed to the Signoria and the gonfalonier and the Otto della Pratica became a council of public security, of national defence and for the detection and punishment of offences. The saying, " andare agli Otto," was synonymous with going to prison.

* Of June 22, 1378.

APPENDICES

II

INDEX

INDEX

INDEX

474

INDEX